Colonial Anglicanism in North America

Colonial Anglicanism
in North America

by John Frederick Woolverton

Wayne State University Press, Detroit 1984

Library of Congress Cataloging in Publication Data

Woolverton, John Frederick, 1926–
   Colonial Anglicanism in North America.

   Bibliography: p.
   Includes index.
   1. Church of England—United States—History—17th Century.   2. Church of England—United States—History—18th Century. 3. United States—Church History—Colonial period, ca. 1600–1775.   I. Title.
B X5881.W65   1984   283′.73   83–27400
ISBN 0–8143–1755–3

IN LOVING MEMORY OF
Ethel Woolverton Cone
and for her friend
Margaret Richardson Woolverton

Contents

Preface

Considering the remarkable sophistication of knowledge about colonial history at the present time in the United States, it is astonishing that no general study of Anglicanism in the long period between the settlement of Jamestown and the outbreak of the American Revolution has ever been written. This book attempts to fill that gap. It will also serve as a foundation for further studies of the denomination which emerged from the colonial Church of England, the Protestant Episcopal Church in the United States.

In writing this book, I have followed my own interests as a historian by dealing with the interaction of theology, politics, and the personality of individuals. Obviously such an approach leaves out a great deal of material. Where it amplified my interests, however, I have incorporated insights which might be called sociological in nature. Perhaps this approach marks this volume as representing more traditional type of history. So be it.

I have tried consistently to avoid a vast compilation of information gleaned from primary sources and the works of other scholars in favor of select lives, ideas, episodes, and contemporary comments. In such selection I have tried, on the one hand, to show something of the relation, however uncomfortable, between what was intended at a particular time and what actually resulted and, on the other hand, to illumine as much as possible the individual in his or her particular circumstances. As a church historian, I have firm theological reasons for doing both of these. It has been my belief that, far from being destructive of sacred cows, these twin attitudes are, on the profoundest Christian basis, the lifeblood of the renewal of institutions.

Thus at the outset I determined not to write a denominationally self-serving history. Indeed, what university press, I asked myself, would ever publish one? And that, of course, did it. In choosing a critical though hardly passionless attitude toward my subject, it seemed to me also that I was following in the steps of an important, if often unrecognized and eclipsed, aspect of my own lifelong church tradition: the willingness to submit all forms not just to human scrutiny but to a transcendent position of criticism from which everything, including authors, are judged. I gained this important insight from two brilliant men who taught me history as an adolescent in an Episcopal school: Richard K. Irons and the late Theodor Mommsen. The memory of both of them in their classrooms is still fresh in my mind. There have been others, similarly free from cant, in whom one detected, amid their deflation of pious and impious pretensions, the deepest currents of humor and grace. Some of their names appear below. Preeminent among them for me was the late Wilhelm Pauck, who indirectly shaped the attitude of this book.

In direct relation to the writing of this volume, I owe a word of gratitude to my former teacher at the Virginia Theological Seminary, William A. Clebsch, now of Stanford University, for his sound initial advice about the form the book should take. There are others who read and criticized this study or with whom I talked about it during the ten-year period of its production. They are: Lawrence L. Brown of the Episcopal Theological Seminary of the Southwest; Nelson R. Burr, retired Librarian of Congress; Robert T. Handy of Union Theological Seminary, New York; Richard D. Miles of Wayne State University; William H. Seiler of Emporia State University; Frank E. Sugeno of the Episcopal Theological Seminary of the Southwest; James J. Talman of the University of Western Ontario; and John Wilson of Princeton University. Above all in very different ways I owe special thanks to two people in the academic world: John K. Nelson of the University of North Carolina, for his unstinting, meticulous, and encouraging criticisms; and to Hans W. Frei of Yale University, whose concern and support are known by an ever-widening circle of friends.

I should like to express my thanks to Professor Jack Goodwin, librarian of the Virginia Theological Seminary, and to his able staff for their remarkable generosity of time and expertise, to Nelle Bellamy at the Archives of the Episcopal Church, to Garner Ranney of the Maryland Diocesan Archives, to Robert H. Land for giving me access to the most hallowed recesses of the Rare Book Room of the Library of Congress, and to the librarians and staffs of the following: the British Museum, the Folger Shakespeare Library, the Lambeth Palace Library, the New-York Historical Society, the St. Mark's Library at the General Theological Seminary, the Swem Library at the College of William and Mary, and the Union Theological Seminary Library, New York. Their many kindnesses in making research pleasurable are not forgotten. I especially wish to recall with gratitude the Department of Religion at the College of William and Mary for providing me with the able services of Phyllis Colman, who typed nearly the entire manuscript. My thanks to Barbara Stafford, my secretary at the *Historical Magazine of the*

Episcopal Church, for typing the bibliography; to Doreen Broder of the editorial staff of Wayne State University Press; to Professor Roland Foster of the General Theological Seminary and Bishop Christopher Keller of Arkansas and the Inglewood Foundation, my appreciation for their efforts and generosity with financial aid in publication.

Acknowledgments would hardly be complete without a word of appreciation to the trustees of the Virginia Theological Seminary for providing the generous sabbatical program which made this undertaking possible. To my many students over a twenty-five-year stint as professor of church history at Virginia Seminary, I can only say that I owe a great deal. Their liveliness, involvement, sometimes incredulity, even their "I'd rather be sailing" expressions are remembered by me with affection.

To my friends on the Board of Directors of the Historical Society of the Episcopal Church and to the Right Reverend Scott Field Bailey, I feel particularly indebted for their endorsement. For his interest, my thanks to Professor Goldwyn Smith of the Editorial Board of the society's *Historical Magazine.*

Finally my love and thankfulness to my own wonderful young people: to Charles and his wife, Diane; to Mary and her husband, David Sims; to Susan and Arthur, all of whom cheered from the bleachers. Above all to my wife, Maggie, whose support, encouragement, reading, proofreading, and generally putting up with often daily replays of the latest progress or regress went beyond the call of anything so trite as duty.

Introduction

In one of those remarkable bursts of literary energy which characterized leading members of his family, in 1821 John Quincy Adams completed his *Report upon Weights and Measures*. For all of the midnight oil burned by that busy and single-minded secretary of state, Adam's admirable essay has lain unread and unappreciated by his fellow countrymen. Behind the detailed discussions of avoirdupois, grains troy, and cubic feet was a political vision of continental American and transatlantic peace, beneficence, and unity. Adams sought a world in which there could be "no final appeal to physical force; no *ultima ratio* of cannon balls." He found it ironic that men "should use the same artillery and musketry, and bayonets and swords and lances, for the wholesale trade of human slaughter, and that they should refuse to weigh by the same pound, to measure by the same rule, to drink from the same cup, to use in fine the same materials for ministering to the wants and contributing to the enjoyments of one another."[1] The world should follow France and adopt the metric system, Adams declared.

But there was additional wisdom in that statesman's essay. Adams knew that uniformity—our boastful and inaccurate *E Pluribus Unum*—remained a pious hope. When law, he judged, "comes to establish its principles of permanency, uniformity, and universality, it has to contend not only with the diversities arising from the nature of things and of man; but with those infinitely more numerous which proceed from existing usages, and delusive language." Peculiar customs—"the tangles of confusion . . . partial standards, and misapplied names"—spread from individuals and families to villages and communities, declared the future president, and were often ignored by those who, such as he, sought to make uniform the laws of nations. The result was conflict between local usage and national aim, between the colloquialisms of villages and the allocutions of statesmen, between the many and the few. "In this conflict between the dominion of

usage and of law," concluded Adams in a tightly packed paragraph perceptive for its irony,

> the last and greatest dangers to the principle of uniformity proceed from the
> laws themselves. The legislator having no distinct idea of the uniformity of
> which the subject is susceptible, not considering how far it should be ex-
> tended, or where it finds its boundary in the nature of things and of man,
> enacts laws inadequate to their purpose, inconsistent with one another; some-
> times stubbornly resisting, at others weakly yielding to inveterate usages and
> abuses; and finishes by increasing the diversities which it was his intention to
> abolish, and by loading his statute book only with the impotence of authority,
> and the uniformity of confusion.[2]

It may seem strange to introduce the history of colonial Anglicanism, or
Episcopalianism, as I shall call it in America, with the reflections of a
Unitarian secretary of state. John Quincy Adams in the context of his essay
on weights and measures invited broader application. He would not be
surprised that his insight into the discrepancy between intention and result
was put to use as a device for describing the progress of religious institutions
and constitutions. His own involvement in the history of mensuration was
itself grounded in biblical and religious history. As in the Bible, so in the
history of the American colonies in the New World, the end of God's
creations was the improvement of man. In 1592, shortly before the settlement of Jamestown, almost providentially it seemed to him, Parliament had
defined the length of the statute mile, and in 1601 new standards for the yard,
ell, bushell, quart, and pint had been deposited at the exchequer. Preparation was thus made for the future in the continent of North America of those
Englishmen who "were arrayed on the side of liberty . . . and who brought
with them all of the rights and none of the servitudes of the parent country."
If Adams's triumphalism and simple belief in providential history no longer
attracts many, his recognition of the inadequacy and impotence of authority,
when it fails to consider inveterate usages, still convinces, if it does not
convict. Moreover, his awareness of the often awesome discrepancies between motivation and result was not surprising in one of his background. He
was, after all, a son of New England. He knew from his Puritan ancestors
what original sin was all about even if he did not care to express himself
formally and doctrinally on the subject.

It is the variance between the desire for religious homogeneity in North
America on the part of the leaders of the colonial Church of England and the
realities of the American scene—its pluralistic usages and abuses—which
is the subject of this study. We will perceive that the laws by which Epis-

copalians sought to implement uniformity proved deleterious. We will discover that Episcopalian legislators on both sides of the Atlantic failed to account for the susceptibility of their subjects, their delusive religious language, and tangles of denominational confusion.

At the same time we shall also see that the Episcopal church contributed important elements to the national religious equation. Her Puritanism in Virginia in the seventeenth century produced new and permanent institutional configurations with respect to the role of the laity in religious affairs. In the eighteenth century, the moderate Enlightenment was brought to bear on the intellectual scene through her theologians, both English and American, with far-reaching and long-lasting results. Ironically, she contributed as well to the revival of Puritan evangelicalism in the Great Awakening in ways which proved anathema to many of her members. For those who increasingly came to yearn for a civilization with more culture and tradition than America afforded at the time, the colonial Church of England provided closer ties with English culture, customs, and even language. In the conduct of Christian worship her liturgical formularies provided a certain stateliness for those who required such a quality. In addition she furnished worshipers with that kind of churchly comfort which assured them that they were part of a long, unhasting tradition, even if in fact it had only begun with the Elizabethan settlement of 1558. That numerous Americans came to uphold the values inherent in king, country, national religion, and empire as the eighteenth century progressed was in part the church's doing.

And, as if these elements were not enough to make her history a matter of moment, there was the principle of uniformity itself. This principle was in retrospect the special "burden"—even curse?—which the colonial Church of England bore in relation to the rest of the country's churches. So acute were the tensions thus created by her establishments, as well as by those in New England of the Congregational churches, that religious uniformity was to find its settled form not in the triumph of one denomination over another but in the condign resolution of civil religion. In that dawning religious light—or was it a waning one?—all denominational distinctions paled, and towards this end the Episcopal church contributed both negatively and positively: negatively, because when her leaders tried to load the statute books for her benefit and at the expense of others, the impotence of her authority became apparent; positively, because in her own lack of theological definitude, in her confusion, and in her comprehensiveness, she declared that the means of grace were many. She thereby anticipated the most basic belief in the religion of the nation.

But we must look more closely at the basic religious outlook of the

Episcopalians. For the ministers and people of the colonial Church of England, God was of course sovereign. He was bound, they were sure, by the constancy of those traditions, sacraments, and governments through which he habitually conveyed his goodness and his promises. Particularly with respect to the divine promises, undue conjecture, it was felt, was not merely bad manners but an affront to God's benevolence and paternal order. As one should not speculate whether the guarantee of salvation applied personally or not, so it was not to be expected that God would rap out disquieting orders at variance with time-honored ways. He was loving to all in the hereafter, it was supposed, just as he was orderly with all here and now. Novel and unpleasant surprises were not to be anticipated in either heaven or earth. For colonial Episcopalians neither the firm-set doctrinal platforms (theoretically at least) of New England Puritans nor the whirling pagodas of the revivalists reflected his ways. Depend upon it, Episcopalians insisted; government was good and necessary. Religion and law went hand in hand. Classes and stations in the mystical body of Christ on earth provided men and women with their identities as well as their purposes. Society with its national traditions preceded individuals. Support of the institutions of government and community by those individuals became a mandatory good work through which the faith might become manifest.

While such an organic view of society in its relation to God did not go unchanged or unchallenged in early America, it is only against some such general view of colonial Episcopalianism that the several religious establishments of the Church of England in the colonies can be understood. These establishments were maintained in whole or in part in six of the thirteen original colonies: Virginia (1619), New York (1693, in New York City and its adjacent counties), North Carolina (1701, 1705, 1711, 1715, and 1720 down to 1765), Maryland (1702), South Carolina (1706), and Georgia (1758).[3] In Pennsylvania the church was small but extremely influential, while in New Jersey and Puritan Connecticut her growth toward the end of the eighteenth century was noteworthy. At the time of the American Revolution all of these establishments were abolished by the new political forces then gaining control over colonial legislatures.[4]

But what is meant by *establishment*? Too often the term has been used loosely, a single word which in fact conveys a double meaning.[5] First, to establish anything means to confirm, settle, permanently sustain, and even build up. Thus the Church of England was given official recognition, certain privileges, and certain immunities. Its adherents, particularly the clergy, benefited from social prestige, the opportunity for higher education in the great universities not open to dissenters and others, and an entrée into the anterooms, and occasionally the very halls, of political power. Most often cited, the church was supported by monies provided by public taxes for many, though by no means all, of its salaries and other expenses. In return for these benefits it was subject to governmental surveillance of its appointments and internal affairs.

But then when we speak of a religious establishment, we have something else in mind as well, namely, the church as a national corporation and communion. Even more than that, we see the church as the state itself considered in its ecclesiastical circumstances and religious frame of mind. The church is not seen here simply as a voluntary body of people who contribute to the settled order of the good society; it is that order. Leaders, parties, and attitudes change, but the sense of the national church's supervision of life, its rhythm, and its permanence remain. As one constitutional historian of this period has said, "The established order of the Church of England is but the ecclesiastical counterpart of the State of England, in which the Church and State are but the spiritual and temporal aspects of the same body politic existing under the rule of an anointed king . . . who is *Fidei Defensor* and *defensor libertatum regni.*"[6] It was the king in whom the two aspects of the single state were lodged, the religious and the secular. In both cases the king was *defensor,* the one in whom was vested both the privilege and the obligation to rule. Thus, in the sixteenth and seventeenth centuries in order to assure the validity of that rule, it was understood that there was but a single apostolic succession, not of bishops whose authority was derived from the crown but of the monarchs themselves whose sovereignty must—but did not always—pass along the double line of blood and grace. They alone were supposed to be supreme (though Richard Hooker was careful to distinguish their supremacy from that of Christ), and through them and their civil governors jurisdiction was maintained over clerical subjects. But the important first point was that in their rule the monarchs came to symbolize the irrevocable binding together—the unity—of church and state. When in the later years of the seventeenth century Parliament came to play an increasingly important role, the custom and precedent emerged in the *Republica Christiana* in which the ministers of the crown in spiritual matters and the ministers of the crown in temporal matters were responsible to Parliament. Increasingly in the period of American colonization, Parliament, if it did not usurp royal prerogative, certainly took over day-to-day control of the church, a control which had once been the domain of the king. Thus if the origin of establishment is to be found in the unity between crown and clergy, its continuation in England is discovered in the equally close relationship between clergy and Parliament.

The increase in parliamentary power is no less true in America than in England—indeed, more so. Part of the significance of the church's American experience in the seventeenth century lay in the accelerating growth of the authority of the legislature over the spiritual corporation of the state. Virginia is a near perfect laboratory in which one may see the process at work. Since there were no lords spiritual in Virginia, the growing domination of the church by the General Assembly may be spoken of in part, though not entirely, as the laicization of the church. At the very time when Archbishop Laud was attempting in England to enhance the power of the religious executive apart from Parliament and in alliance with the monarch alone, Virginia's lay representatives in the colonial parliament in Jamestown were asserting and increasing their control over the church by passing act after act which regulated its affairs, sometimes in the minutest detail. Thus it is perhaps not too much to say that the development of ecclesiastical arrangements in America predate and anticipate similar efforts in England between the Glorious Revolution of 1688 and the First Reform Act of 1832. In that long period "the struggle for Parliamentary control over the executive in secular affairs . . . carried with it an implied struggle for control over the ecclesiastical executive for which Laud's policy was ultimately responsible."[7] In America, though, there was no such struggle. Due to his preoccupation with political affairs in England, Laud was never able to influence Virginia, though he appears to have had plans to make independent New England come to heel. Thus there was no struggle for control over an ecclesiastical executive for the simple reason that there was no such person. Into the vacuum thereby created stepped the General Assembly at Jamestown. From the start, then, it would seem that a more democratic church emerged. Was it so democratic?

Before placing the laurels for perspicacity on American brows the question should be posed: did the Americans and later the English exceed the bounds of Hooker and enter the domain of Hobbes when the legislatures in each case sought control of the church? That is to say, did the nature of the establishment change from one in which lawful and recognized actions of representative government in regard to the church were obtained through mutual agreement to one in which instant statutory control was exercised completely and effectually over purse, appointments, and all else? In America it would seem that earlier than in England a more thoroughgoing Erastianism took over. The reasons for this more rapid change are not hard to find. In the New World tradition and habit, inherited ways of settling churches could not always be followed even by the most conscientious. As a result powerful laymen governed, men who were solicitous for the church's welfare, wanted the timeless and absolute reality of its gospel heard, and wished to enhance its rule by keeping its flag flying over the lives of citizens. In the process of implementing their concern they took control everywhere in the thirteen American colonies where the church was established.

But can we really speak of the Episcopal church's establishments in the same way that we do of England's? Was there not in America within the colonial church itself a dismantling of that second understanding of the word establishment, that is, of the church simply as the state religiously and ecclesiastically considered? Without royal and episcopal powers to toll the bell, regulate life, and provide guidance amid increasing religious pluralism, the sense of the state as a single, corporate religious body was gradually, though unevenly, lost. What was left was the derivative understanding of establishment: official confirmation and recognition, tax support, governmental surveillance, and special benefits and immunities such as in America. It was the demand that these privileges continue to the advantage of Episcopalians which came into conflict with local usage and abusage. But the linchpin had been removed. The principle of uniformity was no longer linked with the profounder, theoretical understanding of establishment as the unity of the entire society. Henceforth it was only a matter of time before a different kind of religious ordering in the New World would emerge. Ironically enough, it was the very Erastianism of the American Episcopalian establishments which served to hasten that process. That Episcopalians in the immediate postrevolutionary era were able to come to a new self-understanding based neither on the oneness of church and state nor on its corollary, the principle of uniformity, is an admirable feat.[8] In the end they came to build and order their own house, one in which kingly, apostolic succession was rejected. For the first time since the early church, they made bishops nonpolitical and so in their eyes "primitive." Episcopalians in the 1780s gave up the principle of uniformity and accepted the permanent presence of local usage and abusage, all the while retaining their stateliness and traditions. Despite the powerful countervailing drive for imperial unity— and perhaps because of it—they were in the end forced to reform themselves in every sense of that word. They did so with astonishing vigor and so took their place in the religious scene as a respected and self-respecting American denomination. The roots of this change lay in the several establishments, in their differences from England and from each other.

Since close examination of the legal intricacies of those establishments has been done elsewhere,[9] it is sufficient to summarize. Unlike the mother church in England, the provincial, American daughter churches had no strong episcopal authority, no hierarchy, as I have stated, no system of ecclesiastical courts to guide expansion and enforce discipline. ''Everywhere," wrote Elizabeth H. Davidson, "clergymen were found officiating in parishes without either presentation or induction, and all too frequently without the Bishop's license."[10] Support from England was irregular and at times insufficient. Differences between colonies were marked. The power of appointment of ministers in Virginia lay with the vestries, except for the church at Jamestown where the governor held that privilege; in New York the practice was for a time similar, though increasingly governors tried to force their appointees on the churches. In Maryland the right of presentation lay with the proprietors and later the governors, and, unlike Virginia, ministers were inducted. In South Carolina, while popular elections of ministers were held in parishes, the twenty lay commissioners of the central government had the right to decide disputed elections, though they were denied full judicatory authority over clergy. The power to induct rectors generally lay with the royal governors, though once again there was an exception: in North Carolina there was no provision at all for induction. Clerical salaries were paid either by voluntary contributions from England, local taxation, or, quite differently in the case of South Carolina, by the colonial government in Charles Town. Similarly the discipline of the clergy varied often from place to place: in Maryland the governor and his council took the place of ecclesiastical courts; in North Carolina, Virginia, and New York the civil courts (in Virginia the General Court and the county courts) had jurisdiction over cases involving clergy. The lay officers of local churches, wardens, and their vestries also operated in different ways in particular colonies: Virginia's vestries were self-perpetuating for most of the colonial period, with wardens elected by and from those bodies; in Maryland the privilege of being a warden depended on longevity as well as service on the vestry. Often in that colony dissenters were elected wardens. Maryland's vestries (ministers themselves were the chief vestrymen) were more democratic and less powerful than Virginia's, while it was North Carolina's which assumed episcopal powers of discipline to an extraordinary degree. Finally, the establishments often differed in general terms. For example, in New York there was no clear statement of Anglican establishment as there was in Virginia.[11]

Without the episcopate, as the high churchmen were forever and correctly arguing, there could be no uniformity. Colonial legislatures were often at odds with those leaders of the church who ultimately emerged to fill the episcopal gap. On numerous occasions proprietary and royal governors, who represented kings and bishops, found themselves at loggerheads with stubborn assemblymen who thought they alone should run the church. In North Carolina a succession of governors made appeals to the General Assembly to establish the national faith of England, but it was not until near the end of the colonial era that establishment really stuck. In New Jersey the provincial legislature, whose consent to gubernatorial initiatives was necessary, resisted and ultimately blocked all efforts to make the Church of England the official religion of that royal colony. There, as well as in the other middle colonies, the forces of dissent were so strong as to make those particular provinces the "huge exception, surely, to *cujus regio ejus religio* anywhere in the New World."[12] In New England of course Puritan Independents "ruled the roast in the [ecclesiastical] kitchen." There members of the Church of England were treated ignominiously and soon found that they were out of place in Massachusetts and Connecticut. It was a novel situation for those who assumed the *ne plus ultra* of their position. Conspicuous enough to begin with, Episcopalians soon found that they had to plead, along with the Baptists and Quakers, for the right to freedom of worship and then for freedom from, of all things, ecclesiastical taxation for the support of an established ministry.

In the southern provinces, where the Church of England was established and had assumed official leadership, conditions varied greatly depending upon time of settlement and religious complexion of the settlers. Virginia and Georgia, the earliest and one of the latest of the Episcopalian establishments, are, because of their marked contrast, particularly good examples of the variety of the church's circumstances.

For well over a century Virginia enjoyed greater religious unity and stability than even Puritan New England could command. No doubt this was due in part to a lack of the theological explicitness which sharpens wits, invites controversy, and ends, likely as not, in schism. Leaders of the church in the Old Dominion until the 1740s often failed to mention the presence of dissenters because such people were either silent or nonexistent. What controversies there were with nonconformists generally fall into the period prior to Cromwell's rule in England. For the most part until the fifth decade of the eighteenth century the church was simply part of the scenery, acknowledged, accepted, and, without undue hysteria, attended. Even after the first arrival of the New Lights of the Great Awakening and the subsequent division of colonial society in the tidewater in the 1740s and 1750s, habits of acceptance, if not loyalty, remained until swamped by the full tide of post-revolutionary disestablishment and spoliation.[13] As late as the 1780s the Reverend Devereux Jarratt (1733–1801) registered profound shock that his fellow Methodists in Virginia and elsewhere had "embraced a new faith," that is, had formed a separate denomination, and rejected "their old mother, to whom they had avowed so much duty and fidelity." Jarratt, who remained in the Episcopal church, became, as a result, "a principal butt—a great eye sore—for to the church I still clave, and ever intend to cleave as long as I live.

You may be sure I have been battered . . . unable to escape the lashes of malignant tongues."[14] Even this most awakened of Virginia parsons disliked change.

In Georgia, on the other hand, no such expressions of distaste occurred at what high churchmen considered the porcine herds which, possessed by the demons of enthusiasm, stampeded and drowned in the Methodist tide. Georgia had been founded by Anglican philanthropists in the early 1730s. Her inspirers, Thomas Bray (1656–1730) and James Oglethorpe (1696–1785), were motivated by the same principles which had guided the founders of Jamestown in 1607—ridding England of her poor and idle debtors. But there the similarity ends. Georgia from the start lacked the religious uniformity of her older neighbor to the north, Virginia. South Carolina's buffer state against Spaniard and Indian alike quickly became a hodgepodge of nationalities and religious traditions. To this Deep South colony came sturdy Lutheran Salzburgers fleeing Catholic persecution, Moravians, Calvinists from both the highlands and lowlands of Scotland, Quakers from North Carolina, Puritans from South Carolina, Baptists, French Catholics from Acadia, and even a few Jews.[15] Moreover, Georgia's Church of England clergy were neither homegrown parsons such as Virginia's Jarratt nor participants in a well-established local tradition. In England's southernmost continental colony, Episcopalian clergy were not primarily maintaining an older, well-defined order but were in fact building novel institutions. Of such a character was Bethesda, the orphanage and trade school of the great revivalist George Whitefield (1714–1770). In Whitefield's train, moreover, came the revivalistic Episcopalian laymen and teachers John Dobell (fl. 1736–1746) and John Habersham (c. 1718–1775). The clergy in Georgia also contributed in background and nationality to the heterogeneity of that Episcopalian establishment. From New England came ex-Congregationalist Samuel Frink (1736–1771); from Switzerland—by way of ordination in England—came the abler and more conscientious Bartholomew Zouberbuhler (d. 1766); Italy furnished in the selfless Jew Joseph Ottolenghe (fl. 1750s) a notable Christian missionary and catechist to black slaves. Like the colony itself, Georgia's Episcopal clergy were a mixed and interesting lot.

The result of such pluralism in the church, as well as in the colony itself, was that Georgia's religious establishment was never as clearly defined a colonial institution as that of either Virginia or South Carolina. Like the church in North Carolina, that of Georgia failed to attract even a strong minority of Episcopalian settlers despite the abilities of men like Habersham, Zouberbuhler, and Ottolenghe, not to mention Whitefield himself.

The result was that the church's authority was greater in print than in reality. What was true of Georgia was also true in part in other colonies.

Nevertheless, the church was an impressive institution. Her roots were deep in American colonial soil. Whatever her differences in outlook with other traditions, she was a solid member of the Protestant establishment in the first British empire. Her welfare was assured, not only by the authority of the crown, parliament, and a long tradition, but also by local support. She possessed a well-organized, superior missionary arm in the Society for the Propagation of the Gospel in Foreign Parts (SPG), founded in 1701. Often under trying circumstances, her clergy remained loyal to the liturgical and ecclesiological traditions of the mother country. As the Reverend William Dawson wrote to the bishop of London in 1751, the ministers of the church were intent upon "the preservation of [the] purity of Doctrine and Discipline in the Church, and the right administration of the Sacraments."[16] These regulatory elements and practices were contained in the church's magnificent Book of Common Prayer, a partially reformed Elizabethan liturgy, which was entrusted to those same ministers.

Examination of the quality of the colonial Episcopal clergy as a whole, moreover, reveals high standards of conduct and in the majority of cases unremitting dedication. It is necessary to emphasize the point, for, until recently, colonial ministers of the Episcopal church have received a bad press. As one historian has judged, the "general low repute of the clergy is a reflection of evangelical domination of source materials." In eighteenth-century Virginia, this writer continues, "ninety per cent of the clergy served without any serious complaint against them, and many were well loved by their congregations. The other ten per cent of the parsons, however, included some truly scandalous men who managed to blemish the reputations of all the clergy by their flagrant actions and refusal to resign quietly."[17] If such commendation seems to damn with faint praise, there is ample evidence to indicate the seriousness with which missionaries of the SPG and others took their task of preaching the gospel. In 1710 the vestry of Caratuck Parish in North Carolina wrote the secretary of the SPG that the Reverend James Adams (d. 1710)

> has during his abode here (which has been for about two years and five months) behaved himself in all respects as a messenger of the mild Jesus, exemplary in his life and blameless in his Conversation; and now being bound for England we with sorrowful hearts and true love and affection take our leave of him; we shall ever bless that providence that placed him among us and shou'd be very unjust to his Character if we did not give him the Testimony of a pious and painful [i.e., industrious] pastor whose sweetness of

temper, diligence in his Calling and Soundness of Doctrine has so much Conduced to promote the great end of his Mission, that we hope the good seed God has enabled him to sow will bear fruit upwards, which has in some measure appeared already, for tho' the Sacrament of the Lord's Supper was never before his arrival administered in this precinct, yet we have had more Communicants than most of Our Neighboring parishes of Virginia who have had the advantage of a settled ministry for many years.[18]

Adam's predecessor at Caratuck, William Gordon (fl. 1708), was similarly commended for his "sweetness of disposition and spotless conversation" and had in addition a "most excellent and practical way of preaching."[19]

While allowance must be made for self-serving reports to authorities in England in order to increase aid for the colonial church, the weight of evidence in letters written to the mother country supports the contention that the church was well cared for by clergymen of high standards. One acute lay observer of the church in New York in the first decade of the eighteenth century declared that

a better clergy were never in any place, there being not one amongst them that has the least Skin or blemish as to his Life or Conversation, & tho' I am not an Eye to witness to any of ye actions of any sort save those in this Comity yet I omit no Opportunity of enquiring into their behaviour both of the friends & Enemys of this Church, & they all agree as to the Character of the Gentlemen.[20]

Similar examples of the conscientiousness of Episcopalian ministers have been noted recently by John K. Nelson in his study of early American SPG missions.[21]

Length of service in the parishes of the church is to some degree another measure of the esteem in which many colonial Episcopalian parsons were held by their congregations. While in seventeenth-century Virginia sickness and death took a heavy toll, there were those who served long and well. George Hopkins held the parish in York County for sixteen years before his death in 1636; Francis Bolton (d. 1652) held a variety of cures in the Old Dominion for thirty-one years, Thomas Hampton for forty-three years, Thomas Teakle (1624–1694) for forty-two years in Northampton County and Accomac County, and George Robertson (d. 1739) at Bristol Parish in Dinwiddie County for forty-six years.[22] Peter Stoupe ministered for thirty-seven years in New Rochelle, New York; George Ross was at Newcastle, Delaware, for forty years; in Rhode Island James Honeyman was at Newport for forty-five years; John Usher was at Bristol for fifty-two years; Ebenezer Miller served Braintree, Massachusetts, for thirty-six years.[23]

What is perhaps of equal interest with the quality and, in some cases at least, longevity of Episcopalian clergy in colonial America is the changing pattern of nationality between 1690 and 1744. As one might suspect, the largest single group of nationals were the English. Among the 272 ministers licensed and unlicensed for the American colonies and the Caribbean islands between 1690 and 1716 whose places of birth can be determined with accuracy—a total of 109—72 were English, 15 Scottish, 7 Irish, 7 Welsh, 6 French, and 2 Americans.[24] Between 1710 and 1744, of the 433 clergy licensed for all of England's overseas colonies—and whose birthplaces are sure (195)—there were 70 English, 44 Americans, 38 Scots, 17 Irish, 9 Welsh, 9 French, 4 Germans, 1 Dutch, 1 Swede, 1 Italian, and 1 Spaniard.[25] From 1690 to 1716 approximately 34 percent were born outside of England (Wales and Scotland included), while from 1710 to 1744—and accounting for the overlap—64 percent came from Wales, Scotland, Ireland, the Continent, and America. But what is of greatest interest is the increase of Americans: in the first period, up to 1716, American-born clergy accounted for less than 2 percent, whereas by 1744 the number of native Americans made up 22.6 percent of the total. In addition, the number of ministers who had been born on the continent of Europe and whose first language was other than English increased from 5.5 percent to 9.3 percent. The ratio of Scottish-, Welsh-, and Irish-born clergy to all others remained the same for both periods, approximately 33 percent.

While it is clear that a study of the colonial clergy as a whole remains to be done, we may draw some tentative conclusions from these figures. First, in the early eighteenth century the church expanded significantly. This was largely due to the founding of the SPG. As a result of the clerical leadership afforded by the society for the betterment of the church in the American colonies, forty-five new churches were erected between 1701 and 1725.[26] Second, the new church was beginning to recruit foreign, that is, non-English and American-born, candidates for service. As Joan Gundersen has pointed out, for Virginia, the largest establishment in America, there was a growing trend to enlist men living in the colony, and, in at least 15 percent of these cases, some or all of their ministerial training was received in Williamsburg at the College of William and Mary.[27] Third, we may remark on the modest effort to incorporate into Episcopalian lay ranks German and Swedish Lutherans, Dutch Calvinists, French Huguenots,[28] as well as Indians and black slaves to a lesser degree.

This last point deserves attention. Throughout the eighteenth century a special effort was made, it would seem, to accommodate the preaching and the liturgy of the imperial church to the languages of non-English-speaking settlers. French, Dutch, and German Palatines heard the Anglican services conducted in their own languages, and in some cases translations were made of the Book of Common Prayer.[29] None of these efforts produced permanent mass conversions. This was partly because non-English-speaking settlers did not wish to give up their inherited ways, and partly because Episcopalians were ambivalent about the use of languages other than English. In 1705 the indecision of churchmen, if not their total censure of the use of foreign languages, was indicated when a group of clergy from the middle colonies, meeting in Burlington, New Jersey, declared that for non-English-speaking people coming into the Church of England "there be no preachers permitted among them but in the English tongue; or at least of Episcopal ordination that can preach both in English and in their own Tongues, nor any Schoolmasters to teach any Vulgar Language but the English without a particular License from the Govr."[30] It was felt that the use of English would in some mysterious way offset the political and ecclesiological nonconformity of prospective Episcopalians, especially, as the ministers continued, the "Dutch and French being of the Presbyterian persuasion and the former generally tainted with Republican Principles." The desire to prove comprehensive won out, and, henceforth, flexibility in matters of language as "a likely means of uniting the Country both in their Religious and Civil Interests" prevailed. Whatever the success or failure of this enterprise, throughout the century there is ample evidence that *Ecclesia Anglicana* was determined to live up to its national and now, to some degree, international tradition.[31]

The desire for uniformity in language and nationality gave way then before prudential considerations. There seemed little wisdom in rejecting potential church members simply because they did not speak English.[32] Legally favoring the church by an attempt to gain more uniform laws on the statute books was one thing; in that case, many royal Episcopalian governors could and did push hard. But when it came to accepting those of different accent, national origin, and even language, the Church of England proved flexible and comprehensive. Clearly it was in her best interest, politically, socially, and in conformity with the universality of her gospel, to be accepting. Building an empire against the French and Spanish required a united people, and that meant bringing diverse groups into a national church. Nor should the specifically Christian prescriptions concerning equality of status before God's majesty be wholly excluded from consideration. There were those in the colonial Church of England who, as we shall see, found in Christian egalitarianism a strong foundation for evenhanded behavior toward either the less fortunate or the ostracized or both.

Nevertheless, inequality in status in the Church of England cannot be denied. There was snobbery. In England itself, whatever desires for flexibility and comprehensiveness existed, they gave way under the weight of the church's caste system. That system operated blatantly and without apology, and it directly affected the American colonies. Simply put, those who could not make it up the ecclesiastical ladder at home were deemed suitable candidates for the overseas provinces of the empire and were dispatched to them. The American church became the recipient of a large number of the offscourings of the mother church. That many of those of lesser rank turned out to be persons of ability and dedication is evident. But how may we determine more accurately the social rank of England's émigré ministers to America?

Even an initial glance at the major figures in colonial Episcopalian history reveals that many, if not most, of the leaders born in the British Isles came from what I shall call the borders of the Anglican community in England, that is, from the north and west of the English nation. The center of the Church of England was London, the universities, and the major see cities such as York and Winchester. Within that limited radius, clerical gentlemen—the term indicated class standing—might expect preferment and eventual elevation into the hierarchy. Others—the plebians—could expect no such opportunity. Those who wisely chose to emigrate and who in the end became the chief spokesmen for the American church were, as a result, a motley collection of outlanders: Scots, Irishmen, Welshmen, Cumberlanders, and Yorkshiremen.[33] These were men who, despite and perhaps because of their own diverse backgrounds, zealously sought uniformity in America. As colonial representatives of the church in America, they had to appeal to the heterodox many rather than to the loyalty of the homogeneous, chosen few. Faced with the antagonism of dissenters and the tide of immigration in the middle of the eighteenth century, these ardent clergymen had nevertheless to broaden their theology and commend the church, not on the basis of explicit doctrine, but by attracting "adherents on the basis of its intrinsic qualities and its ability to appeal to men on differing levels of religious, intellectual, and aesthetic sensitivity."[34] They did not realize that their desire for comprehensiveness had something in common with other people's desire for different religious ends.

That the colonial Episcopal church did not succeed in the monumental task of converting aleady highly pluralistic colonies is not surprising. That her ministers attempted it deserves more attention, if not sympathy, than has hitherto been forthcoming.

It is, of course, common knowledge that the Episcopalians, both SPG missionaries and parochial clergy in the older establishments, failed to draw all men and women into the arms of England's national church. This may be most easily seen in the record of the number of churches for each communion in the colonial period. In the first century of American colonization, Episcopalians were second only to the Congregationalists in New England. In 1700 there were 111 Episcopal churches and 146 Congregational churches.[35] Of the 111, 79 were in Virginia and 10 were in Maryland in that year. The remaining 22 were scattered down the Atlantic coast from Massachusetts to South Carolina. Through the first third of the eighteenth century, numerical leadership remained in the hands of the Episcopalians and Congregationalists.

By 1750, however, the picture had changed sharply due to immigration. While Episcopalians tended to find their greatest strength in the coastal towns and tidewater areas, Calvinist Scots and Ulstermen and Lutheran Germans flooded the back country from Pennsylvania to South Carolina. There the immigrants were caught up in the Great Awakening. Thus, while the Congregationalists still predominated at midcentury with 465 churches, followed by the Episcopalians with 289 churches, close behind were the Presbyterians (233), the Baptists (132), and the Lutherans (138).[36] The Episcopalian breakdown by colonies shows that in 1750, out of the 289 Church of England congregations in America, 90 were in Virginia, 50 in Maryland, 20 in New York, 19 in Connecticut, 19 in Pennsylvania, 18 in New Jersey, 17 in Massachusetts, 16 in South Carolina, 14 in Delaware, 9 in North Carolina, 7 in Rhode Island, 2 in Georgia, and 1 in New Hampshire.[37] What emerges clearly from these figures is the fact that the Chesapeake Bay region was numerically the most significant Episcopalian concentration in all North America. It alone accounted for 140 of the 289 churches, approximately one-half of the total number. And that location could not have been more strategic. In terms of general population distribution by 1775, Maryland and Virginia had over 100,000 more people than the four New England colonies combined. The Chesapeake Bay provinces also outdistanced the aggregate of New York, New Jersey, and Pennsylvania by the same 100,000.[38] Thus it would seem that the Episcopal church was strategically and advantageously located to expand in numbers and possibly influence as well.

Yet expansion did not occur. In the Chesapeake Bay colonies the church was limited largely to the tidewater where the land was controlled by fewer and fewer planters than in the west. Immigrants, either from Europe or from New England and Pennsylvania, first moved west and only then south, down the Shenandoah valley to more plentiful land. To those western reaches, the Episcopal church, with a few exceptions, simply had not moved and did not move. In addition, despite its large population, the Old Dominion was beginning to fall behind the middle colonies and the Deep South in its growth rate as a whole as the Revolution approached.[39] Moreover, when we compare the decades of greatest overall Episcopalian growth throughout the colonies (1675–1683, 1690–1700, and 1765–1775), they do not correspond to the periods of greatest general colonial growth.[40] This would seem to indicate both that the Episcopal church failed to meet arriving immigrants with an effective policy of conversion and that she was not powerful in those areas where the birth rate was highest. The overall colonial picture of the Episcopal church is of a decreasing percentage of the total population. Roughly, from one-fourth of the total population in 1700, she came to represent one-sixth in 1750 and one-ninth in 1775.

Remarkably, just as this low point was reached—in the decade or so prior to Lexington and Concord—there occurred a noteworthy expansion of the church. As one historian has stated, in the fifteen years after 1760 no less than 100 new churches were built, whereas for the longer forty-year period 1720–1760, a relatively smaller number of parishes, 130, were constructed.[41] The most rapid growth occurred in Connecticut, where just prior to the revolution 17 new church buildings were erected for already existing congregations, while 10 other new Episcopalian congregations worshiped in schools, halls, and homes. At the same time, the increase in church buildings was matched by that of numbers of clergy. Between 1745 and 1775, 409 ministers of the Church of England were licensed for service in America; 156 of these received certification prior to 1761, while 253 were licensed from that time until the outbreak of war. Of the 253, 20 went to New England, 71 to the middle colonies, and 142 to the south.[42] As a result of the efforts of these clergymen, the growth rate of the Church of England for the period stood at 30 percent, compared to the national growth rate of 25 percent. Yet 137 of these ministers, over half of the 253, went to those older, more settled colonies where the percentage of the national population had actually begun to decrease at the time of the Revolution (New England and the Chesapeake) or to colonies in which the Church of England was just beginning to gain strength (North Carolina).[43] Limiting ministers to the older colonies meant that expansion occurred to a point but that it could not have continued by taking advantage of new immigration. That number of 137 who went to Connecticut, Maryland, and Virginia must be compared to only 91 who went to the faster growing middle colonies (New York, New Jersey, and Pennsylvania) or to the expanding southern colonies (North and South Carolina and Georgia).[44]

Behind these bare population figures and, to some degree, explaining them lay an ideological story. In their struggle to bring uniformity to the burgeoning and increasingly pluralistic colonies, the Church of England in America was saddled with the politics of imperialism. Part of the church's decreasing popularity in the eighteenth century is to be explained not only by her aversion to Puritanism, and later revivalism, but to the concomitant fear on the part of others of an Episcopalian takeover. This well-known story has been told from the point of view of the American Puritans,[45] yet not from the point of view of the transcolonial and transatlantic Church of England.

To strengthen the national church in the American provinces and to bring into her fold a greater share of the white as well as Indian population, planners in London involved themselves for the better part of the century in a considerable, and even audacious, missionary effort. Let the new toleration of 1689 be what it may, he was a fool who said he could do nothing to bring others into the Episcopalian fold. Charity schools, preaching, and catechetical instruction, in short, education, served to enhance the belief that provincials were—or should consider themselves—Englishmen. Such patriotism, if it could be engendered, in turn entailed obligations. The church sought the acceptance of clear values. Subjects of the crown in America should be loyal to fixed authority, respectful toward appointed officers in both church and state, willing to be instructed by a regularly recited liturgy, and content to take their place and assume their inherited or appointed rank in what was as near a perfect society as had ever been devised. Those who had had the misfortune not to have been born into this Eden, or had rebelled against it, whether English, Dutch, German, Swiss, Swede, or French, could always be shaped by that church which continued to contribute significantly to what it meant to be English.

Nor was the imperial vision—of a homogeneous society in which hitherto pluralistic groups of white settlers lived in peace and worshiped according to the canons of the Church of England—a mean one. With the demise of the Stuart cause in 1745, Maryland's minister-poet-philosopher Thomas Cradock (1718–1770), perhaps as well as any, gave voice to this deep national strain in colonial consciousness. "Americans" might well "congratulate one another at the English victory at Culloden," for, Cradock judged, we are "Englishmen & Britons—born free & with hearts resolved to maintain our freedom & unanimously to relieve & assist each other on account of our National relation."[46] Nearly all colonials rejoiced in the defeat of Charles Stuart's ill-conceived expedition to Scotland. With members of the Church of England, the victory of Hanoverian forces had a particular poignancy; Episcopalians alone need not keep back anything or enter any caveat. The victory of British forces meant the victory of their settlement. Imperial unity was assured. To it the church took the occasion to make its contribution.

Long before 1745, however, the contemplation of American and English-American harmony began with the founding of Thomas Bray's

Society for Promoting Christian Knowledge (SPCK) in 1698. Through the auspices of that effective educational institution, books by churchmen began to flow into America. These volumes were to comprise the intellectual buttresses of the Episcopalian cathedral in which, it was hoped, many American colonists would find that special brand of Anglican peace which had, up to this time, passed Puritans' and others' understanding. The building blocks represented additional values: free will, reasonableness, practical godliness and spirituality, the special value of good conduct, and an emphasis on moral behavior. Within the edifice itself was a historic ministry which, through the sacraments, joined the otherwise separated realms of nature and grace. Puritans—Congregationalists, Quakers, Presbyterians —with their constantly renewed and renewable covenants in which nature and grace were not realms but aspects of each individual, clearly did not like the Church of England. There was nothing they could do. Anglican imperial politics, spirituality, rationalism, and moralism were in America to stay.

Through the auspices of the SPCK, Thomas Bray's copy hit provincial newsstands with full force when, in 1718 at Yale College, unsuspecting librarians unpacked a series of volumes to which he and the organization he had inspired contributed heavily.[47] There, before the startled eyes of tutors and students, appeared not only Locke and Newton but the whole panorama of seventeenth-century Anglican thought.[48] "Seldom, surely has the accumulated literature of a highly important century," wrote one historian, who was thinking primarily of the scientific volumes in the library, "burst so instantaneously upon a group of college men."[49] Not the least were the authors of religious books, and particularly Anglican ones, to exact their retribution from the Standing Order of Connecticut, when most of Yale's Congregational faculty, together with the president of the college, were infected and moved to join the Church of England.

Nor did Episcopalian ideas and ideals lack their own centers of higher education in colonial America. Besides numerous catechists, school teachers, and private tutors, the church could boast three colleges: William and Mary (1693), the College of Philadelphia (1749), and King's College in New York (1754). Moreover, by 1696 William and Mary stood on an equal legal footing with Oxford and Cambridge.[50] Nor did the impetus to educate colonials end with these institutions. George Whitefield sought unsuccessfully to acquire a royal charter to turn Bethesda, his orphanage, into a college.[51] More powerfully backed in England was the scheme of the philosopher George Berkeley (1684–1753). The future bishop of Cloyne undertook the founding of a college in Bermuda from which to "reform the manners of the English in the Western plantations, and to propagate the Gospel among the American 'savages.' "[52] Instead of Bermuda, however,

Berkeley bought one hundred acres of land at Middletown, Rhode Island, during his stay in Newport. By 1731 he had to give up the idea due to the reluctance of the English government to rile colonial political waters by placing a college of the Church of England in New England. In addition there was a shift in philanthropic interest—and money—from Rhode Island to the settlement of Georgia.[53] Yet the English philosopher managed to impart to the Episcopal clergy of New England a degree of stage presence. As a result of his discussions with the American Samuel Johnson (1696–1772) and others, he published a comprehensive defense of Christian faith against skepticism, *Alciphron, or the Minute Philosopher.*[54] For his part, Berkeley added his own share to the principle of uniformity when he mused *On the Prospect of Planting Arts and Learning in America* in words that have become familiar:

> Westward the course of empire takes its way;
> The first four acts already past,
> A fifth shall close the drama of the day:
> Time's noblest offspring is the last.

Neither he nor others could see how much at variance with their cherished wishes that course of empire would be.

In addition to colleges both proposed and founded, catechetical instruction was a major Episcopalian means of education. Here again the ubiquitous Thomas Bray stands preeminent in the Church of England in the early eighteenth century. Bray's *Catechetical Lectures,* designed as theological exegesis of the catechism in the Book of Common Prayer, were widely distributed among those "second class" clergy of the church who resided on the borders of the Anglican world.[55] Early in Bray's ministry, he determined to aid those poorer ministers who had, like himself, been neglected by the church's leaders. The American clergy were specifically included in his concern. As a result of Bray's concern, the catechetical method of instruction was taken up by missionary-minded colonials with renewed energy. Among the more conscientious practitioners of this common method of instruction in America were those who tried to convert black slaves. These men are important to the historian because, in defending their often zealous instruction of blacks, they had to justify their actions against objectors. In doing so, they unwittingly give a clear picture of what instruction was like. Catechist Joseph Hildreth (fl. early 1770s) wrote from New York that in the absence of the clergyman, "I am going through Dr. Bray's catechetical lectures; as they are short I can read one each [Sunday] evening . . . after catechise, [sic] and so conclude with the post Communion Prayers, general Thanksgiving, and singing a Psalm."[56]

At least one clerical catechist in America wrote his own lectures. Samuel Seabury (1729–1796), SPG missionary, loyalist in the Revolution, and future bishop of the Episcopal church in the 1780s, taught Anglican order and serenity with Congregational New England clearly in mind. Unlike Thomas Bray half a century earlier, Seabury was not loath to unchurch other Protestants who failed to agree with him. Authentic churches, taught Seabury in his exegesis of the catechism, were validated by the rule of bishops who, in turn, derived their authority from Christ and his apostles.[57] The future bishop informed his congregation in the 1760s that those in opposition to such a "well-ordered Society, a body of believers of which Jesus Christ is the Head" were "Conventicles of Hereticks & Schismaticks, who, whatsoever they pretend, are really no part of the Catholick Church. . . . They are like a Gangrened Member of the Body which receives no Nourishment from the head."[58] Seabury reminded his auditors that whoever cuts himself off from the rule of bishops "consequently forfeits all Title to the promises of the Gospel."[59]

In addition to preaching, books, colleges, and catechetical instruction, the process of English and Episcopalian education was aided and abetted by the most obvious pedagogical instruments: the liturgy of the church and its architectural setting. The Book of Common Prayer contained the prescribed liturgical formularies. Generally speaking, Morning Prayer was the standard service of the church on Sundays in both the north and south. The Holy Communion was celebrated four times a year, at Christmas, Easter, Whitsunday, and Michaelmas, though the latter seems to have been added later. In some city churches in the northern colonies, the Holy Communion was celebrated monthly.[60] While baptism was universal, confirmation was never practiced since there were no bishops available for the rite.

Church of England ministers performed their liturgical functions in the New World in peculiarly Episcopalian architectural settings. In both north and south, church buildings contained two distinct liturgical centers, one for the Holy Communion and the other for preaching, reading Scripture, and saying the daily office (on Sunday). All Episcopal churches were auditory churches, either rectangular, T-shaped, or cruciform in design. Wherever possible, they had an east-west orientation. Many had galleries together with accompanying double-tier windows. One historian has claimed that "these elements, required by Anglican law, Anglican liturgical practice and Anglican tradition . . . characterized the Anglican church in the northern colonies."[61] Such planning was based on "the accommodation of medieval tradition and the requirements of Prayer Book worship."[62] Within many of these churches the laity—and perhaps the clergy as well—were reminded of the faith of the church through the excellent device of carving the Lord's Prayer, the Ten Commandments, and the Apostles' Creed on panels on either side of the communion table. In one case at least, design gave mute witness to the national character of England's colonial church: at St. James Church, Goose Creek, South Carolina, there was the hymn of praise lettered on the reredos, "Glory to God on High, On Earth Peace, Good Will Towards Men." This admirable exclamation was placed directly under the British coat of arms.[63]

Whatever her fate at the hands of local uses and abuses in opposition to her principles of uniformity, the colonial Church of England was both a proud and significant institution. That she attracted native-born Americans to her ministerial ranks is now a well-known fact. In Connecticut alone, of the 92 ministers who served there from 1702 to 1785, no less than 70 were colonial Americans, and 65 were born in New England itself.[64] In terms of the number of churches constructed in the same period, Episcopalians stood second only to the Congregationalists by 1770.[65] To the increasing number of churches as well as to the expanding number of native American clergy must be added the truly universal representation of the Episcopal church throughout the thirteen colonies. By the eve of the Revolution New England and the middle colonies had drawn abreast of the traditionally Episcopalian Chesapeake Bay area in the number of churches, though not in the number of ministers. By 1775 there were 144 churches from Maine to Pennsylvania with approximately 93 ministers. Virginia and Maryland had 143 churches and 136 ministers. In the colonies south of the Old Dominion—North Carolina, South Carolina, and Georgia—there were 47 churches and 35 ministers.[66] Men and women were attracted to these congregations for a variety of reasons: Some disliked revivalism and found in the broader and more generous orthodoxy of Episcopalianism a religious home which allowed greater urbanity and at times snobbery. No doubt the Englishness of the Episcopal church also proved appealing to those dissatisfied with American provincialism. At the lower end of the social scale, others joined the church's ranks precisely because they were excluded from the more socially prominent, demanding, and limiting covenantalism of the Congregational way.

In the end, however, the Episcopal church failed to draw together the colonies and the empire through her spiritual ministrations. This can be explained largely as a result of American pluralism, the presence of a much stronger ideology in Puritanism, and the colonial Church of England's own too close association with crown and Parliament. When these became overbearing political forces for many, the English church was deemed a dangerous institution in some quarters. What is more, in the end she herself contributed to the very diversity she sought to overcome. Nevertheless, throughout the seventeenth and eighteenth centuries in America, this church was a force to be reckoned with, not only religiously and politically, but also culturally. That she did not simply remain the tool of the London government is to her great credit. It is perhaps surprising that a majority of her people were clearly patriots. In Episcopalianism's most populous province, Virginia, something like three-fifths of the lay members of the church supported the cause of independence from Great Britain. Similarly, a majority of the 286 colonial clergy were revolutionaries, probably about 150.[67] While only one-sixth of Virginia's and South Carolina's parsons were loyalists, all of New York and Connecticut's and most of Maryland's clergy supported the crown. Yet, even so, conditions varied from province to province. New York City and its environs became the focal point of patriot anger, while in Connecticut, as Nelson Burr has shown, loyalism often tended to be passive. The state's "conciliatory policy influenced them [Episcopalian ministers] to stay, and although there was social ostracism, there was no prolonged, official persecution."[68] Certainly those who had been in America the longest tended to support the cause of Congress. This was particularly true of the laity who experienced only a weak sense of obeisance to crown and mitre. And when the crisis of the 1770s was upon them, they did not regard inherited ideas of ecclesiastical authority as indispensable, any more than their secular counterparts considered the inherited ideas of political authority indispensable. Yet, just as in the civic realm revolution did not mean the repudiation of government, so in the church it did not mean the repudiation of episcopacy.

CHAPTER 1
Virginia and the Anti-Roman Grand Alliance

The history of the Church of England in America before 1680 is almost exclusively confined to the Chesapeake Bay region. Within that area Virginia commands the greatest attention. There, after 1607, the foundations of colonial Episcopalianism were laid. The greatest number of Church of England clergy came to Virginia. While Maryland never had more than 5 or 6 ministers of the church before 1690 and Massachusetts Bay had only 1 before 1685—and he was nonpracticing—by 1680 Virginia had attracted the remarkable number of 107. Most of these men were university graduates from such Puritan colleges as King's, Emmanuel, and St. Johns at Cambridge and Magdalen at Oxford. Others came from more royalist and Anglican strongholds, such as St. John's and Corpus at Oxford and Peterhouse, Pembroke, and Caius at Cambridge.[1] The church which these educated clerics founded and served was, moreover, the only tax-supported Episcopalian establishment in North America in the entire seventeenth century. This establishment was underwritten by the laity, was controlled by the colonial government of Virginia, and was in almost perfect lockstep with the farming and planter society of which she was a part. As a result, on the surface at least, her prospects for future influence in America were considerable. Allied with governors and burgesses, the clergy and laity were generally from the Puritan party within the Church of England. Habits of reading and theological reflection were not unknown to them. Indeed, Virginia's ministers and their parishioners kept abreast of English religious literature throughout the century—often to their confusion, as we shall see—and, more importantly, they participated in an imperial strategy whose potent unifying theme was anti–Roman Catholicism. In addition, powerful voices among the ministers were not uncommon—from Alexander Whitaker (1585–1617) at the beginning of the century to the alert and calculating James Blair (1656–1743) at the end. By any standards, Blair in particular, like the Mathers of Boston, must be judged one of the most remarkable ecclesiastical leaders in all colonial America.

Why then has Virginia's religious history not taken a place in American memory with that of New England? The answer lies in part in the now explainable character of the southern colony itself.[2] Unlike the northern colonies in the seventeenth century, Virginia experienced marked social instability and an appallingly high death rate caused by disease, malnutrition, and Indian wars.[3] Nor were the clergy of Virginia's church immune to such depredations; death took its toll of them along with the rest. While the average length of tenure of the 67 ministers who came to the colony between 1607 and 1660 was 8.1 years, the median was only between 4 and 5 years, and 44 of the 67 died before they had held their office for 5 years.[4] Not until the period 1660–1720 did these figures change appreciably. The average length of service of the 144 ministers of the established church who came to Virginia in the second period was 11.4 years, and the median figure was approximately 10 years. Still, 80 of the 144 had incumbencies of only 9 years of less.[5] In addition, the weakness of America's first Anglican establishment may be seen in the sharply declining ratio of ministers to laity throughout most of the seventeenth century.[6] With the mother country in the throes of revolution in the 1640s and undergoing sometimes swift changes of government and religious orientation, Virginia's church was seriously weakened by lack of attention in London until well into the 1670s. Committed to an episcopal polity, she remained without bishops. Espousing the Puritan ideal of a covenanted community in the early days of the Jamestown settlement, she became a generally unzealous, tax-supported establishment, the religious parallel of a tobacco-growing, mercantile society.[7]

In the beginning Virginia's church had been inspired by missionary, educational, and civilizing schemes for the conversion of the native Americans. The varied realities in the tidewater which met this ambitious design became her undoing. While ministers in London pulpits extolled the benefits of Christian faith for the red man, on the banks of the James those same natives—men, women, and children—were being poisoned, drowned, and shot and their corn, though needed by red and white alike, systematically destroyed.[8] To make matters worse, there was little agreement in London with respect to strategy for the conversion of the Indians. On the one hand, there were those who advocated peaceful means. Their voices were to be heard even after the massacre of white settlers on Good Friday 1622. On 13 November of that same year, John Donne had called upon his stunned and shaken auditors in St. Paul's Cathedral to "be . . . a light to these gentiles that sit in darkness." Though a "flood of bloud have broken in" upon white settlers, investors in the Virginia Company of London and colonists in

America should not be discouraged. In the treatment of Indians "enamore them," Donne admonished, "with your *Justice,* and (as farre as may consist with your security) your *Civilitie*; But inflame them with your godlinesse, and your Religion."[9]

On the other hand, there were those who took a harder line. Over a decade earlier Robert Graye, rector of St. Benet Sherehog, had sanctioned holy war against "lewde and wicked men." Sounding the crusader's trumpet, Graye used Joshua as his exemplar. To be sure, Englishmen "must first trie all means before weapons." After all, he asked, had not Saul spared Agag, king of the Amalechites? Nevertheless, when the land of Canaan beckoned the Israelites or, as now, seventeenth-century Englishmen, the tramp of jack-booted, retributive justice was heard. Whoever hesitates, Graye exclaimed, may find himself hindering the building of God's kingdom. As for the natives of the New World, they "have no particular property in any part or parcell of that Countrey." No doubt Englishmen "goe to live peaceablie among them, and not to supplant them. . . . Neither doe wee intend to take anie thing from them, *ex pacto & iure foederis* [by stipulation and binding compact]. [Nevertheless Englishmen will] compound of them for that wee shall have of them." The message was clear enough: a Christian king "may make warre uppon barbarous and Savage people . . . and may make conquest of them."[10]

This history is concerned then with such paradoxes as a large supply of ministers who turned out to be too few, as the sharp contradiction between what was hoped for in London and what could be achieved on the Chesapeake, as the missionary strategy of peace on the one hand and brutal conquest on the other. Perhaps it may be said that these polarities served to keep Virginia's seventeenth-century church from unifying her contemporaries or inspiring subsequent generations of Americans. But if, among the fair prospects of her religious establishment, the church was unable to exert positive and vigorous authority, her history is not less interesting or informative. Indeed the contradictory nature of her theology and religion, of her role in imperial politics, and of her attitude toward subservient races of red and black peoples is worth discovering, not the least because it constitutes a neglected aspect of American colonial history.

The Puritanism of the first decades of the Jamestown settlement, that is, the sweepingly predestinarian theology together with that theology's chronic reforming tendencies, is not to be doubted.[11] Colonists in early Virginia simply reflected the Protestant Christianity of the Church of England in its pre-Laudian days. That expression of Christian faith was Calvinist in theology and episcopal in polity. Few statements illustrate the fundamental character of England's first permanent settlement in America as does the prayer appended to Virginia's *Articles, Lawes, and Orders, Divine Politique and Martiall* . . . (1610–11).[12] Strongly emphasized are the ideas of chosenness, of covenant between God and his peculiar people. Discipline, the ideal of Christian soldiering, anxiety, fearfulness, and expectation were the outward manifestations of the belief that nothing happened to English colonists without God's mercy or anger initiating and attending the event. As Perry Miller showed, the quality of the early Virginians' piety, their sense of their relation to God, their elaborate sermons, and, above all, the dogmas of election moved them to pray in a manner indistinguishable from that of Puritans in England.[13] The prayer following the *Articles, Lawes, and Orders* was no exception. Six printed pages in length, it was to be heard by sick and disorganized colonists every morning and evening: "Father of al mercies . . . pity thy poor servants, we have indeed sinned wondrously." God was angry. Pride of mind, self-love, worldiness, carnal lusts, and unthankfulness were only some of the sins listed. Ironically, the worst sin, idleness, does not appear.[14] Miraculously, God had stayed his revenge, and, though colonists are wretched as a result, it is "our wretchedness sends us unto thee," seeking mercy. In Christ alone pardon was spoken for, mercy given, and saving faith experienced. Next came service, which was to be undertaken with the spiritual equipment suitable for Christian soldiers and pilgrims: meekness, wisdom, godliness, and love. In the Protestant camp preaching had the central place, and, while men might profit from the conversation of saints, since such discourse keeps men wise and maintains discipline, still, after hearing God's word, Englishmen in Virginia would think no company as good as the Lord's. By such means might sin be repressed, Satan confounded, and the gentiles (Indians) receive dubious mercy.

Three notes were struck at the high point of the prayer: first, the conversion of the natives—"may the heathen never say [though they well might] where is now your God?" Second is nostalgia for England: wayfarers in God's service were not meant to look back—but did—to "our warme nests at home. . . . Lord blesse England our sweet native countrey, save it from Popery, this land from heathenisme, & both from Atheisme." The third distinctive mark of the prayer was the covenant. God had called them from their English homes, the devil and the gates of hell were against them, and men, mostly Roman Catholics, scorned them. These are the trials which the Lord puts upon those whom he has chosen, so "confirm the covenant of grace and mercy for the conversion of the heathen." Dagon will fall before the Ark of God. Let Spanish Catholics mock, Englishmen will build the walls of Jerusalem while "such swine wallow in their mire." The final cry for the social realization of that covenant—"Knit our hearts altogether in faith & feare, & love one to another"—fell upon the deaf ears of Virginia's wrangling, lazy, and ill-organized settlers.[15] The rhetoric, unqualifiedly predestinarian, might just as well have been composed in Boston in 1630 or in Plymouth in 1620 as in Jamestown in 1610.

The reality, however, fell far short of the ideal in England's first colony. No united band of saints had been sent out to teach other saints the ways of God with men and women, nor yet had saints been sent by the Protestant lords of the Virginia Company to teach the idle how to work. England's idle adventurers had themselves been assigned the task, under the eye of Puritan clergy, of teaching the unmotivated poor—as it turned out, teaching them how to die in the wilderness.[16] Early Virginians lacked that common spirit their laws sought to impose.

Of course there were exceptions. Soldier-adventurer John Smith (1580–1631), whose Puritan sympathies have only recently been noted, was a firm believer in the "prime authority of the Church of England," and saw, as Jurgen Herbst has written, "the cohesive power of religion, and in every case . . . tended to measure this power by the results achieved."[17] For this remarkable and unfairly maligned man, Christian was as Christian did, and to that belief Smith adhered. He did so not only in an unqualified endorsement of Governor Winthrop and the Massachusetts Bay Colony in the 1630s but with some admiration for separatist Plymouth. "Religion above all things," said Smith, "should move us, especially the clergy, if we are religious, to show our faith by our works." Even Plymouth for all its insularity seemed to fill that bill.

English Calvinist doctrines were read in books as well as heard in prayers, and the first volumes sent to the unsuccessful college at Henrico confirm the Puritan rhetorical stamp upon the colony. These books were Augustine's *De Civitate Dei* and the three volumes of William Perkins's (1558–1602) writings. The latter are particularly significant; they show that the English in Virginia prior to 1624 were probably closer to the mind of Perkins and his strong predestinarianism—that atonement is limited as it issues from God's eternal will—than to the then far less popular Richard Hooker (1554–1600), whose semi-Calvinism saw atonement limited only by God's occasional will. Apparently some Virginians did not believe, as Hooker did, that God's unfailing inclination was to save all mankind.[18] It should be kept in mind, however, that at the time of the settling of Virginia, these two theologians represented two not altogether opposite points of view. Both views were clearly within the Church of England. The split between Puritan and Anglican would come in the 1620s, and even then there were those such as Captain John Smith who refused to acknowledge it. That William Perkins was a theologian respected and read by the largest part of

41

the established church before 1640 meant that there was nothing irregular in sending his works to Jamestown.[19] Moreover, Perkins's ecclesiology showed that this great popularizer as well as alterer of Calvinism was no violent deposer of bishops, though he would reform them by prohibiting nonresidency.[20] Meddling in the affairs of other dioceses was equally anathema to Perkins. Apostolic succession, he went on to argue, must be understood primarily as the succession of the faith of the apostles in the churches they founded and not as a succession of leaders per se. Perkins believed that the apostles had in fact appointed bishops, and he was alive to the fact that the early fathers of the church had urged the antiquity of episcopacy against heretics. Quite correctly, he noted that the church fathers did not commend episcopacy for its own sake, "not respecting it in itself in years and ages but with being joined with the doctrine of prophets and apostles. . . . This good hath antiquitie which was adorned with divine knowledge done unto me."[21]

Besides Perkins's works, the "Ursinear Catechisme," the Bible, and the Book of Common Prayer were sent across the Atlantic in 1622. This catechism was either an English translation of Ursinus's catechism or the Heidelberg Catechism itself.[22] In either case, Calvinism was powerfully represented. The final volume in this early gift of books was the work of John Brinsley (fl. 1633), *A Consolation for our Grammar Schools,* written in 1622 for the Virginia settlement. Brinsley was a graduate of Christ College, Cambridge, in 1584 and a popular Puritan preacher and schoolmaster. His volume was not likely to endear itself to subsequent generations of Virginians, since their colony in Brinsley's estimation was composed "for all those of an inferior sort, and all ruder countries and places, namely . . . Virginia and the Somer Ilands."[23]

The Genevan influence then was basic and pervasive in the literature of the earliest years of the Virginia colony. That influence was represented by the Puritan party, which remained part of the Church of England for eighty years after the accession of Elizabeth I in 1558. Puritans dominated the pulpits, such as they were, of the colony. In addition ties of personal friendship bound Virginia ministers to their counterparts in England. Such was the case of Alexander Whitaker, the "Apostle to Virginia," and William Crashaw (1572–1626), preacher at the Inner Temple in London.[24] Family and economic interests united such Puritan families in England and America as the Sandyses, Bennetts, Chadertons, and others.[25] Preachers in London would have understood the type of prayer accompanying the *Articles, Lawes, and Orders,* and, if the ministers were long-winded in America, the quality of their utterance and the transparency of their rhetoric placed them alongside those fellow Englishmen who were to come to Plymouth and Boston.

They were almost the same, but there were differences. Nothing could be more important than the difference between Jamestown and Massachusetts Bay in the time of migration. Jamestown reflected the English church and nation in 1607, not in 1629. By the latter date reforming tendencies had moved beyond what Virginians had known, or, by the 1630s for that matter, cared to know. The English in Virginia had stood still or gone their own way to a remarkable degree, suspended at first in both time and wilderness, a crude society, which, perhaps because it knew it was crude, came to insist upon religious conformity and the use of the Book of Common Prayer. Until the 1640s, Virginia represented the milder Puritanism which had characterized a significant segment of the Church of England in the first decade of the century. While bishops increasingly proved anathema to Puritans in England, early Virginians presumably held to the qualified ecclesiology of William Perkins; if they did not, there simply was no bishop residing on the James for them to oppose. Compliance, in so far as possible, to the practices of the church in the mother country was demanded of a society which needed all of the assurance of order and structure it could call upon.

Nevertheless, seventeenth-century Episcopalians in Virginia followed the principles of predestinarian spirituality and polemics long after the covenants of the early days had been forgotten. This is not surprising when it is remembered that a number of ministers throughout the seventeenth century showed Puritan leanings.[26] That there were also Laudian clergy should not be overlooked.[27] Moreover, examination of the religious literature which graced the shelves of Chesapeake Bay homes reveals contradictions in theological reading preferences which appear to parallel the churchmanship of Virginia's seventeenth-century clergy. In the absence of sermons, diaries, marginalia, and recommendations, none of which exist for the colony, the historian can only offer a hypothesis, namely, that the wide and diverse taste in theological literature of seventeenth-century farmer-planters shows that the colony was perhaps harboring a variety of religious points of view within its established church. In any event no attempt at classification of religious books has yet been assayed for the period.

Royalist sentimentality vied with antiprelatical propaganda. In the library of Robert Carter, part of which was no doubt inherited from his father John Carter (d. 1669), the famous *Eikon Basilike*[28] sat next to such Puritan volumes as Quaker William Penn's *No Cross, No Crown* (1669) and Richard Baxter's *On the Life of Faith* (1670).[29] Not only did religious literature generally occupy a large place in southern colonial libraries,[30] but, as Charles T. Laugher has pointed out, colonists' books "were dear to them especially when they had to be imported from England or the Continent. . . . [They] were thus carefully chosen to provide many kinds of guidance for conditions in the New World."[31] It is not at all surprising to discover large numbers of Church of England books in the private and public libraries of America's premier Episcopalian colony, especially after 1660. What is unusual, at least at first glance, is the continuing number of nonconformist volumes. Highest on the list of the more Anglican writings was Richard Allestree's popular *Whole Duty of Man* (1657, 1686). This moralizing essay, which George Whitefield found so distasteful, was in nearly every Virginia library whose contents have been recorded.[32] Also from the "holy living and holy dying" school of Caroline high churchmen—which represented a sharp declination from the English reformers' insistence on justification by grace through faith—appeared the works of Henry Hammond, Jeremy Taylor, John Boyse, and John Hales.[33] Hales, an ardent anti-Puritan, had gone to the Synod of Dort to "bid J. Calvin goodnight."[34] While there were some such as William Byrd II who managed to avoid this school altogether, other libraries in Virginia and the Chesapeake Bay area more than compensated by including the works of the later Nonjurors such as John Kettlewell.[35]

More widely represented in colonial Episcopalian libraries in the bay area were a group of Anglican writers who came closer to the thought of Richard Hooker and the classical belief that the "focus of justifying faith is Christ (as Mediator), and this faith is essentially trust in Christ for the remission of sins."[36] Some of these writers were Robert Sanderson; Isaac Barrow, the archenemy of Puritan John Owen, also represented; William Sherlock; George Downame; and James Ussher.[37] The most popular writers, however, were the Neoplatonic Cambridge Platonists and their successors, the Latitudinarians. In the last third of the seventeenth century, these became more representative of colonial Episcopal thought throughout the American colonies than any other group of theologians in the Church of England. After 1635, the Cambridge Platonists stood between Puritans and high church Caroline divines and sought to vindicate theism, advocate tolerance and comprehensiveness in ecclesiology, and arbitrate disputes by reason and the indwelling of God in the mind. The most prominent of this school to appear in southern libraries were Henry Moore, Edward Stillingfleet, and John Tillotson.[38] Finally there were the sixteenth-century Anglican classics: the Book of Homilies, the writings of Thomas Cranmer, and Richard Hooker's *Of the Laws of Ecclesiastical Polity.*[39] All of these were accompanied by numerous copies of the Book of Common Prayer and were surrounded by dictionaries, concordances, legal tomes, and historical works.

The classics of the early church appeared in the writings of Cyprian of Carthage and Augustine. Cicero, Euclid, and Seneca vied with medicine and animal husbandry for attention, particularly as the century drew to a close.

What is remarkable, because it must temper the idea that Chesapeake Bay Episcopalianism sought to isolate itself in loyalty to the crown from English Calvinism, is the number of volumes representing reformed religion. To be sure, Anglican writers later in the century predominate at the expense of the Puritans, yet, even so, the works of John Calvin and those of his associate and successor in Geneva, Francis Turretin, are listed as shipped to America as late as the 1710s. Calvin's *Institutes* appear in 1648 in the small library of Virginian John Kemp.[40] The sermons of Richard Sibbes (1577–1635) were read by Mrs. Sarah Willoughby in 1673–1674, while the writings of William Perkins and Puritan Samuel Purchas graced the shelves of Richard Hickman. Such well-known Puritans as William Ames, later Presbyterians John Owen and Richard Baxter, and the early eighteenth-century Anglican Calvinist John Edwards are all represented.[41] Edwards's *Theologia Reformata* (1713) earned that Cambridge don the title of "the Calvin of his day." Besides the *Institutes,* Ame's *Marrow of Divinity,* and the works of Perkins, Milton was popular in southern colonial libraries, as were such lesser Puritan lights as John Conrad Wendly, and the Lady Margaret Professor of Divinity and later bishop of Lincoln, Thomas Barlow, the teacher of John Owen.[42] William Byrd II's library boasted a copy of John Bastwick's attack on episcopacy, *Flagellum Pontificus* (1641), while in a similar vein, William Prynne's *Prynne against Prelacy* was not unknown.[43] Moreover interest in reformed and evangelical religion continued in Virginia well into the eighteenth century with the writings of Isaac Watts and Philip Doddridge.

As has already been said, these books were bought to be read, not to be placed in reference stacks for the occasional use of scholars who delight in writing history books. That they were indeed read we may believe. Moreover, in colonial times libraries were small, by modern standards tiny. Virginia's private libraries sometimes held only a dozen or so volumes. Harvard, which boasted the largest of two college collections in seventeenth-century America, had only 3,500 books by 1723.[44] Thomas Bray's provincial library at Annapolis had 1,095 volumes. In between the often small shelves of individual families and the larger academic aggregates were the parochial collections of the Episcopal churches. These ranged in size from 10 to 314 different listings.[45] The conclusion is that collections of books reflected colonial minds far more accurately and intensely than the vast holdings of modern libraries reflect popular twentieth-century American taste. Such being the case, it must be concluded further that the colonial

Episcopal church in the Chesapeake Bay area presented a diversity of religious opinion. From the early Stuarts through the Hanoverians, men and women of the denomination read fairly widely in their own tradition, as well as the ideas of those who dissented from their official ecclesiology. The paradox of an established Episcopal church harboring antiprelatical tracts is not to be ignored. As Joan Gundersen has remarked, "In Virginia where there was little need to stress the differences between Anglicanism and other religions, and where the church tried to serve the needs of the whole colony, the moral teachings naturally received great emphasis, not only as a common bond with other Anglicans, but with other Protestant churches."[46]

If in fact these libraries in any way reflect the mind of Virginia's establishment, we may perhaps conclude tentatively that tidewater colonials saw themselves as part of the capacious and, no doubt at times, contumacious Church of England. The writings of England's reformers, Laudians, Puritans, and later latitudinarians all found their way to the colony, but the din of theological battle which of those books represented was barely heard. The great changes in England which occurred in the hundred-year period 1590–1690 were one thing; survival and the building of a workable society in America, however moral or immoral, were quite another. In that struggle for survival which characterized Virginia for most of the seventeenth century, theological conflict was a luxury. Mostly, one accepted whomever came along, if he could swing an axe, fell a tree, and plant tobacco. And if the ministers for their part behaved themselves, not too many questions were asked about nice theological opinions. The attempt to impose stricter uniformity would come later.

Nevertheless something like an anti-Puritan policy emerged under the two governorships of William Berkeley (1606–1677). That policy in itself attests to the strength of a more radical reformed religion at least in Virginia's Upper and Lower Norfolk counties in the 1640s. There a "schismaticall party" emerged whose disloyalty to the spiritual orthodoxy of the colony was condemned by the Assembly in 1648. As a result, two preachers, Thomas Harrison and William Durand, were banished along with other more outspoken predestinarians.[47] Of these ministers and their congregations we have unfortunately "few direct perceptions . . . [either about their] church covenant, or of the settlers' views or theology, their personal or spiritual discipline, or of the conversion experience."[48] Still we know that Virginia Puritans sought religious aid on one occasion from their New England brethren in the form of "such Pastors as shall be selected, nominated and Commended to us by you." While the petitioners of 1642 sought a minister "which shall feed us with knowledge and understanding," they made it clear to their friends in the north that "such Pastors as shall be so Commended and chosen for us [will only be accepted] Provided that being tryed they be found faithfull in purenes of doctrine, and integrity of Life." However highly esteemed Bostonians might be in the eyes of Virginians for their "holy walking in the order of the Gospell," still "wee cannot rest on man's Person or doctrine further than shall be approved by the word of God, and further then his preaching and Government shall be according to the institution of Christ."[49]

Accompanying this unvarnished petition was an earnest letter from William Durand to John Davenport (1597–1670), minister in New Haven. For Durand, who had made Davenport's acquaintance in London, Virginia was yet a "land of darknesse," a "desolate place" in which "if ever the Lord had cause to consume the cittyes of Sodom and Gomorrah he might as justly and more severely execute his wrath upon Virginia." Seeming to undercut the circumscribed plea of the petitioners, Durand accused his fellow Virginians of "so much corruption and false worship . . . that nothing indeed [is] done as it should bee." For him the further reform of the colony's church was as inevitable as it was desirable. Colonists merely awaited the opportunity to do so. Exaggeratedly Durand wrote that new measures "hath beene long in hand and knowen throughout the whole land of Virginia." Against the emergence of a truly holy commonwealth, only one minister, "a wicked priest of Baal," had opened his mouth, and he "is even hated of all that have any good in them, even as he hateth good men, [while] many do approove and like it [reform] singularly well." To be sure, colonists—and here the predictable Puritan rhetoric of sinfulness took over—"are here scattered in the cloudy and darke day of temptation," are "swoln . . . great with the poison of sin," and evidence those "grisly wounds which now begin to affright and astonish us." Yet despite his fears, Durand saw occurring in the tidewater an "enlargement of christs kingdome. . . . It hath pleased the Lord Jehovah who is abundant in goodnesse and trueth, and desireth to magnify the exceeding riches of his grace," wrote Durand, "to worke mightily in cheering up the hearts of many amongst us." For this "schismaticall" Puritan, God "keepes covenant and mercy foreever," and lest the full import of his letter not be clear, he ended with praise for the Long Parliament and its "prosperous proceedings." No longer, he judged, would Virginians send to England for ministers where to be sure there were "enough such as we have already." Therefore "our intentions may be considered as having a further ayme than to seeke after any pastors, then such as onely the lord himselfe prepareth and sendeth to his people"—from New Haven and Boston![50]

Six years later, William Durand was seized by the Lower Norfolk court for illegal preaching and banished from the colony. If Governor Berkeley's astringent policy toward Puritans in Virginia lacked grass roots support, as it did in all probability, Durand's disregard for approved episcopal order and ordination was his undoing. Reformed religion, even moderate Puritanism, was the order of the day for most of the first century of colonial Episcopalian experience. It was perfectly acceptable so long as outward liturgical and political forms were observed.

Colonists' prayers, books, and letters were revealing episodes in a larger imperial religious design and strategy which in 1607 involved England and the continental powers.[51] Conceived nearly 50 years before Jamestown was settled, England's strategy would last for over 150 years despite divarications and contradictions. We must see the early seventeenth-century English invasion of Algonkian Virginia by the Jamestown colonists, then, as the move of a key pawn in a chess game crowded with queens, bishops, and rooks. Nor were the settlers to be a covenanted community in isolation from the chessboard of European politics. They were in the broadest sense an advance guard of what Norman Sykes called "the anti-Roman grand alliance."[52] From 1558 to the cessation of the wars against Louis XIV in 1714, there had been one universally held disposition in the Protestant world: against the Church of Rome, vigilance was the price of survival, ascendency the reward of strategy. Vigilance called for caution and dexterity, qualities which, for the forty-five years of her great reign, Elizabeth possessed naturally and exercised supremely. For all her personal predilections toward outward conformity and catholicity, Elizabeth remained, as Sir John Neale reminds us, Europe's Protestant queen upon whom the hopes of many, and not all of them English, were pinned.[53] Her support and aid in the cause of reformed religion and the powers supporting it were important, her mere presence on the throne of England decisive. Protestant England would outflank Catholic Spain in the New World, and high-mettled English youth, so the romantic saga read, would search the ocean, bring home Spanish treasure, and claim land and natives for their virgin queen, her faith, and England. The more prosaic colonists in Virginia in the 1580s and after 1607 found the experience of the New World anything but blissful. The outflankers were very nearly themselves outflanked, not by Spanish and French Catholics but by Indians and by their own poor planning.

In addition, the anti-Roman grand alliance fell on bitter days after 1628, when sober men despaired of both king and cause. When the alliance began to come apart in England in the 1630s, Puritans emigrated in increasing numbers.[54] The seemingly medieval customs and offices of the Church of England were offensive to the reformers, and when Charles I, desperately seeking an ally in his struggle with Parliament, hit upon the church, her isolation from clerical reformers and the Protestant gentry was assured.[55] The king and his transformed church embraced the "Anglo-Catholicism" of Launcelot Andrewes, Richard Neile, and Archbishop William Laud with its emphasis on authority, ceremony, and free will.[56] At each point Charles and his friends diverged sharply from the Puritan party within the establishment. Whatever the theological and ecclesiological merits of the case, the result was politically devastating for the Church of England. Wedded to a theory not only that the monarch ruled by divine right—that was nothing new here—but also that he could do so without either the people's approbation or esteem, the Church in England found herself increasingly isolated from virtually all centers of power save the court. Showered with royal favor by Charles, the clergy of the Church of England finally had to pay a high price for their part in the suppression of the Puritans when Archbishop Laud was beheaded on the scaffold in 1645. English Puritans, tarrying no longer for the reforms they espoused, became revolutionaries. Four years later they meted out the same punishment to their king. For one who saw himself as the law, it was a strange fate to be condemned as a tyrant masquerading under the forms of law.[57]

More than legalities were afoot, however. After all, Elizabeth too had suppressed Puritans. Christopher Hill offers the suggestion that Laud and Charles were executed as a result of shifting notions of demonology. From associations of the pope with the forces of evil, in the 1630s Calvinist Englishmen came to see their own archbishop as the beast and his clergy as the advanced guard of Satan, "the fifth column of vaster, darker forces abroad."[58] Charles was told to choose whom he would serve, Christ or Antichrist. When his lot was cast with the hierarchy of the church, his fate was sealed. The Caroline bishops had rejected the international Calvinist cabal, persecuted its English adherents, and espoused high views of both monarchy and episcopacy. Then and there the Laudian church seemed to many to imitate nothing so much as the Church of Rome itself. The anti-Roman grand alliance was in a shambles. By 1640, the Elizabethan and Jacobean view of the pope as Antichrist was augmented by the feeling that "the whole hierarchy of the Church of England down to the parish ministers was antichristian."[59] The great enemy had appeared in the heart of God's nation. Charles, with his hankering after the monarchical grandeur of counterreformation nations rather than alliance with a pastiche of Protestant city-states, became one aspect of the problem. No matter that the Caroline theologians considered themselves Protestants and "would have become Protestants in the Continental tradition if that had been their only option besides Catholicism";[60] the time of crisis and the time, in the words of John Winthrop, of "expectations of a new world" had arrived.

Be that as it may, the relevant question is: how did Virginians see themselves, first in relation to the anti-Roman grand alliance and then in terms of the internal political and religious divisions back home in England itself? As in the case of the religious literature purchased for colonial libraries, so in the more inclusive and immediate realm of politics, contradictions are apparent. Not all Virginians were of a single opinion regarding their king, his church, or Parliament. This was especially true in the 1650s. But whatever the paradoxes, they existed quite consistently within the larger and more enduring framework of anti-Catholicism. Clearly, in the 1640s Virginians continued to view the pope and not their own king as Antichrist. As one scholar has suggested, "Virginians' dislike of Maryland may have stemmed in substantial degree from their dislike of Roman Catholicism."[61] Virginia's isolation made for greater consistency of political and religious attitudes. If colonial churchmanship tended to be sealed in a tidewater bottle, so were international political convictions. In both cases, beliefs about the true nature of things were passed along from one generation to another, however subtly changed. Not until the nineteenth century were historians made aware of change as the only constant of history.

In Virginia anti-Roman Catholicism was a fact of political life. The Old Dominion was itself forged as a wedge to be driven into the new and growing Catholic world of sixteenth-century France and Spain. In 1613 Samuel Purchas (1575?–1626), a graduate of St. John's College, Cambridge, and chaplain to "stiffly principled" George Abbott, archbishop of Canterbury, had wondered aloud whether in "the old and decrepit Age of the World" Englishmen might not bestir themselves more "for the further enlargement of the Kingdome of Christ Iesus, and the propagation of his Gospell." If the "Donations of Popes, the Navigations of Papists, the preaching of Friers and Iesuites" were enough to discourage any honest Protestant Englishmen from settling America, Purchas would have it remembered that "the secret dispensation of Divine Providence, which is a co-worker in everie worke, [is] able even out of evill to bring good." Might not the missionary and colonizing machinations of Catholic countries in the new world "be fore-runners of a further and truer manifestation of the Gospell, to the new-found Nations?"[62] In frankly sexual imagery, which has shocked at least one modern scholar, Purchas accused the English of bashfulness and reluctance to cohabit with the beautiful nymph, Virginia. At any moment this native girl stood in danger of being "polluted with Spaniards lust" or of falling into the clutches of those equally sour-faced suitors, the French. Let English "Wooers and Suters" do as Purchas, and "warble sweet Carolls in praise of thy lovely Face. . . . [He] shall get the Bride, [who] laies hold on the Continent."[63]

Nor did such anti-Catholic attitudes change. A hundred years later the Reverend Hugh Jones warned Marylanders of the dangers of "Jesuitical views to distract and subvert the Church of England." While for Jones that colony was "the retirement of Roman Catholicks, . . . Virginia may be justly esteemed the happy retreat of true Britons and true churchmen for the most part; neither soaring too high nor drooping too low, [and] consequently should merit the greater esteem and encouragement."[64] It was all common enough fare.

Within the household of English Protestant faith, it was a different story. While Puritans in England were calling Charles "the Pope's second," their conforming counterparts in Virginia evidenced no such animosity. In the coarse, unstable, and materialistic society of the tidewater where farmers were more interested in the tobacco trade, the fraudulent mixing of wine with water in local inns, the acquisition of land, and simple survival, demonology took a back seat.[65] Nothing shows more clearly the effect of the experience of relative isolation and growing autonomy than the response of the House of Burgesses in October 1649 to the execution of the monarch. Though the event had taken place nine months earlier, the shock and, for these conforming Protestants, the official horror of regicide still communicates itself in the opening condemnatory act of that assembly.[66] Inspired no doubt by Governor Berkeley, whose espousal of the royalist cause is well known, the act was nevertheless approved by a popular assembly. Virginians were clearly behind the times in their knowledge of Antichrist. Innovators and contrivers, it was said, had cast "blemishes of dishonour upon the late most excellent and now undoubtedly sainted king." Charles was called blessed, pious, "deserving ever altars and monuments in the hearts of all good men." But again, rhetoric was one thing, reality another. The lucrative and illegal Dutch trade was more important to local merchants than English politics.[67] As Wilcomb Washburn has written, the "evidence suggests that there was no violent division between royalists and Parliamentarians. . . . The people were Virginians first and royalists and Parliamentarians second."[68] Farmers and merchants quickly dried their eyes, made an abrupt about-face, and, since they were neither Laudian clergy nor cavalier laymen, acknowledged Parliament on 12 March 1652. That surrender was, as has been pointed out, the "whelp of necessity rather than conviction."[69]

Of such religious zeal were these new Americans. Whatever their type, rhetoric was one thing, reality another. Moreover, there was no need either to hide or to emigrate. To be sure, in the decade before, while political storm clouds were thundering in England, Governor Berkeley had begun an effort to rid Virginia of nonconforming Puritans. *Mercurius Civicus,* the London Puritan newspaper, referred darkly in May 1645 to "divers of the most religious and honest inhabitants [who] in Virginia were marked out to be plundered and imprisoned for the refusall of an Oath that was imposed upon the people in reference to the King of England." In Nansemond and neighboring counties on the south side of the James, when the oath was tendered "the people murmured, and most refused to take it: Those few that tooke it did it more for feare then [sic] affection."[70] This act of 1643 also demanded that "the littargie of the Church of England for the administration of the word and sacrament be duely performed according to the booke of Common prayer."[71] Again in 1647 antinonconforming measures were taken by the colonial government: If ministers did not adhere to the prayer book, parishioners need not pay the tithes.[72] Presumably more Anglican parishioners would thus force the offending ministers to leave, taking their disciples with them.[73] But, as Babette Levy suggests, political motives on the part of Berkeley may have operated more strenuously than religious fervor.[74]

Howsoever, by 1650 stricter conformity was nipped in the bud. Everyone was pardoned. The new English government's generous and prudential act of indemnity "and oblivion . . . from all words, actions or writings that have been spoken, acted or writt against the parliament or commonwealth of England" was gratefully accepted in Jamestown.[75] Neither the lord protector nor the colonial government wanted a showdown. After that and throughout the commonwealth period as a whole, nothing was done to provoke conflict. A year of grace was given for continued use of the Book of Common Prayer, minus prayers for the king of course. It is highly likely that even after the lapse of that year the prayer book continued in use in most if not all tidewater churches.[76]

In Virginia the anti-Roman grand alliance held together. It was not, to be sure, a particularly grand affair. Perhaps inertia played as great a role as conviction in the maintenance of what was customary and habitual. Whatever divisions in church and society existed during the rule of Oliver Cromwell are not to be found between Puritans in England and Virginia Episcopalians. Moreover, with the restoration of the monarch in 1660, tidewater settlers proved equally adept at returning to the fold they had never really left.

If indeed one is to search for divergencies, it must be in the area of difference between the returned Laudian high churchmen of 1660 and the colonial church of Virginia. Here dissimilarity appears, and it was sociological rather than doctrinal or ecclesiastical. While restoration churchmen in England, ardent, well-organized, and determined to maintain their anti-Calvinist stance at all costs, prepared to dominate convocation and parliament, Virginians moved in a different direction. Lacking both episcopacy and centralized power, the colonial church drifted into close alliance with local interests and ultimately into lay control. That control was wielded by the vestries of Virginia's thirty-five parishes in 1660.[77] For the remainder of the century—though not thereafter—laymen ruled.[78] Their rule was consistent with the themes of the anti-Roman alliance.

While the shortage of clergy must be taken into account, it is worth noting that more than one parish in Virginia elected Presbyterians as incumbents. At St. Mary's White Chapel and Christ Church in Lancaster County three years before the Toleration Act (1689) itself, the vestry elected Presbyterian Andrew Jackson (d. 1710). So popular was this Scottish follower of John Calvin that his vestry stood by him for twenty-three years. When Sir Edward Northey, the attorney general of England, stated in 1703 that Virginia parishes had the right to call their own ministers but that they must be inducted thereafter by the governor, the vestries of St. Mary's and Christ Church refused to obey the law. Clearly Jackson could not become rector since he was not in Anglican orders. Rather than dismiss him or ask him to change his ordination, the Lancastrians threatened to call a popular assembly if talk of dismissal was not dropped. Jackson quietly went back to work preaching and administering the sacraments according to the prayer book.[79]

It is important to note here that, during the interregnum, forces were set in motion which were to have a profound effect upon the future development of the colonial church. Those forces put the colonial establishment on a course which was in direct conflict with the views of obedience to imperial power which exiled Laudian clergy were struggling to maintain. The issue would be self-government against the spiritual authority of the king and bishop; in America that authority was vested in the royal governor. The roots of self-government in church and state in Virginia can be traced to the establishment of the House of Burgesses in 1619, or to the 1630s, when the unpopular governor, Sir John Harvey, was successfully defied by local interests.[80] After 1650 the House of Burgesses became the center of authority, electing its own governor and upper house or Council of State. In addition, in 1655 the right to vote for representation was extended to all freemen regardless of property ownership.[81] As George McLaren Brydon commented, "The change put into effect by Virginia's surrender to the Commonwealth was a very radical one, in that it placed all power, legislative, executive, and judicial, in the hands of the elected representatives of the people."[82] Those representatives during the interregnum left to individual parishes all matters concerning the vestry, churchwardens, the poor, and the choice of ministers. As one writer has put it, "This *carte blanche* to the parishes must have engendered in the vestries an independent attitude that was later to find expression in open conflict with the governor's prerogative."[83] It seemed that to be English—or was it American?—meant the acquisition of whatever freedom and local responsibilities rulers had not the time to exercise and then sharing the spoils.

After the disarray in the anti-Roman grand alliance in the 1630s and 1640s, the Commonwealth period gave a legacy of permanence and authority to Parliament and so to Protestantism in England. Parliamentary prerogative replaced royal prerogative. Whatever Cromwell's difficulties, both with his own legitimacy and with contentious representative government, the decade of the 1650s ended with the assurance that anti-Catholic forces would remain committed to their calling. Henceforth, the Church of England would rely alone upon royal favor and would depend upon the authority of the state for her legitimacy. Parliament held the key to the state's authority and so to the church's. The church came to realize this, and, in the words of Harold Laski, "taught non-resistance as the condition of her own survival."[84] But if the old order of the Church of England learned the lesson of nonresistance after midcentury, so too did the new order of Puritan revolutionaries.[85] Through no particular virtue of its own, the church in Virginia seems to have anticipated nonresistance and subservience to the state before either Puritans or Anglicans in England.

The Roman Catholicism of James II proved to be the end in the already condemned cause of rapprochement with continental Catholic powers. When that stodgy and grimly retributive monarch actuated the Bloody Assizes of 1685 and hung more than four hundred of the poor who had participated in the rebellion of Charles II's illegitimate son, the duke of Monmouth, a swift and quiet reordering of affairs took place. A reunited Parliament and church acted in unison. By 1688 it was clear that James meant to bring England into alliance with the Counter-Reformation, remaking English institutions as he went.[86] The twin strategies of survival and ascendency drew the Calvinist stadtholder of Holland, Prince William of Orange, together with his wife, Mary, to the throne. Thus, in the 1690s England once again came to assume leadership in the coalition, this time against Louis XIV of France. That leadership against Roman Catholicism would last for the quarter century which separated the accession of William and Mary from the death of Queen Anne. As Norman Sykes wrote, "A corresponding vocation was the lot of the Church of England, to which foreign Protestants, both individually and corporately, looked as the chief and head of the Protestant interest, addressing it, in terms used for example by the *Unitas Fratrum* to Archbishop Wake, as *sancta Ecclesia Anglicana, omnium Protestantium Ecclesiarum praecipua et florentissima.*"[87]

In these remarkable changes of fortune, Virginia's religious establishment played no part. Nor did England take notice of the greater or lesser theological grails sought by the inhabitants of its Chesapeake territories. Not until the end of the century, when the idea of empire became attractive, did Englishmen and Americans, Anglicans and Episcopalians, set out in earnest quest of their hitherto elusive spiritual unity. In the meantime, Virginians' naive loyalty to what they considered a proper and respectable cause helped them to follow English directions without asking embarrassing questions. Since they assumed nobody was for Rome and its "prodigious enormities," they could pay equal respect to Charles I, to the commonwealth of Oliver Cromwell, the restoration of Charles II, and the glorious revolution which ousted James and called in William and Mary. Isolation bred simple Protestant loyalty to what Virginians thought was the cause of monarch, church, and mother country. If in 1649 they had to scratch their heads in puzzlement as to why Charles I lost his on the block, one thing was clear: religiously the change of government made little difference. The lord protector was clearly Protestant and no doubt as staunch a defender of the faith as hapless Charles. Suspicion was reserved for the pontiff of Rome, and, if the idea of *sancta Ecclesia Anglicana* did not exactly set denominational pulses racing, the cry of "popery" was sure to excite political passion. Well might Thomas Cradock (1718–1770) echo, in the next century, the ideals of Christian unity.[88] When it came to Roman Catholicism, he rejoiced that Queen Elizabeth had driven "off the blind Tyranny & usurpation of a Romish Priesthood, & left [us] in the happy liberty to think for ourselves."[89] To Cradock, to be a true Englishman was to be an anti-Romanist. "Oh, let us chiefly remember," he reminded his fellow Protestants, "that we can chuse our religion likewise, & need not tamely, basely submit to the slavish yoke of a Roman pontiff,—a yoke which I hope I may now boldly say our proud enemies attempted to put upon us in vain."[90] Such anti-Catholic sentiments as Cradock's were common enough fare in the household of Protestant faith. They were to remain so for a very long time to come.[91]

CHAPTER 2
Allurement, Laicization, and Authoritarianism in Virginia

Jamestown was founded, if not on a swindle, then on a series of deceptions. In London, leaders of the Virginia Company wished to attract investors and, increasingly, settlers. The leaders' purpose changed with circumstances. First, it was to discover a passage to China, navigable from the west; then the purpose was to plunder the Spaniards, to produce manufactured goods for England, and finally, when all of these failed, to become a land company and sell off their subdivided wilderness real estate.[1] To achieve these shifting goals, the company advertised with varying degrees of intensity between 1606 and 1624. In the process a policy of allurement of investors and settlers through shameless propaganda developed which reached its height in 1608 and 1609. A long period of disillusionment, squabbling within the council of the company, and financial loss ensued. Yet even after 1610, allurement did not fade. It continued almost until 24 May 1624, in the court of Kings Bench, when the original charters were revoked and Virginia became a crown colony.

But in those early, hopeful days before the impact of conditions at Jamestown was felt in London, an animated coalition of religion, ambition, and nationalism prevailed. It was said: "The eyes of all Europe are looking upon our endeavors to spread the Gospell among the heathen people of Virginia, to plant an English nation there, and to settle a trade in those parts." Nobles, bishops, London companies, and astute government servants like Francis Bacon responded. Rhymes and jingles were penned—all of them awful. Advertisements appeared. The clergy preached sermons to whip the fearful into shape, while lotteries tempted the gamier. Pocahontas and her maidens were imported to entice the reluctant. As the crescendo of propaganda increased, abduction of voyagers was sanctioned as the crown, preachers, and the settlers themselves contributed their rhetoric to the national and religious cause.

In addition, the logistics which accompanied the propaganda looked well enough on paper: playing savage tribes against one another, putting England's idle poor to work, and giving the nation a new market. But where logistics faltered in the starving time of 1609–1610, vision took over. No matter that by 1612 adventurers complained that only the name of God was more often profaned in the marketplaces of the capital than was the name of Virginia. No matter that, under the authoritarian rule of Sir Thomas Dale, Jamestown gained the reputation of being almost a penal colony. Missionary opportunity, a return on stock invested, the beauty and profligacy of nature in America, even the absence of clerical surplices were all invoked. The realities, not least the missionary and religious ones, were another, often grim, matter. The failure of Christianization, the prospect of an early death, too many men and not enough women, and a seesawing tobacco economy were the hardships which greeted would-be settlers for the better part of the century. Since Virginia lacked that communal sense of obligation, competency, and the desire for hard work which characterized Massachusetts Bay, an attempt was made, it has been argued, to impose such values by means of dictatorial laws.[2] When authoritarianism too failed to decrease idleness, a peculiarly American "chance for each individual to achieve something on his own" resulted.[3] "New World experience triumphed over Old World customs," and a special American state of mind and work was born. Old World customs remained, though not unchanged, and allurement, authoritarianism, and individualism grew up together in Virginia and remained in curious coalition throughout the seventeenth century.

Samuel Purchas cannot be said to have possessed the literary qualities of his friend and inspirer Richard Hakluyt (1552?–1616), author of the *Divers Voyages touching the discoverie of America*. Nevertheless Purchas's *Pilgrimage* was an immensely popular book in its day, running to four editions in its author's lifetime. The *Pilgrimage* was an armchair travelogue which combined geography with the revelation of God's providence. Purchas was inspired, or so he claimed, by a host of classical and contemporary authors—seven hundred in the first edition and thirteen hundred in the last. With a marked display of academic credentials, he invited his readers to join him

> On the learned Preachers Pilgrimage,
>   Religionis ergo,
> The Body of this Booke is Historie,
> Clad in the quaint garments of Geographie,
> Adorned with Iewells of Chronologie,
> Fetch't from the Treasur's of Antiquitie,

The better part thereof, Theologie,
Soule of the World: Religious Pietie
Addes life to all, and gives Eternitie.[4]

Purchas followed up his invitation with a systematic exposition of England's providential role and with "a magnificent vision of the universal unity of mankind."[5] In 1613 that vision of one world had to begin with Genesis, Adam, the Tower of Babel, and the birth of languages. But what was the first language, Syriac or Hebrew? It seems clear that the vicar of Eastwood thought it Hebrew. Surely it was not Dutch, as "a few Dutch Etymologists" had claimed. To admit such a thing would be, he declared, to make England a colony of Amsterdam, which clearly would not do. But the point was that before the Tower of Babel all people could communicate in linguistic and social harmony. For erecting its proud tower, said Purchas, humanity was scattered throughout the world by a justly wrathful God. But there was an orderliness about the dispersion: men "settled in their proper Habitations." How many habitations are there, he asked; how many nations and languages? Africanus says seventy-two,[6] but that was long ago, and in our time God has so increased our knowledge of the world that should the reader consult the works of Joseph Scaliger, "how easie it were . . . to get down 72 more."[7] What Purchas insisted on was that God had opened up both persons' minds and the highways of the seas, luring them forth to explore the wonderful globe, all for the sake of the unity of humankind in the coming Kingdom of Christ. Even papists, friars, and Jesuits had their part to play in this unfolding mystery of God's grand design. Though the "racke of [Jesuit] Confessions and rabble of Ceremonies" are "Hay and Stubble," and though such rites go to prove that the devil has gotten these "Ignatian Ushers in his hellish schoole," still God uses all persons. The Church of Rome has a role: it is to be the forerunner of the true church. An English expedition to Virginia, he added in an improbable afterthought, might even help convert the Spanish.[8]

But how will God entice the reluctant English Leander to swim the Hellespont to his lovely Hero in the new world?[9] The answer is by the loveliness of her "temperate Clymate, fruitfull Soile, fresh and faire Streames, [and] sweet and holsome Aire."[10] In fact God has so diversified the materials and creatures of the earth that what is absent in one place is present in another. By trade in crops and raw materials, men will be brought into contact with other lands and peoples. The goal of course was not financial return on investors' stock but rather the unity of mankind illumined by providential, divine wisdom and informed by the Church of England. All paled before that great destiny. To that end, defy the terrors of the Atlantic. Let history, chronology, the classics, even theology itself, take a back seat to piety, the "Soule of the World," which alone could add enthusiasm to English enterprise and thus bring all to the eternal kingdom. So spoke Samuel Purchas. Officially the missionary trumpet had sounded.[11]

Even amidst their brutality toward native tribes, Englishmen pronounced their wonder at the rich variety of America. "We did see many squirels," wrote George Percy, "conies, Black Birds with crimson wings, and divers other Fowles and Birds of Divers and sundrie collours of crimson, watchet [light blue], Yellow, Greene, Murry [dark red]."[12] This fifth son of the Earl of Northumberland was appropriately transfixed by the size of Chesapeake waterways, the abundance of trees, fruits, fish, animals, even the physical beauty, pride, and modesty of the Indians he was later to murder.[13] Percy wrote,

wee saw the goodliest Woods as Beech, Oke, Cedar, Cypresse, Walnuts, Sassafras and Vines in great abundance, which hang in great clusters on many Trees, and other Trees unknowne, and all the grounds bespred with Strawber-ries, Mulberries, Rasberries and Fruits unknowne, there are many branches of this River [James], which runne flowing through the Woods with great plentie of Fish of all kinds, as for Sturgeon all the World cannot be compared to it. In this countrey I have seen many great and large Medowes having excellent good pasture for Cattle. There is also great store of Deere both Red and Fallow. There are Beares, Foxes, Otters, Bevers, Muskrats, and wild beasts unknowne.[14]

Allurement was not confined to nature alone. In Alexander Whitaker's well-known invitation to fellow Puritans back home in England, this attractive missionary asked why more of his persuasion now in London and Cambridge "that were so hot against the Surplis and subscription" did not come to America, "where neither are spoken of?"[15] Whitaker's *Good Newes from Virginia,* a lively plea for greater English generosity, spoke of the wisdom of greater exertion and charity on the part of those comfortably back home.[16] Adventurer Ralph Hamor kept up the appeal a year later: "What is more excellent, more precious, more glorious than to convert a heathen nation from worshipping the devil to the saving knowledge and true worship of God in Jesus Christ?"[17] Even in the midst of what Edmund Morgan calls the "Jamestown fiasco" others voiced very similar senti-ments.[18] In addition James I, through the two English primates, sent com-mands to all of the dioceses of the Church of England to raise money for a school and college to further missionary and civilizing efforts among the Indians.[19]

Gradually from 1610 to 1621 disillusionment set in; then, after the mas-

59

sacre of 1624, the influx of men and funds suddenly halted. One of the earliest to voice disenchantment was George Thorpe (1576?–1622). Deeply committed to the task of achieving good relations between white and red, Thorpe became an energetic proponent of the peaceful conversion of Indians. He taught an Indian lad to read and write English and took a healthy interest in native religion. This former member of Parliament and gentleman of the king's privy chamber went to Virginia in 1620 and was made a member of the council of the colony and manager of the college which had been proposed for Henrico. In 1621 Thorpe and John Pory (1570–1636), also a former M.P., a Cambridge graduate, and first speaker of the House of Burgesses in Virginia, composed a letter to Edwyn Sandys. Signed with Thorpe's name, the letter was self-accusatory: "slender hath been the harvest of our Labors . . . insoemuch as I doute not that God is displeased with us that wee doe not as wee ought to doe" in the service of Christ; "scarce any man amongest us," he complained, "that doth soe much as affoorde them [the Indians] a good thought in his hart and most men with theire mouthes give them nothinge but maledictions and bitter execrations." The English think all the wrong and injury, even the devil's malice, has been effected by red men, whereas, he continued, "in my poore understandinge if there bee wronge on any side it is on ours who are not so charitable to them as Christians ought to be." Thorpe's own policy of allurement was a two-way street. Perhaps inviting modern, anti-imperialistic objection, he judged that the "better sort of them [is] of a peaceable and vertuous disposition" and had ability "to affect English fassions." Indians "will be much alured to affect us by gifts . . . they beinge as I think first to be dealt with by the booke of the worlde." On the other hand, Thorpe begged for expressions of good will from the Virginia Company toward the natives, "some publicke declaration of theire intente and desier of the convertion of this people and there withall a testification of theire love and hartie affection towards them. . . . I thanke god," he concluded, "I have testimony of a good conscience."[20] A singularly thoughtful man, Thorpe suffered profound discouragement. Much later, in 1648, Robert Evelin proved as disillusioned as Thorpe had been in 1621. After two major massacres of whites by Indians, Evelin paid no attention to missionary outreach but concerned himself with mere survival. Allurement was hardly in his mind when he described the colony as subject to the "negligence of servants, or treachery of slaves and apprentices, [the] agues and deseases, brackish water to drink or use; and a flat country, [where] standing waters in woods bred a double corrupt air." Virginians were seated in sooty, wooden houses which were subject to fire. There were no forts or stockades to which planters could retreat in time of attack by the Algonkians. Sickness had taken the lives of innumerable settlers, and for all these reasons Evelin flatly asserted, "I on my view of Virginia disliked Virginia,"[21] and returned home.

Despite the bad press, the policy of allurement continued. The following year, in the anonymous *A Perfect Description of Virginia*, the familiar subject reappeared. Colonials, living in a land of plenty, have "20 Churches . . . and Ministers to each, and the Doctrine and Orders after the Church of England: the Ministers' Livings are esteemend worth at least 100/*per annum*. They are paid by each planter so much Tobacco per Pole, and so many bushels of Corn: they live in peace and plenty."[22] In 1650 Edward Williams's *Virgo Triumphant* sounded all of the themes of the 1610s: Virginia "will disburthen this Nation of many indigent persons"; orphans will become wealthy; timber, fish, and crops of all kinds will provide sustenance for disbanded soldiers; revenue thus derived will make England richer, and—it was an old argument—a strong colonial population will be a deterrent to Spanish conquest.[23] In addition, Williams went on, the climate in the Chesapeake and the Carolinas was better than either that of New England or Barbados.

In 1656 the conforming Puritan John Hammond, who had disliked Berkeley's policy of harassment of Independents and who supported the Commonwealth, addressed himself to ship captains bound for the colony. If, Hammond judged, men knew the truth about England's mid-Atlantic colonies of Virginia and Maryland, they would "covet to be your Passengers." Promising not to "speak or write glossingly," Hammond deplored the "odiums and cruell slanders cast on those two famous Countries. . . . Foggy Mists" had hindered many from going there, and while "the Country is reported to be an unhealthy place, a nest of Rogues, whores, desolute and rooking persons; a place of intolerable labor, bad usage and hard Diet etc.," still, he suggested, Virginia was not devoid of honest inhabitants.[24] Combining criticism with hope for a more prosperous future, Hammond sought to entice the godly by making it clear that laws had been passed and vices suppressed, so that Virginians had become "great observers of the Sabbath."[25] In the past "many came, such as wore Black Coats, and could babble in the Pulpit, roare in a Tavern, exact from their Parishioners, and rather by their dissolutenesse destroy then feed their Flocks." Recently, however, "began the Gospel to flourish, civil and honourable, and men of great estates flocked in." Hammond described Virginia as full of sober, godly people who were prospering in a healthy and bountiful environment. Neighbors lived together in peace and enjoyed a measure of self-sufficiency unknown in England. One thing was clear: dissolute ministers, those "wolves in sheeps clothing," had been replaced, so that the "Sabbaoth [was] spent in good exercises."[26]

In the next decade Nathaniel Shrigley continued to feed English curiosity about flora and fauna,[27] while Roger Greene, rector at Jamestown, exposed the sad state of Virginia's church. Greene judged that parishes were too large. Church buildings were scarce, neglected, and dispersed.[28] As Howard Mumford Jones opines, Greene's *Virginia's Cure* "attempts the wellnigh impossible feat of proving that religion requires Christians to live together in cities."[29] As a result of the dispersion of the churches, declared Greene, there was a want "of Christian Neighborliness, or brotherly admonition, of holy Examples of religious Persons, of the Comfort of theirs, and the Ministers Administrations in Sicknesse, and Distresses, of the benefit of Christian Civil Conference and Commerce."[30] Greene, a Cambridge graduate (M.A., 1638), had been ordained in the Church of England but had settled in the Puritan area of Nansemond County. Shocked at the "Vices that reign in . . . Families, [and] of the spiritual defects of their Conversations," he was not above telling his English readers that there were "faithfull and vigilant Pastors, assisted by the most careful Churchwardens," but that these few could not trim Virginia's "plants [which] now grow wilde in that Wildernesse." Greene, perhaps following Governor Berkeley's policy during the latter's second administration, called for more towns to be erected, because the lack tended to "rob God of his due publicke Worshipe and Service . . . so that [they will] continue under the curse of God."[31] Moreover, ministers should be instituted and a bishop sent to the colony.[32] Greene went on to appeal to the comeliness of Virginia's children, who are "generally of more ingenious Spirits than these in England." He also spoke of the missionary opportunity to "remake the Heathen that are men, in love with the Christian Religion." There was also, he pleaded, a continuing need for "Orthodoxe Ministers." In language that could not fail to touch the sensibilities of the restoration episcopate, Greene noted that "in the late times of our Churches Persecution, her people alone, cheerfully and joyfully embraced, encouraged and maintained the Orthodoxe Ministers that went over to them, in their Publicke Conformity to the Church of ENGLAND, in her doctrine and stated manner of Public Worship." In this "very pleasant and fruitful land," the unblushing conclusion was that we hate "Usurpers."[33]

Published reports, pamphlets, and books on the colony, if they did not always attract adventurous Englishmen, continued to interest the inquisitive.[34] Not all were complimentary. The observations on nature in the Chesapeake colony written by the Reverend John Clayton and John Banister in the 1680s were bland enough fare,[35] but the astringent criticisms by contemporaries of treatment of blacks and Indians in the Old Dominion were another matter and caused at least one minister to be sent elsewhere.[36]

Yet appeals to orthodoxy, the salubrious climate, and the opportunity to live in a new, promising environment never died out. As late as 1731, William Byrd was urging the earl of Orrery to come to America and "be a Monarch of a very fine country, and make a very good Soart of People happy." Virginians, commented Byrd, "live in the innocence of the Patriarch under our Vines and our Fig-trees surrounded by our Flocks and Herds. . . . We are all of one Religion and of one Party in Politics."[37] If English merchants keep Virginians from being rich, Byrd continued, the climate assures them they will not be poor. Here there was no "Fogg and Smoake with which your atmosphere is loaded." It was miraculous to Byrd that "any lungs can breathe in Air compounded of so many Vapours and Exhalations like that of dirty London."[38] Virginia, he exclaimed, is Canaan compared to the "Fleshpots of Egypt." It is the innocent land, yet not so innocent that "old maids and old bachelors" are rare and "reckoned as ominous as a Blazing star."[39]

Despite such blanket denunciations of the colony as Lionel Gatford's *Publick Good without Private Interest,* the policy of attraction persisted. Religion played its role in that policy, whether in support of imperial wisdom or local pride. Early in Virginia's history, missionary endeavor sought to bring order and purpose to the colony. In the 1660s Roger Greene provided religious backing for Berkeley's plan to create an urban society and diversify its economy. That Berkeley's and Greene's rhetoric and strategy did not correspond to the realities of royal opposition, to provincial chauvinism, and to overly optimistic estimates of the colony's potential may or may not be morally reprehensible.[40] Certainly they knew what was needed.

Though Greene's criticism of the vastness of parishes and the dispersion of church buildings was well-taken, it should not blind us to the fact that he, as much as Alexander Whitaker, sought to strengthen the religious establishment by attracting English aid. As they could not command that aid, they pled for it. They did so, often by criticizing their environment and just as often by praising it. In the Chesapeake Bay, the landscape of providential history had become choked with the weeds of tobacco culture. Theirs was a mercantile community which took its religion as a matter of course. Because Virginians' expressions of faith were prosaic and their church weak, English aid was necessary. Virginians meant to entice the neglectful by appealing to their curiosity. Their goal was to justify the changes they desired to their rulers across the ocean, to their neighbors, and to themselves as well.

But allurement was not enough. The cudgel of authority was needed to beat the unheeding into obedience. White men and red men alike must hear the voice of religious authority and obey its injunctions. Leaders of the

Virginia Company both in England and America might present appealing propaganda, but, unless they could instill into the minds and hearts of their followers a permanent hunger for work and worship, that propaganda alone would not suffice. The early settlers of Virginia were commoners from the lower class, dispossessed, neither unified by shared distress nor galvanized by strong conviction. Since respect for authority could not be educed from such folk, it had to be imposed upon them. Those who disembarked along the banks of the James in 1607 and thereafter were a different sort than those who migrated to Massachusetts in 1629. Puritans in 1606 and 1610 had merely been thwarted by Elizabeth and James in England. By the summer of 1629 the determined émigrés at Cambridge University had been shaped and toughened by hardship and disappointment. When these later predestinarians decided to leave England, they did so as a community which knew its own mind and was driven by singleness of purpose. The ringing words of John Winthrop's *A Modell of Christian Charity* makes that abundantly clear. For the earlier Virginians no such religious and social singularity existed. Laws must do what manifestos could not: create a people. It was as impossible then as now; Virginia's lawmakers forgot that both manifestos and laws were the creation of society.

In the first years of the Jamestown colony the laws were harsh. Whipping was the cure for disrespect to the clergy. For taking the Lord's name in vain, the hapless offender was liable to have a bodkin thrust through his tongue. Between 1611 and 1619 continued blasphemy against any of the persons of the Trinity was punishable by death. Were these retributions carried out? Certainly they remained on the statute books as grim warnings to all. Historian Richard Morton declares that their enforcement was never in doubt.[41] The most stringent measures were those found in the famous regulations written by Sir Thomas Gates (d. 1621). Gates's work was enlarged upon by the deputy governor, Sir Thomas Dale (d. 1618). The result was *Laws . . . Divine, Politique and Martiall.* Misnamed "Dale's Laws," they exhibit not only the religious emotions of the appended prayer but also proscriptions against stealing of "victuals, or of Arms, Trucking stuffe, Apparell, Linnen, or Wollen, Hose or Shooes, Hats or Caps, Instruments of Steele, Iron &c."[42] An approving Alexander Whitaker found them to be the "sword of the magistrate unsheathed," though only in defense of an honest life, as he was quick to add.

Authority was to reach not only white settlers but the native population as well. Indians were to be "reduced" to the "true worship of God and Christian religion."[43] Reduce—at first—had nothing to do with military operations; it meant *to reclaim, to call a person back,* in short, conversion.

64

Indians were to be brought back to their true God for, as Purchas observed, the "chief God they worship is the Devill, which they call Oke."[44] The principal work of Englishmen—besides obeying the law themselves—was, as the charter of 1609 stated it, "the conversion and reduction of the people in those parts." God ruled King James; James ruled England, Englishmen, and dutiful Indians in America. Not only would "infidels and savages" be initiated into the Protestant faith of England but into "human civility and to a settled and quiet government." However, when Indians proved less than willing to place themselves under the tutelage of England's church and academy, colonists resorted to kidnapping native children from their "Iniocasockes or Priestes by a surprise of them all and detayning them prisoners." By 1618 such ardent missionary and cultural outreach was given an additional fillip in the instructions to the new governor, Sir George Yeardley (1577–1627): a college was to be built "for training up of the Children of those Infidels in true Religion, moral virtue and Civility and other godly uses."[45]

Indian civility, history, and political experience dictated otherwise. Shortly before the English trespassed into their territory, thirty Algonkian tribes had come under the sway of Chief Powhatan's growing confederacy. Eight of the tribes had been inherited by Powhatan, "the others having submitted to his rule by conquest."[46] While these united Algonkians were more advanced than the Iroquoians and the Tuscaroras to the south, still "English settlers encountered some of the most vulnerable and—to European eyes—least 'civilized' Indian cultures, and gradually (greedily) chose to obliterate them."[47] At the moment that English missions and arms threatened, this Chesapeake confederacy was just beginning to achieve what has been termed "primordial unity": a corporate feeling of racial and ethnic oneness.[48] Moreover, the native people in the area had had contact with Europeans before 1607. French and Spanish ships had plied the mid-Atlantic seaboard, and the Spanish had made incursions into the Chesapeake, burning villages and transporting native people to slavery in the West Indies.[49] Some of these may have been the same Algonkians who later came into unhappy contact with Captain John Smith and the first permanent settlers.[50]

While Smith exercised his power and authority with more wisdom than his successors, a pattern had been already established in the two unsuccessful English colonization ventures at Roanoke Island in the 1580s under the leadership of Sir Walter Raleigh (1522–1618) and Sir Richard Grenville (1540–1591). As Samuel Eliot Morison remarked, "Europeans never seemed to learn from one another's experience how to deal with the American Indians intelligently, or even with Christian humanity. Columbus at Hispaniola and Jamaica, Ribaut and Laudonière in Florida, and Cartier in Canada were as bad as the English."[51]

Though the red people's deities, idols, and elaborate rituals were "awesome arrangements and not to be treated lightly,"[52] to the English those deities were uncouth, monstrous, and satanic.[53] To the Jamestown colonists, the American peoples were un-Christian. "From the very beginning of their interest in the New World," writes Taylor, "Englishmen were impressed by the heathenism of the Indians. The immediate result was the early intensification of English religious commitment." As we have already seen, the strategy which accompanied the intensification of religious commitment took two forms. The one, the crusaders' infatuation with conversion by force, vied with the other, the missionaries' ideal—or was it a reverie?—which "consciously countered the idea that the heathenism and barbarism of the Indians justified a Christian nation's attacking them." Those believing in peaceful conversion "called England to a humane but practical mission . . . which emphasized the ultimate worth of Indian souls in God's providential history of mankind."[54] Out of such a worthy sentiment came plans for the college at Henrico. Savages were to be lured from their religious arrangements to the one true God. Other Englishmen responded to the intensification of religious loyalty by fighting the monstrous satanism they convinced themselves characterized Indian religion.

Agreement eluded the strategists of both camps. The quiet dedication to nonviolence by such as Whitaker, Pory, Thorpe, and Donne was answered by Robert Graye's trumpet blast announcing holy war. That call to conquest was delivered less than a month before Admiral Sir George Somers's fleet dropped down the Thames on 15 May 1609. In the same year the confusion was compounded by Robert Johnson, who declared that the purpose of English expeditions into Indian territory was to bring the heathens to the gospel and civilization by gentle persuasion. Johnson would only ask of those heathens "quiet residence to us and ours, that by our owne labour and toyle, we may worke this good unto them." To be sure, the English wished to be recompensed for their investment, but indigenous peoples would be "most friendly welcome to conjoyne their labours with ours, and shall enjoy equall priviledges with us." Englishmen, so it seemed, were to use only "faire and loving meanes suting our English natures."[55] In view of the hostilities which constantly vexed the two peoples throughout the seventeenth century, it is remarkable that peaceful conversion was so often advocated or even advocated at all.

Over a century later, despite the intervening bloodletting between the two races, the voice of Christian humanity could still be heard. As late as 1728,

William Byrd II once again gave voice to the advantages of milder means of conversion. Byrd lamented the antagonism between white and red. The shoe of conscience still pinched. Why had not early colonists married Indian women, asked that lusty autocrat? They were well-proportioned and would make "wholesome, straight bed-fellows" and "honest wives for the first planters." Miscegenation was no problem for Byrd, as it had been for those first English sailors at Roanoke who had refused the offers of native girls.[56] "All nations of men have the same natural dignity," Byrd declared, "and we all know that very bright talents may be lodged under very dark skin." To those who objected, he added elsewhere—though he thought it a shame to count color a reproach—"if a Moor may be washed in three generations, surely an Indian might be blanched in two." Though red and black were not exactly beautiful, such skin colors were certainly no reason for whites not to enter into so good-natured an alliance and thereby convert native Americans. Think of the bloodshed that might have been prevented, Byrd declared, warming to his subject, of Christians made ("a sprightly lover is a prevailing missionary") and of future citizens born not enfeebled by luxury. The "poor Indians would have had less reason to complain that the English took away their land if they had received it by way of a portion for their daughters."[57] While one may delight in Byrd's ingenuousness, the dreary politics of experience decreed another course. The crusaders won out. The authority of England's Christian church would be imposed with military thoroughness.

But Byrd had hit the issue squarely: cohabitation, religious or otherwise, was prevented by prejudices against color and heathenism on the one hand and by conquest on the other. And if there was ever any doubt in the Indian's mind about English bias against native pigmentation and religion, it was soon banished at the end of a musket.

The observation of color differences among the races was of course not new with William Byrd II. "The Tawney Moore," Purchas had written over a century before, "the blacke Negro, duskie Lybian, ash-colored Indian, olive-colored American, should with the Whiter European become *one sheep-fold, under one great Sheepherd, till this mortalitie being swalloed up of Life, wee may all be one as he and the father are one.*"[58] In apocalyptic imagery drawn from Revelation, Purchas declared that together these saints would bear "the Fathers name written in their foreheads, the Lambs song in their mouth, the victorious Palmes in their hands, and their long robes being made white in the bloud of the Lambe." No longer would there be "any more distinction of Colour, Nation, Language, Sexe, Condition [so that] all may be One, onely blessed forever." However, among those who overcame Algonkian heathenism by force of arms, color difference from

67

white, Christian Europeans provided added incentive. Following quickly behind religious and racial differences came servitude.[59] At the beginning of the Virginia colony, heathenism, nonwhite skin color, forceful subjection, and slavery itself were intimately and positively related in the eyes of militant crusaders. For proof of this fact, we need go no further than the most common, available public evidence: Shakespeare's *The Tempest.*[60]

The Tempest appeared on the stage of the Globe Theatre in 1612, three years after Admiral Somers's grand departure down the Thames River, and based upon the shipwreck off Bermuda of the unlucky seaman's flagship, *Sea Adventure.* The American Indian sits for his portrait in the figure of Caliban. That gabbling, ridiculous monster is dark-skinned, heathen, and a slave. He is formed of gross matter, earth-colored, an animal slowly evolving into humanity by the magic of Prospero. Not yet truly human, he is possessed of savage uncontrolled sexuality. He worships as divine the powerful "demons" Trinculo and Stephano. His mother was a pagan witch, and he himself was "got by the devil" of her.[61] Caliban even reminds Trinculo of a dead Indian shown in the Elizabethan equivalent of a side show.[62] Once a heathen "king," he at first shows Prospero—an explorer?—"all the qualities o' th' isle." In return, Prospero educated Caliban: he taught him astronomy and

> Took pains to make thee speak, taught thee each hour
> One thing or other. When thou didst not, savage,
> Know thine own meaning . . .
> . . . I endow'd thy purposes
> With words that made them known.[63]

Prospero, like Purchas, would inform the ignorant native of his role in the providence of God. But Caliban remains unappreciative, continues inhuman, and curses this civilizing missionary:

> You taught me language and my profit on't
> Is, I know how to curse! The red plague rid you
> For learning me your language![64]

For his callous indifference to the benefits of civilization, Caliban is made a slave and is called such time and again.[65] Shakespeare reflects the rhetoric of those who would convert by force when he has Prospero say,

> Thou most lying slave,
> Whom stripes may move, not kindness! I have us'd thee—
> Filth as thou art—with human care and lodg'd thee

In mine own cell, till thou didst seek to violate
The honor of my child.[66]

"Demi-devil," "thing of darkness," "abhorred slave": heathenism, dark skin, and slavery walk hand in hand.[67] Indian slavery thus prepared the way for black slavery.

Nothing could be dramatically sharper than the difference between Caliban and Ariel. In Ariel, Shakespeare depicts the lower class, white immigrant to the New World: the indentured servant. Though both characters share a common servitude, there the similarity ceases. Where Caliban is "A freckled whelp hag-born,—not honour'd with / A human shape[,]"[68] Ariel is a brave spirit, delicate, "Jove's lightning," Prospero's industrious servant, and "tricksy spirit." Ariel does not gabble; he sings. He is not earthbound, but a bird who can change shape or remain invisible. He is not loathed but humored. When he complains, the response is a gentle "How now? moody? / What is't thou canst demand?"[69] Ariel talks about liberty from his master's authority, not as a slave but as one whose freedom is promised upon the successful performance of set tasks.[70]

Not so Caliban. If at the end of the play he repents of his heathenism, determines to become wise, and "seek for grace," he does so as a slave still under Prospero's authority. This "can[n]ibal" who is also "cauliban" (the gypsy word for black) does not have his kingship restored to him either in that "still-vexed Bermoothes" or in Virginia itself.

Beyond this perspicuous drama of early America, we must ask whether the heritage of the Protestant reformation harbored an innate racism which promoted discrimination? Was the larger theological tradition of Puritan Calvinism with its clearly providential assessment of history chiefly responsible for developing racism in Virginia? The answer given by one student of early Virginia is no. There was nothing within the theological convictions of Puritanism which "predetermined the ultimate rejection of Indians and later Negroes by white colonists."[71] Calvin, Ames, and Perkins could in no sense be called racists or the fathers of racial slavery.[72] That unhappy result was caused by the persistence of Indian heathenism, by the contrast of skin color, by the brutality of early white-red relations, and by the lack of the customary restraints of Old World customs. Environment in this case won out over ideology. One thing remains clear: "the Englishmen's treatment of another dark-skinned, non-Christian people—the Indians—further supports the argument that a special and inferior status was accorded the Negro virtually from the first arrival."[73]

Blacks imported from Africa were given a status inferior to that of the Indians. No effort at mass conversion was made in their behalf. The authority of catechism, exhortation, and sacrament did not inform their lives. Baptism, solemnization of marriages, and church membership were increasingly denied them by civil law. The reason was simple: membership in the church might prove to be a first step toward political freedom. White planters and their clergy recognized the egalitarian strain in Christianity in which sinner and saint replaced bondsman and freeman as terms descriptive of the universal human condition. Had the church been stronger or more zealous, slavery at least might not have been passed on from parent to child: "In all the European colonies in America where the leading Christian church was in a position to enforce its demands upon slaveholders, the Negro's position was more secure."[74] As it was, Christian protection, guidance, and freedom from slavery itself were not causes which attracted ministers, subservient as they were in Virginia to political and mercantile leadership. Colonies more purely motivated by religion—Catholic, Quaker, and Puritan—would question the treatment of black slaves and even the institution of slavery itself. Episcopalians did not, and the few who did were given short shrift.

It is not my purpose to rehearse again the evidence of the emergence of slavery in Virginia.[75] My task is to examine those instances in which attempts were made to include blacks within the pale of the church's authority. In doing so, it must be kept clearly in mind that the Episcopal church in Virginia failed as an influence upon the slaveowners with respect to their religious duties toward their human property and as an influence upon the slaves themselves.[76] Nevertheless, those attempts which were made to make the church more inclusive deserve attention.

Initially the question of slavery was tied to the authority of religion. In Virginia in 1665, a slave judged to be a Christian was remitted into his master's care as an indentured servant.[77] Evidently, in the first half-century, to be a Christian meant that one could not perforce be a slave. In 1667, however, the General Assembly reversed this position by an official act which stated that baptism into the church did not imply manumission.[78] Moreover, children born to a black woman by an English father followed the condition of the mother and remained in bondage for life.[79] In 1670 the legislature decreed that neither free blacks nor Indians who were Christians could themselves purchase white, indentured, Christian servants. At the same time that legislation respecting religion tended to separate blacks from the church, civil statutes became sterner. Runaway slaves who were subsequently caught and returned to their masters were punishable by dismemberment as a warning to other slaves. On the other hand, masters who killed a black who offered physical resistance to commands were declared to be guilty—not of murder, but of a felony.[80]

The most revealing evidence of the exclusion of slaves from the law governing whites, and so from the white church, came from the acid pen of the Reverend Morgan Godwyn (1641–1690?), whose *Negro's and Indian's Advocate suing for their Admission into the Church* reveals much, not only about treatment of blacks but about the springs of missionary endeavor that existed in the Church of England at the time. Godwyn was a young Oxonian and an ardent royalist. He came to America in 1666. Son of a canon of Hereford and grandson of the bishiop of that diocese, his removal to Virginia was unusual for one of such connections and prospects in the church. However, during his residence at Christ Church, where he received his degree in 1664, he had read Bede's *The Ecclesiastical History of the English Nation.* From that eighth-century chronicle he had learned how his own country had been converted to the Christian religion. Fired by the stories in Bede of saintly bards and missionary teachers, Godwyn was struck by the similarity of opportunity in Virginia. Were the American Indians and black slaves in English colonies so different from the pagan West Saxons of earlier centuries? Godwyn did not think so. Barbarity did not play favorites. Even "Cesar's account of the Ancient Britains," he wrote, "is not such as should make us proud; For he informs us that they were clad with Skins, and did paint their Bodies." Blacks were not nearly so barbarous as the present-day Irish, who are marked, suggested Godwyn with unfortunate English prejudice, by "doltish Stupidity." No matter that Bede had told how youths had once been sent to Celtic Ireland—the equal of ancient Athens, it was said—for education. Africa too, it was to be remembered, "was once famous for Arts and Arms; while Carthage did rival with Rome for the World's Empire." In fact, reported Godwyn, one Barbadian black had said to him "that if the Irishman's Country had first lighted in the Englishman's way [as a source of slave labor], he might have gone no further to look for Negro's."[81] Godwyn held no brief for racism based on skin color, and later on he would find confirmation for his stand in the writings of Richard Blome.[82]

Morgan Godwyn saw every reason for establishing English missions among blacks and Indians in America. In Bede the Oxonian had read how Gregory the Great had sent Augustine to Kent to preach to the English. Once converted to the faith, those same Englishmen "did themselves become no less zealous *Propagators* thereof, both at home and abroad." Northern Europe and Scandinavia had come to know the power of missionaries like Aidan, Columbanus, Willibrord, and Boniface. "Kenwalchus" (Cenwalh), king of the West Saxons, had Christianized his people, "of which Reformation he soon found the effect, in the Prosperity which thereupon ensued."[83] Following in the footsteps of Bede's heroes, in 1667 this seventeenth-century Boniface arrived at Potomac Parish in Stafford County after short stays in York County and at Jamestown. There at

Potomac Parish the full impact of his teachings was felt. Godwyn was more than ready to point out planters' faults, encourage them to mend their ways, and generally teach them a lesson. The results were, to put it mildly, disappointing.

When Godwyn insisted upon converting and baptizing blacks, he was "laughed to Scorn," for, as he indelicately put it, considerations such as the reform of racist beliefs are *"ridiculous among Atheists."*[84] Jests and scoffs soon turned to *"supercilious* Checks and *Frowns* (to say no worse)." When he urged Virginia masters to do their religious duty by their slaves, Godwyn met with passionate opposition. Some demanded of him indignantly, *"What I had to do with their servants?"*[85] At one time he baptized a thirty-year-old black man who had learned to speak English well. The Virginia lady who owned the slave "caused this message to be delivered to me, *that Baptism, I was to understand, was to one of those no more beneficial, than to her black Bitch."*[86] Godwyn responded that he need look no further for proof of original sin. The American scene offered ample opportunity to observe the results of Adam's fall, and he would lay open the Virginians' *"mystery of iniquity* . . . to the view of the World." For Godwyn there was the *"Common Faith* and the *Common Salvation,"* which was open to all and toward which end *"God had now* commanded all Men every where to repent."[87] While he entertained no thought of black freedom from bondage, he judged that the irreligious and oppressive authority which denied slaves their right to the Christian faith was worse than that "Force which first made them so, Because striking at their *Souls,* and subjecting them to *Hell,* as much (only for a longer time) as to their Tormenters here on Earth." Planters' criminality "marks the Oppressor with the blackest Guilt."[88] God would take severe vengeance upon slaveholders, if not in this life, then in the next. When masters deprived their bondsmen of the sacraments, they renounced their own faith. With a sad heart Godwyn concluded, "These two words, Negro and Slave, being by custom grown Homogeneous and Convertible; even as *Negro* and *Christian, Englishman* and *Heathen,* are by the like corrupt Custom and Partiality made *Opposites*; thereby as it were implying that the one could not be *Christians,* nor the other *Infidels."*[89] Rejecting all such distinctions, Godwyn declared that impartiality was the "ornament and Credit" of Christianity.

But that was not all. Stung by Quaker criticism that, when it came to the treatment of other races, Church of England ministers were men-pleasers and hirelings, Godwyn shot back: blacks were like any others in Episcopalian eyes. In theory it sounded well, but in fact Godwyn knew better. He was engaged on two flanks. On the one hand he had to struggle with planter intransigence in Virginia, while on the other hand he had to ward off Puritan, and particularly Quaker, criticism. To the one he simply stated that baptism did not imply manumission. Indeed Christianity, once accepted by the slave population, provided insurance, it was argued, against insurrection.[90] Having made such a claim, Godwyn then turned to his critics on the left. It was difficult for a royalist like Godwyn to praise any brand of Puritans, much less the Quakers, for their prudence and evenhandedness with "inferior" peoples, but he did it.

Whatever the limitations of his vision of racial harmony and equality, Godwyn's words and actions soon brought him into conflict with his parishioners in Stafford County. The conflict reached a climax when Colonel John Dodman, a leading vestryman of Potomac Parish, caused the minister's possessions to be distrained by the sheriff and given to Dodman himself. The accusation was that the young parson had borrowed a horse from the colonel and failed to return it. Godwyn defended himself before the county court, saying that the horse had run away and that he was unable to recover it.[91] Not surprisingly, the county court found for Dodman. Godwyn then appealed to the General Court, and two years later, in 1670, the decision of the lower court was reversed after lengthy debate. Godwyn's books and possessions were returned. Thereupon he departed Virginia.[92]

But Godwyn never forgot his treatment at the hands of his vestry nor the power of those bodies in the colony, the "Plebian Juntos" as he sarcastically called them in a vehement letter to Governor Berkeley.[93] They reminded him of nothing so much as Cromwell's rule in England during the 1650s.[94] Again in the 1670s Godwyn brought trouble on himself on the Island of Barbados by referring to the "Soul-murthuring and Brutifying-state of Bondage." Once again he was forced to leave, this time to become rector of Woldham Parish in Kent. Thereafter he became a vociferous advocate of the rights of colonial slaves, publishing and preaching in Westminster Abbey and other churches in London. Godwyn's efforts to bring the authority of the church to white and black alike bore little fruit until the last two years of the century, while in the meantime the slave code hardened.[95] The church's authority was used to deny blacks equality, to keep them in bondage, and even to withhold from them her spiritual ministrations.

Despite the efforts of modest reformers like Morgan Godwyn, the Church of England in Virginia proved unable at this time to fulfill her mission of bringing solace, fellowship, and her brand of salvation to all humankind of whatever class or color. It seems likely that at least one reason for this failure was that within her company there was no authority independent of a single-minded laity. Had a respectable portion of that laity or a similar group of ministers or even a combination of both retained some critical attitude, the situation might have been different. By the 1670s critics of ecclesiastical exclusiveness and race prejudice found themselves up against a sticky defensive coverage of the status quo.

Neither the policy of allurement nor the solons' authoritative pronouncements alone can explain the emerging character of Virginia's religious establishment in the seventeenth century. While both attraction and authority remained characteristics of the church, they only become fully meaningful when they are related to the overriding fact of the laicization of the colony's religious life. Without bishops, deans, ecclesiastical courts, or centers for theological direction and education such as Oxford and Cambridge in the mother country, the day-to-day responsibility for colonial church affairs fell into the hands of the laity. Since no English bishop claimed Jamestown as part of his episcopal jurisdiction, such powers as might have been exercised by the leaders of the Church of England fell into the hands of the Virginia Company of London. When the company failed and the colony passed under the control of the king, it was his royal agent, the governor, who assumed the traditional episcopal role of commanding the use of the Book of Common Prayer, granting marriage licenses, and collating benefices.[96] When the governors came to share power with their councils and the General Assembly, the laicization of the church was all but complete. Not until the 1690s, when Henry Compton (1632–1713), bishop of London, assumed a degree of control through his agent, James Blair, was there an attempt to curtail lay power, and even then it was only partially successful. As one scholar has claimed, "the Church of England in Virginia in 1690 was more under the thumb of the King than of the Bishop of London."[97] It may well be said that the church was in fact more under the thumb of local vestries than of either king or bishop.[98] Thus one hundred years before the Church of England itself experienced the emergence of lay power, Virginia's establishment found herself in the coarse, enterprising hands of her laity.[99]

The lack of royal and episcopal control of the church and the rise of the laity can not be explained by reference to supposed English inattention to Virginia. The government in London took a consistent and at times lively interest in the colonies. But interest was one thing, domination another. The great distance between the mother country and the colonies meant that immediate command and regulation of churches were often impossible. In addition the smallness of the church in Virginia made it appear less important than the larger church in England. The result was that Americans made their church "a far more independent body than, say, the Church of England in the county of Kent."[100] It was the laity with their special kind of experience in the New World who simply took over and shaped their own institutions. That formation took place early in colonial history.

As Edmund Morgan has written, the Virginia colony in the 1620s enjoyed a booming economy based on the high price of tobacco. He remarks on the "ugliness of private enterprise operating temporarily without check and . . . greed magnified by opportunity, producing fortunes for a few and misery for many."[101] At the same time a "system of labor that treated men as things" began to emerge, together with a "tightening labor discipline beyond what had been known in Virginia." The magisterial backing given Virginia's lay entrepreneurs extended not merely to labor relations and the economy but to the church as well. Lay control over the church was assured in October 1624, when the governor and his council decided that "all . . . Controversies Concerninge the devidinge of the parishes shall stand as now it doth untill it be decided by A generall Assemble or by some other lawfull heeringe."[102] Where the Virginia Company in London had once controlled the creation of parishes, now that important task was to be taken up by the local government.

But was such lay power in the Church of England so new? At first glance the act of dividing Virginia's counties into parishes, each with its vestry and churchwardens, was not particularly innovative.[103] Indeed, since the fourteenth century, churches in England had had laymen who took care of the church property, elected wardens, and levied ecclesiastical taxes. Traditionally there had been two types of lay vestries, select and open. The select vestries were self-perpetuating and the open vestries elected from and by the parish at large. The rights of advowson, that is, the authority to nominate the minister to the bishop, was held either by the crown, the university, the municipality, or the noble landowner. To be sure, such rights in themselves involved lay power in the church. In 1559 lay authority had been given ultimate expression when it was declared that Elizabeth I was "the only supreme governor of this realm and of all other [of] her Highness' . . . dominions and countries, as well in all spiritual or ecclesiastical things or causes temporal."[104] As a result ecclesiastical authority passed from the crown to the Virginia Company to whomever carried such prerogatives to the New World. In 1609 Sir Thomas Gates was assigned the responsibility for the "principall order and Care for the true and reverent worship of God."[105] Lay interest in church affairs was further developed in "Dale's Laws," where the rudiments of the vestries appear. It was declared that "every Minister where he is resident . . . shall chuse unto him, foure of the most religious and better disposed as well to informe of the abuses and neglects of the people in their duties, and service to God, as also to the due reparation, and keeping of the Church handsome, and fitted with all reverent Observances thereunto belonging."[106] These "better disposed" came after 1619 to occupy places in the General Assembly, and it was that body, together with the governor, which then proceeded to discipline ministers, sequester rights of advowson to themselves as vestrymen in their respective parishes, and generally govern the church.

While the assembly's acts of March 1624 manifest some of the powers of Virignia's entrepreneurs, it is the far more complete set of acts passed by the session of 1632 which display the full power of the laity, even over the ministers themselves. First of all the assembly ordered uniformity to the canons and constitution of the Church of England "as neere as may be."[107] Churchwardens were to levy fines on those absenting themselves from worship without reasonable excuse. They were given authority to "make true presentments" of the profane and the ungodly, that is, "common swearers, drunkards, or blasphemers," especially those who "prophane the saboth dayes or contemne God's holy word, or sacraments." Wardens, the assembly declared, were also to "present all adulterers or fornicators, such as shall abuse their neighbors by slanderinge, tale carryinge or backbitinge, or that shall not behave themselves orderlie and soberlie in the churche duringe devine service."[108]

Such Puritan-sounding regulations as were passed by the laity in 1632 did not exempt the ministry itself. The clergy were to report to the Jamestown court their official yearly acts such as marriages and burials and give account of their financial transactions. They were to preach "one sermon every Sonday of the yeare," catechize children, and see that the Holy Communion was administered three times a year, which was less often than in New England, where once a month was the norm.[109] The "Grand Assembly" further rapped clerical knuckles when it summoned the clergy "not [to] give themselves to excesse or drinkinge or ryott, spending theire tyme idelie by day or by night playinge at dice, cards, or other unlawful game." The laity demanded that their ministers "shall heare or reade somewhat of the holy scriptures, or shall occupie themselves with . . . alwayes doinge the things which shall apperteyne to honestie and endeavor to profit the church of God." They were to excel all others "in puritie of life, & should be examples to the people, to live well and christianlie."[110]

Intermittently for the next seventy-five years successive legislatures sought to exercise disciplinary prerogatives over Virginia's ministers.[111] While the acts passed by later assemblies do not all have to do with discouraging drinking and gambling among the clergy, there are recurring injunctions demanding regular preaching, living within one's cure, proper licensing for marriages, maintaining parish records, catechizing, and keeping within the limits of prescribed fees. As late as 1750 it was expressly stated by the government that ministers were not exempt from regulations respecting sexual behavior. No doubt there were extenuating circumstances surrounding the passage of some of these laws, nor should we imagine that all of the clergy were guilty of reprehensible deportment. Nevertheless, clerical behavior was not always of the highest order.

In 1632 the assembly did not merely remark a lack of zeal in the clergy, they also tried to raise the economic standing of the ministry of the colony's established church in order to attract better men. Not unaware of the low price of tobacco which followed the boom years of the 1620s, legislatures attempted to regulate in a more generous manner the salaries of their preachers and to assure them of proper support. Clergy were to receive the twentieth weanable calf, kid, and pig from the stock of each of their parishioners. Likewise farmers in the tidewater were to bring to the ministers ten pounds of tobacco and a bushel of corn at stated times, and, if planters defaulted in their payments, they were liable for double the amount at a later date. When churchwardens failed to oversee these payments and such were not made, what was owing the ministers was to be paid from the wardens' own estates.[112] In addition, fees were levied for marriages and burials. Finally the local populace was to see that churches were built and kept in repair and burial grounds enclosed and properly cared for.

If the laws of 1632 governing Virginia's church do not reach the level of religious expression of the prayer appended to "Dale's Laws," they do exhibit concern for authority, even regimentation in church and society. Their significance lies, however, in the fact that neither bishop, convocation, nor diocese promulgated or enforced them. They were the creation of the laity. That this event occurred by default as much as by design does not lessen the significance of what had happened in the colony. Henceforth, and until the end of the century, ecclesiastical affairs were firmly in the hands of those yeoman farmers whom one historian has characterized as "tough, unsentimental, quick tempered, crudely ambitious men concerned with profits and increased landholdings, not with the grace of life."[113] There was enough concern with life's graces on the part of the colony's hard-bitten entrepreneurs and their local ministers to move them to organize, and perhaps even reform, their church. Whatever else may be said, Virginia's farmers knew what they wanted in religion. Their laws are ample enough proof. They are also evidence that Virginians remembered with nostalgia the security of English society and wished to re-create that society in the New World as they remembered it in England in the early seventeenth century.

By 1636 the vestry system was firmly entrenched as the source of lay power in the Church of England in Virginia.[114] While the vestry act of that year is no longer extant, it was apparently repeated and added to in 1641 and 1643. By the latter date, churchwardens may well have been chosen by the vestry alone. Vestry, wardens, and ministers were to meet yearly with the local justices of the county courts in what was explicitly described as "in nature of a visitation," meaning that the local magistrate sat in some fashion as a bishop. More important still was the power granted the vestries in choosing their own minister. The law stated that the choice of a minister might or might not be presented to the magistrate for approval. In fact, the vestry presented their own choice to themselves, after they had elected the minister in the first place. The minister was then to be inducted by the governor of the colony. The assembly's act stated that the governor might elect and admit a minister to the church in Jamestown or in such a plantation where he, the governor, already had such rights, provided he or his successors "enjoy not that priviledge but in one parish where he or they have such a plantation." In other words, rights of advowson for the governor were severely limited; beyond his own parish he had none. Elsewhere election of ministers was by popular vote of the vestries. In all cases, removal of ministers was left to the action of the "Grand Assembly."[115]

In the following year it was declared that election of the vestries should be in the hands of "the major part of the parishioners who being warned will appear to make choice of such men as by pluralities of voices shall be thought fitt."[116] Such democratization of the church as the placing of rights of advowson together with election of vestries in the hands of the local citizenry was a result of increasing population and, after 1649, the neglect of Virginia by the government of Oliver Cromwell. Coeval with the remarkable upsurge of immigrants, the number of counties expanded during the commonwealth period from eight to twenty. As a result, the House of Burgesses of the General Assembly together with the courts could not handle the business of organizing the churches and plantations, which swiftly reached west to the fall line.[117] Episcopalian congregationalism reached its peak in 1658, when the aseembly abdicated all responsibility, even for the removal of ministers, and, with what was no doubt a sigh of resignation, declared that "all matters concerning the vestry, their arrangements with their ministers, touching church-wardens, the poore and other things concerninge the parishes or parishoners respectively be referred to their own ordering and disposeing from time to time as they shall think fitt."[118] For better or worse, local power filled the gap caused by the inability of the central government to handle county affairs.

But this government was not destined to develop along such democratic lines as had prevailed in the 1640s. Then vestries were popularly elected; now a more elitist arrangement accompanied decentralization. By 1661 it was clear that strong-willed individuals had come into prominence in both church and state in the new counties.[119] These new leaders were at the head of local governments and, as a result, came to sit in the General Assembly, where in 1662 a law was enacted which limited the vestries of the churches to "twelve of the most able men of each parish." It was further stated that "in case of the death of any vestryman, or his departure out of the parish, that the said minister and vestry [was] to make choice of another to supply his roome."[120] This meant that vestries were less than popular organizations. As one historian put it, "This practice of co-optation continued throughout the remainder of the colonial period with the result that the vestry became self-perpetuating with the parishioners losing the right to elect the vestrymen."[121]

While Nathaniel Bacon's rebellion against the second royal government of Sir William Berkeley produced new church regulations in 1676, these should not be seen as expressions of "proletarian" unrest on the part of those who had lost their franchise in the election of vestrymen. No doubt Bacon's short-lived laws reverted to the more democratic process of electing vestries on a triennial basis, but they reflected the desires of only one political faction and not of democratically inclined masses. Bacon's triumphal entry into Jamestown on 23 June 1676 in the rebellion which bears his name is the stuff from which democratic myths are spun, but recent historians are not inclined toward myth.[122] We may note that Bacon's vestry act still spoke of "substantiall householders" being proper candidates for election to vestries.[123] In 1676 it was a question of which lay power center would assume control and not of restitution of an earlier democracy.

Yet not all were satisfied with aristocratic rule. At St. Stephen's Parish in New Kent County in 1682, certain laymen petitioned the governor and his council for redress of grievances against an "Illegal . . . Illiterate & Ignorant" vestry which had been "made up for the major part without the Knowledge or Consent of the parish as the law Injoynes." One or two leaders had so intimidated the rest that ministers were loath to serve the church. Petitioners complained that "noe Minister Cann or will stay with us or teach amongst us, by which meanes the Service of God is wholly neglected, our Church gon to Ruine and Church Discipline & Government almost Clerely laid aside."[124]

Whatever the merits of the case, it is clear that a power struggle was in progress in which the laity alone were the prime movers. No matter whether it was a case of the many against the few or simply of one powerful faction against another, the minister himself was not in control. To more traditional churchmen in later eras for whom the authority of the clergy was held in high regard, the near-complete laicization of Virginia's seventeenth-century church serves as a fitting denoument to the tragicomic drama of an episcopal church without episcopal or even presbyterial authority. However praise- or blameworthy, it is clear by the 1680s the process of laicization was complete. Yet in another twenty years that process would begin to reverse itself, Then Episcopalians in America would begin to think more intently about what it meant to be a member of the Church of England. In the meantime, the greedy and indomitable laymen of Virginia's establishment were making a lasting contribution to the polity of American Episcopalianism: the vestry system.

So far we have seen allurement, imposition of religious authority, and radical laicization in this history of the church in the Old Dominion. Virginians were committed to the theory of uniformity with respect to the religious habits of white settlers. Concomitantly, they rejected the idea that the church's authority and ministrations should extend to or even attempt to allure Indians and black slaves. Despite the recurring missionary call to convert the unfortunates at the bottom of the social ladder, Indians and blacks were kept at arms length, placed in bondage, or both. They were generally detested, not simply because they did menial labor but for what they were in themselves as human beings—people of a different race.

Yet the church was not devoid of pricked consciences. The visions of racial unity espoused by Purchas, Thorpe, and Donne were echoed by the more modest critiques of colonial society which came from the pens of Morgan Godwyn and William Byrd II. It may be that Godwyn's sermons after he returned to England helped keep alive the missionary enthusiasm which was to surface again in the 1690s in the founding of the College of William and Mary. However, the program of exclusion of nonwhite peoples which was written by the General Assembly and the local vestries came to characterize the church in Virginia.

At the same time clergy and laity alike sought aid from the mother country for their establishment through a policy of allurement. Edward Williams, John Hammond, Lionel Gatford, and Roger Greene were clearly aware of both the weakness and the promise of America's first permanent colony. So too was Morgan Godwyn. That aid was forthcoming at the end of the century, and with it arose renewed missionary concern. But there was to be a price tag on English help: sustenance from the mother country in terms of men and money meant, on paper at least, a greater measure of imperial control, the organizing of clergy into a self-conscious order, and the partial undoing of the lay character of the establishment. To these developments we now turn. They will involve us in a larger drama which took place on a grander geographical stage, including not only Virginia but Maryland, New York, New England, and the Carolinas.

CHAPTER 3
The SPG and Anglican Advancement

No time for ceremony. The Glorious Revolution had begun. Immediately he removed his episcopal robes and donned the uniform he had once worn as a young man in the Life Guards. There was not a moment to lose. Action was called for, and action they would get. In the cockeyed politics of the day, certain arrest faced him and the lady he would rescue if he remained in London any longer. Once astride his horse "in buff coat and jack boots, with a sword at his side, and pistols in his holsters," he rode boldly out of the city before the carriage of Princess Anne. The north and safety beckoned. The date was 26 November 1688. The princess had sought his aid, and, while the circumstances were unusual to say the least, the role he now played was stranger still for a man of God. Later on others would draw attention to the inconsistency.

The soldier-bishop was Henry Compton, bishop of London for thirty-eight years from 1675 until his death in 1713. At Compton's side that November night was his nephew, the earl of Dorset, notorious for his madcap bordello romps and known around the capital as "the biggest rake in town." No doubt some of the reawakened gusto of youth animated the middle-aged Compton as well. Their destination should have been southern England where an army under Sir John Churchill was already welcoming William and Mary to the throne. Unfortunately for Compton, Dorset, and the princess, the forces of James II were between London and the coast. Indeed England's last Stuart King was already returning to the capital and had ordered guards placed before his daughter Anne's house in the small hours of the morning. It was too late; Anne was gone.

All told, the affair of the rescue had the breathless quality of a screen-writer's international who-done-it: secret messages, feigned sleep on Anne's part, a backstairs escape, a hackney coach at midnight, temporary shelter in the city, and a flight through the wilds of Epping Forest. It was all very exciting, and the bishop enjoyed himself immensely. A few days later at

81

Leicester, he told the mayor and aldermen that "he was forced to lay aside the Bible at present, but hoped very suddenly to take it into his hands again." Not alone would the bishop let God's strong right hand gain the victory. An episcopal assist for the Protestant cause never seemed out of place in the divine economy. And Compton, who "talked more like a colonel than a bishop," as James himself put it, had "stood pre-eminent as the determined enemy of Rome, and the head of the Church of England opposition to the king's policy."[1]

Just how Compton came to have a degree of spiritual jurisdiction over the royal colonies in America in the seventeenth century remains something of a mystery. Care for the welfare of American churches by the bishop of London was more a matter of default than incursion, of accident than design.[2] When in 1675 Compton became bishop of that diocese, rumor had it that his title to the American jurisdiction rested upon an order in council issued during the Laudian period. Diligent search produced no such instrument. To be sure there was an order which put London's bishop in charge of English coteries in Delft and Hamburg, but clearly the document of 1633 did not extend to America. Nevertheless the assignment to the bishop of London of overseeing religion in America could not be disputed. It was the beginning of a new Anglican tradition.

Enter upon this scene—quite auspiciously as it turned out—the Reverend John Yeo (fl. 1656–1686), a graduate of Exeter College, Oxford, and the first Episcopalian minister of note in Maryland. On 25 May 1676 Yeo addressed himself in "some rude and indigested lines" to the archbishop of Canterbury, the anti-Puritan, high church Tory Gilbert Sheldon (1598–1677). After judging that there were twenty-thousand persons in the colony in 1676 and only three Protestant ministers conformable to the Church of England, Yeo commenced to treat the ministers of the heterogeneous Puritan settlements caustically:

> Others there are (I must confess) that Runn before they are Sent and Pretend they are ministers of the Gospell that never have a Legall call or Ordination to such holy office. Neither (indeed) are they qualified for it, being for the most part such as never understood any thing of learning and yet take upon them to be Dispencers of the word and to Administer the Sacrament of Baptisme; and sow seeds of division amongst the people, and no law provided for the suppression of such in the Province.[3]

There were, Yeo lamented, no "learned men" to confute the Puritan, the avatars of "Phanaticisme," the Jesuit, and the Quaker, all of whom appeared to this Episcopalian parson to be well defended. Thus "the Lord's day is profaned, Religion despised and all notorious vices committed soe that it is become a Sodom of uncleanness and a Pest house of iniquity." On Yeo's right were the Roman Catholics against whom prejudices, since they could not be aired, ran all the deeper.[4] On his left were Quakers and Presbyterians, the latter greatly strengthened by Scottish and Scots-Irish immigration. In such a fix "fears, [and] suspicions were easily aroused; [while] hatred and anger cut deep into men's souls; [and] trifling incidents [arose] . . . sufficient to arouse doubt and mistrust."[5]

After perusing the contents of Yeo's baleful letter, Archbishop Sheldon decided to forward the colonial complaint to his brother bishop in London. With Henry Compton, the letter stopped. Here in Yeo's screed was what the bishop needed. Was not Compton a privy councillor, a member of the Lords of Trade and Plantation, and a man of intelligence and energy? Into what more capable hands could colonial laments and, as a matter of course, the future of the American colonies fall?

Thus armed, Compton immediately set about placing his assumed jurisdiction upon the firmest legal base he could find. At the same time, he made it a point to gather information about the colonies. In July 1677 he put before the Lords of Trade a vivid *Memorial of Abuses which are crept into the Churches of Plantations.*[6] Thereafter, authority was granted Compton to license—or withhold certification from—ministers of the Church of England who embarked for the colonies. The problem was that this authority was in the nature of a personal favor bestowed by each colonial governor to the bishop of London and had to be renewed with every gubernatorial change. Compton and his successors had to make it their business to persuade royal governors to acknowledge the new ecclesiastical authority. While that in itself was no chore, it meant that the church was neither independent nor, in the eyes of the populace, free from political suspicion. Moreover, once their prerogatives were recognized, the bishops of London then had to take on hefty correspondence with colonial clergy, hear complaints, attend and chair meetings of the SPG, and worry about a good deal more than just the diocese of London. Some incumbents of that episcopal office were lazy and tried to evade the obligations. Such shirking of responsibility for the American churches would have some interesting results. Compton was of no such mind.[7] He applied himself briskly to his new charges.

But politics are an affair of hot plowshares and razor-sharp pruning hooks, and, if the bishop of London was to exercise a degree of control over the church in the colonies, that control had to be shared with the governor. In Virginia low church knavery was already widespread. Indeed, it was the governor who had first been given the power, spiritual as well as temporal, over the king's subjects in America. This power came directly from the

83

crown. In their capacity as rulers over the churches, the governors were expected to organize parishes, assign benefices, ensure competent management, supervise clerical conduct, regulate marriages, and probate wills. By such royal commission the governor became a deputy-bishop as well as a stand-in for the king.[8]

In the 1670s a resurgent church, represented by the energetic Compton, broke into this cozy arrangement and was given a limited share in what had been, up to then, a gubernatorial bailiwick. To better exercise his new authority, Compton sought appointment of a representative who would actually reside in the colony. This person was to be a "Commissary . . . appointed under the Governor to exercise the ecclesiastical jurisdiction."[9] While officials could not assume such episcopal spiritual functions as confirmation of children, ordination of ministers, or consecration of churches and burial grounds, they could constitute ecclesiastical courts for the trial of clergy charged with violating canon law, conduct visitations of parishes, and call conventions of resident ministers.[10] Whatever the limitations of the office of commissary and however lacking in episcopal clout, those who held it possessed both power and, what is more important, a direct line to London and its bishop. When that bishop sat in the Privy Council or among the Lords of Trade, conflict with the provincial governor was not far off, for those same governors also had interests to protect and privy councillors to protect them. Moreover, governors were jealous of their prerogatives of control over ministers and parishes: after all, they held office in an older institution than that of commissary. Nor were any gubernatorial rights over the church abrogated by the appointment of the new religious officers. In fact most of the powers delegated to the commissaries had already been assigned to the older representatives of the church. Nevertheless, Compton's actions with regard to tighter imperial control of the Church of England in America marked a significant stage in that church's development.

Another sort of clergyman now suddenly appeared to advance the church's interests in the colonies. Thomas Bray represented a new reforming age in the church, and his influence on America was to be great. The portrait of Thomas Bray owned by the SPG conveys the impression of a man of modesty and simplicity. Bray holds a book in his hand and is surrounded by other books, an appropriate setting since he founded so many colonial libraries.[11] A pietistic reformer similar to Cotton Mather in his desire to learn "how to do good," Bray also resembled John Wesley, both in his concern for the unchurched and the dispossessed and in his extraordinary administrative ability. He responded with determination to the moral license and social cruelties of late seventeenth-century England. "I am a Projector," he wrote, "(a very mean, contemptible Character with such as are accounted men of Wisdom), upon the count of these designs I am continually forming."[12] A student at Oxford in the 1670s, he read theology and the sciences.[13]

When he took his degree in 1678, he was still three years shy of the canonical age for ordination to the ministry of the Church of England. Once more in the 1680s Bray had to bide his time: he could not marry until he had obtained a living that paid enough to support a family. Preferment came slowly to lower class clergy, if at all.[14] But this *"puer pauper,"* as he was designated at Oxford, resolved to use his considerable energies for the benefit of those who had been denied opportunity. To this end, he organized rural deaneries and founded libraries for country parsons who lacked both fellowship and books. In the 1690s, Bray cast about for a way to make money to finance his schemes. The result was one of the most propitious publishing ventures of the decade. From the parish of Sheldon in Warwickshire, he produced his noted *Catechetical Lectures on the Preliminary Questions and Answers of the Church Catechism Giving an Account of the Covenant of Grace.*[15] The lectures were a popular, solidly contrived statement of the church's theology and religion. Bray presented them to an astonished archbishop of Canterbury, Thomas Tenison (1636–1715), at the very moment when that prelate had enjoined the catechizing of the young in obedience to the church's fifty-ninth canon. Almost overnight, three thousand copies were sold and £700 netted for a now famous Thomas Bray. Characteristically, he used the money for his charitable designs.

In the same year Bray was appointed commissary of Maryland. He had learned to court the rich and influential, and now international ecclesiastical politics became his stock in trade. Bray pleaded with King William for use of arrears of taxes due the crown for the church overseas. When the securities involved proved valueless, he took a fateful step: he "endeavor'd to form a Voluntary Society . . . to propagate Christian Knowledge as well at Home as abroad."[16] This, he felt, would lead to "a Protestant Congregation *pro propaganda Fide* by Charter from the King."[17]

The results were as he had anticipated, and two significant and long-lasting bodies came into existence: the Society for Promoting Christian Knowledge (1698) and the Society for the Propagation of the Gospel in Foreign Parts (1701). The designation for the SPG was "in *Partibus Transmarinis,*" "in transoceanic districts," or, in other words, North America and the Caribbean. The advent of the SPCK and the SPG heralded the fact that the zeal for the expansion of the national church was reawakened. From London a campaign was launched which would take books and missionaries of the now imperially minded church not only into the Chesapeake Bay and its tributaries but up the Merrimack, Charles, and Sakonnet rivers, Narragansett Bay, the Connecticut and Hudson, and along the banks of the Santee, Cooper, Ashley, and Savannah rivers. The waterways of America became the roads to the Anglican city of God. "Transiens Adiuvanos," "helping him across," was the alluring motto of the SPG. That device appeared on the seal of the society as a canopy over a heroic-sized clergyman dressed in gown and bands. He stood in the prow of a man-of-war with a Bible in one hand, while he gestured in response to welcoming natives with the other.

Thomas Bray succeeded in finding "worthy Persons" willing to contribute to defray the expenses of such an expedition. Entrepreneurs such as Sir Humphrey Mackworth, M.P., who was promoting mining and smelting in Wales, Lord Guilford, who eventually became president of the Board of Trade, and the Irish lawyer-politician Justice Hooke heeded the call. Henceforth, businessmen were to work side by side with clerics in the Anglican church.[18] What is more, they were to pay for the privilege. It was precisely that voluntary support, solicited to augment monies sought from the crown, which marked a small but meaningful change: voluntary contributions were to underwrite in part the church's missionary expansion.

The goal was still the same as it had been at Jamestown: to tie economically profitable colonies closer to the mother country; to secure Indian allies against the French and Spanish on the mainland of the continent; and to build a homogeneous society. As we have already seen, in this operation religion was to play a vital role. Without the holy ties of faith and submission, royal command over white and red alike would be incomplete. With England's national, and now stable, religion, imperial unity would be assured. Thus it came about that, in the period between Catholic James and German-speaking George, aid began to flow across the Atlantic from concerned monarchs, colonial proprietors, and voluntary societies. Everywhere on the American continent the potency of the Church of England was on the rise.

To this new era of Anglican advancement, Compton, Bray, the SPG, and its sister organization, the SPCK, contributed significantly. Here a theology of divine benevolence, philanthropy based on religious conviction, the manifestation of faith by its works, inspired a generation and added an attractive increment to religion.[19] Beneath the surface of church politics, brittle cleverness and worldliness gave way to more Christian concerns. Of all churchmen of the period, Bray was the leader in awakening dozing consciences. Through the efforts of this neglected reformer, the plight of the uneducated children of the poor, the sick, the Protestant refugees from the continent, and the savagely treated sailors of the Royal Navy became known. Yet Bray was not alone. He was part of a larger reform movement.

As John Nelson has noted, the influence of German pietism reached England to add to an indigenous reformation already in progress. "Young men pledged to a life of devotion; meeting weekly to sing psalms, pray, and study, they found that their personal exercises compelled them to acts of piety, particularly the relief of destitute people. . . . Individuals involved in this movement played a major role in the formation of the Society for Promoting Christian Knowledge and the Society for the Propagation of the Gospel."[20]

Among the destitute were the poorer clergy in rural England and in the colonies. They became a particular concern of Thomas Bray. Bray's brief sojourn in Maryland in the late spring and early summer of 1700 convinced him of the need for further aid overseas. Both during and after his trip to America, Bray came to think that the church must be established in Maryland and expanded elsewhere. In Annapolis, the observant commissary made good use of his time. While he was received with all the ceremony befitting an episcopal visitor and preached before the assembly, exercises in pomp were not the purpose of his long voyage, and he knew it. More to the point, he called the clergy into convocation, encouraged and disciplined them, issued circular letters, outlined a course for catechizing youth, and devised for the leaders of the church in London *A Memorial Representing the Present State of Religion on the Continent of North America*.[21] Back in England, Bray's activities continued unabated. In London he spoke "as an eyewitness" and called to the attention of his superiors the church's potential for "expansion among the thousands who had lost any tie with organized religion."[22] The result was the chartering of the SPG.

But if social, educational, and charitable concerns motivated the founders of the SPCK and the SPG, so did politics. It should not be surprising to discover that the SPG was an integral part of the anti-Roman grand alliance. "Anti-Catholicism," we are reminded, "was a constant theme in the sermons preached at the anniversary services of the SPG."[23] In 1709, Bishop William Dawes (1671–1724) of Chester reminded his auditors that "we are Protestants" who are

> bound both, to wipe off the foul Reproach, of wanting a Missionary Zeal, for the conversion of Infidels, which our Adversaries of the Church of Rome have been casting in our Teeth: And likewise to prevent Infidels from being made a Prey to the church of Rome, that most unsound and corrupt part of the Christian Church, and which, so industriously compasseth Land and Sea to make Proselytes to it.[24]

In addition, anti-Quakerism motivated the founders of the SPG. Quakers were cut from the same reformed cloth as Anglicans. They were a new patch on an old garment; their very proximity to the common Protestant heritage of the Church of England seemed to tear apart the fabric of true religion. For this reason, Friends were as dangerous as Romanists. To Anglicans, William Penn's (1644–1718) followers resembled nothing so much as that Catholicism which England's national church had repudiated over a century before. So close were Quaker ideas on justification, grace, free will, and Scripture to those of the Church of Rome that many seventeenth-century Englishmen found Friends to be nothing so much "as papists in disguise."[25] This suspicion goes a long way toward explaining why it was that at the initiation of the Society its attention was focused on the Quaker, both in England and America.[26] A truly homogenous national society comprising Englishmen and colonials could only be forged with the extermination of Quaker opinions and the conversion of their misguided purveyors to the true faith. The same held true for Baptists.

In effect, the SPG was a sectarian institution, despite its educational and social concern. But what of the Congregational churches of New England? Thomas Bray left no doubt where he stood on that score: the SPG was not to operate where those churches were established. He wrote:

> Nor do I think myself oblig'd to speak here of *New-England* where *Independency* seems to be the Religion of the Country. My Design is not to intermeddle, where Christianity under any form has obtained Possession; but to represent rather the deplorable State of the *English Colonies*, where they have been in a manner abandoned to *Atheism*; or, which is much at one, to *Quakerism*, for want of a Clergy settled among them.[27]

Such ecumenical comity as Bray envisaged was too much to ask of an institution founded, staffed, and maintained by Anglicans alone. The challenge of stealing eggs from the Puritan nest proved irresistible. While Bray's strategy would have located missionaries of the SPG in those places where there were few churches and many settlers "abandoned to *Atheism*," it was in the heart of New England that some of the society's greatest successes took place. Connecticut, the land of steady, orthodox habits, was to receive far more Anglican attention than the western reaches of the Shenandoah and the Piedmont. The unthinking decision of the SPG to engage nonconformity where it had "obtained Possession" was a fateful one. Thereafter, the colonial Church of England misinterpreted the nature of things and of man: increasingly as the century wore on, she failed to grasp the difference between colonial dissent and colonial disloyalty.

In the meantime the organization of the SPG proceeded rapidly in London after 1701. Meticulous and superior planning brought about a noteworthy approximation of institutional aims and goals.[28] At the society's head was the archbishop of Canterbury, backed by the bishop of London and others of the episcopal bench. The clergy and laity of the capital city, rectors and merchants, took on most of the day-to-day work. The primary function of these assistants was to develop a system of provincial agents who in turn circulated subscription forms throughout the realm. By personal contact with diocesan bishops and wealthy friends, the society's functionaries hoped ''to secure the financial resources to permit the realization of its aim.''[29] The aim, of course, was to select, secure, and maintain missionaries in the field. Inevitably, the gap between expenses and income appeared. The uncertainty of benefactions, the irregularity of bequests, and the inability to create endowment because of fixed operating expenses caused the usual problems.[30] Nevertheless, succeeding generations of organizers managed to subsidize ''a steady and sizable migration to the American colonies of competent and well-trained individuals, [in] a movement of incalculable cultural significance.''[31] Between 1701 and 1783, 329 parsons and teachers founded some three hundred churches in the colonies.[32] All of this occurred outside of self-sustaining Virginia and Maryland.

Of equal importance with the mundane affairs of the society was the religious spirit and style enjoined upon all SPG missionaries. There was no doubt that they were enlisting in a religious order ''pledged to unquestioning obedience and willing to assent to self-sacrificial endeavors to propagate the faith throughout the world.''[33] When Thomas Jefferson referred to the ministers of the SPG as ''Anglican Jesuits'' he was unwittingly close to the truth. The formation of Bray's order of ''good Soldiers of Jesus Christ'' was indeed prompted by jealous and suspicious awareness of the power of the Roman Catholic Congregation *de Propaganda Fide*.[34] Shaped to the contours of reformed religion, the society gave strict instructions to its clergy.[35]

Sound knowledge and strong belief in the Christian religion were demanded, together with ''Apostolic Zeal temper'd with Prudence, Humility, Meekness, and Patience.'' Prayer and Bible reading were mandatory. Ministers were to

> acquaint themselves thorowly with the Doctrine of the Church of England as contain'd in the Articles and Homilies; its worship and Discipline, and Rules for the Behaviour of the Clergy, as contain'd in the Liturgy and Canons; and that they approve themselves accordingly, as genuine Missionaries from this Church.[36]

While they were to conduct themselves in ''a Spirit of Meekness and Gentleness'' toward dissenters, these were manifestly Anglican apologists who sought to ''convince and reclaim'' those not of the national communion. Should any dissenting ''GainSayers'' attempt to lure people from the

Church of England, the clergy were "to make themselves Masters in those Controversies, which are necessary to be understood." In their often extensive American parishes, they were to preach "the great Fundamental Principles of Christianity, and the Duties of a sober, righteous, and godly life, as resulting from those Principles." Missionaries were told to instruct their people in the nature and use of the sacraments as a means of grace. Children and the ignorant were to have the catechism explained to them—wisely enough—in the most simple terms. With what would become characteristic of Anglican apologetic theology in succeeding generations, "Heathens and Infidels" were to be instructed initially in the "Principles of natural religion." Reason and conscience thereby enlightened, the next order of business was to show the "Necessity of Revelation." Then came the certainty of divine self-disclosure in scripture. Here the SPG's instructions bore the unmistakable marks of the Enlightenment.

In terms of the personal conduct of the clergy, little was omitted in the instructions to missionaries. The new Anglican brotherhood was to be marked by sober discipline and strictness of life. Gone was any possibility of carousing at "Publick Houses," idle pastimes, "Gaiming" and gluttony, meddling in politics, and even the use of pretentious titles among the members of the order. Equality, frugality, simple dress, dignified and grave deportment, and regular reports to London were demanded.[37]

For its missionaries, the work of the SPG was a serious business which involved not only the education of others but the clergy's own growth in faith and knowledge. The demands and the program were not for the avaricious or the slovenly but sought to appeal to the high-minded and the firm-hearted. One wonders if the "Opposition to Luxury" gave pause to some of the society's wealthier episcopal leaders. Be that as it may, the call to service in the faith was both clear and attractive, and, as always when it is made with vigor and simplicity, so here: the call was answered.

But audacious planning in London was not enough. The society needed vastly more information on religious as well as physical conditions in the various American colonies. It also needed a permanent cadre of lay officials in America, men of standing in government whose vision reached beyond the boundaries of the particular colonies they served. These men would be able to support the missionaries with encouragement and either create or bend the law to their advantage. Without the aid of secular officials who had a transcolonial and trans-Atlantic perspective, it would be vastly harder to draw together into a spiritual unity the empire England was creating in 1700. Apart from New England and Virginia, there was no strong Church of England tradition with grass roots support anywhere in America. No homogeneous and determined group of Anglicans had migrated en masse, built a colony, fostered their particular expression of religious zeal, and then announced the results of their efforts to their diocesan bishop in London. Rather, members of the church tended to be scattered throughout already existing colonies, living side by side with others not of their tradition. Moreover, state policy since 1689 had decreed toleration of nonconformists to the imperial church. Thus, the home government was faced with the unenviable task of conversion, not by force of arms or even by law, but by persuasion. So far as possible, the church had to be strengthened where it stood, "imposed" from above, and its strategy and actions planned by those with knowledge. These factors clearly pointed to the sort of remote control envisaged by the founders of the SPG. Whatever the difficulties, it was the only way. If these difficulties were not insurmountable, they presented an unusually sharp challenge. New England Puritans had to worry about keeping their precious charters; Episcopalians had to worry about whether they would ever be "chartered" at all.

The first of the Church of England's needs—information about religious conditions in America—was fulfilled in the person of one who had helped draft the instructions for the future missionaries of the SPG, George Keith (1638–1716). He was not a likely candidate for herald of the new Episcopalian advance in the colonies. He was sixty-four years old when he undertook his survey of England's Atlantic coast settlements in 1702. Until 1700, he had not only been a Quaker but also a zealous and argumentative progagandist for Quaker doctrines. Keith's aggressive and ordering mind had sought to fashion Quaker belief, to give it firmness and greater consistency. In his quest he was typical of Protestant reformers in general, for he wished to

> strip away the mighty fabric of human invention accumulated through the centuries and to penetrate to the core of correct belief, the doctrine of the primitive church. He sought an authority for his mind as well as his soul, but he wanted to be absolutely certain that it was the correct one. To link the primitive and genuine spirit, such as he discovered in the Society of Friends, with the primitive creed of the church was his ambition.[38]

His differences with his Quaker peers soon became apparent. Where they held to the "essentially democratic and equalitarian spirit of Quakerism," Keith laid stress on correct dogma, metaphysical subtleties, logical thought, and, of more importance, the church fathers. His writing and preaching were also acerbic and at times violent. These characteristics went against the Quaker teachings of simplicity, quiet emotionalism, and gentleness.[39]

To seek people more receptive to his high church Quakerism, Keith migrated to America with his family in 1685. For ten years he resided in New Jersey and became wealthy. All the while he continued his attempt to reshape Quakerism along more historic, churchly, and rational lines. In 1692 he was opposed, tried for his efforts, and condemned by reprimand. Two years later he returned to England, thoroughly hated by Friends on both sides of the Atlantic. Keith continued to attack Quakers in addresses and pamphlets, much to the delight of Anglican leaders.[40] Thereafter the road to ordination in the Church of England in 1700 was similar to that which he had already trod in his own church: order, authority, historical continuity, and correct formulations of dogma in a larger religious community. This time they led him toward the national church, not toward a new Quakerism.

What better man to send to the New World? Keith knew the country, and, what is more, he knew the lay of the theological terrain occupied by one of the SPG's major adversaries. Yet to send George Keith back to America was a choice loaded with danger. Because of his reputation as an immoderate controversialist, hostility toward dissenters of whatever stripe became a *fait accompli*. The SPG appears to have had a choice: either Thomas Bray's moderation toward nonconformists or George Keith's frontal assault upon all who failed to live by the rubrics of the imperial church. The leaders of the society chose the latter, which was unfortunate.

Keith arrived in Boston on 14 June 1702. He lost no time in engaging Increase Mather (1639–1723) and Harvard's president, Samuel Willard (1640–1707), in theological controversy. At America's premier seat of learning, Harvard College, the former Quaker judged that students had been "poisoned with very bad principles" and that the English universities should contribute "pious and noble scholars" together with a new president in holy orders. Later Keith had gone off to Lynn to engage the Quaker community in debate.[41] He then moved south through colony after colony, the lightning surveyor of the American scene whose thunderclap was never far behind. The result of Keith's trip to America was the *Journal* which the ex-Quaker dedicated to the archbishop of Canterbury and to the rest of the members of the SPG. It was for "the Encouragement of others, who may hereafter be imployed in the like Service."[42] In his "Account of the State of the Church in North America," which he compiled with the help of others in March 1702, Keith gave valuable information to the members of the SPG in London,[43] which they acted upon. Thereafter Keith became one of the major controversialists and apologists of the Church of England.

Of equal, if not ultimately greater, importance than Keith were the permanent colonial officials. These men, lay and clerical alike, were the backbone of the SPG's strategy. They manifested an absorbing interest in the future of England's imperial church in America, and their vision of what that church might become was as transcolonial as it was trans-Atlantic.

Chief among these men in the early eighteenth century was Francis

Nicholson (1655–1728). This remarkable high church, Tory layman spent nearly all of his active political life in America. For some unaccountable reason he has been overlooked and, therefore, undervalued, but to his contemporaries both in and out of the church he was a force to be reckoned with. Nicholson was lieutenant governor of the Dominion of New England (1688–1690) lieutenant governor of Virginia (1690–1692), governor of Maryland (1694–1698), lieutenant governor of Virginia (1698–1705), governor and military commander of Nova Scotia and economic investigator of North America (1712–1714), and governor of South Carolina (1720–1728). There were few who could touch the first-hand knowledge of England's colonies possessed by this official. His praises were often sung by his fellow churchmen without restraint. In 1703, John Talbot (1645–1727), whose high church Tory views coincided with Nicholson's, called him the "chief benefactor" of the church in America and believed that under his leadership the church would "prosper & prevail against all her Enemies."[44]

During his long career in America as a colonial official Francis Nicholson displayed a driving energy, a capacity for organization, generosity, honesty, and a hot temper. As his biographer attests, he was a man of contradictions: markedly religious yet capable of eloquent profanity, obsessed with duty yet a placeman who unabashedly courted favor. A pinchpenny with public funds, he was munificent to the point of carelessness with his own money.[45] Nicholson was illegitimate by birth. As a result, it is likely that he recalled the contingency of life. Time and again he gave money in small acts of charity: to a sick sailor, to deserving ministers, and to the poor. Congregations knew his open-handedness on a larger scale. Thirty pounds went to a church in North Carolina; fifty guineas for libraries in South Carolina; food, books, and furniture for a charity hospital in Maryland; and gifts to King's Chapel in Boston, the SPG in Connecticut, as well as to Huguenots in New York. In 1711 for an expedition against the French in Acadia, Nicholson was responsible for sending four hundred copies each of the Bible, the Book of Common Prayer, and Allestree's *The Whole Duty of Man*, along with other devotional material. These were packed along with twenty-five hundred tomahawks for the Indians of Nova Scotia![46] Due to his extravagance and high gubernatorial living expenses, Nicholson was never wealthy himself. Toward the end of his life a friend said to him, "You spent many thousand pounds in the Country more than you gott."[47]

Everywhere Nicholson's generosity and zeal for royal religion, prerogative, and unity with England were felt. They were accompanied by administrative efficiency. Nicholson sought to reform courts of justice, to improve legislative procedures, to tidy up and care for government records, and to create a better postal service. At the same time, he catalogued clerical

93

libraries, staffed parishes, and, when in England, attended with marked regularity the meetings of the SPG. He made many enemies among the proprietary factions of Virginia and Maryland, as well as among the merchants of South Carolina, but withal he enjoyed the exercise of power, and his liking for politics was accompanied by a talent for keeping informed of local issues. Throughout his life Nicholson tapped a broad range of public opinion in America. As his biographer concludes:

> The basic political idea that Nicholson offered to the developing Empire was the concept of royal prerogative as the essential bond between the colony and the mother country. His devotion to this hoary doctrine did not, however, blind his political insight to the conflict between royal dominance and colonial restlessness. To ease the resulting problems, he actively sought goodwill for the Crown and good gubernatorial working relations with Americans.[48]

Layman though he was, Nicholson, a charter member of the SPG,[49] became the society's roving ambassador in its first difficult years during Queen Anne's reign.[50] As such he was unrivaled.

But there were other ardent supporters of the church in America. Some of these represented an Anglican presence even before the founding of the SPG: Edward Randolph (1632–1703), collector of the customs for New England; Sir Edmund Andros (1637–1714); and Lieutenant Governor Edward Cranfield (d. 1704) of New Hampshire. After the beginning of the SPG other officials arrived who were in close association with Nicholson in his attempt to create a religiously homogeneous group of provinces. Among these were Joseph Dudley (1647–1720), governor of Massachusetts; Edward Hyde (1661–1723), better known as Lord Cornbury, the strange and unpopular governor of New York; Robert Quary (1645–1712), a politician whose interest in the church spanned South Carolina, Virginia, and Pennsylvania; and William Vesey (1647–1746), New York's leading cleric.[51]

Vesey is of particular interest. His steadiness both personally and in his loyalty to royal prerogative made him the natural ally of Francis Nicholson. Described as "of grave, thoughtful, prudent and Discreet Disposition,"[52] he took an interest not only in the church in New York City, but in neighboring New Jersey and Pennsylvania as well.[53] Vesey is of note because he was one of the first native-born Americans to achieve prominence in the church. A New Englander by birth, he graduated from Harvard (1693) and also held a degree from Oxford (1697). He was a Tory, a member of "the positive school of churchmanship [and not of the] temporizing party."[54] For forty-nine years after his appointment as rector of Trinity Church in 1697, he dominated the religious scene in New York. A Jacobite, he remained loyal to the stiff Anglican principle of no dealings with nonconformists. A grateful bishop of London appointed Vesey commissary in 1715. Moderate churchmen campaigned against him. Elias Neau complained that the wealthy rector of Trinity Church was unconcerned about the conversion of blacks, but Neau's evidence was unconvincing.[55] Indeed Vesey displayed his principles on many occasions. He took a strong and unpopular stand against the universal clamor for revenge which followed a slave rebellion on Long Island in 1712. Thereafter the American churchman reported to the bishop of London that of "1362 Indian and Negro Slaves in the province . . . many of them frequent our church and have been baptized, and some of them admitted to the Lord's Table."[56] If the claim that Vesey advanced the càuse of the Church of England by making it universally attractive is open to question, there is no doubt that his presence in New York fortified the high church tradition.

There were other high churchmen in the early eighteenth century whose presence as supporters of the Tories' "court party" aided in the launching of the SPG and the new era of Anglican aggressiveness in America. While the colonies were too scattered along the coastline for close contact, there were shared convictions: the establishment of the church wherever possible, the necessity of the episcopate in America, separation from dissenters and their eventual conformity to the national religion, and always closer ties to England. Among those who achieved prominence for the voicing of these views were John Checkley (1680–1754), Boston's homebred Jacobite; George Pigot (d. 1738) in Rhode Island; Yale's president Timothy Cutler (1684–1765); Samuel Johnson (1696–1772), a Yale tutor and future president of King's College in New York; John Lilliston (1656–1709) of Maryland, who was dubbed the "fittest person America affords for the office of Suffragan [bishop]";[57] and, in South Carolina, Governor Nathaniel ·Johnson (1645–1713), Commissary Gideon Johnston (d. 1716), and later Commissary Alexander Garden (1685–1756). These and others represented a new imperial point of view, one different from Virginia's churchmanship.

But all was not well within the circle of leading Episcopalians. The debates between moderate divines and Tories, which roiled the waters of the Church of England at home in the first two decades of the eighteenth century, muddied the American church as well. Colonial moderates wrote disparagingly of high churchmen and visa versa. Yet both sides wrote to the same secretary of the SPG, and both received English aid. Despite ecclesiological differences, both moderates and Tories sought proselytes. The differences, however, remained. The churchly "Arbitrary Principles" of the high-flyers did not appeal to those who, whether conscious of the fact or not, followed Thomas Bray's churchmanship rather than that of George

95

Keith. These wished to live with greater amicableness toward dissenters, while still seeking to strengthen and expand the church. They were the Whigs.[58] Among their leaders were Colonial Lewis Morris (1671–1746), who became chief justice of New York; Caleb Heathcote (1666–1721); governors Lord John Lovelace (d. 1709) and Robert Hunter (d. 1734), both of New York; the Reverend Joseph Colebatch (1672?–1734) of Maryland, who was once chosen by the bishop of London for an American episcopate (1727);[59] and Virginia's James Blair (1656–1744).

Blair, like his counterpart Vesey in New York, was marked by both physical and political endurance. The Virginian's remarkable ministry covered a period of sixty-four years: for fifty-eight of those years he was a clergyman in the Old Dominion; simultaneously, for fifty-three years he was commissary of the bishop of London; a lifetime member of the governor's council; and president for life of William and Mary College. The life of this solitary Scot and graduate of the University of Edinburgh (M.A. 1673) began during the rule of Oliver Cromwell and ended some years after he had welcomed George Whitefield to his Williamsburg pulpit. In the intervening decades few enemies survived his spleen. In personality Blair was ruthless and ambitious. He loved a political fight and was alternately avaricious and extravagant. More of a politician than a churchman or even an educator, Blair allied himself with the landholders of Virginia in their contention with imperial prerogative. By withholding sponsorship of governors and causing them to be unseated, he acted as a brake upon royal authority. Blair was, as his biographer declares, ''the most articulate spokesman in Virginia against the tightening web of English control.''[60] Incongruous as it may seem, James Blair emerges as a protector of the rights of some Americans against imperial encroachments. Nor was he without a certain idealism when he sought a new moral order for New World planters, a fact not wholly concealed by his argumentativeness. If he never figured in the corridors of the SPG's American campaign, much less in its board rooms (Virginia's church received no SPG aid), Blair nevertheless gave a degree of regularity to the established church he served so long. For this reason alone he symbolizes the new era of Anglican advancement.

None of these men—Blair, Nicholson, Vesey, Johnson, Morris—were members of a close-knit company like the followers of Winthrop and Higginson in the early decades of New England. The Episcopalians' efforts were too diffuse. They arrived on the American scene at a time when pluralism had already gained a firm foothold. Their ventures were not always coordinated, though like Vesey and his Whig vestryman Caleb Heathcote, there was cooperation. United action against dissenters, however much they sought it, eluded them. The divisive character of American life, politics, and geography saw to that. Episcopalian leaders were dealing with a land the length and size of which defied unification. True, the SPG provided a footing for many in the New World from which to explore and then to conquer the interior for the Church of England. If Nicholson, Keith, and Bray were the most experienced Anglican adventurers, they either failed to maintain the campaign or diverted their attention to civic and mercantile concerns. The division between royal and proprietary—and provincial—allegiance also worked to the detriment of a fully unified Anglican advance.

In the final analysis, however, it was religious pluralism within most of the provinces which rendered the cause of conformity to the Church of England questionable. Already by 1700, the diversity of her peoples meant that North America would never as a whole subscribe to Episcopalian faith and practice. Uniformity was impossible, though clearly not unthinkable. Religious comprehensiveness had failed in the mother country in 1662 and again in 1689. In America where traditional English habits and restraints were less in evidence, comprehensiveness stood an even poorer chance. That left toleration; the colonial church reluctantly and hesitatingly submitted.

Nevertheless the leaders of the SPG and the local establishments in America tried to make the larger community respond to the church's dictates, much as English society at home responded to its great religious institution, whether individuals were members of it or not. In the British Isles, the mere existence of the Church of England was taken for granted. To have it otherwise was unthinkable in the eighteenth century; in America this was not so. With a few exceptions, the church had to share virgin territory with others. Everyone had to begin at the same time, and, where such equality of opportunity did not obtain, there were always neighboring colonies to serve as models and show how it could be done. That the colonial Church of England became as powerful an institution as she did may have been due to the imposition of imperial design, but that alone cannot account for her vitality. All disadvantages aside, her order, her history, and her liturgy had their own appeal. In the end, that was the most important factor of all in her survival and development.

The church's guides and supporters in the early eighteenth century in America were politicians, ecclesiastics, and churchmen, not great statesmen or theological thinkers. As politicians, men like Compton, Bray, Keith, Nicholson, Vesey, and Blair proved to be intelligent, energetic, and useful leaders. For the most part, their ideas were in harmony with imperial policy. Drawn into the service of church and crown, they demonstrated talents of innovation, were genuinely interested in America, and were respected by friend and foe alike. Judging from the Puritan opposition to their

97

cause in New England, they were men to be reckoned with. But they saw no deeper into the sensibilities of their own or their opponents' world than the current interpretation of their Elizabethan liturgy and polity—or empire —would allow. One might make the case that Thomas Bray and Elias Neau (and, as we shall see, Francis Le Jau of South Carolina) exhibit deeper stirrings of a religious and critical spirit. Yet in the end because of the chances of birth and background, they lacked opportunities for the exercise of power. Bray never became a bishop; Neau remained a catechist to black slaves and poor sailors in New York.

Despite their lack of advancement, these men of charity also played their parts in the new era of Anglican aggressiveness. For them as well, unity, transcolonial and trans-Atlantic, was not unthinkable. To it they contributed by the very generosity of their actions. Such men as Neau, Richard Charlton (fl. 1731–1747), Samuel Auchmuty, and Robert Jenney (d. 1762) sought to alleviate the lot of the less fortunate. It was not always easy to take the enlightened route in such an enterprise. Neau in particular ran into a good deal of trouble as a result of his efforts with the blacks. In 1712, after a slave rebellion, he was forced to vindicate himself against those who accused him of fomenting insurrection. "Scruples have arisen," he wrote, "in the Minds of our Inhabitants against my School by imputing the Rebellion of their Slaves to the instructing of them, as if the Christian Religion should not Command Obedience to all Inferiors."[61] Whites were full of prejudice, he declared, while "I struggle much more against their bad Notion." Layman Neau wished that the clergy would preach more often the necessity of imparting Christian faith to blacks; they had not been doing so.

Neau's methods of catechizing, which he explained in detail in 1709, sound stilted to us. They were indeed lengthy and thorough. The conscientious former French Huguenot taught uniformity of doctrine and correct deportment in the church. To these he added sensitivity to the educational level of his listeners. The slaves came to him in the evening, he wrote,

> because they are not Masters of their own time. . . . they never come but by Candlelight in Winter and in Summer, except on Sundays, at which time they come at the last Service of the Church. I begin with praying & after my Example all of them fall down up on their Knees using the publick Prayers of the Church which I make them learn by heart to the end that they may mind them the better when they go to the Church; after prayer they all sitt down & I begin at one & finish with the other; when I speak to them they stand up; when there are a great many of them, I Catechize three together.

After rehearsing the basic doctrines of the Church of England as contained in the catechism he continued:

I give myself the liberty to add what I think necessary to make them under-stand what I say to them, suitable to the capacity of those to whom I apply myself, and the time I have to do it in, for Sir, I am obliged to measure my time because their masters want 'em; I don't keep 'em generally above two hours at a time & often less; when I have made my discourse upon the belief I make them all rise & with their faces turn to the East, repeat the Belief or Symbol of the Apostles [Apostles' Creed], after which I make them repeat word for word the Church Catechism as it stands in the Liturgy and all in English; I must acquaint [you] Sir that I proceed after the same manner with the rest of the Catechism, as I do upon the Creed and that they may have a general Idea of the whole Christian Religion, but I don't make them repeat it all at once, because that would take up too much time; When I come to the Lord's Prayer we recite it all Kneeling. After the Sacrament I make them sing two or three verses of a psalm all standing and always repeat the Gloria Patri; and at last I conclude with the evening prayer and Benediction. You may be sure, Sir, that I don't forget their Benefactors for whom there is a particular article in their prayers, and in my discourse I often represent to them their Obligations to the Gentlemen of the Illustrious Society [SPG] towards whom I endeavor to excite their gratitude. I also read to them from time to time the principal stories of the Holy Scriptures that I may give them an Historical Notion of the Creation and Redemption of the World; in a word I conceal nothing from them that is proper to bring them Salvation. I Sett before their eyes the promises and threatenings. God grant them the grace to make good use thereof.[62]

With such diligence the Frenchman sought a more homogeneous and kindlier society.

Throughout the century conscientious men such as Neau made use of Bray's *Catechetical Lectures* as the basic commentary on the church's catechism. As late as the 1770s we find Joseph Hildreth, catechist to blacks, writing from New York to the effect that in the absence of a clergyman, "I am going through Dr. Bray's catechetical lectures; as they are short I can read one each [Sunday] evening . . . after catechise [sic], and so conclude with the post Communion Prayers, general Thanksgiving, and singing a Psalm."[63]

If catechising blacks was one thing, Indian affairs were quite another. Nowhere is the association of church and empire so clearly seen as in the "humanitarianism" which is said to have accompanied—and to a degree did accompany—the church's Indian missions. Here politics of a high order are to be seen. Here, more than in the case of any other Christian commun-ion in America with the exception of New England Congregationalism, the interweaving of church and state is to be discerned. From the earliest days of Virginia to the resurgence of missionary concern for the conversion of the Iroquois on the part of the SPG, the motto was "fur, flag, and faith,"[64] or as it might have been equally aptly put in the days of Jamestown, "corn, crown, and cross."

In 1700, there were four bidders for the loyalty of the Indian: "the British Government, which desired him as an outpost of empire [against the French and Spanish]; the trader who wanted him as a consumer of alcohol and other goods, and as a supplier of furs and various products; the colonist who craved his lands; and the missionary who wished his conversion to Christianity and who in fact softened the impact of the new order."[65] Against such a muster of political and religious forces, the Indian was, if not powerless, deprived and harassed. There is something pathetic in the response of England's "civilized" Iroquois allies to the accession of Queen Anne in 1702. In their no doubt puzzled response to the elevation of a "Squaw Sachem vizt. a woman King," they managed to express themselves as happy enough, but they hoped in movingly ingenuous words that "she would be a good mother, & send them some to teach them Religion, & Abolish Traffick amongst them that they might be able to purchase a Coat and not go to Church in Bear Skins."[66] "Traffick" of course meant primarily alcohol.

In the same decade, George Muirson, SPG missionary in Westchester County, bemoaned the fate of "a decaying people. . . . We have not now in all this Parish," declared this perceptive minister,

> 20 Families whereas not many years agoe there were several Hundreds. I have frequently conversed with some of them and been at their great meetings of *powowing* as they call it. I have taken some pains to teach some of them but to no purpose, for they seem regardless of Instruction and when I have told them of the Evil Consequences of their hard drinking & they replyed that English Men do the same; and that it is not so great a sin in an Indian as in an Englishman because the Englishman's religion forbids it, but an Indian's does not: they further say they will not be Christians nor do they see the necessity for so being because we do not live according to the Precepts of our Religion.[67]

Muirson was "heartily sorry that we shou'd give them such a bad example and fill their mouths with such Objections against our blessed Religion." He felt it was time for the English to set a better example, and he pleaded for a bishop for the church in America, a better governor, and magistrates who would not be "a great Stop to the Growth of piety and Godliness among us." Awareness of the plight of the Indian was coupled with the knowledge of what might be the predicament of the English in the early eighteenth century if the French converted the Iroquois before Queen Anne's missionaries got to them. From the Lords of Trade and Plantation in London to the missionary on the Hudson River—and particularly at the strategic town of Albany—the realization dawned that New York was "the defensive keystone of British North America."[68] Without the friendship of the Five Nations of the Iroquois, that is, the Mohawks, Oneidas, Onondagas, Cayugas, Senecas, and later the Tuscaroras, there was the imminent and significant danger of the loss of Albany. With that disaster "the French might overwhelm the colony, drive a wedge between New England and the South, and thereby pave the way for the ultimate conquest of all the British colonies."[69] If the Five Nations could be converted to England's Protestant faith, then political allegiance would follow, and French designs would be thwarted.

As early as October 1700, the Lords of Trade and Plantation addressed the archbishop of Canterbury concerning the conversion of these Indians. The Lords wanted missionaries to instruct the "five nations of Indians on the Frontiers of New York and prevent their being practised upon by French priests and Jesuits who are . . . very industrious in persuading them by pretences of Religion to espouse the French Interest."[70] There was no doubt in the Lords' minds that "Propagation of the Reformed Religion" paralleled "Improving the Interest of England." Two years later, Godfrey Dellius put the case for conversion as succinctly as anyone. In a letter to the secretary of the SPG, he declared that he wished "to serve the Prince as his Subject, and to edify the Church of Jesus, and to extend conquests by converting the Barbarians as a minister . . . for the Honor of God as for the Benefit of the English Crowne."[71] He thought it would be wise to reach the "Remote Indians" since "in case of need, as in time of warr or otherwise, these Christians are good guides in the woods."[72] Faith and flag went together; fur was never far behind. Imperial strategy called for that less-than-holy alliance, not only in the province of New York, but in Virginia as well. In 1715 the governor of the Old Dominion wrote the bishop of London of a "new design of converting" Indians through the promotion of the fur trade.[73]

Always in the background of conversion of the native peoples by Church of England missionaries loomed the "Exhorbitant Power of France," as the SPG's address to Queen Anne at her accession to the throne in 1702 put it.[74] English missionaries were seen to be in direct competition with French Roman Catholic priests.[75] In 1703, New York's secretary for Indian affairs, Robert Livingston (1654–1728), viewed with alarm the presence of Catholic missionaries in the Mohawk territory. There a French Jesuit called "Jacob Bryas (now Superior in Canada) . . . used all Diligence Possible to make Proselytes among them." Attempts had been made on the part of authorities in Albany "to diswade the Indians to receive Popish Priests in their Country." Nevertheless the Jesuits "have drawn over a Considerable Number of our Indians." Many "who were true to the English . . . were Poyson'd . . . [and] seduced to goe to Canada to be Instructed in the Popish Religion by the Jesuits, & tis feared more will follow, unless they have ministers in their Castles to Instruct them." It is, Livingston continued, the French, not the English who cloak their true intentions and "too frequently visit those Nations upon Religious Pretenses, and by that means Corrupt their Affections from the English."[76] The secretary concluded that "no better Recompense" could be afforded the Mohawks "for all their Faithful Services than the bringing them into the Bosom of the Protestant Church," for they have "Fought our Battles for us, and been a Constant Barrier of Defense between Her Majesties Plantations of Virginy, & Maryland and the French." Nor was the military problem confined to New York and the Chesapeake Bay colonies. In 1708, Robert Stevens wrote from Goose Creek, South Carolina, of the necessity of getting the French off the Mississippi.[77]

In 1710 there occurred one of those strange events in which so much confidence is placed and so few lasting results obtained: a summit conference. The chief sachems of the Mohawks were received in London by Queen Anne amid all the pomp and dazzle of the court. It was the sort of thing done supremely well by the English, with a stateliness and reserve perfectly suited to the English character. On that occasion in 1710, however, British restraint met Indian gravity and nobody snickered. The princely sachems addressed the queen with a dignity few could miss:

> We have undertaken a long and dangerous Voyage which none of our Predecessors cou'd be prevailed upon to do; The Motive that brought us was that we might have the Honour to see and relate to Our Great Queen, what we thought absolutely necessary for the good of her and us her Allies, which are on the other side of the great Water.[78]

Indians of the Mohawk tribe had always been "a firm wall," they reminded Anne, against the French and for the security of England's colonies "even to the loss of our best Men." They had "readily embraced our Great Queen's Institutions," and, they concluded,

> since we were in Covenant with our Great Queen's Children, we have had some knowledge of the Saviour of the World, and have been importuned by the French Priests and presents, but ever esteemed them as men of Falsehood, but if Our Great Queen would send us some to Instruct us, they would find a most hearty welcome.[79]

It was a highly politic address, one which put the burden firmly on the British.

As if to drive home the point, on 22 May the Mohawk princes followed this with a further request to the archbishop of Canterbury that he forward "what has been promised to us in behalf of the Six Nations viz, that the Ministers designed to Instruct us in the knowledge of the Saviour of the World . . . with as much speed as possible be sent over to us."[80] On the same day Sir Francis Nicholson, one of the most powerful English civil servants in America, warned the archbishop that the promised missionaries must be sent, for the Indians "fully rely thereupon and nothing will convince them but Peculiar Demonstration and they are quick for dispatch in all affairs. . . . If there be not a speedy beginning made," Nicholson added, "I fear they will at least suspect that what was promised them will not be performed." It was not until two years later that the society finally found a suitable candidate in the Reverend William Andrews (d. 1719).

Like those before him and those who would come after him, Andrews, for all his courage and seriousness, failed. Neither he nor others possessed spiritual and psychological sensitivity to the culture and folkways of the Indians. They were simply "Barbarians," savages, and "heretics"—like the Quakers. John Talbot lumped Indians, Roman Catholics, and Quakers together as equally and indiscriminately despicable and therefore fitting inhabitants for "these dark places" of America. (Under the circumstances, why he should have bothered to try and convert any of them remains something of a mystery.) For Talbot, the natives needed nothing so much as an Anglican bishop. Projecting his own wishes upon the hapless natives, Talbot had them cry out with him: "Send us a God Father or rather a Father in God with Apostolical Gravity & Authority to bless us that we may also be a Church"—and here he inadvertently slipped back into the first person singular—"for I count No Bishop, No Church as true as No Church, No King."[81] It is doubtful if the Indians were aware of the internal difficulties that had attended the use of any such dictums in seventeenth-century England.

Though he was still as blind to the Indian mind-set as John Talbot, the Reverend Patrick Gordon (d. 1702) was more realistic when it came to providing the spiritual aid needed by the Iroquois. Gordon wanted schools in which poor white youths and young Indians could be taught together. How else, asked Gordon, could the "Extirpation of Indian Jargon and the Propagation of the English Tongue" be accomplished?[82]

Only a few in the early eighteenth century raised objections to the predominance given the process of "civilizing" the more independent tribes of the frontier. In 1704 Elias Neau thought the conversion of the Iroquois a "great and glorious work," but, with his habitual concern and good sense, Neau wondered why more relief and assistance had not been given those Indians closer to home, particularly those in slavery to whites.[83]

The majority, however, went along with the demands of imperial politics.[84] As late as 1770, Governor John Wentworth (1736–1820) of New Hampshire judged that the "Principles of obedience and attachment to the British Government carefully inculcated upon their [the Indians'] minds and the arts of Society gradually introduced among them" would serve the advancement of British civilization. Then artlessly tying the faith to the flag, he pointed out that this was "a most critical and happy time to disseminate the Church of England in these colonies that ever did or ever will happen."[85] The gospel and "arts of Society" went hand in hand.

For their part, Indians throughout the century remained wary, if not crafty. After the initial disappointment of 1710 over not being sent either lords spiritual or temporal by Anne's government, many chose neutrality in the colonial wars between the English and the French. At midcentury as that conflict sharpened, English Protestant Iroquois joined their French and Catholic brothers. Together they sought nothing so much as "to Destroy both English and French and to Observe a strict Neutrality between themselves."[86] With good reason, self-preservation had become a prime consideration. Upon that premise and upon the mistaken idea that "civilizing" the savage was a necessary preparation for conversion to Christianity, the missionary enterprise foundered. As Gerald Goodwin has observed, the attempt to westernize the Indian was in fact "a confession of missionary failure."[87]

Some "humanitarianism" existed, however. Awareness of and sensitivity toward what was happening to native peoples when they were caught between government, trader, colonist, and missionary were seen in the attitudes of Muirson, Neau, and Samuel Thomas and Francis Le Jau of South Carolina. Yet in the end the politics of imperialism won out. Rivalry with France, the Jesuits, and the Church of Rome might produce summit conferences with the sachems, but it also abetted insensitivity on the part of the English religious leaders toward native Americans. For the English, uniformity, temporal as well as spiritual, cultural as well as religious, secular as well as ecclesiastical, remained.

But the Indians were not the only ones who, it was felt, should be made fit subjects for the "Principles of Obedience and attachment to the British Government . . . and to the arts of Society." the Anglicization and unification of the white population was of equal, and perhaps greater, concern. Here once again imperial planning and local custom collided. John Quincy

Adams's realization that the legislator in his search for symmetry and orthodoxy invariably ends by "increasing the diversities which it was his intention to abolish" was proved true. Conformity in the minds of the leaders of the Church of England both here and in the mother country in 1710 had not yet fully accepted the new policy of toleration. Respect for diverse religious and cultural traditions was still a long way off. Full religious freedom and the separation of church and state were ideas hardly worth contemplating, understandably preposterous to those whose vision involved other things.

To strengthen the national church in the American provinces and to bring into her fold a greater share of the white as well as Indian population, planners in London involved themselves for the better part of the century in a considerable and even audacious missionary effort. Let the new toleration of 1689 be what it may, only a fool could do nothing to bring others into the Episcopalian fold. Charity schools, preaching, and catechetical instruction—in short, education—served to enhance the belief that provincials were—or should consider themselves—Englishmen. Such patriotism, if it could be engendered, in turn entailed obligations. The church sought the acceptance of certain clearly stated values. Subjects of the crown in America should be loyal to fixed authority, respectful toward appointed officers in both church and state, willing to be instructed by a regularly recited liturgy, and content to take their place and assume their inherited or appointed rank in what was as near a perfect society as had ever been devised. Those who had had the misfortune not to have been born into this Eden, or had rebelled against it, could always be shaped by that church which continued to contribute significantly to what it meant to be English.

Nor was the imperial vision of a homogeneous society in which pluralistic groups of white settlers lived in harmony and worshiped the Christian God according to the canons of the Church of England a mean one. With the demise of the Stuart cause in 1745 and at the end of the era here discussed, Maryland's minister-poet-philosopher Thomas Cradock gave voice to this deep national strain in colonial consciousness. Well might the British in America "congratulate one another at the English victory at Culloden," for, Cradock judged, we are "Englishmen & Britons—born free & with hearts resolved to maintain our freedom & unanimously to relieve & assist each other on account of our National relation."[88] Nearly all colonials rejoiced in the defeat of Charles Stuart's ill-conceived expedition to Scotland. With members of the Church of England, the victory of Hanoverian forces had a particular poignancy. They alone need not keep back anything or enter any caveat. The victory of British forces meant the victory of *their*

105

settlement. Imperial unity was assured, or so it seemed. The efforts of bishops like Compton, reformers such as Bray, royal governors such as Nicholson, and clergymen and missionaries like Keith, Vesey, Talbot, and Neau appeared to be paying off. But in this epoch of American colonial history, we must discern more than the contributions of individuals. We must examine the struggle of rival elites for control of an unsettled social system—Episcopalian vs. Puritan, imperial vs. proprietary, provincial vs. local. To that struggle in the northern and southern colonies we now turn.

CHAPTER 4
Religious Imperialism in the North

"The Common-Prayer-Worship [is] being sett up in this Country," wrote Cotton Mather in his diary in November 1686; "I would procure and assist the Publication of a Discourse written by my Father, that shall enlighten the *rising Generation*, in the *Unlawfulness* of that Worship, and antidote them against Apostasy from the Principles of our First Settlement."[1] On 19 December of the same year, Samuel Sewall recorded the arrival of the HMS *Kingfisher* which carried James II's new royal governor, Sir Edmund Andros. The ship had been sighted off Boston harbor "with the Flagg in the main Top." That day being the sabbath, Samuel Willard preached to his congregation from Heb. 11:12, "Therefore sprang there, even of one, and him as good as dead, so many as the stars of the sky in multitude, and as the sand which is by the sea shore innumerable." Bostonians—the promised innumerable multitude—should not lose heart, declared Willard, but be "fully persuaded and confident God would not forget the Faith of those who came first to New England, but would remember their posterity with kindness."[2] If the message was momentarily comforting, it failed to convince for long. Three days later the *Kingfisher* entered the harbor. As if to match the sullen mood of the citizens of the town, the frigate fired no customary salute to the Castle. The day before, 21 December, the Puritan ministers of four Boston congregations had met and decided that they "could not with good conscience consent that our Meeting-Houses should be made use of for Common-Prayer Worship." They proceeded to inform the new governor of their decision.[3]

For Bostonians Mather, Sewall, Willard and the rest, the arrival of Andros, Nicholson, and their red-coated, Irish, Roman Catholic troops aroused seldom absent fears. Once again New Englanders were reminded of Stuart despotism, Court of Star Chamber, and now the loss of the colony's charter. Thereafter, noted a somber Sewall, there were many guns fired for the Queen's birthday, bells rung "respecting the beheading of Charles the first," and on 6 February Puritan sacraments were rudely interrupted by the "ratling of Guns during almost all the time, [which] gave them great disturbance."[4] In addition to smallpox and the death of his son, Sewall recorded the erection of May poles and later the celebration of Christmas. "'Twas never so in Boston," was his grim conclusion.[5] A new epoch in America had begun. It was to be a time of imperial politics and Anglican assertiveness. Andros's arrival in Massachusetts was only the beginning.

Common-prayer worship, May poles, and Christmas: since the founding of Massachusetts in the 1620s, Pilgrims and Puritans had experienced such affronts to their reformed, covenanting religion. While they had not put up for long with the perpetrators of these offenses, there was always the whisper of the presence of members of the Church of England in their midst. When the whisper became an audible declaration of intent, the visible saints sent the offenders packing. Not until June 1686, two years after the original charter of Massachusetts had been annulled by royal command, was there to be a parish of the Church of England in the Bay Colony. Then the congregation of what would become King's Chapel was organized, and that October some four hundred worshipers gathered to use the Book of Common Prayer.[6] Until that day, the Standing Order of New World Congregationalism stopped the mouths of whichever lone Anglican lions dared roam the forests of New England. Still the threat was always there, and political vigilance was demanding and difficult, more so, since all acknowledged—or tried to—a continuing membership in the Church of England. She was the nurturing mother of Puritans, John Winthrop had claimed, "from whence we rise . . . ever acknowledging that such hope and part as we have obtained in the common salvation we have received in her bosom, and sucked it from her breasts."[7] If such bill-of-fare no longer enticed, Winthrop at least did not loath "that milk wherewith we were nourished," or so he said.

None of the few Anglican clergy, all conforming Puritans who chanced to settle in Massachusetts, remained for long. William Blackstone (1597?–1675), Boston's first settler before the arrival of Winthrop and his followers in 1629, moved to Rhode Island in 1634. He had, as he stated, "left England to escape the power of the Lord's Bishops, but found himself in the hands of the Lord's Brethren."[8] Earlier, John Lyford (1580?–1641), a graduate of the strongly Puritan Magdalen College, Oxford, left Massachusetts in 1627 to become minister of Martin's Hundred Parish in James City County, Virginia.[9] William Morrell (1594–1625) of Magdalene College, Cambridge, who had arrived in Massachusetts at the same time as Lyford, returned to England.[10] None of these exercised his ministry in the Bay Colony in either Pilgrim or Puritan surroundings.

Church of England laity fared no better. The story of the licentious carryings-on of Thomas Morton (1593?–1646) of Merry Mount has been told numerous times.[11] The erotic energy and sexual revels between Englishmen and Indian squaws at Morton's plantation are well known. What is not often realized from Morton's *The New English Canaan* is his protestation that those at Merry Mount read the Bible and used the Book of Common Prayer. When Pilgrims declared the prayer book to be a "poore thinge" and that he who "hath the guiftes of the spirit [needs] not a booke in hand," Morton replied that they were "like the Serpent . . . [and] did creepe and winde into the opinion of the illiterate multitude."[12] In 1630 the impasse between this renaissance Anglican lawyer and Elder William Bradford came to a head, and the "Lord of misrule" was banished. As Kenneth Murdoch long ago suggested, the rites of the Church of England were as much a bone of contention as Morton's loose behavior.[13]

Nor was Morton the only son of England's national church in the land of Pilgrim separatists. Within Plymouth Plantation were those who kept the Anglican holy day of Christmas. Bradford disciplined them and stated that there would be no play on Christmas Day while others worked. Sports were banned, and the governor "tooke away their implements." While he allowed these members of the Church of England to "kepe their houses," that is, stay in the colony, "ther should be no gameing or revelling in ye streets." To this Bradford added darkly, "Since which time nothing hath been attempted that way, at least openly."[14] If a few Anglicans were allowed, it was an exception to the usual practice of Massachusetts Pilgrims and Puritans. Expulsion was the rule. Only those who kept silent and bided their time survived, and they were not many.

Less fortunate was Thomas Lechford (fl. 1629–1642). Lechford, a lawyer and member of Clement's Inn, had distinct Puritan leanings, even "as tending to subvert Episcopacie, and the settled government of England."[15] At first imprisoned and then banished, he landed in Boston in 1638. He did not, however, own the covenant or join the church of the visible saints. Indeed, Lechford engaged John Cotton, then Thomas Dudley, and finally Governor Winthrop in theological debate. The Clement's Inn lawyer now called Massachusetts's bluff regarding the colony's continuing loyalty to the Church of England and judged that "Apostles ought to remaine in the Churches, likewise Evangelists and Prophets, as well as Pastors and Teachers, else we must be beholden to the sins of men for the propagation of the Gospel."[16] Because of this unpopular opinion, "I saw," wrote Lechford, "seven shepherds and eight principall men called out against me, as if I were an Assyrian." Two years later, in May 1640, Thomas Lechford's views of episcopacy appear to have undergone radical change. Life in the bosom of the visible saints had altered his opinions. He now professed that Christians could not live happily without bishops, nor Englishmen without a king. Moreover the "people here, in short time, if the course here hold long, (which God forbid!) are like to be most unchristian, and the rest erroneous and ignorant enough." He had not received the sacrament in two years, "nor am I like to doe, for . . . I am not of them, in church or common weal."[17] Popular elections of pastors and teachers in the church and of magistrates in the commonwealth—or so it seemed to Lechford in comparison with England—meant only trouble in America. How, he asked, can New Englanders make themselves a church without the presence and approbation of a properly designated ecclesiastical authority? Ordinary Christians did not have the power to choose and ordain their own officers. Furthermore ministers had no right to ordain anyone without the presence of a bishop. Puritans "strain at gnats, the cap, tippet, surplice, cross, kneeling at the Sacrament," but in their church government they "swallow such camels as departe from Christ and his Apostles and Evangelists."[18]

When Lechford turned to the subject of the conversion of the Indians, he decided that the Book of Common Prayer was a much needed formulary of worship. If the "best and the learnedest are and have been beholden to forms," then surely "the poor Indians are to be taught . . . by forms." Repetition of set prayers was necessary. If churches allowed "extempore long prayers in publique . . . the generation following will be more ignorant, if not erronious."[19] Furthermore, lectionaries, holy days, ceremonies, bowing at the name of Jesus, private discipline of offenders, and universal admission to the sacraments were more agreeable to scripture and God's word. By such means might colonists have peace and orderliness, he judged, both for themselves and with the native people to whom they were to preach. "When they [New Englanders] urge the example of Geneva, some churches in Germany, both the Higher and Lower, Scotland, &c," Lechford continued, "I then propound to them to consider what experience any of these churches had in mission to convert and plant churches among pagans and heathens." It was a remarkable reversal for one banished from England for anti-episcopal tendencies. Lechford himself recognized the inconsistency and wrote in conclusion, "You may wonder how I am reformed: Truly, Sir, I was forced for my owne satisfaction to studie these things."[20] Lechford was also forced to leave Boston as a result of his study. Back in England, he published his uncomplimentary findings on New England.[21]

There were other members of the Church of England in seventeenth-century Massachusetts who, if they were not forced to leave the Puritan colony, found life there not at all to their liking. Among the earliest of whom we have record was layman John Oldham (fl. 1624), the Reverend Francis

Bright (fl. 1629), the Reverend Ralph Smith (fl. 1630), and possibly the unstable and avaricious Nathaniel Eaton (1610–1674), first "head" and professor at Harvard College from 1637 to 1639.[22] Among the colonists who in May 1646 submitted to the General Court of Massachusetts a petition in behalf of religious liberty were at least two members of the Church of England: the Reverend Samuel Maverick (ca. 1602–1676), who, like Blackstone, had settled early (1624) in the Boston area,[23] and Dr. Robert Child (1612–1654), a graduate of Corpus Christi, Cambridge.[24] These two, along with five other petitioners, declared that they, although unfit for high office, could perceive from their vantage point "those leaks which will inevitably sink this weak and ill-compacted vessel [Massachusetts], if not opportunely prevented."[25] Child, the author of the remonstrance, declared that he and the other petitioners were "of a linsiwolsie [variegated] disposition; some for prelacy, some for presbytery, and some for plebsbytery." Those, he went on, who were members of the Church of England were like sheep without a shepherd, and, unless their wants were speedily met by the General Court, would be compelled to petition parliament for redress.[26] In Judge William Pynchon (1590–1662), the petitioners met their match. Pynchon suggested to John Winthrop that henceforth all warrants should be issued in the name of the king, whose evenhanded laws Child had declared all should obey. For Pynchon, "though the King be never so corrupt in Religion and manners yet if his subjects will be faithfull to the lawes of England he cannot hurt his subjectes" since all laws are made not in the name of the monarch's personal prerogative but in that of his power "which is his lawes."[27] It was a neat piece of circular argument, and it landed Child in jail and ultimately brought about his banishment. Massachusetts could— if it so desired, and it did—write its own laws, call them the king's, and organize its churches to exclude any other manner of worship. Once again noisy members of the Church of England were the losers.

With the restoration of the monarchy in 1660, the desire for freedom of worship on the part of the members of the Church of England in Massachusetts received royal support. King Charles II, in response to the greetings of the Congregational magistrates of the General Court, declared that "freedom and liberty be duely admitted and allowed, so that they that desire to use the Booke of Common Prayer . . . be not denied the Exercise thereof or undergoe any prejudice or disadvantage thereby."[28] Massachusetts authorities found it convenient to ignore this injunction. The London government and the General Court were on a collision course. In 1664, royal commissioners arrived in the Bay Colony, but, until the advent of Edward Randolph in 1676 as collector and surveyor of the customs, matters were at a standstill. It was one thing for commissioners to come and go and report to

London; it was quite another to have a permanent official of the crown keeping Puritans under close surveillance.

In October, the busy and observant Randolph wrote to the Privy Council's Committee on Trade and Plantations that while the number of Church of England folk in Massachusetts was scarcely a sixth of the population, there were many waiting in the wings who had little real commitment to the Congregational way. "It is nothing but Interest & designe," wrote the sanguine official, "that draws most of that people into their [dissenters'] Churchmanship & to think well of that religion and Government they thrive under."[29] No doubt emboldened by Randolph's presence, a number of Bostonians, already members of the Church of England, petitioned the king *"That a Church might be allowed in that City, for the Exercise of Religion according to the Church of England."*[30] Charles II responded rather lamely in the same year (1679) that it was his intention to tolerate all in his colonies except papists. It was hardly enough. In the meantime Massachusetts resolutely continued its policy of nontoleration.

Yet Randolph was busy. This "chief architect of the Dominion" of New England[31] not only tried to keep Americans from breaking English trade laws, but at a later date he sought to have royal gubernatorial inaugurations attended with Episcopal ceremonies and solemnities.[32] As a result, Randolph wound up the most hated man in the northern colonies. By 1684, his machinations on behalf of the annulment of the Massachusetts charter bore fruit. The deed was accomplished in June of that year, while consternation spread throughout the bay area. Two years later, Puritan grief in Massachusetts was added to by the arrival of Joseph Dudley on the *Rose,* a ship destined to bring trouble. Dudley came as "President" of Massachusetts, Maine, and Nova Scotia. The fact that he was a native of Roxbury, son of Puritan governor Thomas Dudley, and a graduate of Harvard (1665), did not help matters. While Dudley did not become a member of the Church of England until 1693, he soon proved himself offensive to Bostonians. With him on the *Rose* was the Reverend Robert Ratcliffe (fl. 1657–1700), who proceeded at once to read common prayer in the hated surplice. But Dudley did not press religious matters and, as it turned out, failed to arrange financial support for Ratcliffe. Randolph complained bitterly to the archbishop of Canterbury. The following year (1686) Andros became the first royal governor of all New England.

Edmund Andros could have learned some important lessons from Lieutenant Governor Edward Cranfield of New Hampshire. Beginning in 1684, Governor Cranfield had attempted to impose the Anglican liturgy upon Puritans, the remnants of Anne Hutchinson's movement, and a few Quakers. Cranfield had met with stiff resistance. In this first direct confrontation between royal gubernatorial will and local custom, the insistence upon uniformity ended in increasing diversity, or at the very least making the Book of Common Prayer even more of an issue than it had been before. The governor's demand that New Hampshire's colonists fast on the day of Charles I's decapitation, refrain from manual labor on Christmas, and perform baptisms and celebrate the Lord's Supper according to the national formularies was not popular. Cranfield went on to make local heroes out of resisting Puritan ministers Seaborn Cotton (1633–1686) and Joshua Moody (1632–1697). Cotton was threatened with expulsion and Moody with imprisonment.[33] The next year Cranfield was forced to return to England to answer charges against his conduct as governor; he never returned.

New Hampshire was a test case. It was observed by Bostonians with foreboding, and the arrival of Andros and his soldiers in 1686 did nothing to calm fears. Massachusetts was proud of its heritage. Despite its well-documented and much discussed tensions, the colony had a degree of stability unmatched by any other province in the late seventeenth century, except perhaps Virginia. The bay area, and indeed New England as a whole, was well on the way to becoming clannish. Unlike New York and the middle colonies, her population was not made up of congeries of Dutch, Swedes, Germans, and French.[34] Massachusetts, moreover, had its own establishment of Congregational churches, and it was assumed that all would give their tax money and at least nominal allegiance to those privileged bodies. The alternative was to leave. Thus it came about that Episcopalians found themselves in the exotic position of being thought, at best, dissenters or, if they refused to pay, tax dodgers. If that were not enough to enliven the missionary enterprise in the hearts of men like Randolph, Andros, Keith, and Dudley, there was an additional challenge. Throughout New England, the legal fiction was maintained that if any town or meeting house cast a majority of votes for an Episcopal minister, he could be legally instituted and his salary paid by the taxes which ordinarily would have gone to the Congregational minister.[35] Since Congregationalists were unwilling to deny the orthodoxy of the Church of England, tax exemption for the mother church was not long in coming (1727).[36] Such were the opportunities afforded Episcopalians. Few could resist taking advantage of them.

With these three imperially minded officials—Randolph, Dudley, and Andros—the promotion of the Church of England proceeded rapidly. Their efforts, supported by the crown, made the growth of the church modest but steady. Beginning with King's Chapel and then Christ Church (1723) in Boston, Episcopalian parishes sprang up in the surrounding areas of the Bay Colony.[37] Not only did these doughty officials strengthen their church in Massachusetts, they also attempted to tie that colony closer to England by

113

appointing military officers. Thus, they tended to displace the provincial militia with a royal army which was local in character. Such a move could hardly be expected to appeal to citizens used to having a free hand in such matters. From the imperial point of view, however, a united and effective fighting force against French Canada was increasingly attractive.[38] In addition, both Dudley and Andros sought to revise and change the court system of Massachusetts and to make it more like that of England.[39] New justices of the peace replaced the older colonial magistrates. Trial by jury in criminal cases was forced on the province despite the fact that it went against in-grained local custom. In addition, paper money was issued over Bostonians' protests, and, in general, royal patronage was greatly increased.[40] While New England alternately resisted, absorbed, and compromised in these matters, a clear transformation was taking place. In this metamorphosis, the colonial Church of England played a distinct and increasingly unpopular role.

To make matters worse, from the Puritan point of view the quality of Massachusetts Episcopalians, both lay and clerical, was of a high caliber by midcentury. In her presbyters, especially at King's Chapel, the church was singularly fortunate. Ministers such as Ebenezer Miller (1703–1762) of Dedham and Scituate, Peter Bours (1726–1762) of Marblehead, William McGilchrist (d. 1779) of Salem, and Gideon Bastwick (1742–1793) of Great Barrington and Lanesborough were well educated and highly responsible. Moreover all these were native New Englanders, educated at Harvard and Yale. None of them displayed high-flown contentiousness against their Congregational counterparts. Miller was a thoughtful and socially concerned missionary, whose "truly religious life and conversation" included concern for West Indian blacks.[41] Peter Bours, the much-loved rector of St. Michael's Church, Marblehead, has been described as never contemptuous of Congregationalists.[42] Gideon Bastwick, the charitable and missionary-minded rector at Great Barrington for twenty-three years, became pastor for the entire village. During his incumbency at St. James Church and in his many travels into the province of New York, he baptized 2,274 children during a busy ministry.[43] These and others were part of Massachusetts's aspiring intellectual and social aristocracy.

Among Episcopalian laity were a cross section of colonial life and endeavor. At the upper end of the social scale were newspapermen, doctors, and merchants, such as Samuel Colburn (d. 1761?) of Dedham whose generosity made possible the building of Christ Church in that town. Others were farmers, fishermen, and militiamen. While Edward Randolph drew attention to a number of gentlemen who had a hand in founding King's Chapel in the 1680s, he also noted that there were "tradesmen, [and] others of mechanick profession." Among them were William Harrison (d. 1686), a coach maker, Goodman Needham, and Smith and Hill, a joiner and a shoemaker, respectively, who were "very busy about prayer-book worship."[44] Others like "Major Howard" and Benjamin Bullivant were clearly slightly higher on the economic ladder.[45]

In the first two decades of the eighteenth century and before the arrival of more moderate Episcopal clergy, there appeared in the heart of the citadel of Massachusetts, in Boston itself, a polemicist of rare wit. His name was John Checkley, and he was to prove one of the most contentious churchmen in New England. On Christmas Eve, 1720, Checkley, apothecary, bookseller, and layman at Episcopalian King's Chapel, wrote to his legal counselor and fellow parishioner John Read. In "Obedience to the Commands of my holy Mother the Church of England, (that most excellent Branch of the Church catholic)," wrote Checkley, "I am endeavoring to prepare myself for the ensuing Festival, the ungrateful Commemoration of the Nativity of our great & glorious Redeemer." Though the Christmas season, judged this popularizer of the Church of England, called for solemnity, it was hard to suppress a natural exuberance, "the swelling Exultations of my Soul which are rais'd by looking forward to the coming Day." Joy, even a degree of mirth, was suitable for the occasion wherein was seen the "astonishing Love of the Deity, in sending his only-begotten into the World, for the redemption of lost Mankind." Warming still further to his subject, Checkley found himself fairly swept away with emotion. "I glow, I burn, my heart strikes quick," he rhapsodized, "and every Pulse beats Joy!" But then how dreadful to behold those unhappy wretches, Boston's ministers and magistrates, who, by not celebrating Christmas, crucified afresh, and added new sufferings to their Lord. Checkley's tears flowed, he confessed, for disobedient New Englanders. He would henceforth avoid the tents of the wicked. Surely John Read too would "preserve inviolate the Unity of Faith in the Bond of Peace."[46]

One wonders how Read, "Leather-Jacket John" as Bostonians called him in his day, reacted to his client's hyperbole. Read, the brilliant lawyer, avoided the tents of none. He would travel throughout the dominion incognito and appear before magistrates in defense of the poor; at such times, he astonished observers with his procedural dexterity and legal knowledge. If one were to judge from his character alone, Read would have preferred discrimination in speech to extravagant expression. Whereas Checkley was ambitious for the Church of England in the northern colonies, Read had little appetite for ecclesiastical gain. Read would defend the missionaries of the SPG in the courts, watch out for the church's welfare, but, along with an increasing number of eighteenth-century laymen, he would take his religion

115

in stride. Originally a Congregational minister in Stratford, Connecticut, Read had considered ordination in the Chruch of England.[47] Instead he settled on the law, became a vestryman at King's Chapel, and befriended legally disadvantaged missionaries of the SPG in Massachusetts.[48]

Something of John Read's true reputation crept into his obituary when in February 1749 the *Boston Post-Boy* esteemed him simply as one of the greatest lawyers in the country.[49] The most famous case taken on by Read was that involving a libel suit against Checkley himself. Checkley had republished a book—not his own—deemed to be scurrilous in its treatment of the New England ministry. Read won the case; Checkley was acquitted. In his summation before the Suffolk Court which tried Checkley in 1724, he, unlike his client, brooked no "harsh censures of those of the Congregational or Presbyterian persuasion; for I honor their persons and reverence their Ministry." Evenhandedly, Read warned the court which sought the indictment of Checkley that somehow justice must transcend the hearsay and prejudices of the moment. When "such a Case as this at barr," Read exclaimed, "stands upon Innuendos, I look upon it dangerous to admit such power in an Innuendo as to make crimes and scandals of such matters as are not so without an Innuendo; for this is to make cruel and dangerous Engines for the punishment of the Innocent; for no man can be so innocent as to stand before an Innuendo. Therefore for the Example of it, I pray . . . that he may be acquitted."[50]

But if Read knew the importance of obedience to law, he also knew the privilege of rebelliousness against mere custom. In nothing so much as his membership in the Church of England did he make the point. Beyond that, the approbation he received as a citizen of Massachusetts showed that accommodation was possible. Read was preparing the way for the settled ministries of such men as Miller, Bours, McGilchrist, and Bastwick. As early as the 1720s, Read was showing fellow New Englanders that one could be a loyal citizen and an Episcopalian.

The adaptation which Read achieved eluded John Checkley. No son of New England was so fervently detested by the Standing Order as was this American Oxonian. As an outspoken apologist for the mother church, he fell heir to traditional Puritan mistrust. The shadow cast by his figure seemed to the older generation of Puritans to resemble an apparition of Archbishop Laud. In the land of Sewall, Willard, and the Mathers, Checkley was a bad influence, the purveyor of scandalous libels, the editor and publisher of scurrilous material. He was seen as one of a group out "to gett our Colledge into their Hands; which will be a most compendious Way to bring quick Ruine on our Churches."[51] To make matters worse, this Tory was snaring Mather's own nephew, Thomas Walter (1696–1725), of Roxbury.[52] The stupidity of such a promising young man baffled and worried Mather. As early as 1716, Walter, under Checkley's influence, had been attracted by the high church faction.[53] While in the end the young man came around to the faith of the fathers and even provided theological grist for the Puritan mill,[54] his flirtation with Episcopalianism caused anxiety in Boston.

At the same time that Walter was being enticed toward the Church of England, a new danger was perceived by the Puritans. In October 1713, Francis Nicholson reappeared on the scene. Nicholson's reputation as a supporter of the national church preceded him. Though this time he came to America as governor of Nova Scotia, Whitehall gave Nicholson additional, broad powers to investigate economic matters in all colonies north of Virginia.[55] Boston was chosen as his headquarters. Cotton Mather was suspicious and feared for the Puritan meeting houses, but, when Nicholson produced his commissions and instructions, there was a sigh of relief, for they contained no "hurtful Aspect on these Colonies or Churches."[56] As if to show his good intentions, the day after his arrival the new governor of Nova Scotia attended a Congregational ordination service in Charlestown. With great assurance, the preacher of the occasion declared the validity of Congregational ordination and the legitimate vocation of the New England ministry. The service over, Nicholson, "not without Appearance of Impression," remarked that "*he had never seen such a Spectacle before; and it was a solemn, serious affecting Transaction.*"[57] Two months later, however, when the Massachusetts authorities proclaimed a fast day, the new economic investigator grumbled. No proper authority had commanded such an act; the Queen was head of the church and only she or her deputies could order a fast day. Nicholson's hitherto restrained temper began to flare: he "seem'd to be Warm," remarked Samuel Sewall dryly.[58] For their part, Episcopalians complained that they were treated as if they were heathen.

To add to the outrage of Governor Nicholson, in February of 1714 his secretary John Netmaker was arrested and fined for the profane cursing of an assistant constable—"God damn ye"—when that New England officer refused to drink the queen's health with Netmaker in a local tavern. Netmaker was then charged with "Contempt for Her Majesties Government in this Province," which no doubt caused him considerable surprise. The next day, the secretary "Offer'd not so much as his own Bond" and was promptly sent off to jail. It would seem that the transformation of the Massachusetts court system was incomplete. Since he had twisted the lion's— Nicholson's—tail, Judge Sewall had to endure a roaring noise. It was not long in coming. Did the judge know that General Nicholson was in America with "the Broad Seal of England"? Yes, replied Sewall. Did he know that "Mr. Netmaker was his Secretary"? Again Sewall was forced to respond,

"Tis generally so received." Then "I demand JUSTICE," yelped Nicholson. At this "so furiously Loud . . . Noise," Governor Joseph Dudley appeared at the door of the council chamber and pleaded for Netmaker's release. Sewall held his ground: "I objected to that; saying, we had committed him: but I did not know that we had the power to release him." Power or no power, Dudley then took matters into his own hands and ordered the council to draw up an order releasing Netmaker, thus slipping around the court and due process of law. Sewall acidly remarked that those who voted in favor of the order were "hardly drawn to it."[59] The Dudleys, it seems, never did things by halves and were conspicuously concerned for their own prerogatives.[60] So too were Nicholson and Sewall.

None of the officials who sought to control the Puritans were theological controversialists, however. That role fell to Checkley, who assumed the mantle of George Keith. Whereas the former Quaker had sailed away on his grand tour of the colonies, Checkley remained permanently in the heart of Massachusetts. He was a homegrown thorn in the flesh of the "Bostoneers," as Randolph had called them. Checkley's intimacy with Thomas Walter led to a vigorous tilt on theological and ecclesiastical questions. As a result, in 1720 Checkley published *Choice Dialogues Between A Godly Minister and an Honest Country Man Concerning Election and Predestination.* In his *Choice Dialogues,* this Episcopalian apologist promised "the meanest Plough-man, the very meanest of God's People" fresh religious understanding in the form of a "rich and precious store of spiritual Knowledge and godly Comfort."[61] The author viewed with alarm the intellectual and religious state of his native province. "Wicked Books written (by the instigation of the *Old Serpent* who goes about to deceive) . . . were putting false Comments and horrid *Anti-Christian* Glosses upon the *best of Books,* the Fountain of all true and *Divine Wisdom.*" Checkley referred not only to the Bible but to Calvinist publications appearing in the book stores of Boston from the pens of Dutch, English, and Scottish authors.

Especially galling to John Checkley were the Church of England Calvinists, particularly John Edwards. It would hardly do, if one wanted to maintain Episcopalian distinctiveness in Calvinist New England, to have Edwards held up as a paragon of theological probity. Better anticipate trouble before it arose. There were other advantages in attacking Edwards. Might not Checkley be able to say that he was simply dealing with an in-house, Anglican squabble? To mask one's intentions, however thinly, gave one a certain leverage. As one historian suggests, the use of Edwards as antagonist might be a way of alluding to the New England claim that Congregational churches were part of the Church of England.[62] In his preface to *Choice Dialogues,* Checkley had judged that those "who call themselves, Church of England Men . . . won't like what these Papers contain." There was another front besides that "blessed Confederacy" of Calvinists "which would have us *reform'd* backwards"; it was the Church of Rome. She was the *"great Whore, the Scarlet Whore,* the *Whore of Babylon,* the *Anti-Christ."* While such eloquence was common enough to all Protestants, it served Checkley's purpose by providing him with the opportunity to place his own church midway between Calvinist wickedness and Roman lechery. Anglicanism offered a well-illumined high road, free of the dark vales of Romanism and dissent on either side. Here in fact was a tradition which served as "the Example of the *primitive Church* . . . and which bade others give Ear to those *pious* and *godly Fathers* of the *Church* who will teach us the Truth in Sincerity."[63]

While Checkley's fellow countryman must have had little idea of the writings of the early church fathers, Checkley did and made appropriate use of them. Ignatius was an obvious choice.[64] Attached to *Choice Dialogues* and the American edition of Charles Leslie's *Short and Easie Method with Deists,* which Checkley had contracted to be published in 1719, were Ignatius's letters to the Magnesians and the Trallians. Both epistles, for reasons different from Checkley's, affirmed the primitive authority of bishops. The inferences were obvious: Congregationalists lacked bishops; the Church of England had them. At first glance, Leslie's work seems an unlikely cudgel with which to belabor the sons of the Puritan saints. After all, neither Quakers nor Calvinists were deists in the strict sense of the word.[65] What was significant—and it was hardly to be missed—was that Leslie appealed to "what might be termed tradition, or the concurrent testimony of the church" against skepticism. Such a weapon now used against New England had its advantages. Without actually saying no, Checkley could smoke out the "Bostoneers" from their ecclesiastical lairs, "for Leslie's method of argument made the sacraments, the liturgy, the priesthood and its succession the great evidences of the truth of Christianity."[66] These were the strong points of Anglicanism—at least for Checkley.

While I will deal with John Checkley's theological apologetics in chapter 7, it is important here to pursue his ecclesiological thought and its uncompromising character. The furious controversy which he started was carried on as much upon institutional grounds as along the theological lines of grace and free will. For Puritan and Episcopalian alike, church polity was an integral part of the fabric of social life, and, if it did not come first in the religious order of things, it was a close second to the great theological doctrines. Thus, after the publication of Leslie's *Short and Easie Method* and his own *Choice Dialogues,* Checkley got down to ecclesiological business. In 1723, with the impact of the Yale conversions fresh in New England minds, he brought forth his *Modest Proof of the Order & Government Settled by Christ and his Apostles in the Church.* This tract was followed in the next year by *A Defence of . . . A Modest Proof.* These compositions took up where Ignatius left off and presented arguments for diocesan episcopacy. While *Modest Proof* made the usual appeal to the "apostolic" origins of the episcopate, i.e., instituted by Christ and the apostles, the three orders of ministry—bishops, presbyters, and deacons—were declared to have always been clearly distinguished from one another. That the Church of England carefully maintained the distinctions was obvious. Moreover, her bishops were in unbroken succession with the apostles themselves.[67] Dissenters in New England could make no such claim. They were *"Carnal Libertines"* and, therefore, enemies of Christianity.[68]

At the same time that Checkley made this astounding assertion, he also welded Christian faith to episcopacy. In his "A Discourse concerning Episcopacy," which he appended to yet another reprint of Leslie's *Short and Easie Method,* Checkley asserted that not only were all sacraments of no avail without proper bishops but that those who pretended to their efficacy were guilty of conducting ministrations which were "Sacriligeous, and . . . [in] Rebellion against the Lord." Lawful authority was necessary; without it ordination was a "vile Prostitution" of Christ's priesthood. The apostles called themselves ambassadors of Christ. But now, he screamed, "every Tag, Rag, and Long-tail call themselves his Ambassadors too, by a call from the People! Good God!—Good God!—How has the Priesthood been vilify'd of late!"[69]

Except for his vehemence, there was no originality in his thought. Checkley said what any early eighteenth-century Anglican Tory might have claimed. Yet this American apologist clearly earned for himself the dubious honor of being the first person to publish anti-Puritan tracts in New England. The phenomenon of such publication was striking enough. But Checkley also mixed politics into his ecclesiological brew. In the *Defence,* he spoke of the alliance of prelacy with royalty. Presbyterianism, he charged, was established on the ruins of kings and kingdoms.[70] Kings ruled by divine right, and subjects must be passively obedient to their pleasure. In the light of the Glorious Revolution, it was clearly a discarded notion in England. Equally as clear, John Checkley continued to espouse the cause. He was in fact a Nonjuror.[71] That he remained so until 1738—and in the heart of New England at that—is one of the more captivating anomalies of colonial religious history. Checkley, it would appear, gives credence to the judgment of one historian who baldly states that "New England Anglicans never mastered the secret of the Hanoverian establishment, to avoid action of any kind except when no alternative remained."[72] Passive and distant

Anglicans elicited curiosity, while aggressive and nearby Episcopalians aroused fears.

Such fears produced results. Instead of hanging out crepe, latter-day Puritans responded: Thomas Walter, Harvard's Edward Wigglesworth (1693–1765), Jonathan Dickinson (1688–1747), Nathan Prince (1698–1748), Samuel Mather (1706–1785), and the urbane Thomas Foxcroft (1697–1769). Controversy developed on a broad front. There was no way of avoiding a controversialist who could quote Calvin in support of episcopacy.[73] From Boston's point of view, Checkley's attack could not have come at a worse time. In the second decade of the eighteenth century, the descendents of John Winthrop were just beginning to learn the significance of the events of the Glorious Revolution. It took twenty-five years for the implications of toleration and a new era of trans-Atlantic relations to register on the colonial mind.[74]

Ever since 1689, New England, like New York and Maryland, had experienced a strong sense of dislocation and anger caused by the crisis of the revolution. Checkley contributed significantly to this disarray. He presented a case for the Church of England with ability and effectiveness,[75] considering the climate of political and religious uncertainty. We need not retell here the story of the witchcraft trials, the yearning to reestablish the old Puritan Zion, or the desire to put faith to work once again as Cotton Mather attempted in his *Bonifacius* (1710).[76] In his way Checkley tried to do just that. He was more like Mather than he ever would have cared to admit.

Perhaps John Checkley, a son of New England and her pious thoughts, drank deeper than he knew at the bitter spring of Puritan uncertainty. He too could and did speak of national crime and the necessity of national repentance. He too could pray with ardor to "the God of Mercy to avert that Wrath which is so justly due." He too could lie on his study floor and pound the dust out of the carpet with his fists and beg forgiveness for "those unhappy, wretch'd Men who, by abetting . . . wicked Principles, react [sic] the horrid Crime." As much as any of them he would "endeavor with my Family to keep a Fast unto the Lord."[77] But the crime which Checkley's Puritan earnestness abhorred was not that of sexual license or the execution of old ladies as witches, it was regicide. We must take him at his word.

> There are too, too many who defend the horrid Regicides, and glory in their being of their King-killing, hellish Principles: and there are too many others, who, tho' they do not avowedly poses these diabolical Tenets, are unhappily deluded by the crafty but specious Pretences of cunning, wicked Men, to entertain such mischievous Principles, as, were they pursued to their full Length, wou'd inevitably involve them in the same Guilt, and make them (even these moderate Men) react the impious Crime. Therefore O my Soul,

121

come not into their Secret, unto their Assembly, mine Honour, be not thou united: for in their Anger they slew a Man.[78]

So spoke the father of the high church movement in colonial America, the expounder, clarifier, and elaborator of the imperfect ideas of George Keith.[79] In doing so he looked forward with unblushing confidence to that day when all would be of one mind.

Boston's Episcopalian community was perhaps better served by the Reverend Samuel Myles (1664–1728), rector of King's Chapel from 1689 to 1728. Myles was, like Checkley, a native New Englander. He was a man of "moral integrity, temperate disposition and outstanding gifts as a preacher."[80] The rector of King's Chapel aided Episcopalians in Swansea and Braintree. Myles's own congregation was made up of recent Anglican immigrants, merchants, professional people, and government officials.[81] Some of these proved to be a good deal less temperate than their rector. Indeed, the leading laity at King's Chapel made up a circle of political and literary polemicists who wished to defy personally the Puritans. James Franklin (1697–1735), the elder brother of Benjamin Franklin (1706–1790), presided over this Episcopalian junta. Its chief organ of communication was the *New England Courant*, to which young Benjamin was apprenticed in the early 1720s. With James Franklin as editor was Checkley himself, who has been called the founding "author" of the *Courant*.[82] There were other high churchmen in the group: Dr. John Gibbins (1687–1743), a convert from the Reverend Benjamin Colman's (1673–1747) liberal and Episcopalian-leaning Brattle Street Church; Dr. William Douglass (1691–1752); Dr. George Steward (fl. 1735), future treasurer of the Episcopal Charitable Society; John Eyre (1700–1753), a wealthy merchant who became one of the leading laymen at Queen's Chapel, Portsmouth, New Hampshire; Thomas Fleet (1685–1758), printer for King's Chapel and future editor of *The Weekly Rehearsal* (1733) and *The Boston Evening Post* (1735), and John Valentine (d. 1722), one of Boston's leading lawyers and warden at King's.[83]

To the future sage, self-promoter, and former Puritan Benjamin Franklin, these men made up the circle of what he called brother James's "Writing Friends."[84] That they soon gave young Benjamin a partiality toward the Episcopal church is not to be doubted.[85] He wrote for the *Courant* under the pseudonym "Mrs. Silence Dogood," though only after the paper had passed from an early high church stage to a more congenial latitudinarianism inspired by the Reverend Henry Harris (1689–1729), the assistant rector at King's Chapel.[86] But whatever its theological bias, the *New England Courant* annoyed Bostonians. It was felt that Checkley, the Franklins, and their medical friends had no business starting another newspaper. The capital of the Bay Colony already had two: the venerable *Boston News-Letter*, founded in 1704, and *The Boston Gazette* (1719). Both represented the Standing Order. When compared with them, the *Courant*, as Benjamin Franklin suggested, "gain'd . . . Credit, and made it more in Demand." Because the columns of the *Courant* contained anti-Congregational, and therefore scurrilous, material, it was fun to read. Of course, there was never any doubt about the readers' loyalty to Congregationalism. It was just that one should keep up with what the opposition was thinking and saying. Whatever the rationale, Boston's nosy Parkers found it racy and bought it—that is, until the Franklins got run out of town.

In the meantime, in the 1710s and early 1720s, the SPG was up to worthier things. The society found adherents to the church among the commercial interests of Newbury and among the fishermen at Marblehead. Clergy were sent to these towns, but progress was slow in Massachusetts. Not until after 1723 did that vigorous growth begin which would give England's church twenty-two congregations by 1775.

Meanwhile, to the south in New York events were occurring which would further the church's expansion into New England. This time it would be Connecticut which beckoned. But there was also to be a march into the middle colonies as well. Far more than Boston, Philadelphia, or Annapolis, after 1700 New York would become the key to the expansion of the Church of England in all directions north of the Potomac.

At first glance it is difficult to surmise why such promise initially should have been recognized and then developed. There was little homogeneity in New York. Factious politics characterized the colony, and extremes of wealth and poverty further divided settlers. Different nationalities and languages existed side by side. Common ideology was lacking. The promise intrinsic in the province and its port city at the mouth of the Hudson was not due to any preeminence of population. New York was then a third the size of Virginia, half that of Massachusetts, and comprised somewhere between 20,000 and 30,000 population.[87] In terms of religious allegiance, Episcopalians were outnumbered seventeen to one by English dissenters, French Calvinists, Lutherans, and Dutch Reformed families.[88] Nevertheless, beginning in the 1690s the colony's governors were all Anglicans, subject to a settled policy to guide their religious attitudes. After the mob rebellion against New York's aristocracy which occurred from 1689 to 1691 under Jacob Leisler (1640–1691),[89] the governorship alternated between the "Court Party" and the moderates. Between 1693 and 1720, Benjamin Fletcher (Tory); Richard Coote, earl of Bellomont (Whig); Lord Cornbury, earl of Clarendon (Tory); Lord Lovelace, baron Hurley (Whig); and finally

Robert Hunter (Whig) served as governors. Such shifting between those who wished to live amicably with dissenters and those who would disadvantage them as much as possible not only embroiled the province unnecessarily but divided the Episcopalians.

Generally high church governors such as Fletcher and Cornbury favored the aristocracy of the colony by giving them—as well as the church—large tracts of land. Cornbury, who had an exceedingly curious penchant for dressing up in his wife's clothes, even on the day of her funeral procession, was notoriously overbearing and arbitrary.[90] He inducted clergy into parishes against popular will, imprisoned his enemies whether Presbyterian or Episcopalian, and, in John Nelson's judgment, "demonstrated what seemed to be extensive powers residing in the governor's office to advance the interest of the Church."[91] Other governors such as Coote, Lovelace, and Hunter attempted to be more evenhanded.

Around these successive officials, opposing factions grew up in the church. High churchmen such as William Vesey, Thomas Prichard (d. 1705), and John Talbot approved of the tactics of such men as Lord Cornbury. To Prichard, Cornbury exhibited "Unparallel'd and Uninterrupted Zeal" for the high church cause.[92] On the other hand, to Lewis Morris, the leader of the Episcopalian moderates, the Earl of Clarendon was "the greatest Obstacle that either has or is likely to prevent the growth of the Church in these parts." Morris scored the "pernicious effects of his arbitrary Conduct, [which] if not prevented by the Society will render it, (humanly speaking) impossible to propagate the Church in this part if not in any part of America."[93] Cornbury, claimed Morris, was making the SPG ineffectual by his obstinate high churchmanship. Thus by 1709, just before Hunter's administration was to begin, an altercation within Episcopalian ranks had descended to name-calling and informing.

It was a two-way street, however. If Morris told tales on the leaders of the high church movement, they gave in kind. To high churchmen, the members of the Whig cabal—Morris, Heathcote, and the Reverends Thoroughgood Moore (d. 1707) and Christopher Bridge (d. 1719)—were nothing better than "a pack of Rascals and Knaves, never a Barrel of them better Herring."[94] Vesey, the Reverends Jacob Henderson (fl. 1751) and Thomas Poyer (1685–1732), and the lay leadership of Trinity Church found Governor Hunter to be nothing less than a traitor to the church he was supposed to protect.[95] The SPG in London did its best to mediate and not respond by taking sides. Nevertheless, given the realities of New York's mixed religious affiliations, the burden of proof seemed to lie with the Cornbury faction, for wisdom favored the Whig course despite the loud noises of their opponents.

Even with these debilitating factors, New York emerged as a highly important base for the church's advancement. There were a number of reasons for this unlikely development. First, of course, was the string of powerful Anglican governors. If they were not particularly tactful, they were clearly able to play the game of politics with some freedom. Whichever Episcopalian party they belonged to, they could always find an articulate and determined minority behind them. Second, the SPG responded with alacrity to appeals from the province for ministers. The strategic military importance of converting Indians west of the Hudson as a barrier against French expansion figured, as we have seen, in London's planning. The result was to focus attention on New York and its needs. In addition, the religious makeup of the colony was unlike that of its neighbors. In New England, an entrenched majority opposed the spread of the Church of England at every opportunity. In western New Jersey and Pennsylvania, the Quakers were in control. In New York, there was no such unified opposition, because New Yorkers had never emigrated to the New World as a single body of believers. The religious makeup of the province was, as a result, a tessellated affair, ready for some ecclesiastical craftsman to give it form, even if it were only to declare a settled policy of toleration. No one ever appeared with the proper perspective. Robert Hunter with his powerful and even pious allies, Lewis Morris and Caleb Heathcote, might have proved to be that man, but, by the time he reached the governorship, too many divergent hands had been at work. Still there were those with perseverance and energy who were willing to devote themselves to the interests of the church.

The final key to understanding why New York became of consequence to Episcopalians was the vestry act of 1693. This piece of legislation was passed through the General Assembly by means of compromise and pressure. What emerged was an ambiguously worded statement which seemed to favor the interests of the Church of England without actually saying so. The act left everyone unsure of whether churches had to call men in Anglican orders or whether dissenting ministers might do just as nicely as incumbents of Episcopal churches. Vestrymen were to be elected, which sounded Anglican enough, but, in nearly every case, members of other denominations served as lay officers and often predominated in the vestries. In 1694 the vestrymen of Trinity Church even took the step of electing a dissenting minister to be its rector.[96] Only the speedy intervention of Governor Fletcher and his Episcopalian advisors saved the day. Bound as he was by his instructions to protect the church, Fletcher did two things. He "found" a substitute in William Vesey who was sent scurrying across the Atlantic for ordination in the Church of England. Secondly, Fletcher permitted the

125

Episcopalians at Trinity Church to elect a second vestry.[97] While the first vestry continued to exist and collect parish taxes, to the second body fell the privilege of choosing the rector. Since the new body was elected only by the immediate congregation of communicants of the church and not by the citizens of the parish at large, the future of the Anglican ministry was assured. Here was a bit of legerdemain designed, it seems, to astound the credulous as well as to elect ministers.

Behind such moves were New York's prominent Episcopalian families, a determined minority, who saw to it that they were well represented in the assembly and in the courts, as well as in their churches in the city and in Westchester, Queens, and Richmond counties. Among those laymen was one whose planning and actions set missionary forces in motion which would have no little consequence for the future of New England. To the "King's Province" of New England then we must once again return, but this time to its southern region, Connecticut.

In 1705, the first rays of light seemed to Caleb Heathcote to be shining into the darkness of Calvinist Connecticut. From his home in Scarsdale, Judge Heathcote had written to the secretary of the SPG regarding the prospects for the Church of England to the northeast.[98] This gentleman colonist, besides being a member of the SPG, was judge of the Court of Admiralty for New York, New Jersey, and Connecticut and Receiver General for the Customs for North America. Such offices no doubt contributed to the judge's larger imperial perspective. In 1705, Heathcote came to the opinion that Connecticut was a land guilty of the "sin of schism." To end such a deplorable condition, the judge wished to have settled there the Reverend George Muirson, a young Scot who had been ordained in the Church of England. To this end, in 1706 the judge and Muirson toured Connecticut as far as Stratford. They found the colony ignorant of the ways of the national establishment. Again in 1707 they sallied forth to Stratford, where they bent the willing ear of John Read, whom Heathcote called a very ingenious gentleman.[99] The three musts have conferred on how to best minister to Anglican immigrants recently settled in Stratford. It is probable that John Read was at this time converted. His willingness to listen to Heathcote and Muirson was a portent of things to come. Efforts to organize an Episcopal church in Stratford were, however, cut short in 1708 by the death of Muirson.[100]

In the meantime, news had spread to Boston about the missionary journeys of the two Episcopalians from Scarsdale. As a result, in the following year Stratford received a Congregational minister of ability and conviction, a new Puritan champion against Episcopalian inroads, Timothy Cutler. From the point of view of the Standing Order, it was an ill-fated choice.

Like Heathcote, Cutler was not a man to stand still. Getting out of the Cambridge-Boston area after his graduation from Harvard in 1701 might be a wise move. There had been just a whiff of scandal which clung to Cutler as a result of his undergraduate years at Harvard: a few college fines and a bill which remained unpaid and was later forgiven. He had proved himself to be a student of marked ability in languages as well as in other studies and was admitted to the New England ministry in January 1709.[101] Cutler immediately departed for Stratford where a fresh start, a new and significant challenge, and elbow room to exercise his talents awaited him. He did not disappoint: nine years later when Yale College finally settled in New Haven, he was chosen to succeed his father-in-law as its president. There Timothy Cutler won the approbation of students. No less an acute observer than Jonathan Edwards (1703–1758) found, during his undergraduate years, that President Cutler was an "extraordinarily courteous [man] . . . loved and respected by all who are under him."[102]

In the meantime, Episcopalians were not idle. The northern branch of the Church of England moved into Connecticut in the person of George Pigot, a native Rhode Islander and an SPG missionary. From Stratford in 1716, he traveled a circuit which included Norwalk, North Haven, Fairfield, Ripton, West Haven, and Newtown. Full of high and, as it turned out, unrealistic hopes, Pigot wrote glowingly of the Episcopalian cause. It flourished in the province. Puritans began to fear once again for their churches as word spread of the renewed Church of England activity. Pigot had no sympathy for dissenters. Congregationalists were to him "inveterate schismatics" who lived in a "deluded country." In spite of his apparent distaste for the land of Thomas Hooker, this SPG missionary had a vision of rejuvenation: a bishop arriving, wardens appointed in all Congregational churches, and the whole phalanx of reformed saints safe at last in the Episcopalian camp. What led Pigot to such an "apocalyptic" turn of mind was a surprising and friendly visit from five of the leading Congregational ministers in Connecticut. Timothy Cutler, newly appointed president of Yale, was among them. In August 1722, a justifiably elated missionary wrote to the secretary of the SPG: "I have great expectations of a glorious revolution of ecclesiastics of this country, because the most distinguished gentlemen among them are resolvedly bent to promote her the Church of England's welfare and embrace her baptism and discipline."[103]

The moment of triumph had come. Its sweetness was savored to the full by Pigot. Massachusetts with the new liberalism of the Brattle Street Church and, in the western part of the colony, Stoddardian revivalism was one thing.[104] To imagine the entire northern tier of colonies becoming Episcopalian was quite another. Pigot did not shrink from such a thought. "If," he wrote, "the leaders fall in, there is no doubt to be made of the people." Then, soaring to the heights of expectation of a general reformation in all North America, he declared that there were others in unnamed provinces who were ready to renounce separation and follow the example of Cutler and his friends. The end of dismal nonconformity was at hand, or so it seemed. Pigot had, however, overestimated his good fortune and underestimated his opponents.

The story of the famous September graduation at Yale in 1722 is beloved of colonial historians. The moment of truth involved just seven words, spoken at the close of the graduation ceremonies: "And let all the people say, Amen." Without them, Timothy Cutler would have remained Edwards's courteous, respected Puritan leader, secure in the stronghold of arch-Calvinist Connecticut. With them, Cutler became an ugly apostate in the minds of many. The significance of the Episcopalian manner of ending public prayers was not lost—either on those who heard it or on those who heard about it. As Perry Miller aptly observed, "In 1722 the heavens opened and consternation rained down: the Rector of Yale, two tutors, and four neighboring ministers announced their conversion to the Church of England."[105]

New England was in an uproar. "The effect on the colony," writes Henry May, "was similar to that which might have been produced in 1925 if the Yale football team had suddenly joined the Communist Party."[106] Young Benjamin Franklin, who could not resist appearing in print in the *Courant*, suggested the wisdom of moderation. In the meantime, Pigot, who had been warned in advance of what was to occur on "Black Tuesday," had himself been unable to resist attending and so "repaired to the Commencement of Yale College in New-Haven, where in the face of the whole country, the afore-said gentlemen and six others . . . declared themselves in this wise, that they could no longer keep out of the communion of the Church of England."[107] The group by no means presented a solid front to the trustees of Yale, however, and Pigot's prediction that the college commencement was a "great outset towards a reformation" and that it "has brought in vast numbers to favor the Church of England" proved false.[108] When the apostates made their appearance before Governor Saltonstall in the college library the following day, three of the seven backed down in the face of determined opposition.[109]

Nevertheless the door to Connecticut had been opened. The revolt of the young clerical scholars at Yale provided, in Professor Goodwin's words, "striking and indisputable evidence that the Church of England posed an intellectual threat to colonial Dissent."[110] Henceforth, Episcopalianism would appear as an alternative to Puritanism and the New England way.

At the end of the year, Cutler led his insurgents to England and ordination in the imperial church. Upon his return to America as a priest in the service of the SPG, he assumed the rectorship of Christ Church—Longfellow's "Old North"—in Boston. There, from 1723 until a stroke incapacitated him in 1756, he harangued his enemies, built the high church party among Episcopalians, and, by political maneuver, sought to strengthen his cause at every opportunity. Feared and respected, he held "to the conviction," as Nelson Burr has pointed out, "that episcopacy is of *divine appointment, unalterably established upon Christ's gift to his Apostles, which fixed a particular constitution for His Church.*"[111] While others such as Samuel Johnson found themselves moving toward a position of greater toleration of other polities, Cutler never wavered. The sooner the Bay Colony was brought into total submission and Harvard turned into an Episcopalian seminary the better.

Cutler's tenaciousness of purpose was amply illustrated in 1725 when he questioned the right of the Standing Order to hold a church synod under English law. If Massachusetts had in fact gone Presbyterian, Cutler meant to call their bluff. It was an astonishing challenge. Who, if not the New England aristocracy, had a better right, established over a hundred years, to meet together in solemn deliberation? To the delight of Cutler, royal attorneys-at-law thought otherwise. They deemed that such a synod "would be a violation of the King's prerogative."[112] Boston was stunned; Cutler had clearly scored a victory. However, when he tried to gain admission to the Board of Overseers of Harvard College for his fellow churchmen, he failed conspicuously. After that, the most he could expect from his fellow citizens was grudging respect.

There is no doubt that Cutler could not distinguish men from ideas. His caustic tongue constantly got him into trouble, and at times he demeaned himself and his cause. He called Cambridge a "Snotty Town." Politics were forever getting in the way of better religious sense. A woman in Boston who was a sometime parishioner of Cutler's wrote him words of criticism, all the more devastating because of their gentleness.

> I pray preach more on true conversion and the life of Christianity, and not so much on passive obedience and nonresistance. Pray in your little prayer before the Sermon for King George and Royal Family, and for the Governor, as our Ministers do, and I will come more often. I know many others of my mind; and I am sure your Church will be full.[113]

In addition to his endlessly expressed political convictions, there was a ripe sensuality in Cutler's makeup. In an untasteful letter to his college classmate George Curwin (1683–1717), Cutler affected the salacious dig in the ribs. Marriage was full of "Dangerous Depths"; there were the "usual troubles of it, as that of the Pewking of my Spouse, care to get the Baby clowts ready," and all of the other domestic chores. Otherwise it was "Pure Sport." He never knew there could be such "Intimate Fellowship and noble Happiness found in the world." But Cutler could not leave well enough alone, and while "she hath the Softest lips in the world next to your wife or Dear," still she was extravagant. Finally marriage was a "Mire [and he] who has fallen in would have as many others fall in as he could." He hoped that another married classmate would "give way to his betters and let me get a boy before him."[114] The letter to Curwin just missed the tone of straightforward heartiness for which its author sought. Perhaps it was because he chose to speak openly of that most intimate relation between husband and wife. Later in that same year (1711), Mrs. Cutler with exquisite and gentle reprisal presented her husband not with a son but with twin girls. With such parables did Providence seek to teach Timothy Cutler.

There was no lack of courage in this leader of Massachusetts Episcopalianism. He stood his ground in a hostile environment. He was kindly disposed to youth and befriended young people on many occasions. His devotion to his own sons and his generosity to them were marked.[115] Cutler was undoubtedly learned, orderly, and precise. He "has a very good spirit of government . . . and seems to increase in learning," wrote Jonathan Edwards.[116] Yet Cutler was unable to bring about unity, whether among Episcopalians in Boston or in Massachusetts as a whole.

The high church movement which Cutler and Checkley fostered was an American movement in part, and, for both of them, there was never a question that after ordination they would once again live in their native land. No doubt they traveled to England to see the beauty of Anglican holiness in great cathedrals, university colleges, and other stately buildings of the mother country. By contrast America came to be perceived as devoid of history, culture, and tradition.[117] Nevertheless, their abiding interest was in their province of New England, and to it they both returned.

After ordination in England, John Checkley came back to an interracial mission in Rhode Island. There Checkley appeared at his best when he sought to convert the leaders of the most powerful tribe of eastern Indians, beginning with the Iroquoisan sagamores "Sanguaasam, Arexus, Francois Xavier, and Meganumba." When his old enemies in the Bay Colony suggested that his mission to the Piscataways was only a front for further Episcopalian troublemaking, Checkley let it be known to authorities in the mother country that Boston would rather have the chiefs remain French Catholics or relapse into paganism than "be reconciled to the Church of England."[118] Checkley lost no time in baptizing not only the Indian chiefs but also blacks as well.[119] Like any other New Englander, he complained of the cold that froze the blood in winter and at the same time relished informing his superiors in London of his use of "Snow Shooes, to visit the sick and bury the dead at the Distance of 6, 8, & 12 miles . . . [which] few others could undergo."[120] If his tracts had proved controversial, Checkley could display another side to his character when he remarked on the kindness of his own people and the little presents they brought to him.[121] The "Posture of Affairs" in America never ceased to enthrall him. Cutler too, for all of his disparaging remarks about Cambridge, kept himself well informed on affairs in New England.[122]

In the meantime, Anglican expansion from New York was moving north and east into Connecticut and, simultaneously, south and west into New Jersey. Unless the common character of these moves to expand the church is recognized, the larger picture of the development of the church in the North as a whole will not be perceived.

At the end of the seventeenth century, Burlington, New Jersey, was full of rich Quakers. Members of the Delaware River Society of Friends had built themselves "a fine Market-Town . . . having several Fairs kept yearly in it. . . . Assemblies and chief Courts [are] kept there; and by that means it is become a very famous Town, having a great many Brick-Houses in it. . . . There are many Fair and Great Brick Houses on the outside of the Town which the Gentry have built for their Country Houses." Trade was brisk in Burlington and occasioned the building of wharves, timber yards, breweries, and bakeries. By 1698, prosperity allowed Quaker John Tatham to build a "Great and Stately Palace" surrounded by orchards and a formal garden full of "July Flowers."[123]

But Quaker prosperity was not accompanied by Quaker harmony. Six years before Tatham built his mansion, no less a figure than George Keith had shattered the unity of Friends by leading a sizeable rebellion at the Burlington Yearly Meeting of Keithian or Christian Quakers. Keith's exodus from the meeting presaged the religious collapse of Quaker rule. In addition, shortly before the Burlington meeting, proprietary rights in West Jersey were sold to a group of London businessmen who allowed stock in their newly formed company to be bought by associates regardless of religious allegiance.

Political hegemony began slipping through Quaker fingers. In 1698 the mantle of New Jersey's governorship passed to Keithian Quaker Jeremiah Bass. Old-time Friends were furious, but there was little they could do. They had merely to await the sad denouement. It came soon enough in 1702 with the simultaneous arrivals of George Keith, now in Anglican orders, and Lord Cornbury, newly appointed governor, not only of New York but of

New Jersey as well. A year later, the cornerstone was laid in Burlington for an Episcopal church. The church was to be known as St. Mary's. Possibly to nettle old line Quaker sensibilities still further, the cornerstone was laid on the "Feast of the Annunciation of the blessed Virgin Mary."[124] It was hoped that "Christian" or Keithian Quakers might be pointed to the true church. Among those who heeded the injunction was Jeremiah Bass who attended the laying of the cornerstone as a convert to the Church of England. Later he was to become a vestryman.[125]

Burlington's Episcopalian minister for the next twenty years was to be Keith's friend, the formidable John Talbot.[126] Initially, Talbot did not come to America as a missionary of the SPG. He was chaplain aboard the ship which Keith took in 1702 to make his survey of the colonies for the Venerable Society. At sea the two men became fast friends, and it was decided that Talbot should join the American expedition. Two of their key objectives were the New York-Philadelphia axis and along the banks of the Delaware where Keith's former Quaker followers had already been diminishing the status of Friends' power. Within the larger geographical area, Burlington, with its yearly meeting, was a principal town, particularly of West Jersey. There John Talbot was to remain. In early 1704, the vestry of St. Mary's petitioned the society to appoint Talbot as their rector. A year later the request was realized.[127]

At first with both Talbot and Keith working, the task of conversion went well enough and, as Keith wrote Thomas Bray, "our labor has had very good success."[128] But thereafter, the task of attracting worshipers fell to Talbot alone. His efforts were strenuous, his correspondence in behalf of the cause of the Church of England in New Jersey unflagging in its regularity. His letters, writes one historian, had "an effervescence found nowhere else in the bundles of SPG correspondence: High Church and Tory, he represented the Anglican interest with fervor.[129] But fervor seems to have made Talbot a stranger to subtlety. With more than usual passion, even in that passionately religious day, he lambasted his enemies, the Quakers. "Last month," Talbot wrote, "I attack't ye great Synagogue of ye Quakers at their yearly meeting in Burlington; we gave them a broad side with some honest Francis Buggs Bombs, but could not get them to dispute by no means; then I upbraided them with their charges."[130] Once Friends "used to challenge all priests," said Talbot, but "now they could not answer one." That one, meaning John Talbot himself, might now "defy a thousand, and put ten thousand to flights."[131] But the Lord's warfare was not to prove so simple; New Jersey's "heathen" stood their ground.[132] The faithful of the Church of England had no other choice than to become part of the pluralistic population. In the entire formative period of Episcopalianism in New Jersey, the

SPG was able to sustain no more than four missionaries in the colony, and usually only two.

Nevertheless, the hopes of the imperially minded Talbot were high in the first decade of the eighteenth century. Well might he expect preferential treatment from New York's Episcopalian officials, an increase of church members from English and Scottish immigrants, and always the addition of Keithian Quaker converts.[133] Zeal for episcopal prerogative burned in Talbot with a steady flame. If the church was to "att last take Care of her Children," a suffragan must be sent, for the "Poor Church in America [is worse off] in this Respect than any of her Adversaries."[134] Time and again he made the point throughout his long career: Episcopalians in America must have the full measure of their church government.[135] In 1712, Talbot purchased the mansion of John Tatham for the considerable sum of £600. The SPG paid for what was to be, so they hoped, the first episcopal palace in the colonies.[136]

Did John Talbot ever occupy the Tatham mansion as a bishop? The general consensus is that in the years 1720–1722 when Talbot, then aged seventy-seven, was on one of his trips to England, he received consecration from Nonjuring bishops. Such a step, if indeed it was ever taken by Talbot and the rebellious bishops, would have placed him outside the pale of the national church and beyond the fellowship of even the Hanoverian Tories. This in turn would corroborate the accusation of Talbot's Whig opponents in the New York-New Jersey government that the Burlington minister was a Jacobite.[137] More recently, the consensus that Talbot was the first Episcopal bishop in America has been challenged.[138] Since the one piece of incontrovertible evidence—the certificate of consecration—is missing, one historian has implied that Talbot was the innocent victim of "the charge of Jacobitism [which] could always be made and generally with some effect."[139] On 9 April 1715, Governor Hunter, who had consistently sought cooperation with the Quakers for the sake of provincial amity, complained to the SPG that "Mr. Talbot has Incorporated the Jacobites in the Jerseys under the Name of a Church in order to sanctifye his sedition and Insolence to the Government."[140] When notified of Hunter's serious charge, Talbot replied:

> I am very sorry that I should be accused of sedition after I have travelled more than any body to keep peace in church and state. . . . Let them consult the admiralty office and they will find I took all the oaths to King George I necessary to qualify me for the service which I have performed faithfully abroad and at home. . . .
>
> The Lord rebuke that evil spirit of lying and slander that is gone out against the Church. Here and there they spare none. I suffer like my Lord and Master

between two at Philadelphia and New York, but God has been my succor and I doubt not but he will still deliver me from the snare of the Hunter.[141]

No doubt to the satisfaction of New York's governor, Talbot's salary was suspended. Nine years later, in 1724, Talbot was permanently separated from the SPG on the same charges.[142]

Yet the question still nags: did the septegenarian minister of St. Mary's receive ordination to the episcopate in the two years he was in England? Surely Talbot knew the dangerous consequences of such a move. It is doubtful that he would have risked the permanent schism which inevitably would have come had he donned episcopal robes in New Jersey and begun the ordination of deacons and presbyters for the church. We know that Talbot as early as 1708 felt deeply discouraged. The variety of sects in New Jersey troubled him. Unless the Episcopal church was manned by missionaries "the Gate of Heaven be shut, [and] the Gates of Hell will soon prevail against us."[143] To add to his dismay, the Presbyterians with their doctrine of double predestination and their questionable ordination of elders were no better than Quakers in Talbot's eyes.[144] Only members of the national church were true Christians, and they at present were not well provided for.[145]

As a result of what for him was the frightful pluralism of the American scene, Talbot began to sound like St. Paul or like one upon whose shoulders the saint had laid the mantle and burden of episcopal authority. "I am forced to turn Itinerant agen," he wrote to the SPG, "for the care of all the Churches from East Jersey to West Jersey is upon me; what is worst I can't confirm any nor have not a Deacon to help me."[146] Certainly Talbot himself would have welcomed consecration and would have gladly performed the office of a bishop. Even though he found an ally in the Reverend William Skinner (1687–1758), a fellow "Jacobite," by 1722 it was too late. Nevertheless, the inspiration for New Jersey's high church tradition was due in no small measure to the efforts of vigorous John Talbot. Without his presence it is doubtful that the Episcopal church in the southern tier of the middle colonies would have gained the foothold it did.

The Episcopalian presence was not limited to New York and New Jersey. Both the church in New York and Talbot in Burlington made no real distinction between the east and west banks of the Delaware. Philadelphia and the lower Delaware figured indiscriminately and prominently in Episcopalian missionary planning. The religious scene in Pennsylvania (see chap. 9) in the early eighteenth century closely resembles that of New Jersey. Here, similarly, no establishment is to be found, but rather Quaker control of a colony in which diverse people found a haven and in which freedom of worship prevailed. As in Rhode Island, New York, and the Jerseys, so in Pennsylvania the denominational pattern was established quite early. The Church of England took its place among Pennsylvania's many religious traditions. Once again, the presence of George Keith and John Talbot proved of great importance to the achievement of this position, and once again the SPG provided the missionaries and paid the bills. In Pennsylvania Keithian Quakers, Anglican immigrants, and Swedish episcopal Lutherans to the south provided a prospective minority of worshipers at first eager to live in accord with the rites of England's church. With Christ Church, Philadelphia (1695), as its first and most prominent parish, Episcopalian growth proceeded. Clusters of church folk made possible the formation of other parishes at Montgomery, Oxford, and Radnor to the north of Philadelphia, Dover Hundred and New Castle (now Delaware), Lewes Town, Apponquinimy, and Chester. In the years before 1708, the growth and staffing of these churches proceeded even more rapidly than in the Jerseys.

Early successes were, however, deceptive. Pennsylvania's seven churches were not to be blessed with long and consistent service on the part of their ministers, and by 1725 there were only four clergymen in the colony. Chester, New Castle, and Apponquinimy in particular failed to keep rectors. No less than four SPG missionaries left for the financially greener pastures of Maryland's wealthy establishment. Among them was the rector of Christ Church, Philadelphia, Evan Evans. As a result, the Church of England failed to draw dissenters in any large numbers. The Episcopal church in Pennsylvania remained until midcentury a small minority, one denomination among many.

135

CHAPTER 5
The Church's Progress in Maryland and Virginia

When Thomas Bray arrived at Annapolis in the spring of 1700, seventeen ministers of the Church of England were on hand to greet him. At the new capital of Maryland, a degree of pomp and solemnity—fit for a bishop—accompanied their ministerial salute. Bray was welcomed and courted as "Your Reverence." In a single decade, the number of Episcopal parsons in Maryland had jumped from three to well over a dozen. While these clerical émigrés had never had "gent." (gentleman) affixed after their names on university rolls, but rather "pleb." (plebian, or commoner), or "p.p." (*puer pauper*, poor boy), they, like Bray himself, were university men. Many hailed from All Souls, Brasenose, Queens, Jesus, and Oriel at Oxford, and Peterhouse and Christ's at Cambridge.[1] Together they comprised a potent religious force for crown and mitre in the promising, if contentious, colony on the Chesapeake.

Maryland had been marked from its inception by the most intense competition among religious and political factions. Originally founded in 1630 as a refuge for persecuted Roman Catholics, it shared with Rhode Island both the chaos and freedom of a reasonably open society. Toleration had become the accepted policy, if not the practice. Whereas Roger Williams would have allowed Jews and would have shaken hands with a Turk had such an exotic foreigner presented himself on the shores of the Naragansett, Marylanders limited their welcome on the Chesapeake to trinitarian Christians. That in itself was ahead of the times. The result of such "openness" was that all sorts of riffraff arrived, making these particular colonials a "people sensitive and excitable and reflecting in so many ways the restlessness and discontent prevailing in England during the seventeenth century."[2] Like Rhode Island, Maryland knew little stability.

Resistance to Caecilius Calvert (c. 1605–1675), the second Lord Baltimore, increased. "The habit of attack on the prerogatives and privileges of the lord proprietor," wrote Charles Barker, "had begun when the colony began, and in the seventeenth century had led to . . . violence."[3] Calvert had wanted all of his settlers to live in mutual toleration. At a desperate moment, this skilled and sincere English nobleman had caused a toleration act to be passed by the Maryland legislature. The date was 1649, a bad year for Catholics and Anglicans: Cromwell's rule was about to begin in earnest. Calvert's generous gesture was not enough to save the colony's charter. It was revoked the following year. However, when Maryland Puritans, following what they believed to be an international English policy established by Cromwell in his treatment of Ireland, began to persecute Catholics in Maryland, the lord protector surprised them. Cromwell sent back word in 1655 that all persecution must cease, that toleration should be reestablished, and that Lord Baltimore was to be restored to his proprietary rule. Marylanders were "not to busy themselves," said Cromwell, "about religion."[4] Colonials could not have been more surprised: the policy of live-and-let-live came not only from Catholic Calvert but from Protestant Cromwell. It proved to be a policy which the clergy of the Church of England in Maryland were slow to grasp. Nevertheless, it had been set once and for all in 1649 and was to be maintained in the 1690s, even if that maintenance required imperial intervention.

With the restoration of royal government in England in 1660, proprietary government in the colony remained. Religious differences among Quakers, Puritans, Jesuits, and Episcopalians continued to diminish. No doubt a host of sociological and economic reasons may be adduced to explain Maryland's chaotic condition from the 1660s through the 1680s.[5] Still, the lack of a common religious, and thus ideological, identity must not be discounted.

Doubt and mistrust persisted in the years following the Glorious Revolution, when Maryland found itself—for a time (1692–1715) at least—no longer a royal colony under the proprietary rule of the Catholic Calverts. As a result of this new status, the colony moved slowly and with difficulty toward the establishment of the Church of England. The process was complicated by the fact that Protestant dissenters made up the bulk of the population. These, together with the Roman Catholic minority, were, as Francis Nicholson complained to the bishop of London, "joyntly bent against our Church."[6] Before 1689, the Catholic issue had always been present in the conflicts between the lower house of the legislature and the council and between the proprietary party and the people, which caused further dissent.[7] In addition, as we shall see, Episcopalians themselves were by no means united. Thus the religious and political situation in Maryland was complex and volatile in the 1690s, quite unlike that of Virginia.

The revolution of 1689 was no trifling incident in Maryland. In the confusion which reigned in its aftermath, Protestant Englishmen found that they had fled from the Roman Catholic, Stuart lion only to fall into the embrace of the imperial, Anglican bear. Three religious groups predominated in the 1690s. First was the obstinate proprietary faction made up of the Roman Catholic minority plus the Quakers, who had found in Maryland a haven of religious sufferance. Second, there was the insurgent, antiproprietary commonwealth faction made up of incipient democrats. Strong among this group were the Puritans of the lower Eastern Shore in Somerset County.[8] Third, there appeared the upright royal governors, Lionel Copley (c. 1650–1693) and Francis Nicholson, together with the increasing number of Episcopalian clergy. This confusion was further complicated by the fact that not all Maryland's Episcopalians presented a united front.

In April 1689, after news reached the colony of the arrival in England of William and Mary rumors of a Catholic and Indian alliance and a possible massacre were rife. At the time "an Association in arms for the defense of the Protestant Religion, and for the Asserting the Right of King William and Queen Mary to the Province of Maryland and all the English Dominions" was formed.[9] The leadership of this cabal fell to the former Anglican priest, John Coode (1648–1708). Coode, like John Yeo before him, had matriculated at Exeter College, Oxford, in 1664 at the age of 16.[10] He was subsequently ordained and served briefly at his home church in Penryn, Cornwall. For undetermined reasons, he was removed from that parish and traveled to Maryland to try his ecclesiastical hand in a new setting. This too failed. Thereupon, Coode became a militia captain, married a rich widow twenty years his senior, and ran successfully for the assembly. In 1689, he headed the rebellion against Governor William Joseph, an intrepid believer in the divine right of James II to rule. The Protestant majority in the legislature insisted that they were denied the rights of Englishmen by the proprietary council. No longer would they remain tenants in the private domain of the Calverts.[11] Under Coode's leadership they dispatched Joseph easily and proclaimed a "great and general Jubilee." Coode boasted of his act of revenge against the proprietors.[12] It is clear that he was an "aristocrat" who chafed under foreign control. In addition this spiny Episcopalian seems to have personally invited imbroglio with nearly all with whom he came in contact. He incurred the wrath of four royal governors and was eventually forced to flee to Virginia, however, not before he carried to England a list of colonial grievances drawn up by the revolutionaries. This was the *Declaration of the Protestant Association*. It was a bombastic discourse, full of comments about "nullyfeying and suspending power," illegal impressments, fears of Jesuits, "popish youth," and arbitrary power. Members of the association had taken up arms to defend the Protestant religion, so that Marylanders might enjoy their "liberties and properties."[13] That Coode

138

and his followers outnumbered the "popish youth" by twenty to one was of course not mentioned.

That was not all: there were some members of the Church of England in Maryland who stood by the Calvert government rather than support the rebellion. Among these was the future speaker of the legislature, Thomas Smithson (fl. 1689–1717). Smithson found Coode's uprising illegal and immoral. He wrote the bishop of London, saying that "only the sence of our duty and the doctrine of our Church obliges us nott to stand in the [Associators'] Councill."[14] No doubt Smithson's religion was stiffened by self-interest: he had only recently, in September 1689, been appointed justice of the peace for Talbot County. A "great many supporters of the Proprietor were petty officeholders appointed by [Calvert's] deputies." When Smithson spoke for the "True sonnes of the Church of England," he clearly did not have John Coode in mind.[15]

The majority of Episcopalians, however, supported efforts on the part of the royal government toward obtaining a religious establishment. What is surprising is that five bills to this end were disallowed by Whitehall (1692, 1694, 1695, 1696, and 1700). The English reaction seems strange at first, but London was cautious. More could not be required in Maryland than was permitted in England. The new rights of nonconformists, assured by the Bill of Rights of 1689 and the Toleration Act of 1690, must be protected. Kensington Palace dispatched a clear message to Annapolis when King William caused the bills passed by the Maryland legislature to be vetoed. The message was ignored, however. The colonial assembly's acts instead became tougher on dissenters and, as a result, increasingly out of line with the broad principles of toleration laid down in the mother country.

Caught up in their own problems as a minority and troubled by the disorders of the recent past, Maryland Episcopalians were determined to seize the opportunity to assert what they judged to be their prerogatives. Against Presbyterians, Quakers, and Roman Catholics, they rang the tocsin. The final act to originate in the assembly in 1700 even went so far as to declare that the Book of Common Prayer must be used in every church or house of public worship. That took care of Catholic mass and Protestant meeting. It is probable that such a requirement was made in direct response to the open flaunting of all restrictions on religious freedom, particularly on the part of the now proscribed Roman Catholics.[16] Clearly the policy of Maryland Episcopalians was to demand liturgical uniformity and universal tax support for the Church of England and its ministry in the colony. In short, the right of dissenters to freedom of worship was not to be honored.[17] The government in London had different ideas. There a coalition of low church, Whig bishops and Protestant nonconformists was determined to withhold its support for any bill of establishment which granted less toleration to Maryland's Protestants than they had attained at home.[18]

It was this decade-long altercation between colony and mother country which brought Thomas Bray to America. He, like his friend and collaborator Francis Nicholson, was eager to see establishment made a fact of political and religious life. Bray himself influenced the act of 1700, but when it passed the assembly, it was as clear as it had been in the past that the legislators had once again overreached themselves and included the offensive clause regarding the use of the prayer book in all churches. Bray's return to London in the same year was essential. He alone could undo the damage done in Annapolis. Into that cause he threw himself with customary energy. He conferred with the bishop of London, haggled with the Board of Trade and Plantations, and in the end settled the course of the Church of England in Maryland. There would be an establishment, but the act which completed it was dictated in 1702 by the royal government. A hitherto recalcitrant Maryland assembly had no other choice but to go along. Imperial policy emerged victorious. Toleration, and with it prudence, no doubt saved Maryland from further rebellion and thereby added to the belief, in England at least, that if Americans could not set their own house in order then it was up to crown and parliament to do it for them.

In the meantine, an ever-observant Thomas Bray had been gathering knowledge of colonial conditions. More specifically, Maryland became the source from which that provident clergyman developed the Society for the Propagation of the Gospel. What Bray learned became the starting point for the religious part of the endeavor to make America "a functioning part of England's commercial empire."[19] To counteract Charles Carroll's Jesuits, the church needed "Anglican Jesuits." In addition, like the Society of Jesus, the Society of Friends was thought to pose an equally dangerous threat. Indeed, Quakers were often seen by seventeenth-century Englishmen as "papists in disguise" so close were their ideas on justification, grace and free will, and scripture to those of the Romanists.[20] What better way then to counteract Quaker influence than to employ former Quaker George Keith as apologist and missionary? In 1699 Bray interviewed that well-traveled controversialist and reported favorably to the SPCK on Keith's activities. Shortly thereafter came Bray's own first hand experience at Annapolis. Once again, as in the case of Roman Catholics, Bray's knowledge of Quakers came from his more immediate concern with Maryland and the church's antipathy to the *Quakers* there. To weaken the positions in Maryland of both Catholics and Quakers, declared Bray, "Paternal Care and Pious Assistance" were needed.[21] The church must be strengthened. Clergy wanted relief from debt. Those who had left wives in England pined for their conjugal rights as much as they did for their civil ones.

Maryland's Episcopal ministers were discouraged and sought a commissary "to redress what is amiss and to supply what is wanting."[22] The council and assembly complained as early as 1694 that Virginia was better off. No doubt with the incipient William and Mary College in mind, they pled for schools and a college in Maryland.[23] In addition, in 1696 the eight Maryland ministers complained of low salaries and of what a "hard shift [it is] to live here."[24] In 1698, these same Church of England clergymen again petitioned London. Unless their needs were met, they would be prohibited from combating "popish priests" and those Puritans from New England who "wandered about without so much as license to preach."[25] Money and men, not only for Maryland but for neighboring Pennsylvania, were on the mind of Francis Nicholson when he advised Archbishop Tenison in 1695 that he was "in great expectation of your Grace's sending a minister and a schoolmaster for Philadelphia . . . [together with] ye penny and pound for their maintenance."[26]

Such transcolonial concern is fully echoed in Bray's own *Memorial*. His arrival in Maryland in 1700 was met with all the ceremony of an episcopal visitation. Bray preached before the assembly, called the clergy into convocation, issued circular letters, suggested a course for catechizing youth, and outlined "The Present State of the Protestant Religion in Maryland."[27] After returning to England, he turned his attention to the larger task of founding the SPG. That society was to accomplish its greatest work of evangelization in the north in general and in New England in particular, rather than in Maryland. Nevertheless, it was the immediate situation in Maryland with its Puritan minority, strong Catholic tradition, and persistent Quaker presence which gave rise to the SPG.

In the meantime Virginia's church faced a different problem. If in Maryland the issue was how and in what manner the church was to be established in a pluralistic society, in Virginia the question was who was to control an already established church in a homogeneous society. Would the church be controlled by the governor, vestries, clergy, the commissary, or a combination of these? In addition, the events which occurred in both of these Chesapeake Bay colonies in the late seventeenth century were to have repercussions of trans-Atlantic significance within Britain's first empire. Curiously those events were of an almost antithetical nature, directly related to the lives and attitudes of two remarkable leaders, the two commissaries, Thomas Bray and James Blair. If Bray's visit to Maryland in 1700 directly resulted in the founding of the SPG and indirectly until the Revolution in the long attempt to draw the colonies closer to the mother country, Blair's actions produced a decidedly different result. By allying himself with the lay power of the vestries against the governor, council, and even the clergy, Blair thereby heralded not a new imperialism but precisely its opposite, local rights and privileges.

James Blair was a Whig and a Scot, and, like many other leading Episcopalian clergy in the eighteenth century, he came from the borders of the Anglican community in the British Isles. Blair was, ecclesiastically speaking, something of an outsider in England. He came to America early in his ministerial career, at the age of 29. For the next five decades in Virginia, he shaped a tradition, built a strong church, got rid of governors, reformed manners, scolded clergy and laity alike, and generally made a nuisance of himself. By the time he died in 1743 he had held every office in the colony worth holding, including that of acting governor for eight months in 1740.

Blair was a *politique par excellence*. As such, he knew that "God and the world are like two Masters of contrary Tempers and Dispositions, whose Commands do generally interfere."[28] His sermons made him appear as vicar of a strongly moralistic God, while his politics were of such a nature as to cause disaffected clergy in 1705 to wonder "how dangerous a thing it is for a priest to be trusted with too much power."[29] To those who crossed him, he showed flashing annoyance that arose from his wounded feelings and afterward had the gall to suggest that he did not mean it! Anger was but a means of "putting some Life and Vigour into the cooler and slower Cunsultations of Reason." It should be used, he suggested, "to bark, to frighten and scare People to their Duty, without hurting them: at other Times giving them a gentle Pinch of Punishment, if the Bark of Reproof won't reclaim them."[30]

Was his bark all conscious bluff? His enemies claimed that Blair was forever seeing plots. What did he expect? Cromwell's mounted infantry? Fifth monarchy men? Was Virginia to be delivered into the hands of out-of-work militia? Perhaps, suggested his mocking fellow clergy, the soldiers were going "to lay a bridge over the Bay & let in the Accomackians." Or maybe they would make the mouth of the Potomac fordable so that the "New York-kians" could invade. Were the slaves rising? Maybe the schoolboys of William and Mary were turning the college into an arsenal with intent to murder Blair in his bed. No doubt there was "a plot to cast off the Yoke of Engld, to erect a fifth Monarchy on this northern Continent of America & make Govr Nicholson Emperor in the West, & who should have been at the bottom of this plot, but the English Clergy of the Colony of Virginia."[31] Only the loyal Scots supported Blair, it was said.[32]

For two years prior to the summer of 1705, Blair's political enemies had been after him: "'Shall a Scotch Commissary have ye making & unmaking of our Governors?'"[33] Many of the ministers spoke bitterly of "'that Scotchman & his gang.'"[34] Pointedly, Blair preached on humility and meekness to his clergy. The text from Matthew (11:29) ran, "'Take my yoke upon you, and learn of me, for I am meek and lowly in heart: and ye will find rest unto your souls." The ministers remained unconvinced and accused their commissary of *"overawing* methods": they had decided that the yoke was Blair's, not Christ's. Moreover the commissary, they judged, stuffed every page of his reports to England with stealthy, half-finished insinuations, "'crambo Stories of Govr Nicholson's *overawing* methods.'"[35] Those who wanted to get rid of Governor Nicholson—and Blair was the chief one—were a "few malcontents" who, to satisfy their "pride [and] avaricious humour," had done their worst. Blair, the ministers complained, used extravagant language, hard words and had brought contempt "'upon his Nation," dissatisfaction in the colony, and had generally exceeded the bounds of his authority.[36]

Historians have shown some puzzlement regarding Blair's place in the larger currents of colonial history.[37] He allied himself with the planter class, the tidewater rulers of vestries, courts of law, and the assembly, who so controlled the council itself as to make of it "'a body of uncles, cousins, and brothers-in-law, who, when they put up a united front were able to guide their relatives and supporters in the lower house, checkmate the governor at any hostile move, and run the colony generally in the interests of their own extremely privileged class.'"[38] Thus Virginia's ministry as a body never wholly trusted Blair, the bishop of London's emissary, and never gained a measure of cohesion until midcentury when the power of the commissary declined in the Old Dominion.[39] Only James Blair and a few others managed to attain full membership in the planter class. The clergy remained, at least in the minds of the laity, liegemen of the king, and, as a result, their loyalty to provincial interests was nearly always suspect.[40]

Blair advanced "the Whig doctrine that executive power should remain subject to parliamentary checks.[41] Blair observed that "'Frequent Assemblies are Esteemed as necessary there [in America] as parliaments in England and they reckon that if they gave away ye power of Levying & maintaining . . . , there would be no more Occation for Assemblys, because the Governor might do what he pleased without them.'"[42] The rights of the colonial legislature, the welfare of Virginia and the slaveholding landowners of the tidewater who sat on the vestries were what interested Blair. If he displayed interest in empire, it was on the basis of uniform rights and enjoyments for Virginians. Upon the basis of self- and class-interest, he became entirely a constitutional and parliamentary man. He allied himself

143

with the powerful families of the colony when he married the daughter of Benjamin Harrison (1645–1712). After that came close association on the council with those of the "college faction," Philip Ludwell II (1672–1727), Robert "King" Carter, Matthew Page (1659–1703), William Bassett (d. 1744?), and later Nathaniel Burwell (1680–1721) and William Byrd II. Beyond personalities, a question of principle was bared in the fights with imperial governors: "'was Virginia to be dominated by England, or was the maturing colony entitled to increased self-determination?'"[43]

Each of the governors of Virginia whom Blair got rid of at regular intervals through his invectives and accusations were themselves staunch Tories: Edmund Andros (1698), Francis Nicholson (1705), and Alexander Spotswood (1722).[44] Conversely, the governors with whom Blair got along well were either weak, like Edward Nott (1705–1706), or Whigs, like Hugh Drysdale (1722–1726) and William Gooch (1727–1749).[45] Whatever the truth of his allegations against Nicholson, Blair showed his own addiction to parliamentary principles when he accused that governor of favoring martial law.[46] Surely such a one as Nicholson, the commissary slyly observed, could not be in the true service of an English sovereign. To the charge that Virginians were out to feather their own nests, Blair argued that they were loyal subjects. His fellow citizens were not growing rich and haughty, he confided. Nor were they tainted with "republican notions & principles, uneasy under every Governmt & . . . ready to shake off their obedience to England."[47] Blair accused the governor of interfering in local appointments, currying favorites, irritating the House of Burgesses with long speeches, bribing judges, keeping irregular hours, threatening to cut the throat of the speaker of the House, exhibiting rudeness to gentlewomen, and so forth. It was a long and undifferentiated list of abuses, even by eighteenth-century standards. A month later, on 1 May 1704, the commissary repeated the charges in a further affidavit to the Lords of Trade.

Behind the smoke of accusation burned the fire of royal prerogative vs. colonial perquisite, as Tory design clashed with Whig ambition. Nicholson, it was said, had appointed men of "inferior stations" to the militia where gentlemen used to serve. Additional sparks were struck in Williamsburg when the governor insisted upon attending personally the legislative sessions of the house. That, the burgesses declared, was an infringement of parliamentary rights. Nicholson persisted. He then grew impatient with debate and sought rubber-stamp approval for measures already drawn up by himself. Outside of the assembly, he made unpopular appointments without benefit of the council. Robert Quary, ever the imperial enthusiast, received the post of Surveyor General of the Customs. In the early 1690s, when

Nicholson had been the lieutenant governor, he had realized that the art of politics was the timing. Such perspicacity had even won him the friendship of Blair himself. In the early 1700s, in Nicholson's second administration, however, diplomacy took flight. By 1703 the governor had lambasted the council, declaring its members to be a pack of "Rogues, Villains, [and] Rascalls," nothing but "commonwealth men."[48] He then lost his head further and fell in love with Lucy Burwell, the seventeen-year-old daughter of Colonel Lewis Burwell, who was allied with the hated Harrison family, thus playing into the hands of his enemies. To his great disappointment, Lucy Burwell rejected his suit and married a "commonwealth" man, a young Berkeley from Virginia.

The war of words was on. Affidavit was met by affidavit, accusation by accusation. The noise was deafening. As the clerical supporters of Nicholson queried: with such a commissary as Blair, what governor "should be able to be any longer quiet?"[49] Blair and his Whig allies won; Nicholson, the Tory, lost. The trouble was that both men wished to be governor and both men wished to be commissary.

After Queen Anne's War (1706–1710), the aged and absentminded Edmund Jenings (1659–1727) was replaced as governor by the dashing Alexander Spotswood.[50] This soldier, mathematician, and architect had fought with John Churchill, duke of Marlborough, at Blenheim. Spotswood's first impression of Virginia and the Carolinas in June 1710 was one of distress over "the incapacity of this Country for an Offensive or Defensive war." Tuscarora Indians on the frontier of North Carolina had massacred English, Swiss, and German settlers. Among whites in that colony, there was evidenced "that spirit of disobedience to which they have been long accustomed." Virginia seemed to be little better off. "Our militia," he added to the Lords of Trade, "are in a manner wholly destitute of ammunition and [are] ill provided with arms." As a soldier, Spotswood's first concern was "to secure Her Majesty's people & Territories from the Heathen."[51] But military preparations demanded attention to matters of religion as well as ordnance.

At first there was cooperation between Governor Spotswood and Commissary Blair. The two Scotsmen shared a concern for the renewal of Indian education at the College of William and Mary.[52] In white parochial affairs they also joined forces when the vestry of South Farnham Parish tried to rid themselves of their French, Calvinist parson, Lewis Latané. Uncharacteristically, Blair sided with his fellow presbyter and with the governor.[53] But peace between Tory and Whig forces, represented by the governor and the commissary, did not last long. From 1714 to 1718, Spotswood, ever one to seek greater uniformity with English law, made a strong attempt to break the power of the planter class over the courts, the purse, and the council. Whatever the wider implications, the contest between the two sides was joined on the particular issue of the governor's claim to the power of collation as well as induction. Here Spotswood challenged the laity, who were supported by Blair on the most sensitive point: the vestries' right to elect their own ministers.[54] Appeals were made by both sides to England. While the litigation was pending before the Privy Council, Spotswood was recalled. Subsequent governors, Hugh Drysdale and William Gooch, decided that discretion with vestries was the better part of colonial surveillance. Whig localism won out: those who paid the ministers should have the right to select them.

At the same time that Spotswood sought to undo the power of the vestries, he was plotting the overthrow of Blair. James Blair's most dangerous political hour occurred on 8 April 1719 when he called to order a convention of his clergy in the great hall at the College of William and Mary. There Blair had to read aloud three letters, two from John Robinson (1650–1723), Tory bishop of London, and one from Spotswood. The issue was "Presbyterianism" in Virginia's church, together with the questioning of the episcopal validity of Blair's own ordination in Scotland in the 1670s.[55] Spotswood and Robinson had been in close correspondence since 1713.[56] Their joint purpose was the removal of Blair from office and the bringing of Virginia's church into conformity with English ecclesiastical custom.

Behind the action of those who in 1719 attempted to suspend Blair lay suspicion "of a Scottish Church system they did not understand."[57] As early as 1697, the commissary was accused of trying to fill "the Church and the College [William and Mary] with Scotchmen and to make a national faction by the name of the Scottish party."[58] Blair was the son of a Scottish minister who had conformed to the episcopal organization erected in that country at the Restoration.[59] The church in which the elder Blair served was characterized by the theology of John Calvin (1509–1564) and John Knox (1505–1572). It was not ruled by bishops but by "democratically chosen presbyters of equal rank."[60] With the Restoration, however, and the imposition of episcopal government upon the Church of Scotland, ministers who had all along been in favor of moderate episcopacy came to the fore. The ordination which James Blair sought in 1679 involved both episcopal and presbyterian elements. First came presbyterial examination, then episcopal laying on of hands, and finally presbyterial and episcopal approval and installation into a parish. The church in Scotland was in fact governed by a dual system but one which was marked by the absence of episcopal visitation, confirmation, and immediate supervision, a situation strikingly similar to that in America.[61]

There seems little doubt that Blair "remained a Scottish churchman throughout his life."[62] He had inherited Calvinist ideals of order and discipline and was a pragmatist. Virginia's churches were rural; they were without episcopal authority and the clerical fellowship that accompanied it.[63] When Blair found himself in a position to shape Virginia's church, he drew upon the Scottish Presbyterian tradition. Blair adapted Scotland's kirk-session, presbytery, and synod to America, where they evolved into the vestry, precinct, and yearly meeting with the commissary in Williamsburg.[64] It was the intermediate body, the precinct, which marked a departure from Anglican practice and which decentralized authority in the church. In 1691 and 1697, Blair had proposed that Virginia's scattered churches be organized into precincts and that a "Standing number of Visitors be appointed, (vizt.) two of the Clergy in every precinct who with the Commissary shall have power to try all cases."[65] Visitors were to be the "Learnedest Ministers" and were to be elected by their peers. Visitors were to conduct visitations of every parish in their precinct at least once every three years. They were to have the authority to execute church laws in all things pertaining to church buildings and their contents, vestries, salaries, the ministry, and the poor of the parish.[66] In addition, precinct meetings were to be held quarterly. The advantages of orderliness, fellowship, and education were obvious and were so recognized by Blair.[67]

The similarity between Blair's plan of organization and the Scottish system are noteworthy. At the quarterly meetings and at the synods in both countries, the clergy were to be examined in Scripture by their superiors, and handle "commone heads of controversie . . . espciallie wher Poprie is most preached."[68] Blair's desire to examine Virginia's licensed ministers at the yearly meeting of the clergy had its equivalent in the Scottish "tryalls . . . at the Synod" which followed the bishop's licensing of the ordinand. Such practices held an honored place in the *First Book of Discipline* of John Knox and others.[69] Blair carried on that tradition in America. Finally, Blair must have felt at home with the strong role of the laity in his adopted country, for it was similar to that of the land of his birth. While the claim has been made that in Scotland there is "no evidence that elders and deacons were elected by vote of the congregation," the facts appear to be otherwise.[70] Certainly congregations in the Church of Scotland had their say regarding the choice of their "lay" leaders. Though the "matter of voting was left to local arrangement," there is no doubt that it took place.[71] The parallel here with Virginia's vestrymen is clear: they too were elected regularly. The myth of Virginia's self-perpetuating vestries is not more tenable than the notion that deacons and elders in Scotland were presbyterially or synodally appointed.[72] Once elected, leaders of parishes in both countries had the right to signify assent—or in some cases denial—before the formal institution of a minister took place.[73]

James Blair's long career in the colony of Virginia remains an enigma unless his Scottish background is taken into account. Certainly as commissary he was concerned with his own power, as his constant battles with early governors attests. That he often sided with the vestries is equally obvious; he had married into their ranks and fought for their rights within the low church atmosphere he helped to nurture. But just as often he contended for the rights of his clergy for better salaries, improved housing, education, and security.[74] He refused to allow vestries to dismiss their ministers at will. If Blair's schemes for regular visitations floundered in the politics of clerical resistance and imperial conflict,[75] if his "balanced" diplomacy often confused his contemporaries as to whose side he was on, there is no doubt that when it came to imperial control without respect for local custom, Blair was adamant. He was not in any way anti-episcopal. Indeed he thought a bishop in America "would con[tribute] very much to the Good Government of the Clergy."[76] The endorsement was mild enough, far from the Tory absolutism of northern episcopal clergy.

Finally, the Scottish influence upon the education of the clergy in the colony's established church was notable. The College of William and Mary was modeled on the Scottish system of granting degrees: a bachelor of arts after two years and a master of arts after another four years. In addition, a third of the ministers in Virginia's church in the eighteenth century were educated in Scotland. When this figure (forty-six) is added to the increasing number of ministers educated at William and Mary (forty-five) the result is nearly double those educated at English universities.[77]

"Presbyterianism" was the accusation thrown at the commissary in the spring of 1719. An unsteady alliance of Tory officials and conservative English Whigs led by the Reverend Hugh Jones threatened Blair's efforts to build his Scottish-American church. Well known for his invaluable essay, *The Present State of Virginia,* the urbane Jones wished nothing so much as to make Virginia conform more to England.[78] Religion in the tidewater was not Anglican enough to suit even that low church, Hanoverian Whig. While Jones reported that Virginians favored neither "popery nor . . . presbyterianism," and were "firm adherents to the present constitution in state, Hanoverian succession and the Episcopal Church in England as by law established," still there was a certain bite in his hope that no "true Englishman" in Virginia would ever refuse to say,

God bless the Church, and George its defender,
Convert the fanaticks, and baulk the Pretender.[79]

Jones, ever Blair's enemy, wondered about such things as clerical dress and ceremonies. Surplices, he noted, "were disused there for a long time in most churches." People received communion in their seats, "a custom introduced for opportunity for such as are inclined to Presbytery." Jones did not like the diffuseness of Blair's precinct system and wanted to make uniform all liturgy and practice. "Every minister," he remarked, "is a kind of independent in his own parish, in respect of some little particular circumstances and customs."[80]

In the end, neither Bishop Robinson's imperious warning to his commissary about "deviations from our rule" nor Spotswood's and Jones's casting of doubt on Blair's ordination were able to unseat him: the clergy assembled in Williamsburg simply refused a majority vote requesting gubernatorial removal of the commissary.[81] There the matter rested. Blair had won again, though barely.[82] Thereafter, none pressed tactical advantage. The commissary stayed on in Virginia under wiser—and Whig—governors. Spotswood had jeopardized his position by fanning the flames of discontent and was retired. Jones left for England, and Bishop Robinson was called to his heavenly reward.

Behind the politics and outward maneuvering during the church crisis of 1719 lay deeper religious concerns about what sort of a church Virginia would have. Would it be a replica of Queen Anne's Tory establishment? Would it be a Whig, Hanoverian church, or something different from both: a "Scottish" church in which presbytery took up episcopal slack? The answer is none of these. What emerged was distinctly Virginian, Whig and low church to be sure, certainly influenced by her Scots ministers but lacking the explicit theological and ecclesiological stamp of Scotland's church.

Not all of Virginia's ministers achieved the deserved fame of Commissary Blair. Generally the clergy were part of the lower echelons of the gentry, both in worldly goods and in attitude. Though many aspired to reach the social and economic level of their lay patrons, most did not. Ministers served their lay congregations as clients and those congregations often denied the preachers the independence their calling enjoyed in England. Only a very few attained economic prosperity. Most clergy who did not bring wives and children with them married the daughters of locally respected, though not wealthy or prominent, householders. They were among, but not strictly part of, the gentry. Hugh Jones description of the attitude of Virginia clergymen suggests that as a group they were to possess middle-class virtues. They were to be men of the world, be able to converse in more than

149

"philosophy and speculative ethicks, and have studied men and business in some measure as well as books." They should act "like gentlemen," but not overstep their calling, be "facetious and good-humoured, without too much freedom and licentiousness." They may be "good Christians without appearing stoicks." Jones remarked that there "are many such worthy, prudent, and pious clergymen as these in Virginia, who meet with love, reputation, and success."[83] Ninety percent served their people faithfully and creditably; ten percent did not.[84] The majority were practical, hard-working men who stayed on in their parishes and generally shunned theological phillipics.[85] If they burned no theological brand into the hides of their parishioners, it was because they had neither iron nor fire in their souls. Morally they were no worse—and perhaps better—than many of their neighbors.

There were those who were something less than a credit to their profession: the boring, the scandalous, and the tragic. William Byrd II referred to the Reverend Peter Fontaine (1691–1757) as "the Reverend Doctor Humdrum" who "would never be concerned with a plot [plan] that was like to cost him five pistoles."[86] Drinking and adultery were the occasional charges made against others, while the physically and mentally sick were to be found in the ministry as elsewhere. One of the saddest cases was that of Joseph Smith (fl. 1728–1738), an ugly hunchback, poor, with a family to support, but with "so little to say for himself that no Parish would receive him."[87] Unable physically to serve two churches thirty miles apart, he read prayers for Blair in Williamsburg and was then given the job of lecturer in the capital through the kind offices of Governor Gooch. In a final parish where he served a short four years, the vestry tried to get rid of him. As a result Smith took to drink. Blair did not know what to do with him and remarked that "he is fit only for an infirmary." Shortly thereafter Smith died, "decayed in both body and mind."[88] These were some who simply could not help themselves.

There were also those like Adam Dickie (1706?–1745), minister at Drysdale Parish, who were credits to their profession. Dickie came from Edinburgh University to America in 1727, licensed by the bishop of London and with nothing to his name but £20 of the king's bounty.[89] Once in King and Queen County, however, he did not remain poor but married Anne Thacker of St. Mary's White Chapel on 7 May 1735.[90] The bride had a sizeable fortune and came from a good family. Parson Dickie, who had once been reprimanded by the governor for wearing clothes too loud in color for a minister—it was the only suit he then owned—was now rich. Dickie, however, remained a troubled man. His problem was the treatment of black slaves which he observed in Drysdale Parish. From the days of Morgan

Godwyn in 1660 when blacks accounted for only 5 to 10 percent of the total population, the ratio in 1730 had changed radically with blacks at about 40 percent or sixty-one thousand.[91] Adam Dickie, conscientious in his ministry, found white attitudes toward the Christianizing of these blacks intolerable. Against the usual palaver that slaves were unteachable, Dickie remarked to the bishop of London that the newer arrivals among the blacks were "able to Repeat the whole Catechism very Inteligibly tho not so very plain as those who Speak nothing but English." As the Drysdale parson scanned the planters' fields and slave quarters, he discovered that there was a "very great Harvest of Souls to be reaped among those poor creatures." Many were "very Serious and Devout attenders upon the worship of God and very Earnest of being more and more Instructed in Christian Knowledge."[92] Persuaded that conversion was possible, Dickie began to catechize slaves before divine service.

He could not have chosen a more inauspicious moment. There had been several threatened slave revolts, and, in 1730, Virginia's tranquility was momentarily shattered by the discovery of planned insurrection. Slaves spread the rumor that, despite Virginia's law to the contrary, baptism meant manumission. When those who were baptized among blacks heard no word from the king of England announcing their release from bondage, anger replaced patience, and the revolt was planned. Patrols, however, apprehended the leaders.[93]

Two years later, Dickie appeared on the scene. With a degree of ingenuousness, he wrote to the bishop of London that "some of the more Loose and unthinking" of the planters discovered in their new minister "an over active Zeal in instructing and Baptizing Negroe Slaves." Dickie surmised that his critics were "Rather to be pittied and prayed for," since, he continued, they deserve "I fear too Justly that woe Denounced by our Saviour [in] Matthew 23:13 against the Scribes and the Pharisees for Shutting up the Kingdom of Heaven against men."[94] The minister continued to teach the catechism to black and white children together. In the eyes of many, it was "a Mighty Scandal." Dickie then had to separate the two groups, but he continued his examination of blacks with baptism in view. Gossip ensued, but the parson would not back down. Accusations against him, he remarked, "never had and I hope never will [have] any Influence upon me to Desist from a Design which I believe answers so Good an End." He then set before his superiors three questions.

> Query 1st. If Christian Slaves ought not to Marry and not live after their own manner, or (which is very often the Case) if they Marry being of two Different white Families and the master of the one Removes off or sells one so that they

have no opportunity of coming together whether then the party may not marry again, they being as Effectually Separated as by Death, not of Choice but necessity?

2nd. If Christian Slaves mey not be admitted as Sureties at Baptism for one anothers Children, because very few People will stand for their Slaves? And if persons of Riper Years may not be admitted to Baptism without Sureties, when they can Distinctly Answer for themselves and can not get Sureties?

Lastly if Christian Slaves ought not to be allowed to be Churched and Enjoy the other Privileges of Christianity when they Desire it?[95]

The questions elicited no definitive answers. Dickie continued to engage "some . . . Gentlemen with whom I have had some Conversation upon this subject and happen to Differ." With simple eloquence this not-too-lettered parson saw that it was "a very easy matter to Read the life of the Master or overseer in the knowledge of the slave." The SPCK and the SPG judged that he was "like to do good in the station where providence has cast him" and sent him "a present of a handsome packet of Books."[96]

Nearly seven hundred slaves were baptized by Thomas Dell (fl. 1724), John Brunskill (fl. 1715–1758) of Wilmington Parish, William Black (fl. 1709–1738, and the Spanish minister John Garzia (fl. 1724–1744) of North Farnham Parish.[97] Yet the efforts of these enlightened few were meagre when compared with the whole. While the laity were digging in their heels against clerical zeal for the underprivileged, the slaves were finding little to commend Virginia's Episcopal church. Its cherished Elizabethan formularies of worship spoke with a cadence wholly foreign to black African experience. Insistence upon memorization of the catechism and acceptance of its alien moral admonition proved an almost insurmountable barrier to meaningful membership. Had the church begun with her original, reformed theological position as held in the sixteenth century, matters might have been different. As it was, not until the evangelical revival of the 1820s, when theology once again came to dominate liturgy and morality, did a portion of the black population begin to participate in the life of the Episcopal church in Virginia.[98] In the meantime, other authoritarian churches, such as those organized in Quaker, Puritan, and Roman Catholic colonies, afforded blacks a greater measure of nurture and protection.[99]

By the 1730s, despite her failure with blacks, Virginia's mother church entered a period of harmony and balance with the society of which she was an important part. While it would not be accurate to speak of Virginia's pattern as a union of church and state, still, as one historian has emphasized, legal and social authority coincided closely with, and were, at least at the local level, intimately related to, the Church. Vestrymen were officeholders with civil functions, and civil magistrates were usually vestrymen. The community and the congregation were one; church attendance was still compulsory, and grand jury presentments for repeated absence were not unusual.[100]

The physical arrangements for compulsory Sunday morning worship reflected the coincidence of secular and religious authority, and, incidentally, the stratification of the community. The magistrate-vestrymen sat forward, nearest the chancel and in the seats of honor. Children, the poor, and black slaves occupied the back benches. Churchgoing was an affair of the total community. There was no sense of crisis.

Such complacency was not to survive, however, and, with the coming of the Great Awakening in the 1750s and 1760s, previously controlled clerical resentment at the rule of the vestries burst into flame. By then there was no man of James Blair's strength and presence to put out the fire.

CHAPTER 6
The Church's Southern Establishments

In July 1710, Gideon Johnston, SPG missionary and commissary to South Carolina, wrote of the dangers and difficulties facing him. "The Salary and Subscriptions indeed make a great shew at a distance . . . and P[er]quisites besides sound great," but, he continued, hardship, poverty, and constant disease is cloaked by talk of "the hope of Subscriptions, the goodness of the Climate, the fertility of the Soil, the plenty of all things necessary for the life of Man."[1] Sometimes his hand shook so from fever, Johnston complained, that he had to use two hands to write. His "Small and numerous family, which it has pleased God to bless me" were only a notch above starvation, but help had been provided by kind friends and an unselfish French doctor. He needed prayer books. Indian traders were "a Wretched sort of Men" who obstructed his efforts to convert the aborigines. Yet, though poverty and disease hounded his steps, the commissary assured his superiors he would not quit the post to which he had been appointed in 1708.

Johnston came to view his new home unenthusiastically. After an initial impression of the population of Charles Town, he wrote the bishop of Salisbury of his new charges. They are, Johnston remarked, "the Vilest race of Men upon the earth. . . . they have neither honour, nor honesty nor Religion enough to entitle them to any tolerable Character, being a perfect Medley or Hotch potch made up of Bank[r]upts, pirates, decayed Libertines, Sectaries and Enthusiasts." South Carolinians, he added, came from such outlying districts in England's first empire as Bermuda, Jamaica, Barbados, New England, and Pennsylvania. They were "the most factious and Seditious people in the whole world."[2]

What lay behind Johnston's resentfulness toward South Carolina? Undoubtedly there was the cultural shock of entering a different and, in this case, highly pluralistic society. Class distinctions were equally sharp. With a population smaller than England's and only one-seventh the size of Virginia's, South Carolina's religious, racial, and class differences among a few

154

thousand people appeared to the unprepared observer to be far more sharply etched than what could be seen in the mother country.

There was also the fact that the promise and the zeal of the SPG outstripped its ability to sustain its mission in terms of salaries and other means of support. Early in the same decade in which Gideon Johnston came to America, the society had sent another missionary whose idealism ran into the harsh realities of Roman Catholic and Indian enemies on the frontier. As in the case of New York, there was the desire to offset Catholic influence in South Carolina. In the minds of the London planners, this was coupled with a degree of benevolent concern for the conversion of white, black, and red peoples. To further this design, in 1702 the SPG sent the Reverend Samuel Thomas (d. 1706) to preach to the Yamassee Indians. Thomas immediately ran into the endemic facts of colonial life. South Carolinians were at war with the Yamassees. Instead, Thomas became missionary to the whites along the Cooper River. In 1704 he wrote to the disappointed members of the society in England that he found greater need to convert the blacks and Indian slaves within the English settlements. The warlike Yamassees, he judged correctly, were not likely to listen to him, even if they could understand his language, which they could not. On the other hand, he claimed that of the one thousand slaves in South Carolina, eight hundred could speak English. With words that sound genuine rather than self-serving, Thomas wrote, "I beg any impartial man who knoweth our American Plantations, must and will say, that it is as great a Charity, and much more practicable to propagate Christianity among our poor Slaves in our own Plantations as among the wild Indians in the woods."[3]

While the SPG considered Thomas's dismissal for failure to fulfill his mission, three factors contributed to a change of mind in London. First, South Carolina's governor, Sir Nathaniel Johnson, intervened in Thomas's behalf. Second, the passage of a church act by the colonial legislature in 1704 gave assurance to the London organizers of local support for the church. Third, Thomas himself returned to England to argue the case for more realistic aid to the church in the southern colony. It was no doubt this last factor which swung the SPG. With a mixture of political dexterity and selflessness, the South Carolina missionary convinced his superiors that here was an opportunity not to be missed. He appealed to the highest and the lowest motives simultaneously when he wrote in a memorial:

> it is sadly evident how destitute our Brethren of the Church of England in South Carolina are of spiritual guides and Publick Ordinances, and [in] how much danger they are of famishing in grace for want of the word and sacrament, or to be led aside to error while destitute of the public ministry to confirm them in the truth, for as circumstances are at present in this our

155

Province not one person in 20 among those who profess themselves of the Church of England can have . . . benefit of the word and sacraments from a church of England minister, the Dissenters have at present 4 ministers among them besides one Anabaptist Preacher lately gone to Carolina . . . and I am informed that 3 or 4 more dissenting Ministers are going . . . in the Spring.[4]

The call of the destitute and the chance for new opportunities to compete with their rivals caused the London planners to change their minds. With the aid of Governor Johnson's own chaplain—for such Indian missionary Thomas had become—the SPG drew up a remarkable blueprint for six parishes in South Carolina. With an alacrity fed by high hopes, four appointments were made in December of 1705. The SPG constantly desired to "transform the creation of worldly men and motives into an instrument of genuine moral and spiritual growth."[5] Gideon Johnston's hardships and disillusionments were not new; they were part of an already emerging pattern of experience.

There was a third and perhaps more important reason for the new commissary's resentment of the people and habits of South Carolina. Johnston was a high church Tory; South Carolina's church was lay controlled, low church, and traditionally Whig. Moreover, these same laity sought political power, economic gain, and social distinction for themselves, not the altruistic ideals of the SPG. Johnston was well aware of the past religious history of the colony, first in terms of the Episcopalian faction and second in terms of the nonconformist tradition.

Shortly after the SPG appointments of 1705, there were second thoughts as church officials in England began to read the fine print in the colony's church act of 1704. That act had as its goal the exclusion of nonconformists from political office. In addition, the English officials discovered to their intense annoyance that the laity in the colony had retained the power to dismiss their ministers at will. It was too much. The imperially minded church and Parliament in England were little used to such freewheeling, low church authority. The society wished to retain the powers of appointment and of dismissal for itself. There matters stood. The SPG could not recall its appointments; it refused to make any more. A royal veto of the church act saw to that. Not until 1707 would the SPG again move in South Carolina's behalf and then only after a new church act (1706) was passed by the colonial legislature. The offending clause which allowed lay vestries to control their clergy was removed from this new piece of legislation. Even so, South Carolinians demanded and got by compromise the permission for a trial period for all appointments to their churches. It was an unpleasant concession for the English church.

In 1708, with legal matters cleared up, Gideon Johnston was appointed commissary, The choice, as we have seen, was not an altogether satisfactory one. Despite the church act and the strong Episcopalian faction in the colony, Johnston was poorly equipped to deal with a strong nonconformist tradition and religious diversity. Among what he termed that "vile race of factious people" was New Englander John Cotton, Jr. (1639–1669), a noted biblical scholar as well as an authority on American Indian languages.[6] There was also in South Carolina's congregationalist minority Joseph Lord (1672–1725), Harvard graduate and son-in-law of Governor Thomas Hinckley (fl. 1685) of Plymouth Colony. Of enviable reputation in Charles Town's presbyterian community after 1686 was the future principal of the University of Glasgow, William Dunlop (1649–1700).[7] From Bermuda came the colony's first governor, Captain William Sayle, a Calvinist who received his commission from fellow nonconformist Anthony Ashley Cooper (1621–1683), the first earl of Shaftesbury. Cooper, along with John Locke, had originally drawn up the elaborate Fundamental Constitutions for the colony in 1669. The constitutions had declared that "No person whatever shall disturbe, molest or persecute another for his speculative opinions in Religion or his way of Worship."[8] No doubt Cooper's experience as a prominent figure in the Commonwealth and Protectorate and his subsequent delicate position in the Restoration made him aware of the values of toleration.[9]

South Carolina was marked by a variety of religious and national groups: English, French, New England nonconformists, African and Barbadian blacks, Irish, Swiss, Dutch, and Germans. Anabaptists and Quakers from England rubbed elbows with Dutch Calvinists from New York, while a decade later the first French Huguenots began to arrive (1680). Gradually during the first decades of colonization after 1670, the proprietors in England called for and were granted distinct religious conditions added to their basically tolerant constitution.[10] At first each colonist had to be a member of some church in order to hold public office. Almost immediately this was tightened and the Church of England was roundly declared to be "the only true and Orthodox, and National Religion of all the King's Dominions . . . [and] so also of Carolina."[11] Planter William Owen writing to England in 1671 suggested that a leader in the new plantation should be "of moderate zeale not strict episcopalle not yet licentious nor rigid presbiterian nor yet hypocritic all but swayinge himselfe in an even Ballance between all opinions but especially turneing his face to the Liturgie of the Church of England."[12]

Swaying himself in an even balance proved to be hard for Gideon Johnston, and he expressed decided distaste for evenhanded toleration.

"Many of those who pretend to be Churchmen," he wrote the bishop, "are strangely cripled in their goings between Church and Presbytery." They are "of large and loose principles . . . sometimes going openly with the Dissenters." As if latitudinarian toleration were not enough, Johnston would bend the bishop's ear and "speak a little of the Dissenters [themselves, who] I must Observe to your Lop [Lordship] . . . are the most unreasonable in all the British Monarchy, [for] they have Liberty & property to the full and enjoy the free and undisturbed Exercise of their Religion in all respects."[13] Johnston must have suffered from a momentary mental lapse, for his episcopal correspondent, his "Lop" of Salisbury, Gilbert Burnet, had voted against the Occasional Conformity Bill of 1703. Had it passed the House of Lords, this act would have disfavored dissenters.[14] No doubt Johnston, a Tory, soon became aware of the fact that in the thirty-nine-year history of South Carolina no less than seven of the thirteen governors between 1669 and 1708 had "turned their faces away from the Church of England liturgy in various degrees of dissent."[15]

Nevertheless, in this hinge epoch, 1689–1730, South Carolina provides ample, if often confusing, evidence of the new Anglican aggressiveness. Johnston took pains to assure Bishop Burnet that the "'Contests, that are on foot here, are not between High and Low Churchmen; but between dissenters and the Church"; in the eyes of the new commissary the "Mammon" of Erastian expediency which attracted "half faced Churchmen" was being served. Such ecclesiastical restrictiveness as Johnston hoped for was simply not an option amid the heterogeneity of early eighteenth-century Carolina, not unless imperially minded proprietors were willing to pay a high price. Gideon Johnston never quite learned that lesson.[16]

Anglican Erastianism was as much a factor in England as it was in South Carolina. In both lands, the politicians were in charge. Churchmen might occasionally complain, but they had no power in the Hanoverian succession. If, as along the Carolina gold coast, politicians had "gotten . . . Strange Notions & Whims in their heads . . . and have fallen into such a Comprehensive and Latitudinarian way," they were surely well within Anglican tradition. That tradition, whatever its theological latitude, called for state control. Early politicians in South Carolina knew that and acted accordingly; Johnston missed the point. The new commissary was on firm ground when he marked the disparity between the lay-controlled establishment in South Carolina and episcopal government in the church in England. Clearly, there was a difference. It was shocking to hear the bishop of London attacked as "a Pope, nay worse than a Pope because (as they said) he would feign Extend his Diocese and Authority farther than the Pope ever did." If the ecclesiastical powers in London refused to settle a bishop in Carolina as had always happened elsewhere "in Apostolical and primitive times . . . It is but reason," judged the laity, "that we should do Justice to our Selves."[17]

Early in his eight-year residence in South Carolina, Johnston recognized the diversity of religion and nationality as well as the comprehensive and latitudinarian views of Episcopalians. He also bore witness to another set of contrasts in the Carolina tidewater: the division between rich and poor. The large proportions of aristocratic wealth so evident by the 1730s, when cards, dice, balls, bottles, and horses occupied the leisure time of South Carolinians, were only just emerging in 1708 when Johnston first arrived. In the initial decade of the eighteenth century, the alliance between the urban merchants of Charles Town and the planters of the tidewater counties was already well founded. Charles Andrews remarked that "the merchant had his estate in the country as the planter had his house in the town, so that to a greater extent than in any other colony town and country were bound together in a common interest."[18]

None other than Henrietta Johnston, wife of the commissary, proved to be the first artist to record the growing aristocratic atmosphere in America. Her small pastel portraits of such leading Episcopalians as Colonel William Rhett in Charles Town and the daughter of Cadwallader Colden of New York were technically competent even though she was self-taught. Her husband was to write in 1709, "Were it not for the Assistance my wife gives me by drawing pictures . . . I should not have been able to live."[19] Henrietta Johnston also assisted the commissary in his illnesses by acting as his secretary, a not inconsiderable accomplishment in those days when few women were known to write.

The fact that Henrietta Johnston had to go to work to help support a growing family is testimony to the relative poverty of Carolina clergy. Gideon Johnston complained to London of the scarcity of goods, resulting inflation, and insufficient clerical salaries in nearly every letter he addressed to his superiors. South Carolina was "the dearest Place in the whole world, & every thing, generally speaking, being Sold at Such an Extravagant Price, as if it were closely blocked up on all Sides, and reduced to the last Extremity of a long Siege."[20]

If inflation, a result of the Yamassee War (1715), hurt the poor and the middling sort like the Johnstons, it helped the seekers after wealth. Some ten years before, the Reverend Francis Le Jau spoke of the "topping men" for whom not religion but "revenge, self-interest, engrossing of trade, places of profit and things of that nature are the Motive that gives a turn . . . to our affairs."[21] The interests of business and profit motivated the wealthy to a degree which was only equaled by the grandees of New York.

Nevertheless, religion played a vital part in the lives of these merchants and planters. "How a man worshiped," observes one recent historian, "and where he came from became matters of importance in South Carolina politics."[22] Those who supported the Church of England were Barbadian royalists, often the younger sons of substantial island sugar planters.[23] These were unable to inherit land or wealth in the increasingly crowded Barbados due to the custom of primogeniture. Thus they came to settle the larger and more felicitous tidewater area of South Carolina and its estuaries from the Pee Dee in the north to the Savannah in the south. There, in the counties of Berkeley, Craven, and Colleton, they hoped to establish a community and church similar to that which they had left in Barbados. At the center of the colony was Charles Town, compact, defensible, and possessed of a magnificent harbor, the only navigable estuary waterway along the entire coast. While Virginia's deeper rivers made it possible for ocean-going ships to dock at the wharves of dispersed plantations, in South Carolina all business and immigration passed through the one port town. Economic and political centralization resulted in what, as Richard Dunn has shown, became the most fully developed agricultural production system of rice and indigo in English America.[24]

The founders of this sytem were Le Jau's "topping men," or, as they came to be known, the "Goose Creek men." They became the nucleus of the upper class, that privileged class to which other immigrants of lesser stature aspired, often successfully.[25] For these men the Church of England was immensely attractive. It meant civilization, the chance to associate with men of prestige and wealth, government officials and lawyers, as well as with the artisans who served them. To St. Phillip's parish church in the capital of Charles Town came the elite. From the firm base of that parish, orderly expansion of the church was possible.

Such promise and orderliness concealed the stark contrast between rich and poor. If the clergy at first suffered strained circumstances, they were not alone.[26] At the bottom of the economic ladder were the blacks who already outnumbered whites by 1708.[27] Our knowledge of the Afro-Americans of colonial South Carolina rests heavily upon the letters of SPG ministers. Within these letters the conditions under which slaves lived, their treatment by white masters, and the attitudes expressed towards them are closely tied to the church's major concern—conversion. Here as in Virginia, the ministers raised the subjects of baptism, marriage, and admission to the sacrament of the Lord's Supper. Between black bewilderment and white intransigence lay the clergy's altogether natural concern, stated in the charter of the SPG itself, for the salvation of the souls of heathens and infidels, whether black persons or red persons. Generally, admission to the church and sacraments was postponed or prohibited by whites. Gideon Johnston complained at the "rubbs and impediments that lye in the way" of conversion: the slave was not given time for worship on the Sabbath when he "has work enough from the White Folk on his hands." In addition, a shocked commissary noted that on Sundays slaves had to clear land and produce for themselves that food and clothing which planters did not choose to provide. Visits to black families, continued Johnston, were made difficult for the clergy because of the great distances between plantations. Masters were against conversion in the first place, and their legislature "does not Encourage a work of this Importance."[28] There seems little doubt that Johnston's jaundiced view of his new home in America was colored by slave owners' treatment of their human chattels. The owners seemed to Johnston to care little for the welfare of the slaves, much less Christian principles.

Other clergy lamented white treatment of blacks, much as the more enlightened did in Virginia. Whether one were a high church Tory such as Johnston or a Calvinist seemed to make little difference. For many, basic Christian attitudes overcame the political ways in which men and women expressed the faith. Among the Calvinist clergy in South Carolina's Episcopalian establishment, none was more notable than the Frenchman Francis Le Jau. Le Jau voiced complaints similar to those of Commissary Johnston.[29] His theology was, however, quite different. For example, when smallpox broke out in 1712, this remarkable minister decided that surgeons who believed that the infection had been incubating for more than a decade did not know what they were talking about. Irreligion and lewdness, Le Jau declared, had loosed the hand of an angry Providence against the people of South Carolina. The chief reason for the smallpox epidemic was the "Barbarous usage of ye poor Slaves." Le Jau urged restraint and mercy in the treatment of blacks. For those masters who had not heeded his admonitions, he hoped that the smallpox would make them "mind better things than worldly advantages." Le Jau boldly set biblical law against provincial statute when he remarked:

> it is in Relation to run away Negroes by Law enacted in this Province some yeares before I came; such an Negroe must be mutilated by amputation of Testicles if it be a man and of Ears if a Woman. I have openly declared against such punishment grounded upon the Law of God, which setts slaves at Liberty if they should loose [sic] an Eye or a tooth when he is corrected.[30]

He was deeply shocked by the coffin, a device in which live blacks were placed for twenty-four-hour punishment, their feet chained and the lid press-

161

ing cruelly into their stomachs. When the Frenchman "invited the Children, Servants and Slaves to come to be instructed in the Church," his parishioners were afraid to face him with their objections. Instead, they whispered behind his back and by their coolness toward him let him know that they had no desire of "contributing to the Salvation, Instruction and human usage of Slaves and free Indians."[31]

Generally, such horrors as castration, which was sanctioned by law in 1712, burning alive of slavewomen, and torture of the innocent as well as the guilty give grim credence to the assertion of one historian that the constant exposure to the realities of slavery reminded the South Carolina planter never to allow another man to assume uncontrolled power over him. It was in such a climate that personal independence became the constant concern of the white aristocracy.[32] At times the clear commandments of the Gospel were sounded by the ministers of the establishment. "All Men shall speak well of us," wrote one, "if we give them [the planters] Liberty to be as badd as they please; but I am sure I never was sent here for that end, and I thank God I've resolution enough to call evil, evil; let it be where it will."[33]

There was a consistently patronizing quality to the remarks made about Indians and blacks by the South Carolina ministers. Clergy were often prone to caution, even obsequiousness, before slaveholders who held the power of hiring and firing. Ministers demanded familial, cultural, and sabbatical conformity which conflicted with African patterns of relationship and, on Sundays, with the blacks' brief hours for rest and fraternization.[34] Yet it is unfair to say that "Proper observance of the Sabbath seemed a more important problem to the ministers than dismemberment of black recalcitrants."[35] If Le Jau complained more of the confinement of slaves at home on the Lord's day than he did of "Mutilation and Death," it was because simply seeing blacks in the church conveyed, however weakly, a plea for religious equality and gentler treatment. Caught between rich and poor in colonial South Carolina, the clergy professed to work for the conversion of those in direst circumstances, often in the face of outright denunciation from the leaders who controlled their own church.[36] While aid might come from England in the form of helpful pronouncements on the necessity of masters and mistresses to instruct their slaves, there was no binding force to mere words.[37]

Blacks were not the only objects of religious concern on the part of the South Carolina clergy. Such men as Le Jau were interested in Indian converts as well. Language difficulties, war, and the ubiquitous frontier traders from Virginia who dealt in human chattel served to discourage efforts to this end.[38] Le Jau complained strongly to London about

162

the Indian traders [who] have always discouraged me by raising a world of Difficultyes when I proposed anything to them relating to the Conversion of the Indians. It appears they do not care to have Clergymen so near them who doubtless would never approve those perpetual warrs they promote amongst the Indians for the onely reason of making slaves to pay for their trading goods; and what slaves! poor women and children; for the men taken prisoners are burnt most barbarously.[39]

A change of heart appears to have taken place among whites toward the Indians. In the early eighteenth century, the red man began to emerge in the southern colonial mind as worthy of attention, not only for his culture but as a candidate for conversion. The old Purchasian view of Indians as "bad people, ignorant of Civilitie, or Art or Religion" gave way to the basic assumption that the Indians, rather than being cultureless, had a culture that was worth examining.[40] Le Jau came to admire their "sobriety, patience and content in their Condition."[41] They "make us ashamed," he wrote elsewhere, "by their life, Conversation and Sense of Religion quite different from ours; ours consists in words and appearance, their[s] in reality."[42] In white society men and women were marked by ambition often to the exclusion of other qualities of mind and heart, he felt. By comparison, the Indians were better. During the Yamassee War, many of the South Carolina ministers reverted to the older point of view. Gideon Johnston joined the rest of his clergy in describing the Cherokees as having only "the shape of Men to distinguish them from Wolves & Tygers." Even so the ministers gave them grudging respect, for they were "a very populous and warlike Nation."[43]

Under the initial influence of Governor Nathaniel Johnson and Commissary Gideon Johnston, the clergy of the colony came to see themselves as part of the imperial Church of England, rather than as members of a local establishment. Most of South Carolina's clergy were supplied by the SPG. As a result, nearly all of them disliked dissenting ministers, Presbyterians, Baptists, and Congregationalists, especially those from New England and Scotland by whom they were outnumbered. For reasons of self-interest, in 1720 the Episcopal clergy of the province supported a popular assembly of the people which had petitioned the crown in the previous year to accept South Carolina as a royal colony.[44]

Despite ministerial rivalry with dissenters and the desire to conform to Anglican liturgical standards, the Episcopalian ministers of South Carolina were in many cases theological Calvinists and not Latitudinarians or high churchmen. While Francis Le Jau gave voice to Calvinist theology, he remained a stickler for Episcopalian ceremony and at times could be quite anti-Presbyterian. His sharp sense of divine blessing and retribution came from his own older Huguenot experience in the land of his birth. Le Jau's eyes were not fixed simply upon the horizon of empire but also upon the urgencies of South Carolina.

Le Jau was not alone in his theology. French Calvinists made up one-tenth of the population of the colony.[45] While in itself that is not a remarkable figure, what is of note is that out of the twenty-six Episcopalian ministers who held cures in South Carolina for more than one year between 1702 and 1740, more than one-third were Calvinists, French, or both: Samuel Thomas, John Maitland, Ebenezer Taylor, Philip De Richebourg, James Gignillat, John La Pierre, Lewis Jones, Francis Varnod, and Le Jau.[46] The colony's church bore a peculiar stamp of its own which made it different religiously from the other Episcopalian establishments.[47] When we speak of the church in colonial South Carolina, we should not speak only of the "Americanization" of an English institution but of the maintenance of a particular theological tradition which had been and to this day remains within the larger circle of Anglicanism. Gideon Johnston's dislike of the "bad tenets of . . . heterodox, libertine, or fantastical persons" was not only a response to what the American environment did to England's church, but his foot stamping testified to a continuing debate on the very nature of Anglicanism.

The trouble with Gideon Johnston's position in South Carolina was that he could do very little without gubernatorial backing. Unlike Blair in Virginia, the South Carolina commissary had no political base among the laity. When confronted with the pragmatic, tolerating policies of Governor Charles Craven, there was little he could do. Johnston must, if he wished to survive the shifts of colonial politics, cajole rather than subvert. One may have some sympathy for the courage with which this Irish Tory churchman faced his situation: he had neither influential friends at court nor powerful allies among the local nabobs of the Gold Coast. Thus it came about that Johnston's desire for stricter conformity to the rubrics of English ecclesiology went unheeded.[48]

Never was the life of the Episcopal church in South Carolina a matter only of the theology and ecclesiology of clerics. This was as much a church of and for the laity. By the time Francis Nicholson took over as royal governor in the 1720s, laymen were firmly in charge. Their power was greater than that of their counterparts in Virginia. The more southerly colony's Commons House, where ecclesiastical control resided, met more often than the House of Burgesses in Virginia, developed more rapidly, and exerted more power. As a result, nowhere were governors in Episcopalian colonies, whether proprietary or royal, stripped of their patronage of church offices more speedily. In the first decade of the eighteenth century, the

Commons twice confirmed the right of a majority of parishioners who were taxpayers and freeholders to choose their minister. Such elections had to take place in an open meeting. Permission to hold such meetings was granted by a board of twenty-four lay commissioners who had charge of the ten South Carolina parishes.[49] Lay commissioners, according to the Act of Establishment of 1704, also retained the right of appointing duly elected parsons to their cures. In case of "any immoral or imprudent conduct" on the part of the minister, the commissionars could remove the incumbent from his cure upon the notification of nine parishioners and after a hearing.[50] Veto power was given to Sir Nathaniel Johnson, but that power would expire when he was succeeded by another governor. Neither the commissaries nor the SPG could change a thing. For a time laymen chose the ministers, laymen appointed them, laymen disciplined them, and laymen removed them from office. Laymen had assumed the powers which were supposed to belong to the bishop of London—the powers of institution, induction, suspension, and deprivation.[51] Even after a compromise was worked out in 1707, the lay commissioners could still, according to the law of 1712, "hear and settle all differences concerning the election of ministers, and, in case of a vacancy in a parish . . . appoint someone to take care of the property."[52]

Nevertheless, there were challenges to this arrangement and not only from the House of Lords at Westminster. The South Carolina laity's usurpation of episcopal powers was challenged by Edward Marston, the rector of St. Philip's Church in Charles Town. Clearly Marston was not in the Calvinist camp at all, but was a Nonjuror. He objected vociferously to the Act of Establishment of 1704. Priests, judged Marston, had their authority from Christ and were superior to legislatures. The clergy were "in no way obliged to the Government for the bountiful Revenues . . . due them . . . of Divine Right." Those who objected, Marston roundly declared, were not better than "Korah and his rebellious companions."[53] Reaction was swift. In an immediate show of determination, the Commons House deprived Marston of his "bountiful Revenues," i.e., his salary. Four months later, when that doughty clergyman still refused to bridle his Tory tongue, the Commons removed him from office.

Nonconformists posed a more difficult problem. They did not seek the divine right of the priesthood but the political "right" of provincial settlers to order their own religious ways. Thus the Episcopalian laymen who had come to dominate the Commons House just prior to 1704 found themselves fighting on two fronts: against high churchmen like Marston on the one hand and the dissenters from all Episcopalian ways on the other. Some five months before the passage of the first establishment bill in 1704 and with the cooperation of Governor Johnson, a special session of the Commons was called. By means of a rigged election, the house was packed with a majority of Episcopalians. A bill was introduced which would exclude nonchurchmen from membership. As was charged later, "'the election was managed with very great partiality and injustice, and all sorts of people, even alien Jews, servants, common sailors and negroes were admitted to vote."[54] Even so, the exclusion bill passed by only one vote. From then on, dissenters had to abjure their own sacraments for a year prior to election—and on oath—before they could sit in the Commons House.

The presence of non-Episcopalians in the Commons "'hath often cause[d] great contentions and animosities," but they were nothing like the condemnation which emanated from the Whig lords and bishops in the English Parliament when news of the shenanigans in Carolina reached them. For them, the preservation of toleration, national unity, and their own power were elemental facts of eighteenth-century life. The lords were also supported by the dissenters, both colonial and English. The South Carolina act was clearly at odds with Parliament's rejection of occasional conformity in the mother country.

It was into this uneasy alliance that Edward Marston came: he objected to the Carolinian act of 1704, not because it inhibited the political rights of dissenters but because it put power over the clergy into the hands of colonial laymen. The dissenters latched on to Marston's objection. These strange, political bedfellows were unsuccessfully opposed by the Anglican proprietors, led by Sir John Granville, a Tory who had barely supported William III and was against the Hanoverian succession. He and Bishop Compton were willing to trade episcopal power for an exclusive establishment, even if that establishment were controlled by the laity. On 12 March 1706, however, the lords begged the queen to reject the South Carolina establishment act "'as not being consonant to Reason, repugnant to the Laws of this Realm, and destructive to the constitution of the Church of England." They further pressed Anne to "'deliver the said Province from the arbitrary oppressions under which it now lies, and to order the Authors thereof to be prosecuted according to Law."[55] The South Carolina assembly quickly repealed the offensive measure and on 30 November 1706 passed the establishment act which became the legal basis of the Episcopal church's existence until the American revolution.

Hereafter, dissenters could hold office. Lay commissioners were still in charge, though they could no longer discipline recalcitrant clergy. French Calvinists could now sit on the lay commission. The people of the ten parishes could still elect their ministers, but, and this was a bonus for the clergy, rectors could sit as voting members of vestries and join in the election of the wardens. The act benefited everyone, but primarily it was a low church affair with the laity making the largest gains. Even a systematic governor like Francis Nicholson could not tidy up South Carolina's establishment, but, when compared with North Carolina, the church of South Carolina looked like the work of professionals.

In 1670, some seven years after the first settlement in what is now North Carolina, a young German adventurer named John Lederer recorded in Latin the story of his trips from Virginia to Carolina.[56] Carolina was a "pleasant and advantageous Seat [with] spacious plains and beautiful air."[57] The Indians were superior to those of Virginia, for they were "governed by an absolute Monarch; the People [being] of a high stature, warlike and rich" were to be preferred to Virginia's rude tribes.[58]

Thirty-five years later, in 1709, interest in the land and its native population still ran high. John Lawson (d. 1711), an astute and sympathetic observer of Indian character, declared that "these Indians [the Tuscaroras] are the freest People in the World . . . so far from being Intruders upon us, that we have abandoned our own Native Soil, to drive them out, and possess theirs; neither have we any true Balance in Judging of these poor Heathens, because we neither give Allowance for their Natural Dispositions, nor the Sylvan Education, and strange Customs, (uncouth to us) they lie under and have ever been trained up to."[59] Lawson advised thinking of the benefits that would come from the Tuscaroras becoming "Members of the same Ecclesiastical and Civil Government we are under. . . . the whole Body of these People would arrive to the Knowledge of our Religion and Customs, and become as one People with us." The English in their turn would gain "a true Knowledge of all the *Indians* Skill in Medicine and Surgery. . . . They would inform us of the Situation of our Rivers, Lakes, and Tracts of Land in the Lords Dominions, where, by their Assistance, greater Discoveries may be made than has been hitherto found out." Lawson envisioned the Christian and Indian living side by side in peace. Were such a society to be achieved, Lawson wrote, "we might be sufficiently enabled to conquer, or maintain our Ground, against all the Enemies of the Crown of *England* in America."[60]

What spoiled this peaceful kingdom for Lawson were the methods used by English settlers and their governments when dealing with red men. In a scathing passage he rapped out his resentments.

We trade with them, it's true but to what End? Not to shew them the Steps of Vertue, and the Golden Rule, to do as we would be done by. No, we have furnished them with the Vice of Drunkenness, which is the open Road to all others, and daily cheat them in every thing we sell, and esteem it a Gift of

Christianity, not to sell to them so cheap as we do to the Christians, as we call our selves. Pray let me know where is there to be found one Sacred Commandment or Precept of our Master, that counsels us to such Behaviour?[61]

All of the wars fought against the Indians of North Carolina "were occasioned by the unjust Dealings of the Christians towards them." He could name numerous instances of such injustices. Surely there was a "more reasonable Method of converting the *Indians*, than to set up our Christian Banner in a Field of Blood."[62] Two years later the North Carolina Indians took to the warpath. John Lawson died at their hands, the slow agonizing death by scalping and torture which he had so graphically described in his book.

Indian warfare in North Carolina was worse than that between the Yamassees and the South Carolinians. Whereas settlers along the Gold Coast maintained Charles Town, the capital, as a compact defensible refuge in times of trouble, no such urbanization occurred to the north in the Albermarle colony.[63] While the population of the two was approximately equal by 1700, between five thousand and seven thousand, there the similarity ceased.[64] Colonists in North Carolina were scattered far and wide, making them easy prey to Indian attack. There were no towns to speak of. Central agencies of government lacked any permanent location; there was no fixed residence for the governor.[65] Settlers in the early decades had merely drifted in from Virginia. The Cape Fear area could not boast an aristocracy like the Barbadian émigrés who came to the coastal regions of South Carolina. Indeed, few North Carolinians came from anywhere beyond the seas.[66] Not until the turn of the century did the province evidence the kind of pluralism of the middle colonies. Beginning in the 1690s and continuing to the early 1750s came French, Swiss, Germans, English, and Scots highlanders.[67] These swelled the ranks of the popular party in the House of Commons which, as in Virginia, sooner or later triumphed over the governor and his council.[68]

There were also religious differences between the two Carolinas. Before 1700, only the Quakers supported any kind of organized religious life in the colony. While Quakers were neither numerous nor clustered in groups in settlements, there had been a sizeable number of converts in the 1670s as a result of visits by Quaker missionary William Edmundson (1627–1712) and by George Fox (1624–1691). Historian John Nelson suggests that the "appeal of the Society of Friends is understandable; requiring no paid ministry, no church building, a minimum of organizational apparatus, and offering a faith shorn of liturgy, sacraments, and an intricate theology, it was peculiarly suited to the conditions and dispositions of North Carolina's early settlers."[69]

When Anglicans arrived in North Carolina, long after the Quakers had gained a foothold, they found no organized laity of their own persuasion awaiting them. This was not the case in South Carolina, where the Church of England was present from the start. Moreover, the Quakers were at the opposite pole from England's national church. The proprietary governors[70] sought "'Proper respect for form and order, the worship of God in decent surroundings, and the civilizing influence of the church";[71] Quakers wished freedom from oaths sworn to the "civilizing" state and exemption from taxation for the support of an Episcopalian establishment. With that, the clash of religious interests commenced. In South Carolina, the issue was not whether there would be an establishment but whether dissenters from the faith of the national church might retain positions of secular power and the right of representation in the colony. In North Carolina, where the Quaker minority had controlled the colony for a decade prior to the arrival of the Anglicans, the issue was whether there would be an Episcopalian establishment at all.

The history of the efforts of the Church of England and of the SPG to form parishes and build churches in North Carolina from 1700 to roughly 1740 is one of failure. After nearly three decades of attempts to establish the church in the province, William Byrd II reported in 1729 that there were no ministers to be found. As a result, magistrates performed marriages. There were no Church of England baptisms. Byrd feared that Jesuits from Maryland or New England might invade North Carolina.[72] The squire of Westover caused the Virginia commissioners to write North Carolina's commissioners on the matter of the dividing line between the two colonies and at the same time offered the services of the Reverend Peter Fontaine (1691–1757) for religious ministrations. No matter that Byrd referred to that unfortunate minister as "the Reverend Doctor Humdrum [who] would never be concerned with a plot [plan] that was like to cost him five pistoles."[73] He was in Byrd's estimation good enough for Tar Heels. With a haughtiness born of the consciousness of his own superiority, Byrd decided that North Carolinians were "content their offspring should remain as arrant pagans as themselves." Where else, he asked himself, were people less "troubled with any religious fumes"? They believed in nothing. "They do not know Sunday from any other day any more than Robinson Crusoe did, which," he added with a not untypical Byrdian afterthought, "would give them a great advantage were they given to be industrious."[74] So spoke businessman Byrd.

Although attempts were made, the church failed to supply her own worshipers with ministers. In 1701 after a vicious political struggle with Quakers, the Episcopalian planters with the cooperation of the governor proposed a vestry act which barely passed the North Carolina House of Commons. In 1703 the proprietors in London vetoed it, but for the moment the Church of England was the official religion in the colony. Quakers hated the 1701 legislation for it made possible the limitation of non-Anglicans in political life.[75] While the act created three or four paper parishes, there were still no ministers to man them.

Then, in April 1703, Thomas Bray entered the picture. The great planner of Anglican expansion privately commissioned the Reverend John Blair (d. 1706?) to survey the North Carolinian religious scene. At the end of January 1704, Blair was in the colony. Referring to the vestry act of 1701, he reported that Quakers "will endeavor to prevent any such law passing for the future, for they are the greatest number in the Assembly, and are unanimous, and stand truly to one another in whatsoever be their interest."[76] To Blair, there appeared to be four sorts of people in the colony: first, the Quakers, "the most powerful enemies to Church government"; second, those who have no religion; third, those who "are something like Presbyterians . . . some idle fellows who have left their lawful empoloyment, and preach and baptize through the country, without any manner of orders from any sect or pretended Church." Fourth were the relatively wealthy, "who are really zealous for the interest of the Church." They were, Blair noted, the fewest in number with the other three groups standing against them. Neither Quakers, "Presbyterians," nor the irreligious wanted an Episcopalian establishment. To add to this bleak scene was the sheer vastness of the territory, the "solitary, toilsome, and hard living," terrible roads, "whole nights [spent] in the woods," and the people scattered.[77] Blair's report was not good public relations; for himself, he vowed never to return.

Other clergy came to feel the same way, and no doubt Blair's report colored their outlook. As a result, the SPG did not act for three years, despite the entreaties of Episcopalians in the colony for clerical aid. Thereafter, from 1708 to 1723, the society sent a total of six missionaries to this hardship post. Only one remained for more than two years. The rest packed their bags and left.

That one was John Urmstone (1662–1725) who remained in North Carolina for eleven years. Generally, Urmstone has received a bad press.[78] He appears to have been avaricious, ill-tempered, and unattractive, though not all accounts agree. What is perhaps most instructive about his ministry is that it reflected over a period of years the conditions under which he labored.

Whatever his personal failings, Urmstone's life and actions provide a perfect mirror of the hardships facing all SPG missionaries to North Carolina, but, whereas others fled the colony, Urmstone remained—to struggle, to grumble, and to keep the political pot boiling. He had three widely scattered communities to serve. He found parishioners in them to be tightfisted and indifferent. He had difficulty learning how to farm his glebe. Added to this was the ever present Quaker influence. As a result Urmstone's letters and reports to the society were full of his "Obscure Corner of the world . . . inhabited by the dreggs and Gleanings of all the other Inglish Colonies." He wailed at being "Buried Alive in this hell of a hole," and then roundly declared that he "had rather be Vicar to the Bear Garden than Bp. to No. Carolina."[79]

In the meantime, Episcopalians continued in their efforts to impose an establishment upon Quakers. John Blair's prediction of a united front against purveyors of the national religion of England became a reality after 1707. When oaths were demanded of nonswearing Friends which forced their removal from the House of Commons, Quaker interests in London secured the appointment of another governor. But Thomas Cary (fl. 1710), the original governor, refused to yield, leaving two governors and two governments. Warfare among whites ensued, and marines from Virginia had to be called to install the proprietors' new commander. To the Indians it seemed a good time to attack. On 22 September 1711, the Tuscaroras in the coastal plain struck in what appeared to them to be their last opportunity to rid their country of its invaders.[80] The entire colony was nearly wiped out.

From this deplorable situation both in the church and in North Carolina's desperate social circumstances, some stability emerged, but it was never on the order of either Virginia or South Carolina. Within the orbit of religious affairs, pluralism remained with freedom of worship allowed for dissenters. With respect to the establishment of the Church of England as the official, tax-supported religion of the colony, controversy with the government and the crown persisted down to the eve of the Revolution.

The main point of contention was patronage of church offices. In the establishment act of 1715, the right to fill church offices was transferred from the governor to the local vestries. Not only could the vestries displace an unwelcome minister as the 1704 act stipulated, but they could now choose their parsons as well. Henceforth, laymen controlled the ministers whom they alone chose. However, each time that a new act was passed by the colonial legislature which provided such allowances for the laity (1741, 1755, 1760, and 1762), the crown disallowed the measure, since in the eyes of the Board of Trade, the right of patronage belonged to the governor.

Finally, in 1765, the colonial House of Commons wrote a bill which was silent on the matter altogether; London approved.[81] By then it was too late, and North Carolina's low church tradition had been secured. The SPG's failure from 1701 to 1723 to gain a solid foothold in Albermarle was the laity's gain. Not until the 1760s did North Carolina obtain a strong Episcopal church.

CHAPTER 7

Samuel Johnson and the Exponents of Free Will

Samuel Johnson's career as academician at Yale and King's College, preacher, and leader of the northern high church movement spanned nearly the entire eighteenth-century colonial period. Second only to Jonathan Edwards in the keenness of his mind and the breadth of his interest, Johnson remains one of the most important intellectual figures in the history of the Episcopal church.

In 1714, when he was 18 years old, Johnson, then a young Puritan aspirant, came across a book which was to change the course of his life. The book was Francis Bacon's *Advancement of Learning,* first published in 1605.[1] In his volume, Bacon sought a new regimen for education. He suggested that, instead of imposing their own arbitrary systems on nature, humans should observe the complexities of the universe in an attitude of passive receptivity.[2] Johnson, who had always sought to improve his mind, became convinced that by Baconian wisdom he might suspend his Puritan, schoolman's judgment and learn to treat the content of nature and the sciences with new respect.[3] Over forty years later, he still recalled some of the intoxication of fresh discovery. Johnson noted that *Advancement of Learning* "brought down his towering imaginations." He immediately bought the book and began studying it. Without equivocation and with unusual enthusiasm, Johnson reported that he was like one "emerging out of the glimmer of twilight into the full sunshine of open day."[4] The incredulous young student apparently felt that if he was to advance in knowledge he would have to begin again without "enslaving" Puritan preconceptions. As far as the sciences were concerned this meant the rejection of those endless, formal schemes of classification inspired in Puritan circles by the anti-Aristotelian, French Protestant martyr, Petrus Ramus (1515–1572). Henceforth the material content of the sciences came to outweigh their imagined relationships to each other, to human reason, and above all to the mind of God. Johnson was led by Bacon to set aside his own series of such propositions published in 1714 and called *Technologia*.[5] Bacon had caused him to reject his "little system of all parts of learning then known in nothing but a curious cobweb of distributions and definitions."[6] Johnson did not see his move as a threat to divine authority. He saw that in Bacon's universe, God's "signature," his mark of ultimate authorship, was on every leaf and blade of grass. Rather than ignore nature's empirical messages, observers were encouraged to look at leaves and grasses: first, for what they were, second, for what they—to the naked eye at least—were not. By this means rational acuity was wedded to spiritual discernment.

Johnson perceived that history was among the sciences which required this new attitude of docility before the facts. Here as elsewhere, if one reflected sufficiently, he claimed, the divine touch could be discerned. More than that: the very facts of history were expressions of the will of God. It was this belief, perhaps more than anything else, which led the young American to take the claims of apologists for the Church of England to antiquity, universality, and consent with the utmost seriousness. History seemed to be on the side of the Anglicans not the Puritans.

At the same time as he was reading Bacon's *Advancement of Learning*, Johnson was carrying on a correspondence with his friend and Yale classmate, Daniel Brown. Brown thought that the "several objects that are handled in history, are reducible to some of the other sciences."[7] Since history's only distinctive subject matter for Brown was politics, he saw no reason to designate history as a separate science. Johnson disagreed. He questioned whether it was advisable on Brown's part to ignore the study of the effects of divine providence, that is, history itself. Surely human actions, as they are subject to the will of the world's governor, are of a different character than the physical and chemical composition of bodies. It would not do to "jumble history among your policy [polity] or natural philosophy."[8] While all sciences were ultimately related to ontology or *philosophia prima*, as it was called by Bacon, still in the order of creation one could distinguish large families of sciences: those of quantity, those of quality, and then "Providence, hence History, which is either civil, ecclesiastical, natural."[9]

Having given a large place to history in academic studies, what did Johnson find? The answer was the visible unity of the catholic church. He discovered it by reading the early church fathers who were as much plagued with problems of disunity as he. Nevertheless, in their appeals for oneness, Johnson discerned the signature of God. The unity of the early Christians was assured, Johnson judged, by "Episcopacy [which] was truly the primitive and apostolical form of church government, and that . . . apostolic office was designed to be a settled standing office in the church to the end of the world."[10] There were of course difficulties in making the early church fathers perspicuous: the primitive church was remote from the eighteenth century, its accounts often obscure, its lessons remote, and so on. In addition to the problem of time, for Johnson there were also other matters which appeared to inhibit full theological understanding: American provincial ignorance on the one hand and the darkness of popery on the other. In the middle ages and even among the great Protestant reformers, there had been insufficient examination of the origin and facts of episcopacy. With all this went defense of the surplice, the "middle way of Erasmus, Melancthon and the Augsburg . . . Confession," and "bodily worship," that is, "bowing at the name of Jesus . . . [and] kneeling at the Sacrament."[11]

Such concerns as these were not at first apparent; they came later. The initial transition was far less assured, more painful, and even poignant. In the late 1710s Johnson felt that while the necessity of living in Connecticut could justify disobedience—remaining in "presbyterian" orders—still at some point he must *Fiat justitia ruat coelum* (Make justice roll down from heaven).[12] If divine providence had placed him in such a position under such circumstances, then divine providence would tell him when it was practicable to open the heavenly floodgates. In the meantime, he had argued in 1718, he must make a distinction between the positive and moral laws of God. The evidences and facts of episcopacy, he momentarily concluded, were in the first category, "for they have no intrinsic good or evil in them, but our duty with relation to them is merely built up on the arbitrary will of the lawgiver."[13] In a short time episcopacy would be a moral good.

If Bacon provided Samuel Johnson with a method and an intellectual attitude, others supplied the theological content which moved this young Puritan thinker toward ordination in the Church of England. In the years between 1718 and 1722, Johnson began his theological reading with the works of those urbane avatars of liberal Anglicanism, the Cambridge Platonists. Their works had come to America packed in Jeremiah Dummer's (1679–1739) "Pandora's Box of Books," that thousand volume cache which had been sent from England to Yale by the Connecticut agent and which was to change the course of American intellectual history. Among the ecclesiological and liturgical volumes in this collection, which Johnson read at Saybrook and after 1718 at New Haven, were the works of William Chillingworth (1602–1644), Ralph Cudworth (1617–1688), Henry More (1614–1687), Edward Stillingfleet (1635–1699) and John Tillotson (1630–1694). These latitudinarians had tired of the interminable theological disputes between Presbyterians and Anglicans in the seventeenth century. The Cambridge Platonists sought refuge in quieter, broader, less exposed theological pastures. A sympathetic God, tolerance for human kind, and practical morality were attitudes which they found congenial. These they tried to place in some sort of systematic arrangement. Johnson found in them kindred spirits who were as suggestive and liberating as Bacon had been. Indeed the Cambridge men held views of the church similar to Bacon's views, though derived from different premises. Both spoke of the comprehensiveness of the Christian community.[14] That Cudworth, More, Stillingfleet, and Tillotson were men of high culture, wit, and polite manners also appealed to Johnson.

Samuel Johnson was not destined to loiter in the delightful pastures of latitudinarianism. The heights of high church polity beckoned. He was the first American heir of any consequence to the renaissance of Anglo-Catholic historical writing which took place in England between 1660 and 1730.[15] What inspired the writing of church history within Anglican circles at that time was the necessity for countering Presbyterian pretensions, the difficulty of a Roman Catholic king after 1685, and the continuing problem of defining the church and Anglicanism. England's royal church was not sure, or at least as sure, of its identity after 1689. Its common cause with continental Protestantism in the days of Thomas Cranmer (1489–1556) had been thwarted. Somehow in 1559 Anglicanism must occupy a special place between Rome and Anabaptism. From there it was a short step to the declaration in the 1590s that that place was most productive of Christian life and morals. But Richard Hooker's mediation between Puritan and Catholic failed when Laud drove out once and for all the church's own more ardent reforming spirits. The hundred years which separated the apogee of Elizabeth's power in 1589 and the glorious events of 1689 show a shrinkage in the percentage of adherents to the established church. For a while, after the restoration of the monarchy in 1660, a policy of comprehensiveness was tried, but that gave way to the inevitable acceptance of simple toleration. By the Glorious Revolution there was no alternative. By toleration, the Protestant front against Rome might yet be saved even if in a less unified condition. But if toleration meant the acceptance of the facts of political life and a smaller establishment, the lack was more than made up for in expanded ideology. Self-authentication, the rediscovery of roots, justification, and the effort to prove to themselves who they really were was irresistible to Anglicans. It was to this inventory of the Catholic heritage of Anglicanism that the young American Puritan, Samuel Johnson, fell heir at a time when his own reformed tradition was experiencing a crisis of definition. In the lively ecclesiological debate in the first two decades of the eighteenth century, high church Tories, the legatees of Laud, were answered by dissenters as well as by latitudinarians. Increasingly embarrassed by the rigid Calvinistic notions of his native Connecticut, Johnson devoured this literature.

In 1715, he came across William King's (1650–1729) *A Discourse Concerning the Inventions of Men in the Worship of God*. This work by the archbishop of Dublin, an Irish patriot and friend of Jonathan Swift, skillfully took to task the Puritan neglect of Anglican liturgical forms. With abundant reference to historical precedent, Archbishop King judged that nonconformists gave "human wit too great liberty of treating the word of God as men please."[16] Neglect of set forms of prayer was out of keeping with ancient precedent. King suggested that if in the past anyone had the temerity to pray in such an undisciplined manner as Puritans did, he "must have separated from all the established churches of the world at the time." With "uncontrolled" prayer went the abolition of a set lectionary, so that Puritans had cast out as well the reading of God's word. It was an astonishing assertion which King made when he declared, "the voice of God is never publicly heard amongst them."[17] Johnson, with specific reference to King's *Discourse*, suggested to his compatriots in New England that extemporaneous prayer was a "human invention, and of late date too."[18] Similarly when the archbishop enjoined "the Lord's Supper . . . as a constant part of the ordinary service of the Church,"[19] Johnson was not far behind. He himself came to speak of the sacrament "as a duty incumbent upon us sinful mortals."[20] Bodily adoration was part and parcel of that act. With the Cambridge Platonists, with historian-apologist King, and, increasingly, with the young American there was a common assumption that the apostolic church in all of these matters must serve as the permanent model of ecclesiology.[21]

What became crucial for Johnson was not whether the apostolic church should serve as the bellwether for the eighteenth century, but which group in the present most faithfully reflected its tenets. From the side of the dissenters appeared Peter King (1669–1734), who would eventually become Anglican and, in 1727, assume the position of England's lord chancellor. In 1691, however, Peter King, as an independent, published *An Enquiry into the Constitution, Discipline, Unity and Worship of the Primitive Church*. In it, King argued that apostolic constitutions supported congregational principles.[22] This mainstay of the Whig party was answered by William Sclater (d. 1717?), a Nonjuring clergyman, whose decidedly Cyprianic, high church views were presented with learning and piety in his *The Original Draught of the Primitive Church* (1717). This repairer of "the breaches of this Holy city of God" sought "perfect unity" and an end to "litigious volumes of controversy" which plagued the early eighteenth century. Let "all the divided parties in the reformed churches of this age," he wrote, "have the same awful fear of the dreadful guilt and danger of schism." Though Sclater barely mentioned the Church of England,[23] the inference was clear throughout that that body came closest to primitive ecclesiology.

177

Sclater's work became the standard in theological education in the established church until 1880.[24]

Sclater had written *Original Draught* in the midst of the "Bangorian controversy," an ecclesiastical scrap initiated by the Whig, civil libertarian, Benjamin Hoadly (1676–1761), bishop of Bangor. Hoadly's low views on the powers of the visible church and its ministry made him the *bête noir* of the high church party. Hoadly "denied in set terms," wrote Norman Sykes, "that God could possibly require as a condition of salvation that all men should belong to one external communion, and that He could commit the power of absolution to any society of fallible mortals."[25] This alarming notion was first proposed in a homily delivered on 31 March 1717, the text of which was "My kingdom is not of this world."[26] That a member of the Anglican episcopate should have denied the priestly character of his own office and have enthroned upon the ruins of the visible church the right of unlimited private judgment was as astonishing as it was frightening. In New Haven, Congregational minister Samuel Johnson scratched his head in perplexity. While later revolutionary Americans would cheer Hoadly,[27] and while the Church of England proceeded to honor the prodigal son by elevating him to the see of Winchester, Johnson, with better Episcopalian sense, followed William Sclater. For a time Johnson stated that he was in danger of being influenced by Hoadly's reasoning and arguments.[28]

In the end, he sided with the higher churchmen, yet he did not embrace an exclusive view of the church. After his ordination in the Church of England, Samuel Johnson was unwilling to repudiate either the churches of New England or their ministries. Unlike other high churchmen of the time, he felt other ecclesiastical traditions were also bearers of the Christian gospel, however lacking they were in proper order. Johnson refused to endorse an interpretation of scripture that demanded conformity from all others. Perhaps in part drawing from the Cambridge Platonists, he preferred to emphasize, at least initially, that which was held in common by Puritans and Episcopalians alike, especially in points of belief. The great exception here was the doctrine of absolute reprobation and the divine foreknowledge of it.[29] While for him the Church of England was the best and most true church, it and the Congregational churches of New England "have the same religion, the same Gospel, and the same hope."[30] Johnson remained a moderate high churchman who was not intolerant of others.

But his moderation had definite roots in the writings of the Anglican controversialists of the early eighteenth century. John Scott (1639–1695), canon of St. Paul's Cathedral and debater with both Presbyterians and Roman Catholics, was particularly influential on the young American.[31] Of even greater impact on Johnson was John Potter (1674?–1747), Regius

Professor of Divinity at Oxford and, later, archbishop of Canterbury (1737).[32] Potter's *Discourse on Church-Government* was appreciated by Johnson.[33] The American found in this conservative Whig a kindred spirit. Potter believed that bishops had spiritual authority only, and he judged that "they who govern the church, can claim no civil prerogative, nor enforce their laws with civil rewards and punishments nor exercise any part of the power which belongs to magistrates of temporal kingdoms."[34] Johnson adopted such a position officially, and, when in 1760 he wrote a long and careful letter to the archbishop of Canterbury, Thomas Secker (1693–1768), pleading for a bishop for America, he made it clear that an episcopate should not interfere "with any civil matters as they now stand" in this country.[35] In the church, however, no Hoadlian libertinism was allowed by John Potter, for Christ had "left so complete a system of all religious and moral duties, that no addition of new duties could be made to it." In the early church, bishops were part of that system, appointed by God, and that office must be preserved "till it shall please God to change or wholly lay them aside."[36] The terms *presbyter* and *bishop* were interchangeable in the earliest church—even Sclater admitted as much.[37] Still the three offices did emerge, and men, Potter asserted, were not permitted to tamper with them.

By 1719 Johnson believed that his Puritan churches already possessed the first two orders in the elders and deacons; they lacked the final capstone, the episcopate.[38] Johnson, following Potter's lead, wrote: "Christ and his Apostles did establish a certain form of government in his church, as to the essentials of it, and not leave it to be variously modelled and settled by human authority as might best suit worldly conveniences."[39] Johnson was inconsistent in claiming that the true church was episcopal and then proving reluctant to unchurch his nonepiscopal, Puritan neighbors in Stratford. However, he was no worse than Potter who claimed that bishops were purely spiritual officers and had no business in civil power and then accepted the not inconsiderable positions in the House of Lords consecutively as bishop of Oxford and archbishop of Canterbury. Word and deed were not always the same, and God's signature, on the pages of current events at least, was not always clear.

While the reading which Johnson did before 1722 was more extensive than I have indicated, what emerges from this analysis of the major ecclesiological works to which he gave his attention is that he rejected emphatically the Hoadlian position. Johnson came closest to the conservative Whig stance announced by John Potter, and his high church inclinations were modified by it. That modification was also affected by the latitudinarian attitudes of sympathy and toleration. Johnson's high church inclinations were fed by the historical writings of William King, Sclater, and Potter, but

179

the way had been prepared by his own Puritan desire to systematize and unify and by the new system of Francis Bacon, characterized by "historical materialism." Henceforth, when he consulted the divine will, he would pay close attention to facts and evidences of divine activity.

Yet Johnson, unlike his contemporary Jonathan Edwards, began not with God himself but with the human mind, its design, its definition, consciousness, memory, and its degree of progress toward perfection. Rationality, not the mercurial kinetics of experimental religion, became his focal point. Johnson's *Elementa Philosophica* in this respect became the *magnum opus* of colonial rationalism. The former Puritan bade his followers tramp through the lowlands of scripture "and other excellent pieces of oratory, history, poetry, and morality." Great works of literary genius must be consulted by those who would be educated, for they "have stood the test of time, and been handed down to us thro' the several ages of mankind."[40] In order to know God's ways one must first consult man's ways. Through the inspiring expressions of the best minds and spirits of the past and by the study of languages themselves, we may come to see that God condescends to our low, human capacities to teach us the lessons of moral happiness. God "uses various types and emblems . . . wherewith to represent and shadow forth his perfections and dispensations, which are vastly above our comprehension." By attention to such divine "signatures" will we be guarded from the ravings of religious enthusiasm, those "impressions of sense, and solicitations of imagination and appetite, which continually divert our attention . . . strongly tempting us to the violations of order and law, both moral and political."[41] Johnson himself had trudged through the educational flatlands of history, worked his way up through the foothills of polity and morality, and found himself freed and disengaged "from fleeting and sensible things, and low animal pursuits and gratifications which we are shortly to leave." From such scenic escarpments he, from time to time, surveyed the pleasant landscape of moral happiness. However arduous the trek, there was always the promise of the summit where God's majestic light shone clear, though not dazzling, upon human travelers. "Here then," he wrote, "we arrive at our perfect consummation and bliss; our highest perfection and happiness, both intellectual and moral, in the clearest knowledge of Him and ourselves, that our minds can admit of." There was to be then an "entire union of our wills, affections and behaviour to his will." To this end mankind was to practice "holy discipline . . . due disengagedness from this uncertain sensible scene, and to improve ourselves in the knowledge and love of things unchangeable . . . [through] the exercise of devotion . . . [and] imitation of Him."[42]

For Edwards, on the other hand, there was no such long journey. As he had gone to the summit of religious exaltation, so he promised his awakened followers that they too could vault directly to that pinnacle where the blazing glory of God's beauty stunned and at first blinded the sight. Once having leaped the chasm of darkness and sin one could, upon regaining one's vision, look below or within, it did not matter which, and see that beauty reflected in ordinary, even uneducated, men and women in New England or Africa or wherever. One was to see that divine splendor, taste it, sense it in nature. All else was derivative from that one experience of being grasped by the power of Beauty. It was not so with Samuel Johnson. He himself would seize and comprehend, not incautiously and with no little courage, whatever promptings he could discern which emanated from the pages of holy history. If his quest was not radiant with adventure and risk, if it did not make the blood run fast, it was thoughtful and persistent.

Samuel Johnson was, without exception among Episcopalians, the most perspicacious churchman in eighteenth-century America. Above all others in the high church party, he gave copious expression to those values for which the church stood: "veneration for tradition and the Fathers of the church, a conception of the church as an organic unity of dogma, liturgy, and life, and . . . the necessity of an edifying, orderly, and uniform liturgy . . . found in the Book of Common Prayer."[43] With the exception of the church fathers, who were remote from most American Episcopalians, the remaining values were held in common. Episcopalians might and did disagree about the advisability of colonial bishops, the role of the laity in the affairs of provincial churches, and whether or not to unchurch dissenters, but the majority sought a unity of belief, conduct, and worship which centered on the use of the Book of Common Prayer. Beyond that, there was, as Samuel Johnson knew, a common mind with other American Protestants. "For you join with us," he wrote to his opponents, "in teaching the necessity of repentance towards God, and faith in our Lord Jesus Christ, and a sober, godly and righteous life, and of the supernatural grace of the Holy Spirit, to enable us to repent, believe and obey the Gospel, and that our acceptance with God wholly depends on the free grace of God, and the merits and intercession of Jesus Christ. It is happy," he concluded, "that we agree thus far."[44]

Nor was Johnson alone in such commonly shared Protestant sentiments. Missionary George Keith spoke of "good *Protestant Principles* of true Divinity maintained by the most Pious and learned *Protestant Writers*."[45] Whether sincerely or for propaganda purposes, Keith spoke of joining New Englanders in their own churches "in most external Acts of Worship . . . as some of Us have lately done at the charitable Christian Request of some Ministers of some New-England Churches."[46] They had, he noted, been

181

kindly received and thanked for their Christian doctrine and labor of love. When Keith and John Talbot were not admitted to the Congregational Lord's Supper, the charity ended, the imposed rules were attacked, and the practice of taking communion while seated without removing hats was criticized. Time and again, however, former Quaker Keith placed his new Episcopal church alongside that of dissenters and in opposition to Quakerism. There are, he wrote "many Pious and Learned Men [who] are judged to be found in this nation, not only of the Church of *England*, but among Dissenters and Nonconformists."[47]

Throughout the eighteenth century, similar expressions of the commonality of Christians appear in Episcopalian sermons. Thomas Cradock, the respected Marylander and rector of St. Paul's Church in Baltimore, wished

> that in all Churches of Christians in the World, if we would put by the points wherein we differ from one another, we shall find that in those propositions which without all controversy are universally received in the Christian world, so much truth is contained, as being joined to holy obedience, may be sufficient to bring a man to everlasting life.[48]

Edward Bass (1726–1803), future bishop of Massachusetts and an evangelical preacher, sounded similar yet deeper notes in the Christian gospel in 1759 when he judged that many follow Christ's religion as established by human authority, "but how few receive him heartily & to any saving purpose." Few in any church live as the Gospel prescribes, and were Christ to come again, he would not be welcome. Bass felt that "when by the grace of God we are brought to a sincere & hearty love of the gracious words which proceeded out of the mouth of our dear Lord & Savr, our love will not be confined there."[49] Such expressions transcended—at least momentarily—the rival agendas of opposing camps.

In the north, Episcopalians found their greatest differences with their Puritan neighbors over the tenets of Calvinism and the doctrine of predestination. While Samuel Johnson, like Keith, Cradock, Bass, and others, repeatedly asserted that the Church of England and the New England churches preached the same gospel, the idea of absolute reprobation as officially held in American Calvinist circles proved abhorrent to northern Episcopalians.[50] Samuel Johnson declared that the Thirty-nine Articles evinced no such notion. "Our reformers," he wrote, "did not aim at expressing Calvin's sense."[51] If one were to arrive at Anglican thought on this subject, then one must take all of it and compare passages in the articles, liturgy, and homilies. In prayer, he declared, we address the one "who hast compassion on all men and hatest nothing that thou hast made, and wouldst not the death of a sinner, but rather that he should be converted and live." In

182

the catechism, he went on, we are taught that Christ came to redeem all mankind. In the seventeenth article of the thirty-nine, "Of Predestination and Election," Johnson drew his opponents' attention to that article's final paragraph which stated in part that "God's promises must be received in such wise as they be generally set forth to us in Holy Scripture."[52] No sooner had Johnson marshaled the scripture passages which implied a universal atonement than he was accused of being an Arminian, which immediately labeled him as theologically suspect.[53]

Johnson did not negate divine assistance: "God over-rules the sins and follies of men in such a manner as to bring good out of evil," he wrote, "and make them turn to the advancing of his own ends in the government of the world."[54] Later he spelled out his ideas in more detail. Speaking in very nearly Edwardsean terms of God's visibility, he declared:

> We see him in every shape and form, in all his works, throughout the whole creation, in all which he is everywhere present, clothed with light as with a garment, whereby he renders Himself to our senses. We should moreover seriously consider, wherever we are and whatever we behold, that it is God who by means of the sensible light of this world, renders all things visible to us; and wherever we go and whatever we do we should bethink ourselves that it is God who surrounds us with this light and directs us in all our steps, and how to act with advantage in all our exertions.[55]

The Calvinist doctrine of predestination was unreasonable as well as unscriptural to Johnson. While he made no effort to get away from "the mysterious and inscrutable features of the Deity," he nevertheless wanted to avoid declarations of God's sovereignty in the sense of uncontrolled power. For Johnson, God was a rational model for his people, and while he could do whatever he pleased, "he pleased to do what is just and fair."[56]

In most cases, American Episcopalians of the eighteenth century assumed the freedom of the will and studied the works of moral perfection in themselves as well as in others. James Blair warned his parishioners at Bruton Parish that the deity allows "no decline or shift off Duty." Remember, he charged, "that *God is not mocked, and he that doth Righteousness is righteous,* and no other." Between the too bright landscape of the "Solifidian, Antinomian and rigid Predestinarian"[57] and the dark tangles of the "Casuist and the Delayer of Repentance," the true practitioner of Christianity must thread his way warily, cautioned Blair. The proper attitude he called "Evangelical Righteousness." This righteousness allowed no "evasions of Subterfuges," and at its heart was a moral code and a new legalism. There was a great deal of emphasis on the pitfalls of "Cares and Lusts, and Bad Examples . . . all trick and Fraud and Dissimulation of Duty."[58] Something of the majesty of the law was missing from Blair's homilies, however. His presentation of the prickly path of righteousness presupposed and took for granted free will. While the invitation to this arduous journey was soberly and even solemnly proffered, there was little spiritual pluck and stamina demanded. Blair did not electrify by either stern or frightening command. He was no Jeremiah crying out in indignation from his Williamsburg pulpit. Instead of biblical fiat, prudence became the greatest virtue in Virginia where "Christianity had become respectable morality, polished by restraint and moderation."[59]

Of perhaps wider influence than the published sermons of Virginia's commissary were the *Catechetical Lectures* of Thomas Bray. These found their way into nearly every Episcopalian library in America and into all those libraries sent to the colonies by the SPCK. Bray frankly stated that obedience to moral and divine law was a condition of salvation. By such obedience, Christians, he added, "come to have a right to Salvation." So no one would think him out of step with acceptable Protestant doctrine, Bray hastened to add that evangelical obedience was not a work, since it was an effect of God's grace and was produced by grace as well as by faith.

While the term *pietist* fits Thomas Bray well, it is harder to so designate James Blair.[60] The warm personal faith, social concern, abiding missionary endeavor, and liturgical interest so marked in true pietism was lacking in Blair. Nevertheless, both voiced an evangelical moralism which placed their church squarely in the Protestant camp. Their point of view—that of low church obedience to moral law—was shared by others south of the Potomac.

To the north, sharper theological wits were bred than in Virginia because of competition with articulate Congregational churchmen. Here amidst the minority of high church Episcopalians, free will and moral law provided the framework of their theological unity. In 1698 while still in England, George Keith had declared in his *Christian Catechisme* that believers are not to rely upon obedience to any law "either Outwardly or Inwardly given them as the Foundation of their Justification."[61] Justification came through God's grace and favor alone. Repentence could not be called the cause of forgiveness. Christ alone caused human beings to be justified. The problem for Calvinist New England, as it turned out, was that Keith's consent was made by a free act of the will in which the faithful themselves chose God. That choice, however, was not made in a religious and moral vacuum. At Annapolis in 1703, Keith declared that conversion came about through the converting power of the Gospel. When worshipers beheld Christ's free sacrifice of himself on the cross, they were moved to obedience.[62] Elsewhere he made clear that such movement was the work of the Holy Spirit.[63]

Where then was the issue between Keith and President Samuel Willard of Harvard in the famous debate begun in 1702? The issue was not so much over the process of justification with respect to man, at least initially, as with respect to God. Keith rejected God's immutable decree, the seemingly necessary fall of Adam, and God's determination of every event thereafter. To Keith and other Episcopalians, this made God appear to be the author of evil. Worse, men and women came to be seen as puppets. Are we ''Tennis-balls of Destiny,'' Keith asked, pounded by ''Rackets . . . those second Causes and outward Objects?'' Willard's Calvinist premise about God's irresistible grace led, Keith was sure, to ''Ranter'' conclusions.[64]

Freedom of the will, the call to a sense of duty, and the cause of a benevolent deity were continued in New England by John Checkley. In terms that any New England farmer could understand, Checkley declared that God was necessary for the attainment of a responsible, moral life. ''If I manure my ground, never so well,'' wrote Checkley, ''yet without the Sun, it will not bear.'' Few would care to dispraise such a sentiment. ''On the other hand,'' he continued, ''if I do not *prepare* my Ground, the *Sun* will not bring a *Crop* I did not sow. Nay it is the *Sun* too, which with my Labour, do's prepare the Ground and fit it to receive the Seed.''[65] God and man work together, God so ordaining.

If, among high churchmen, Keith and Checkley emerge as prime exam-ples of Episcopalian leadership in their day, they did not say much that was new. Free will, moral responsibility, and quiet reasonableness in a national church were the ideals esteemed by Anglicans for the better part of the seventeenth century. These attitudes were imported to America by Keith, Bray, Checkley, and others. They were the *sine qua non* of the imperial church. The leaders of that church had had enough of the Puritans' irresisti-ble grace. Thomas Bray declared that to claim knowledge of an unalterable predestination to communion with God was to give way to that surge of curiosity ''to know *Hidden things* such as are not proper for Man to know.'' Those who peered into ''the Decrees of Predestination, and the Counsels of God's Will'' were no less guilty of ''a *sinful Lust of the flesh.*''[66]

There was also the political angle to predestination. Over the preceding century, the Puritan's declaration of God's irresistible grace and the perse-verance of the saints had seemed to Anglicans to rationalize rejection of established morality and dishonesty, a convenient device for turning one's not-so-private desires into the will of God. Anglicans wanted obedience to God, king, lords and bishops—and in that order—so that the traditional structures and distinctions within society might be maintained. John Checkley spoke for all of his fellow churchmen on both sides of the Atlan-tic, when he declared that ''the more absolute and the more unlimited Sense

185

the Principles of Obedience and Submission are understood in, the safer the Government."[67] The Puritans' irresistible grace was inappropriate to traditional structures of obedience, for, in theory at least, it knew no class distinctions but sustained whomever it chose, whether rich or poor. If for the Puritans submission meant an altogether passive acceptance of whatever God's free will might be, for the Anglicans it meant an active and freely given allegiance to God and king. Anglicans simply did not trust the common herd to behave patriotically of their own accord. They did not trust readings of God's grace unless those readings were well within the carefully defined safeguards of the establishment. Without those safeguards, anyone could call himself God's chosen vessel and persevere in endless and stubborn independence. The result of such willful rejection of duly constituted powers of court and convocation was, as Anglicans had seen, disorder, wild chiliasm, prophesyings, and finally in the 1640s, political chaos. If only subjects would put corporate peace ahead of their own selfish inclinations, the state would be secure.[68] Apparently there was no stopping those "saints" who had confused their own obstinacy with the steady and conventional work of the Holy Spirit in a well-ordered society.

In Puritan ideology, ethical duty was directed to "higher" ends and only then was it worked into an interconnected structure of social values.[69] Moral behavior for the Puritan was the result of the covenant; for the Anglican it led to the realization that one was in the covenant. Thus, in a sense, in Anglicanism one moved from the "world" to God, from moral behavior to acceptance by deity.

That much was clear from the writings of Bray, Blair, Keith, Checkley, and others. With Samuel Johnson, the Episcopalian "this-worldly" relationship with God underwent a decisive change, however. What Johnson did was "shift the basis of morals from the idea of sin to the desire for happiness."[70] Men and women naturally desire true happiness, Johnson declared. That joy was not to be found in the transient amusements of this world but in dedication and devotion to God.[71] The happiness which accrued to the individual from such a dedication was primarily intellectual happiness. Since both God and man were intelligent beings and since man's intellectual light was akin to God's, it was again possible to declare that humans had the power to choose the good.[72] Where Johnson differed from his predecessors was in making the choices which faced everyone more intellectual than voluntary. Election depended on intelligence, not fealty. Reprobation was more the result of ignorance than disobedience.

Samuel Johnson affirmed the power to act or not as men please in consequence of their perceptions. Of course, no one could control the sight or sound of evil: theft, murder, bad habits, and sexual license would surface sooner or later across the tea tables of Connecticut or in the newspapers. None remained innocent long. Once God had exposed humanity to either vice or virtue, then God's task was, if not done, at least interrupted while he awaited the outcome of human reaction. Here freedom, understood as "neutrality" and "objectivity," took over. In no way were men and women irrevocably conditioned by those vices and virtues they had been caused to observe. Astonishingly enough, for Johnson the human spirit was immune from the forces of custom and habit.[73] The mind stood above environment, inclination, and even its own perceptions. Subsequent will and action were free and under no constraint. Johnson's moral theology provided the mind a moment of clean air amidst the general pollution of events. Just how this exemption was achieved he did not say. Even if the mind was "ever so much necessitated to assent to evident truth," the visible actions of sanctity were another matter entirely. A separate act was required by a self-determining will to do the works which assent commanded, or as Johnson put it, "I am . . . free to choose or refuse, to act or not to act, in consequence of this assent; for action according to the frame of our nature, ever springs from a self-asserting power."[74] To Johnson it appeared that without such freedom "virtue and vice, praise and blame, reward and punishment, can have no meaning, but are empty names." Let theologians doubt and quibble, Johnson would simply refer them to their consciences. He was "astonished if what I contend for be not self-evident."

It was not. He had driven a wedge between the mind and the actions of the will, between assent to truth and conduct, between theology and ethics. That wedge, because it made belief an opinion at first isolated from action, would have domesticated Christian faith by doing away with theology as a serious matter. That this did not happen until much later was in part due to the fact that Johnson's *Elementa Philosophica* received little attention and few readers. This was so because the thunderclap of experiential religion, the Great Awakening, drowned out the hitherto voiceless Berkeleyanism of his system.[75]

In more general terms, Johnson's metaphysical speculations made their author appear less interested in human cravings than in human limitations, less affirming of human capacities and capabilities than in accommodation to the debilitating circumstances of life.[76] In the 1740s, covenant hope had been reawakened and reformed for all classes in the Puritan land. Johnson's promise that Christ "hath appointed an order of men to administer sacred rites . . . preside in the exercise of this social religion and worship, and to explain and inculcate the divine philosophy" paled by comparison.[77] The revivals promised more than Johnson's pledge that the teachings of his order of men would qualify and prepare them for eternal happiness. The majority wanted happiness now. God and religion did something in the present.

But beyond matters of free will and the character of grace, Johnson's wish to systematize Anglican thought had much in common with the Calvinist desire to mark the steps to salvation. Johnson was not content to let matters rest with the general Protestant theology held by Bray, nor with that loyalty to crown and episcopate envisioned by imperial Anglicans Nicholson and Checkley. There remained in his mind the Puritan desire for a cosmic view governed by prescribed, logical laws. In addition, if William Wollaston's deistic *Religion of Nature Delineated* led Johnson to believe that he could use his reason to discover God's moral law in nature no less than in scripture, he was "unwilling to allow his 'just sense of God' to be sacrificed to rational inquiry."[78] Samuel Johnson wanted to maintain the sovereign God of reformed religion as well as present to his generation a unified system of knowledge.

Finally, it is not accurate to place Samuel Johnson in opposition to Jonathan Edwards and to say that for Edwards "man's obligation was to seek the salvation of his soul," while for the Episcopalian duty called for one to fulfill the normal desire for happiness in this world.[79] For both, happiness, or, to use Edwards's terms, delight, beauty, enjoyment, complacency, and pleasure in God were central. Johnson's intellectualism and his espousal of a human will free to act either for or against that spirit set him apart from Edwards and the great revival which Edwards had helped to initiate and then struggled to direct.

CHAPTER 8
Reactions to the Great Awakening

In the fall of 1740 Episcopal clergy in New England were frightened. To Charles Brockwell (1696–1755), rector at Salem, the question of proper behavior in such perilous times was a problem serious enough to seek instructions from the SPG in London. The cause of alarm was neither an invasion of the French nor any legal threat against churchmen by Massachusetts' authorities. It was the landing in Rhode Island of one of the church's own sons, George Whitefield. Of all Anglicans in colonial America, this single-minded Christian, masterful preacher, and tireless itinerant commanded universal attention. Perhaps even more than Jonathan Edwards, it can be fairly said that he set in motion forces which would thereafter influence American popular religion. In his seven American journeys, Whitefield became the unifier of those scattered awakenings which, in the late 1730s, flared up in Massachusetts, Connecticut, Pennsylvania, New Jersey, and elsewhere. His visit to Boston and New England would be the grand, Parsifalian triumph of his first American tour, a journey the "guileless fool" had begun a year earlier in Philadelphia. There and elsewhere, however, his presence healed few wounds. On the contrary, his preaching opened new ones. He also set the pattern for subsequent American revivals with his unflagging zeal, his constant self-promotion, and his fervid oratory with its promise of release from sin and its pledge of union with Christ.

In addition, Whitefield showed his disdain for cherished Anglican forms. Where his Episcopalian contemporaries talked of the apostolic succession of bishops, priests, and deacons, Whitefield took higher ground and styled himself an apostle. When defenders of Episcopalian faith and practice like Timothy Cutler unchurched those outside of England's establishment, Whitefield declared, "I bless God, the partition wall of bigotry and sect-religion was soon broken down in my heart; for as soon as the love of God was shed abroad in my soul, I loved all of whatsoever denomination, who

189

loved the Lord Jesus in sincerity of heart." When his fellow clergy disagreed with him and identified God's will as nearly as possible with a particular institution, Whitefield promptly unchurched them. He was sure that the Holy Spirit led him to truth "even in the minutest circumstances, as plainly as the Jews were, when consulting the Urim and Thummin at the High Priest's breast."[1] There was no arguing with such a man. As avenging angel of the Lord, he simply swept aside what habit and custom held dear. The doctrines which the high churchmen of the seventeenth century had rejected—free forgiveness, justification by grace through faith alone, closing with Christ, and the perseverance of the saints—became the principles of which Whitefield approved. Where one of his keenest critics, Timothy Cutler, the former provincial Congregationalist, had found in English religion the churchly beauty which passed American understanding, Whitefield, the Oxford graduate, found in America that freedom to enjoy the forgiveness of sins—imaginary and otherwise—which passed churchly patience. Where Cutler, Johnson, and Checkley had sprung from the New England aristocracy, this first American folk hero was the son of an English tavern proprietress.

Whitefield's bitterest enemies were his fellow Episcopalian clergy, whom he consistently attacked. Among them he was known as the "Slanderer of the Brethren." Because of his unwillingness to meet other clergy halfway, the whole parcel of Whitefieldian religion and the awakenings he nurtured and led were rejected by a considerable number of the laity and a majority of the clergy.[2] Whitefield's first detailed confrontation with the clergy occurred early in his career in New England. On 19 September 1740, the great evangelist met his fellow Episcopalian presbyters at the home of Commissary Roger Price (1696–1762) in Boston.[3] Whitefield noted that they received him courteously.[4] They fell to arguing two issues: the doctrine of the ministry on one hand and grace and free will on the other. The revivalist readily admitted that he considered Presbyterian ordination valid, that he had communed with a Baptist minister, and that the "catholic spirit was best" in such matters. Whitefield advised his fellow clergy "to preach new birth, and the power of godliness and not insist so much on form."[5] It was clear that each side knew the lines along which the other would speak.

New birth and baptismal regeneration were tackled next. Whitefield led with the loaded question, "Whether conversion was not instantaneous?" At the moment that he "sprinkled the child with water," he asked Timothy Cutler, did he believe that "the Holy Ghost fell upon the child?" Answer, yes. Then regeneration is instantaneous? Suppose, Whitefield asked "every child was really born again in baptism, then every baptized infant would be saved." "And so they are," returned Cutler dryly. "How do you prove that?" asked the revivalist? Because, replied the Massachusetts rector, the rubric says so![6] When Whitefield asked for a text of scripture to prove the point, Cutler held up the prayer book and responded, "The Church says so."[7] Predictably the conversation steered toward predestination and the possibility or impossibility of falling away from grace.

> Whitefield: "A true child of God, though he might fall foully, yet could never fall finally."
>
> Cutler: But "Men may fall away from grace given."
>
> Whitefield: But then observe what follows, "and by the grace of God they may rise again."[8]

The evangelist then took his leave, nor "did he ever visit our Persons or our Churches more, tho He was in Town 3 Sundays, where we had two successive Sacraments."[9] That afternoon he preached to four thousand people in Benjamin Coleman's meetinghouse.

Whitefield's unpopularity with many Episcopalians grew. He proceeded to reproach "the Church [of England] universally for her corruptions in ye Faith and deviation from her Articles." He further angered northern clerics when he recommended that his auditors read Willard's *Body of Divinity,* Shepherd's *Sound Believer,* and Stoddard's *Safety of Appearing in the Righteousness of Christ,* rather than Anglican authors.[10] While for Episcopalians in Puritan New England there was nothing new in the recommendation of these volumes, when testimonial was offered by one of their own, it was more than patience could endure. Churchmen were well aware of the details of previous awakenings from Edwards's *A Faithful Narrative of the Surprising Work of God in Conversion of Many Hundred Souls in Northampton,* which by 1738 had run into three editions.

Timothy Cutler, writing to the bishop of London over a year before Whitefield arrived, gave a full, and for the most part fair, appraisal of the religious revival. Some of the converted were sincere enough; others simply followed the crowd. Still others—of whom Cutler highly approved—"remain serious and unblemisht." On the whole the awakenings gave for him only a "great Appearance of Religion. . . . People in those parts unbyast by their [revivalists'] popular Schemes, think there was [a] great deal fantastical and foolish in those shows. . . ." The most susceptible were "the meanest of the Teachers, here and there, and scarce any other Teachers, fall into them." Quite incorrectly, Cutler judged in 1739 that "the Talk of these [th]ings [revivals] is now generally dropt."[11] It was in fact only the beginning.

Enthusiasm, lack of concern for church order, the castigation of "worldly" ministers of the Church of England, and his alliance with American dissenters led to Whitefield's rejection by his fellow priests. His continuing presence in the land in which he felt most at home was a constant irritant, especially to high churchmen. By early 1742 with the revival in full swing, the cool appraisals by Timothy Cutler gave way to bitter, universal castigations. Charles Brockwell spoke of the "convulsions into which the whole Country is thrown by a set of Enthusiasts . . . [who] strole about haranguing the admiring Vulgar in *extempore* nonsense." To make matters worse, "Men, Women, Children, Servants & Nigros are now become (as they phrase it) Exhorters." Their behavior was shocking: "groans, cries, screams, & agonies . . . tears . . . ridiculous & frantic gestures . . . some leaping, some laughing, some singing, some clapping one another upon the back."[12] The Great Awakening was in full swing. To Henry Caner (1700–1792), then at Fairfield and Norwalk, Connecticut (1744), the prospect "of a new storm from the daily irregular excursions of Mr. Whitefield" was grim indeed. "His sickness stil continues" and was contrasted with the "visible deadness and formality" of others. For Caner, zeal for God's cause lay somewhere between the ragings of the turned-on preachers and the "cold Laodician dispositions" of the lukewarm.[13]

Further south in New York, the adverse reaction of Episcopalians to Whitefield was equally strong.[14] Whitefield had been invited there by a Presbyterian, a "Mr. Noble (a spiritual man) . . . [who appeared to cry] 'Come over to Macedonia, and help us.' "[15] When Noble and the evangelist visited William Vesey to request the pulpit of Trinity Church, the commissary turned to Noble and remarked, "as you sent for this gentleman, so I desire you will find him a pulpit." Noble did. Whitefield prayed that Vesey's darkness would be lightened and that he would be "obedient to the faith."[16]

At least one other New York Episcopalian perceived Whitefield as being outside the pale of that faith. Powerful lay councilman Cadwallader Colden (1688–1776) found Whitefield and his fellow enthusiasts, the Presbyterians, to be "Men without Charity [who] give ground to doubt their being Christians." For Colden, the Whitefieldians set God's revealed will against the dictates of conscience and oppose religion to reason and morality. The principles of the exhorters, Colden argued, "are the invention & imposture of Popery & can only be defended on popish principles." The twice-born, he thought, will become Pied Pipers to lead the people back to Rome. "It is for this reason that Popish Emissaries have directions to join with & promote all the Enthusiastic Sects & principles among the Protestants."[17]

The story was nearly the same in Pennsylvania, New Jersey, and Delaware.[18] Maryland and Virginia were not sufficiently urban for Whitefield to gather large crowds. In addition, Maryland's parsons were simply too worldly to bother or be bothered by a single evangelist, no matter how able.[19] In Virginia the reception was warmer. Blair praised Whitefield, ushered him into the pulpit of Bruton Parish, and showed him around the College of William and Mary. Later, Blair shrewdly hedged his bets with the bishop of London with respect to Whitefield.[20]

Adverse Episcopalian criticism of the English evangelist had already reached something of a crescendo in South Carolina early in the summer of 1740. There the revivalist encountered the hot anger of Commissary Alexander Garden (1685–1756). The story of their confrontation is well known.[21] It provides no new insights into either the theology of Whitefield or the objections to his preaching. Yet there was a certain sharpening of the debate between the great preacher and his Episcopalian enemies. In the journalistic warfare carried on by Whitefield and Garden, all that had been implicit in the religious attitudes of both sides in terms of faith, election, baptism, and works finally came down to one crucial issue: the nature of regeneration.[22]

That regeneration was the work of God as sustaining spirit neither doubted. That the Holy Spirit bound himself to a ministry and through that ministry to a particular body of believers few questioned. But when one inquired into the nature of that ministry, canvassed its extent, and scrutinized the body of believers, then the differences became clear. In the collision between Garden and Whitefield, the question was not so much whether God bound himself to a liturgy, a three-fold ministry, and a national church. Whitefield never attacked those pillars of Anglicanism. The issue was whether in any Christian tradition God had bound himself to deal with his creatures in an outwardly prescribed form. Garden thought so; Whitefield did not. For the great revivalist the motions of the Holy Spirit in the world were sudden, convulsive, and exempt from human calculation, and in that the commissary of South Carolina thought he saw a flaw.

Alexander Garden recognized the inherent weakness of Whitefield's evangelicalism: impulsiveness. Regeneration for the commissary was not abrupt but protracted and enduring: *"first the Blade, then the Ear, then the full Corn in the Ear;*—in a Word, gently *Co-operating,* assisting, . . . that they may *grow in Grace.*" Sudden regeneration, while he admitted its biblical foundation, appeared to have no place in the Episcopalian scheme of things.

Thus, my Brethren, the Work of *Regeneration* is not the Work of a *Moment,* a sudden *instantaneous* Work, like the *miraculous* Conversion of St. *Paul* or the

> *Thief* on the Cross; but a *gradual* and *co-operative* Work of the *Holy Spirit,* joining in our *Understandings,* and leading us on by *Reason* and *Persuasion,* from one Degree to another, of Faith, good Dispositions, Acts, and Habits of Piety.[23]

The commissary charged the revivalist with enthusiasm and pride and threatened suspension. Whitefield replied that he cared as much for Garden's threats as he would a papal bull. After preaching in Baptist and Presbyterian meeting houses, the evangelist went to his superior's church on Sunday, 3 July 1740. There he was barred from the Holy Communion and promptly told the world about it through his journal. Whitefield rejoiced "that I was accounted worthy to suffer this further degree of contempt for my dear Lord's sake." As if that were not enough to make Garden bristle, Whitefield then went on to pray out loud, "Blessed Jesus, lay it not to the Commissary's charge."[24]

Eventually Garden took it upon himself, quite unsuccessfully, to suspend Whitefield from the ministry of the Church of England. The attempt created a great deal of legal clatter but resolved nothing.[25] The "Great Itinerant" went on wayfaring for another three decades.

Modern derogatory assessments of Whitefield follow much the same pattern. One historian recently noted the self-serving character of Whitefield's evangelism: "George Whitefield was so much the actor that he produced a large body of self-promotional literature intended to detail God's special dispensation toward him and serve as an avenue of defense in any disputation in which he became involved."[26] Commercialization of the faith was not simply the work of the press; it was that which motivated the evangelist himself. His marketable humility paid high dividends to his unrelenting egotism.

Another modern historian takes a different position: however much debunking Whitefield deserves and has received, the "basic core of the Whitefield personality was the fact that he had experienced the new birth." Thus, whatever contradictions studded his personality, however much controversy attached itself to him, there is no doubting the "abiding conviction that he knew God." Everything he said sprang from that certainty. If he was a charlatan who dispensed rhetoric to colonial rubes, then he duped himself more than them, for his "basic honesty was one factor that made it possible for many to gloss over or forgive his surface errors and faults, however grave."[27]

Whitefield had many enemies among the Episcopal clergy, but he also had friends. First, there were the crowds. In Boston at the end of his visit to New England in early autumn 1740, twenty thousand citizens thronged the Boston Common to hear him. It was to that date the largest crowd ever to assemble in America. The trumpet voice sounded until dusk. "Numbers, great numbers, melted into tears, when I talked of leaving them," he recorded.[28] That evening the evangelist was visited privately by a little girl from Roxbury who had followed Whitefield to the Common. The text of the sermon he had preached was "The Lord our Righteousness," and, recorded the soul winner, "she was enabled to say, 'The Lord *my* Righteousness.' "[29]

In addition, the ministers and laity of dissenting churches greeted Whitefield warmly. It was almost too good to be true to have an Anglican priest as the champion of a revived Puritanism. When that priest took his own church to task, delight was almost universal. Thus, when Whitefield arrived in Boston, dissenting ministers turned out in force to greet him: Governor Jonathan Belcher (1681–1757), Judge Joseph Willard (1681–1756), President William Cooper (1694–1743) of Harvard, and Benjamin Coleman (1673–1747), famed minister of the Brattle Street Church.[30] Some months earlier Jonathan Edwards had written a letter of welcome. "It has been with refreshment of Soul," he wrote,

> that I have heard of one raised up in the Church of England to revive the mysterious, Spiritual, despised and exploded Doctrines of the Gospel, and full of a Spirit of Zeal for the promotion of real vital piety, whose Labours have been attended with such Success. Blessed be God that hath done it! who is with you, and helps you, and makes the weapons of your warfare mighty. . . . I hope this is the dawning of a day of God's mighty Power and glorious grace to the world of mankind. May you go on Rev. Sir![31]

He did indeed go on winning many more to his side.

It has been claimed that Whitefield had no allies in his own church.[32] It is true that a majority of the clergy were, with some notable exceptions, both anti-Whitefieldian and antirevivalist, but the laity by no means presented a solid phalanx against the renewal of covenantal religion. As in other churches, the movement of revival proved to be astonishingly complex: divisive but also unifying, creating new alignments, and presenting stunning ironies. Nor have these been examined sufficiently with respect to Episcopalians.

First, the laity in the Episcopal church were simply curious. They wished to see Whitefield in action, learn what all the fuss was about, and perhaps even experience the promised conversion themselves. There is some good evidence about these lay people. In Virginia, the Reverend Patrick Henry (d. 1777), uncle of the patriot, remarked to Commissary Dawson in 1745 that he had allowed Whitefield to preach in his church, for had he not done so the evangelist "would have preached in the Church yard, or very near it and then the whole congregation would have gone over to him." Henry surmised that though the revivalist's followers were few, "yet all the people to a man had great desire to hear the famous Whitefield."[33] Elsewhere the laity were more than titillated. George Ross at Newcastle, Delaware, reported in 1741 that Whitefield "could not sow his tares in the field of our Church so plentifully as elsewhere."[34] Yet the next year Ross was forced to admit that "under the notion of New Light & conviction" several "made away with themselves." These were "weak creatures who have absented for some time from Public worship."[35] Three years later, in 1745, Ross complained that his flock had "little strength in Apocalyps . . . [though] This ebb of the church here can be by no means laid to my charge."[36] To what extent economics as much as revivalism caused the ebb in Ross's congregation is difficult to say. Certainly revivalism did not help.

There are other reports of similar parish divisions over religious enthusiasm among Episcopalians. In Lewes, Delaware, John Pugh reported that his congregation was cut in half in the autumn of 1740 by the turmoil.[37] The next spring William Beckett was reporting, also from Lewes, that a religious society had been set up.[38] At Oxford, Pennsylvania, Alexander Howie complained that a number of his church members had been attracted to the awakening.[39] From Radnor, William Currie spoke of Whitefield's "Brazen Forehead, Impertinent asseverations, uncharitable assertions, & impious imprecations [which have] raised such a confusion among the people of this province . . . & (which I am most troubled about) [have] made a very great rent in all the congregations belonging to the church of England." Currie judged that the "generality of my hearers not only run after, but adore him as an oracle from heaven."[40] What was equally appalling was that they "look upon all he says to be, the immediate dictates of the holy Ghost." In New Jersey, Thomas Bradbury Chandler (1726–1790), rector of the church in Elizabeth Town found himself in trouble with his parishioners when he refused his pulpit to Whitefield,[41] while from Marblehead, Massachusetts, Alexander Malcolm reported that not a few of his flock were pro-Whitefield and so prorevival.[42] Clearly the two were interchangeable.

On one notable occasion, a leading layman realigned himself with the Episcopalians because of the great revivalist. The man's name was Benjamin Rush (1745–1813), patriot signer of the Declaration of Independence. Rush heard Whitefield preach, and was convinced.[43] The Philadelphia doctor then and there felt himself obligated "to retreat from their [New Light Presbyterians'] society to the church of my ancestors and in which I was born, viz., the Church of England."[44] Rush liked the "Calvinistical" theology of the Thirty-nine Articles, and that, coupled with Whitefield's eloquence, brought about his entry into the Episcopal fold.[45] Rush later was to "refuse to be a slave to any sect," but his subsequent deviation from the faith of his childhood was not due to revulsion against Episcopalian reformation doctrine or anti-Whitefieldianism but to high church claims to the exclusive validity of Anglican orders.[46]

Whitefield's influence on colonial youth met more permanent success with Devereux Jarratt, who became one of the leading southern evangelists of the late colonial and early national period.[47] As a young man in the early 1750s, Jarratt came across "Mr. Whitefield's eight sermons, preached in *Glasgow.*"[48] When this unlettered Virginian, who "understood little of what I read," asked about the author of the sermons, he was told that Whitefield "was a *New-light,* and consequently what *he* said was nothing to *Churchmen.*"[49] His first awakening to "vital religion" was augmented by one who "became my favorite author," James Hervey (1714–1758), an Oxford associate of Wesley and Whitefield who has been described as a Calvinist of a "gentle, pious, and unworldly" stamp.[50] But above all Whitefield, along with John Wesley, "caused me to judge more favourably of the Church [of England] than I had done."[51] While Jarratt later founded Methodist societies in Virginia and North Carolina, he avoided the theological debate over grace and predestination which ultimately separated Whitefield and Wesley. Throughout his life, Jarratt retained a modified Calvinism which struck closely to Article Seventeen of the Thirty-nine.[52]

Later in the eighteenth century, there were other lay inheritors of the kind of evangelicalism maintained within the church in Virginia by such disciples of Whitefield as Jarratt. These were the "believing wives," as one historian has dubbed them. Such women as Mary Randolph Meade practiced and taught her children the "evangelical asceticism of the English evangelicals."[53] Nor was Mary Meade the only representative of a planter family to embrace evangelicalism. Frances Tasker Carter, wife of Robert Carter, hired a young, New Light Princetonian, Philip Fithian, as tutor for the Carter household. Presbyterian Fithian soon discovered that the Episcopal church near Nomini Hall on the Northern Neck did not wear the same serious theological face as his own church in the north. On the other hand he soon found out that Mrs. Carter herself was by no means religiously ignorant. On Sunday, 30 January 1774, after a violent storm made church-going impossible, this woman of beauty, uncommon intelligence, and wide reading engaged her young instructor in "a long conversation on religious affairs." Fithian found himself surprised at Frances Carter's "very extensive Knowledge," for "indeed she converses with great propriety on these things." Fithian also ascertained that his employer "thinks the Religion of the established Church without Exception the best of any invented or practised in the world." Mrs. Carter, however, allowed "the difference between the Church, & Presbyterianism to be only exceeding small, & wishes they were both intirely [sic] united."[54]

There were others. Along the coast of South Carolina, as well as in Georgia, there were members of the church who were stirred by the Great Awakening in general and George Whitefield in particular. Hugh and Jonathan Bryan, successful South Carolinian planters in the 1740s, visited Whitefield in Savannah and were converted.[55] There were Episcopalian clergy who by Whitefield's own account supported him: in South Carolina Lewis Jones (c. 1700–1744) of St. Helena's Parish and Thomas Thompson (fl. 1740s) of St. Bartholomew's Parish who "refused to preach or sit in judgment against me."[56] In Connecticut the rector of the church in Hebron, Samuel Peters (1735–1826), heaped praise on Whitefield. Peters wrote that he "ever viewed him [Whitefield] as an instrument of Heaven, as the greatest Boanerges and blessing America ever knew."[57]

There were those who appreciated Whitefield but never accepted his theology or his style. Among the more famous of these was Benjamin Franklin. Franklin saw the utility of Whitefield's spiritual power and wrote of a grand scheme of settling the great valley of the Ohio with Whitefield as chaplain of an American army of settlers.[58] If Franklin's political aspirations intruded themselves upon his friendships, he, who genuinely disliked all sermons, found the Englishman to be a stirring orator.[59] When news of the evangelist's death reached Franklin, it drew forth a complimentary, if calculating, response. Franklin wrote, "I knew him intimately upwards of 30 years: His Integrity, Disinterestedness, and indefatigable Zeal in prosecuting every good Work, I have never seen equalled, I shall never see exceeded."[60] William White (1748–1836) was more artlessly admiring. This churchman, destined to be the future bishop of Pennsylvania and chief architect of the Episcopal church in the 1780s, was no lover of Calvinism in general.[61] Yet White readily acknowledged that when, as a young man, he met Whitefield, the great preacher "added to the existing tendency in my mind" toward religion. He subsequently heard Whitefield preach "with great delight."[62]

What was the secret of Whitefield's astonishing fame as the revivifier of Christian faith in the colonies? No doubt it is correct to say that one reason for his triumph was that "the man spoke freely."[63] He replaced the tightly woven manuscripts of Puritan preaching with an emotional directness and dramatic simplicity which stunned his audiences. One of the secrets of Whitefield's power was that he had a vivid, personal faith that he had been chosen by God to do the work that God willed him to do. Whitefield was one of that small band of men and women that is possessed by a compulson to take religion with utmost seriousness. "If," as one modern writer has put it, "they are atheists, they will have no part in religious ritual. If they believe in God, they hunger to know as much as they can about what God would have them believe and do."[64] Whitefield was one of those latter souls, and his desire to know God's will for himself led him to a rigorous discipline of prayer and Bible study.[65]

Second, Whitefield fitted himself into the narrative of scripture. That narrative mediated his identity for him. Figuratively he became, for instance, the boy Samuel standing before the Lord in his ephod or Elisha over whom Elijah cast the prophet's mantle or Timothy whom Paul told not to be ashamed of his youth.[66] Having once experienced the dramatic impact of scripture, Whitefield went on to preach what he had seen with his own eyes. In doing so, he did not argue the relevance of Christian faith, he simply declared its glories.[67]

Third, he rediscovered the Thirty-nine Articles of the Church of England. For the most part those articles had lain unheeded and disused theologically until Whitefield revived them. They became the prism through which the soul winner viewed his sacred texts. To South Carolinian, Congregationalist Josiah Smith (1704–1781), Whitefield was the reincarnation of reformed Anglicanism. Smith noted perceptively that the doctrines which Whitefield insisted upon in his sermons were those agreeable to "the dictates of reason; evidently founded upon scripture; exactly corresponding to the articles of the establishment; of great use and necessity in forming the Christian life." For Smith, Whitefield appeared to have "revived the ancient spirit and doctrines."[68]

The personal call of God, the Bible, and theology: with these firmly in place, the evangelist had only to add his own native dramatic ability and remarkable sense of timing to produce the desired results in his auditors. Before episcopal thrones and childrens' cradles alike, the Wonder of the Age demanded conformity. Whitefield saw ancient truth where others were blind. They might ridicule his call and authorization to speak for God; he never wavered in the conviction that he possessed both the summons and the right. Time was too short and the sense of urgency too great for him to absorb the lessons of utility which politicians and statesmen taught. Though he received their disdain and derision, he did not care. Thus he strode through the moral tangles of existence, impervious to the brambles which clawed and scratched at the armor of God. It is perhaps Whitefield's unqualified assurance and pietistic simplicity which have led both admiring and hostile critics alike to assume that he was a theological illiterate.[69] Such was not the case; he knew his theology well enough. From that position whose centerpiece was the free, unmerited grace of God to sinners, he took aim and launched his theological barbs in two directions. On the one hand he attacked unrelentingly the latitudinarianism of Archbishop Tillotson, while on the other hand he entered the lists against the high church moralism, as it seemed to him, of Richard Allestree's *Whole Duty of Man*.[70]

It would be nice to think that Americans recognized Whitefield's theology and clasped him to their bosoms because of it. But, for whatever reason, they lauded him. They found in him not merely Franklin's "Chaplain to an American Army" but one in episcopal orders at that. It is a remarkable fact that awakened Calvinists in the late 1760s looked favorably on the idea of a bishop for America so long as Whitefield was appointed.[71] Twice it was reported in the American press that Whitefield might be considered a suitable American bishop. The first time, late in 1739 and early in 1740, newspapers in Virginia and Pennsylvania carried the story—it was really a joke—to the effect that

> the Rev. Mr. Whitefield's Preaching is becoming so very offensive to the Clergy of this Kingdom [England], that 'tis said one of my Lords the Bishops a few Days since, went to the King to desire his Majesty to silence him: Upon which his Majesty enquired whether he preach'd Treason, Sedition, &c. but none of these Things being alleg'd against him, his Majesty seem'd at a Loss how to satisfy the Bishop; which a Noble Duke present observing, humbly proposed, that in order to prevent Mr. Whitefield's preaching for the future, his Majesty would be graciously pleased to *make him a Bishop*.[72]

Again twenty-nine years later in 1769, the droll idea was bruited about that Whitefield's presence in America as a bishop would be a great improvement upon high church schemes to land someone far less well known and, even more important, less pleasing to the majority of Americans. Whitefield, so the "Intelligence Extraordinary" ran, would be "Archbishop of Boston . . . Rev. Mr. [John] Wesley, Bishop of Pennsylvania . . . Rev. Charles Wesley, Bishop of Nova Scotia, &c." There would be others, six bishops in all, from Massachusetts to the Carolinas.[73] The king, it was announced, would foot the bill. He never did. Whitefield was never elevated to that exalted rank. If the idea was calculated to amuse, it was also in its way informative of the American mind, and there was in it just a hint of seriousness.

Though he did not have the opportunity to benefit his church as a resident bishop, Whitefield contributed in an ironic way to the growth of his church by virtue of his presence. There were those in other churches to whom the religious upheaval was disquieting and its demands for personal testimony of true conversion intimidating. For not a few New England townspeople, the reappearance of covenant requirements was abhorrent. Since many of these were "excluded from the New England churches by the membership requirements, [they] drifted back toward Anglicanism in gratifying numbers." Additional accessions occurred when many of all classes "who were offended by the excesses of enthusiastic religion embraced Anglicanism as a serene and orderly alternative."[74] The loss of three or four to the evangelical infection, reported Arthur Browne (1699–1773), rector at Portsmouth, New Hampshire, was more than offset "by ye addition of thirty-six to our Communion notwithstanding the indefatigable Industry of some crackbrained zealotts to disturb our Peace and promote Division."[75]

Far from appealing to the lavishly genteel or to those with more modest roots in New England's revived covenant, the Church of England came to offer a haven for the economically impoverished and the theologically bewildered. The result was that "New England Anglicanism in its area of greatest numerical strength—the farm community and the rural village—was in good part a lower class movement."[76] It was a lower class movement allied with those of education, with political connections with the SPG, and with Britain herself. Along the coast of Maine, clergy joined forces with leading laymen to found new congregations among the poor and middle class and to ease the way into the church for dissatisfied members of Congregational meeting houses. Jacob Bailey (d. 1818), the first itinerating clergyman as well as the first permanent Episcopalian parson in Maine, either served existing groups of Church of England folk or founded new congregations in Pownalboro (now Dresden), George Town, Harpswell, Brunswick, Gardiner, and Falmouth (now Portland). Bailey's efforts were so successful that in 1764 the minister of the Casco Congregational Church at Falmouth began to conduct services according to the Book of Common Prayer and ended up as the Episcopalian rector of that congregation.[77] To these and others, the church offered an opportunity for social standing which evangelical, provincial civilization denied them and which, because of their low economic standing, they might otherwise fail to attain. To be welcomed into the dignified surroundings of Anglican worship became a source of assurance.

Elsewhere, the antirevivalist alliance between the Episcopalian wealthy and the unchurched poor gained adherents. In 1769, New Hampshire's Governor John Wentworth (1736–1820), an ardent churchman and later loyalist, was sure that, if he had a chaplain under his direction, he could establish a permanent system of forty parishes in the province.[78] Wentworth, whose allies were "of the principal families and the richest merchants" of Portsmouth,[79] was aware that in the interior of the province the people were very poor and had no public worship. The governor was optimistic enough to believe that "if the Church service was performed without Expense or any zealous attempts to proselyte, the People would naturally flock to it, and from the regularity, good order, and native Merit of the Church would soon be attached to it sufficiently."[80] In North Carolina, Governor William Tryon had earlier said the same thing.[81] Both governors failed to make an appreciable dent in the poorer parts of their respective colonies.

In South Carolina, greater success attended the footsteps of the remarkable gentleman missionary, Charles Woodmason (fl. 1772). Woodmason sought to bring into the Episcopal church the poor of the Carolina Piedmont. In the same year that Wentworth urged caution with respect to proselytizing New Hampshire farmers, Woodmason was throwing caution to the winds. He began by lambasting the clergy of the Gold Coast and demanding that they cease their cringing before the powerful of Charles Town. He became the champion of the desolated settlers of the vast upland St. Mark's Parish and the peerless leader of that uprising of frontier people in the Carolinas between 1768 and 1771 known as the Regulator Movement.

Such had not been his initial intent. Hating Presbyterians, Baptists, and other revivalistic riffraff, as he judged them to be, Woodmason labored for the acceptance of the Church of England with all of its genteel accoutrements in the lawless backcountry. It was a hopeless task. People jeered at his efforts, brought dogs and set them barking during services, and ignored liturgical injunctions. Converts to the church were few and far between. Slowly, however, the uplanders came to find in Woodmason "a man of some learning, eager for conversation," and above all a friend.[82] Woodmason put his clear literary ability to work for the cause of relief of poverty and fear. He argued in the press for lower food prices, justice in the courts for rich and poor alike, protection of Piedmont farmers from the violence of roving bands of white criminals, equitable distribution of tax benefits, and the founding of schools and churches in the interior. His voice and pen proved to be eloquent.

His choicest invectives were reserved for South Carolina's insouciant clergy, those parasites who lived off the largesse of the low country planters. In a sermon preached in 1769, Woodmason's use of the Bible took on that simple and direct application to contemporary events which marks the most convincing preachers in time of crisis. Vagrant outlaws, hired by the magistrates of the tidewater to act as "police," had been stealing livestock, plundering and burning settlers' houses, and torturing and raping women and children.[83] To this accusation, he added a searingly biblical reproof:

Speak O Ye Charlestown Gentry, who go in Scarlet and fine Linen and fare sumptuously ev'ry day. Speak O Ye overgrown Planters who wallow in Luxury, Ease, and Plenty. Would you, Could you, Can you see or suffer Poor helpless, pretty Boys—Beautiful, unguarded, promising Young Girls, for want of Timely Care and Instructions to be united with a Crew of Profligate Wretches, *Whose Mouth is full of Cun[n]ing Deceit and Lyes,* from whom they must unavoidably learn Idleness, Lewdness, Theft, Rapine, Violence, and it may be, Murder . . . ?

"Thus we live," he declared, "and have liv'd for Years past as if without *Law* or *Gospel, Esteem* or Credit."[84]

When these same gentry began to discuss revolutionary ideas against Great Britain, Woodmason's scorn knew no bounds: "Lo! such are the Men who bounce, and make such Noise about Liberty! Liberty! Freedom! Property! Rights! Privileges! and what not; And at the same time keep half their fellow Subjects in a State of Slavery."[85] Had it not been for Woodmason's demand for reform and the backing he received from Lieutenant Governor William Bull (1710–1791), it is doubtful whether the upland areas of South Carolina would have chosen the patriot side in 1776. If the Episcopal church in South Carolina did not gain in numbers from Woodmason's efforts, it can at least be said that in this antirevivalist, yet prophetic figure, she produced a worthy minister.

Elsewhere in the south, the church lost adherents because of the awakenings. Despite the later evangelicalism of Virginia's Randolphs and Meades, the church increasingly lost whatever hold it had maintained on the common run of humanity. The poor left the church of the aristocracy and formed distinct religious communities, an entire alternative society. That society was characterized by prudence and biblical sobriety.

The most devastating loss of prestige on the part of the Church of England occasioned by the Great Awakening was in Virginia. Here, in the oldest and presumably most "settled" Episcopalian colony, forces of social change from 1740 to 1760 weakened the church and led to the disestablishment of 1776–1785. In Hanover County, a traditionally Episcopalian area,

> numbers of ordinary people led by Samuel Morris, a "Bricklayer," began reading religious tracts and absenting themselves from church. The group grew, was inspired by readings from George Whitefield's sermons, and eventually reached such a size that it felt compelled to build a meetinghouse. Disaffection from the Church seems to have been general so that "when the Report of these Sermons and the Effects occasioned by reading them was spread Abroad [Samuel Morris] was invited to several Places . . . at a considerable Distance."[86]

Whatever their lack in terms of religious enthusiasm, Virginia's parsons did not deserve the almost brutal treatment afforded them by awakened dissenters. Along with the clergy's traditional desire for equality with the planter vestrymen went an equally understandable yearning for greater independence. They were solicitous for the integrity of their own order, for its sense of corporateness and dignity. In short, Virginia's ministers wanted to participate in the control of the lay-ruled establishment. To share authority under royal supremacy and to bring a measure of uniformity along English lines, not American ones, became their goal. To the vestrymen, such thinking appeared at first ungrateful, then treacherous. To the ministers, it appeared altogether proper.

As long as the laity remained loyal to the Church of England, however, resentment on the part of the ministers toward their employers only smoked and smoldered. When at midcentury the gentry began to join the dissenters, clerical anger burst into flame. To have renegade laymen sitting on juries and handing down judgments against ministers of the established church was unacceptable. The traditional order began to fracture as the old rivalry between the clergy and vestries erupted in the 1740s. Intense litigation went on in the courts of the colony, taking the immediate form of demands for financial security, higher salaries, respect for the gentlemanly stature of ministers, and greater independence.[87]

Fierce quarrels broke out between laity and clergy over the twopenny acts of 1755 and 1758 which stated that the annual salary of sixteen thousand pounds of tobacco due each minister was to be paid at twopence per pound no matter what price tobacco might sell for on the rising London market. To achieve their aim of taking advantage of fluctuations on the exchange, the ministers of Virginia empowered the Reverend John Camm (1718–1778), former professor of divinity at William and Mary, to lobby for the disallowance of the act. When the act of 1758 was disallowed by the crown, the parsons were seen as enemies of the colony. The bishop of London supported his clergy by declaring that to have made such an act in times past without "Royal assent . . . would have been called Treason." The Virginia legislature had assumed a "power to bind the King's hands, and to say how far his power shall go, and where it shall stop [which] is such an act of Supremacy as is inconsistent with the Dignity of the Crown of England." Might not Virginians, the bishop continued all too prophetically, be drawn away from their allegiance to the monarchy, "when they find that they have a higher power to protect them?"[88]

No sooner had news of the disallowance reached Virginia than the Reverend James Maury (1718–1769) brought suit to recover his salary.[89] Maury was no parvenu outsider to Virginia and its ways. A graduate of William and Mary, this "ingenious young man," as he was described, proved to be a "bright example of diligence in his studies, and of good behaviour in his morals."[90] In 1763, Maury's ingeniousness and diligence did not desert him. He took it upon himself to demand a degree of autonomy and clerical independence for himself and his fellow clergy. It was a dangerous move, for Virginia's planter-legislators, whether in the church or under the influence of the dissenters, were not a body to be trifled with. Maury proceeded against the collectors of parish levies in Hanover County. The defendents procured the services of Patrick Henry (1736–1799) who had the temerity to announce that the colony had a right to pass laws in defiance of royal prerogative when its own welfare was at stake. Henry stunned the jury, brought tears to the eyes of the judge, lost the case, and gained a reputation. The damage to the standing of the clergy, however, was irreparable. Henry declared that "the clergy, by thus declining to abide by the law of the land[,] counteracted the great object of their institution, and therefore instead of being regarded as useful members of the state, ought to be looked upon as enemies of the community.[91] Their seemingly greedy desire for the advancement of their own economic and social position marked one step along the road to disestablishment.

Yet there was something to be said for these ministers. As we have seen they sought freedom for their own order from the all-powerful control of the vestries. They also wished to enhance their reputations as "Gentlemen, Christians and Clergymen,"[92] not only for selfish reasons but in order to gain sufficient authority in the community that they might reverse the trend away from the establishment which had been initiated by the revivalists.[93] If there was something odious in ministers of the Gospel engaging in litigation which time and again appeared self-serving, there was something less than loftiness of purpose in the demands of wealthy laity that their ministers observe apostolic poverty.

In the end nearly everyone lost something. The Virginia legislature was restricted in its right to regulate the clergy. The colony's ministers found that the crown was a slender reed upon which to lean in America. The gentry who controlled the vestries had their activities curtailed for seeking too hard to make the clergy dependent, and the church as a whole became discredited.[94] The only winners were the evangelical enthusiasts of the Great Awakening, who looked "upon Mr. Whitefield as a zealous and successful minister of Christ; and as such to countenance him."[95] The church in Virginia forgot that whatever emoluments might come their way from kings, bishops, and privy councillors, the basis of political power throughout the

English-speaking world of the eighteenth century was in local government. In this, provincial America was no different from Georgian England.[96] In relying on the legal rulings of the crown, the clergymen succumbed to those "last and greatest dangers to the principle of uniformity which proceed from the laws themselves." The Great Awakening did the rest.

CHAPTER 9
The Enlightenment, Education, and Politics

High churchman Samuel Johnson and evangelical George Whitefield seldom agreed on religious and theological matters. On one point they were in perfect accord: the Christian rationalism of Archbishop Tillotson and Dr. Samuel Clarke (1675–1729) was unacceptable.[1] Johnson was fully aware of Tillotson's popularity in America and remarked, "It will not do here to speak against him with much acrimony except among Methodists." Johnson was as captivated by the style of the archbishop's sermons as were other Americans. But "for these several years [I] have been sensible of the ill effects of them in these parts . . . and done my best to guard against them."[2] Men and women were meant to live by faith, not by sight, he declared, an injunction which Tillotson and his followers ignored. The Connecticut Episcopalian felt that "the more gentlemen pretended to reason and deep speculation the more they dwindled in faith." As a result "Arianism and Latitudinarianism so much in vogue often issued in Socinianism and that in Deism and that in atheism and the most dissolute living."[3] Johnson confessed that he was shocked by the artifice and subtleties of Clarke and others. In 1757, he declared that "Dr. Clarke, etc., had led me far many years ago into the reasoning humour now so fashionable in matters of religion."[4] But if Johnson was reluctant to take on the mighty Tillotson, Whitefield was not. In his reply to the Harvard faculty in 1745, Whitefield pronounced that in the colleges "tutors neglect to pray with and examine the Hearts of Pupils. —Discipline is at a low Ebb: Bad Books are become fashionable among them: *Tillotson* and *Clarke* are read instead of *Shepard*, *Stoddard*, and such like evangelical Writers."[5] The reaction to rationalism sometimes produced strange companions.

For both Johnson and Whitefield, the latitudinarians, however orthodox they sounded, claimed too much for human reason and gave it a veto power over divine revelation which it should not in their view have had. Of course God existed: no one, deists included, ever doubted that. For those of the

207

moderate Enlightenment, any ideas God might convey to his creatures must be believed even if those ideas were previously unknown. But once God's words had been witnessed, repeated, and recorded by believers, then human reason stepped in and judged the accuracy and even the validity of that witness. The same tests which were applied to any piece of evidence must be applied to that of the witnesses of revelation.[6] Not yet had it occurred to any that judgment of the witnesses themselves and their "evidence" might be more complicated than the "simple" act of determining facticity. Not until the novels of Fielding and Richardson and, to a lesser extent, the paintings of Hogarth in England and John Smibert in America did anyone try to preserve "reality" and the marvelous, though not the incredible, concurrently.[7]

Tillotson and Clarke knew no such possibility. By their "rationalism," they shocked not only the orthodox in England but in America as well. Their trust in the utility and success of natural religion against atheist and infidel alike, their notion that creation offered the most sensible argument for the existence of deity, and their shared belief that the mother suckling her child was a more pious and important act than that of kneeling before an altar rail, proved anathema to high churchmen and evangelicals alike.[8] For Johnson the keen desire on the part of latitudinarians to stress the mightiness of divine being at the expense of his relationship to Christ and the tradition-bearing church led to Arianism. Henceforth theology and mathematics, an Arian Christ, and the laws of nature, or so Clarke thought, would walk hand in hand. There were those who felt that with him the work of apology was complete. Others, including Johnson and Whitefield, dissented and saw in Clarke a nascent deism.[9] For neither Johnson nor Whitefield did the new synthesis of Tillotson and Clarke or any of the rest provide a proper answer to the question of how to live in the new world of the eighteenth century.

Of a quite different attitude was William Smith (1727–1803) who, from the mid-1750s to the Revolution, was provost of the College of Philadelphia. This liberal Episcopalian clergyman was "one of the major figures of the Moderate Enlightenment."[10] In his famous pamphlet, *A General Idea of the College of Mirania* (1753), a utopian vision of education in the land of Mirania, Smith spoke of the great objective of civilized instruction: "the easiest, simplest and most natural Method of forming Youth to the Knowledge and Exercise of private and public Virtue." Miranians and William Smith "often had this Sentence in their Mouth, which I think, in other Words, I have read in TILLOTSON,—That the Knowledge of what tends neither directly nor indirectly to make better Men and better Citizens, is but Knowledge of Trifles."[11] With that statement, latitudinarian education was launched for the middle colonies of New York and Pennsylvania.

The author of *Mirania* banished to the sidelines all Calvinists and Arminians whose "polemic Writings about Grace, Predestination, moral Agency, the Trinity &c. . . . so enflame the World at this Day, to the Disgrace of Christian Meekness and Charity."[12] To achieve that unbiased mentality for which he sought, Smith withdrew the investigation of the Bible from his curriculum. For the purpose of examining scripture "the Sunday Evenings are set apart; when about an Hour is spent," he continued, "in all the Classes, in the Study of the Old and New Testament."[13] Otherwise the Bible was to be read privately. One historian of American education has noted that "Smith's *Mirania* is easily the most characteristic and comprehensive formulation of the altered conceptions of piety, civility, and learning that underlay the development of education in eighteenth-century America."[14] In that alteration, Ciceronian eloquence replaced Pauline persuasiveness. Smith's program of studies was the first systematic course in America "not deriving from the medieval tradition nor intending to serve a religious purpose."[15] It was a new attitude in American education which came to fruition particularly in Episcopalian, colonial colleges.

At the time that William Smith wrote *Mirania* he was a tutor to the two sons of Colonel Josiah Martin (fl. 1740–1761), the baronial master of Rockhall, an estate on Long Island. Smith had arrived in America in 1751 after he had studied at King's College, University of Aberdeen, then one of the more enlightened centers of education in the British Isles. The young tutor was aware that in both Pennsylvania and New York men of power were promoting education. He had absorbed Benjamin Franklin's *Proposals Relating to Education of Youth in Pensilvania* (1749).[16] He also knew that there were plans for a college in New York. One historian has suggested that James DeLancey (1703–1760), the ardently Episcopalian lieutenant governor of New York, had requested that Smith draw up a paper for the proposed college in that province; *Mirania* was the result.[17] After Franklin read the pamphlet, he immediately requested that Smith pay him a visit. The "job interview" went well: Franklin was charmed by the twenty-six year old Scot, who could converse with ease on music, literature, religion, and education.[18] In possession of Franklin's blessing, Smith sailed for England where he obtained ordination in the church and the additional laying on of hands of the Penn family. Proprietary approval subsequently assured him of the provostship of the new college. Franklin would soon regret the day he met his new professor for Smith did not turn out to be the tractable corporation man, the gilded clerk whom Franklin sought.

The Philadelphia to which William Smith returned was fast becoming in the 1750s the largest and most culturally diverse city in colonial America.[19] That he contributed significantly to its refinement and enlightenment there is no doubt. Smith gathered around him the first literary and artistic circle in America.[20] Within its circumference was Francis Hopkinson (1737–1791), musician, poet, and scientist, a signer of the Declaration of Independence and later a federal judge.[21] There was Benjamin West (1738–1820), the painter, in whom Smith stimulated an interest in history and the arts, and for whom the provost of Philadelphia's college obtained the money for that passage to England which was to bring West international fame as an artist. In addition to these two best known Philadelphians, there was Thomas Godfrey (1736–1763), a lyric poet and author of the first—and one of the worst—plays ever produced in a colonial American theatre, *The Prince of Parthia*.[22] Smith's circle of students later claimed able clergymen: Jacob Duché (1737–1798), Episcopalian and then Swedenborgian who changed his politics as he did his religion when he entered the revolution as a patriot and emerged as a Tory. There was also William White and the promising young poet and preacher Nathaniel Evans (1742–1767). These young men spent a great deal of time together and with Smith, tramping along the Schuylkill, composing verses, and conversing with the master.[23]

Smith's prominence is attested by his membership in the American Philosophical Society and his editorship of the short-lived but stimulating *American Magazine and Monthly Chronicle for the British Colonies* (1757). In 1765 he wrote his *Historical Account of the Expedition Against the Ohio Indians,* "one of the most significant studies of wilderness life and warfare in colonial America."[24] In it Smith contrasted the "gentlemanly" tradition of warfare in eighteenth-century Europe with the "American campaign [where] everything is terrible; the face of the country, the climate, the enemy." In the wilderness there was no "refreshment for the healthy, nor relief for the sick. . . . victories are not decisive, but defeats are ruinous; and simple death is the least misfortune which can happen."[25] Ostensibly written in order to describe new methods of fighting Indians, Smith's work goes against prevailing images and prejudices and "suggests that the proper way to live in America is to imitate the Indian, and conversely, that the Indian's patriotism, independence, and love of liberty make him the model of the ideal American."[26]

William Smith was not the only purveyor of culture and inspirer of closer ties with England in the Philadelphia of the 1750s. There Benjamin Franklin had founded the first public library in 1731.[27] There too Franklin had been a leader in enhancing the cause of liberal education when he sought to make Philadelphia's academy into a college. Franklin also had a desire for closer ties with England. Neither that wish nor his ideas of a free college and university were those of the provost he had so precipitously chosen. William Smith, whose chair at the college had been endowed by the now Anglican

Penn family, supported the proprietary government. Franklin did not. Smith further sought an aristocratic colony, supported by the Church of England, and over which he himself might preside as lord bishop. Franklin wanted an English commonwealth in the province where the assembly, not lords, would rule.

As a result Franklin supported the Quaker dominated legislature. He hoped that Pennsylvania would cease to be a proprietary colony altogether and would revert to the crown. To William Smith, all Quakers, along with New Light Presbyterians, were "Infatuated Enthusiasts," a category to which he would later consign Methodists as well. So intense was Smith's dislike of all forms of revivalism that at one point, when a group of Episcopalian laymen sought to elect as their rector an "awakened" Church of England parson, William McClenachan (fl. 1755), Smith deemed the candidate to be of an "impudent and restless Temper,"[28] and tried unsuccessfully to deprive the laymen of their right to elect their minister. Franklin, on the other hand, had no such religious scruples. He welcomed George Whitefield to Philadelphia and, so long as it suited him, remained friendly. Franklin found Smith's cabal of Episcopalians and Old Light Presbyterians to be infatuated establishmentarians. Benjamin Franklin despised religious schemes of all kinds, found them senseless, and refused to support his own brainchild—the college—when he discovered that it "had become a battlefield on which an only partially submerged religious war was being waged."[29]

On the other hand Smith saw the college as part of an eminently sensible and patrician ecclesiastical scheme which would Anglicize Philadelphia's motley citizenry by training the sons of her wealthy leaders in Church of England graces. Smith wished all might become loyal members of an enlightened British Empire. So too did Franklin, but not in the same way. For the sage of Philadelphia the church was a utilitarian institution, not a political one, whose "usefulness to society" was evidenced in "social worship" the purpose of which was to "further religion, increase unanimity and occasion [by shortening its prayers, homilies, and so forth] a more frequent attendance on the worship of God."[30] Both men wished to exercise control, and alternately they fumed and pouted at each other in one of the more famous colonial quarrels.[31] It was an argument to some degree within the household of Episcopalian faith and Pennsylvanian politics and for that all the more rancorous.[32]

There was no doubt that William Smith was a cantankerous person. In his personality he had a "love of battle, zeal for a cause and inability to concede any virtue in his opponents."[33] To Franklin he was a "common Scribbler of Libels and false abusive papers . . . against Publick Bodies and private

Persons, and thereby keeping up Party Heats in the Province."[34] To another contemporary, Presbyterian Samuel Purviance (fl. 1766), he was an equally dangerous character. Purviance rued the fact that "the Flower of our Youth are every Day perverted by the Intrigues of that designing, subtile Mortal Dr. Smith."[35] John Adams in 1774 confided in his diary that "there is an Appearance of Art" about him, and, two years later in the summer of 1776, the Massachusetts' patriot wrote his beloved Abigail, "I have never heard a single person speak well of any Thing about him but his Abilities which are generally allowed to be good."[36] Elsewhere Adams wrote in 1774 that he had met "Dr. Smith, Provost of the Colledge, who is looking up to Government for an American Episcopate and a Pair of lawn Sleeves. Soft, polite, insinuating, adulating, sensible, learned, industrious, indefatigable; he has art enough and refinement upon art, to make impressions."[37] Battle, intrigue, and art: to these one must add a predilection to more than an occasional pull at the madeira bottle. Perhaps teetotaling Benjamin Rush best summed up Smith's character, when he wrote,

> He possessed genius, taste, and learning. As a teacher he was perspicuous and agreeable, and as a preacher solemn, eloquent, and expressive in a high degree. Unhappily his conduct in all his relations and situations was opposed to his talents and profession. . . . He appears to have been a nondescript in the history of man.[38]

William Smith's most lasting contribution to colonial life lay in the educational goals he pursued. His *Mirania* not only set the stage for higher learning in Philadelphia, but its emphasis on gentlemanly education influenced Samuel Johnson at King's College as well. Despite their theological differences, epitomized by diverging judgments of Samuel Clarke and Archbishop Tillotson, Smith's and Johnson's institutions were remarkably similar. That similarity was to continue until the mid-1760s. Johnson even went so far as to place the works of the suspect Clarke on his students' reading list. Between them, the two men restored the this-worldly, Renaissance idea that the Greek and Latin classics provided the proper setting for the acquisition of virtue and wisdom. Of course, there was nothing new in the study of the classics: all American colleges demanded their mastery until the end of the nineteenth century.[39] What was new with Smith and Johnson was the fact that Puritan suspicion of the snares and vanities of pagan literature was missing. Gone were the disjunctions between God and humankind which could only be overcome by a laboriously wrought series of covenants. God was now a friend, not an adversary. Now in his benignity God seemed to encourage in his creatures the development of those very qualities commended by Cicero: eloquence, independence of character, and self-control. In these colleges, the study of Greek and Latin authors was carried on within a world described by Samuel Johnson as "one harmonious, beautiful, and useful system." That system was governed, not by the "harsh" God of Calvin and Edwards, but by a benevolent deity who himself infused into his creatures a sense of amiability and altruism. As a result, mutual dependence, well-being, and happiness were ends sought by the presidents of King's College and the College of Philadelphia and, they sincerely hoped, by their students as well.[40]

Behind the curricula of the three Episcopalian institutions of higher learning lay the common tradition of the moderate English Enlightenment. It was represented by the Cambridge Platonists: John Locke (1632–1704); Bishop Berkeley; William Wollaston (1660–1724); Anthony Cooper, earl of Shaftesbury; Francis Hutcheson (1694–1746); Bishop Joseph Butler (1692–1752); Paul de Rapin (1661–1725); and even Clarke.[41] These provided the general intellectual atmosphere. There were others who specifically shaped educational attitudes and programs of the Episcopalian institutions in novel ways: Robert Dodsley, an educational reformer; David Fordyce of the University of Aberdeen; the Frenchman Charles Rollin; and again Locke, whose treatise of 1693, *Some Thoughts Concerning Education*, they all read.[42] It was Fordyce's revamping of the curriculum of Marischal College which inspired William Smith to create an institution in America along similar lines. Both Johnson and Franklin were aware of Fordyce's reforming tract, *Dialogues Concerning Education*.[43] All three Americans read the works of these European educational reformers as well as each other's writings on the subject.[44]

The classics of Greece and Rome were necessary for the proper training of clerics and lawyers, but the curriculum, Samuel Johnson judged, "must train them in all the virtuous habits and all such useful knowledge as may render them creditable to their families and friends, ornaments to their country, and useful to the public weal in their generations."[45] What should be taught? It was the "practical arts": agriculture, surveying, accounting, navigation, and, at the College of Philadelphia, astronomy and chemistry. In addition, both at Philadelphia and New York, modern languages, belles lettres, politics, and the sciences of geography and chronology were taught at the expense of the more traditional metaphysics.[46] With these new curricula, Johnson, Smith, and Franklin were developing institutions which paralleled other American colleges, notably Harvard, Yale, and Princeton, though King's and the College of Philadelphia were smaller than these Puritan schools.[47]

Smith's and Johnson's institutions differed from the older schools in that they were founded at a time when the new sciences of Newton, Locke, and others had become a fact of American intellectual life. Neither in New York or Philadelphia did an older tradition exist which had to be elbowed aside to make way for the new learning. Together with the College of William and Mary, the Episcopal schools were more explicit in their purpose of educating young men to be "useful members of society." To this end at Smith's college a third or more of students' time was spent studying some form of science.[48] In addition, the College of Philadelphia and William and Mary introduced courses in law and government earlier than Harvard and Yale. Of such a utilitarian bent was William and Mary that a professorship in "law and police" was founded.[49] Moreover, at Philadelphia and at King's, in 1765 and 1767, respectively, the first medical schools in America were started.[50]

Here the similarities between the two new, northern Episcopalian colleges ended. Quite different lines of development emerged in the 1760s. The College of Philadelphia, despite the fact that a cleric served as its leader, became the most "secular" center of higher education in colonial America, more so than either Harvard or William and Mary.[51] This was due to William Smith himself, who produced no such work as Johnson's *Elementa Philosophica* from which to teach his senior students those "metaphysical notions," as Smith termed his friend's system. When Smith wrote a careful and somewhat grudging introduction to the English edition of the *Elementa*, he noted Johnson's "sincere zeal to vindicate the rights of Deity, and a just abhorrence of the absurd system of the materialists." But, he judged, Johnson had gone farther toward Berkeleyan idealism "than will be justified by some philosophers." Clearly Smith felt so for, he continued, "If he [Johnson] errs . . . it is on the safe side, by referring all to God and considering him as all in all. This, if it is an error, is an error of piety, into which some men of the purest hearts, most exalted virtue, and sprightly genii of this age have fallen before him."[52] Smith's own "cool, dispassionate mind" would, he hoped, be followed by others who would prove equally appreciative though remain equally critical.

In terms of the development of the College of Philadelphia over which this dispassionate critic reigned for over twenty-five years, it is clear that he did not declare as explicitly as Johnson did for King's that "the Chief thing that is aimed at in this college is to teach and engage the children to know God in Jesus Christ, and to love and serve Him in all sobriety, godliness, and righteousness of life."[53] No doubt the cosmopolitan character of Philadelphia necessitated caution in such matters lest a similar statement of conviction lead others in that denominationally variegated city to discover an Episcopalian plot. In some measure the lack of a clear statement of faith was due to the fact that the college depended upon an alliance between Episcopalians and Presbyterians for its existence. In this respect it has been said that "either of these two strong Protestant groups served to check any obvious shifts to favor one over the other."[54] The result was a lack of denominational distinctiveness.

King's, on the other hand, had been founded by a group of aristocratic Episcopalians whose Anglican esprit de corps was marked. Their purpose was to provide higher education for their privileged children within the pale of England's established religion. Most of the trustees were either Episcopalians or "good friends" of the church.[55] When Myles Cooper (1737–1785) succeeded Johnson as president of the college in 1763, this process of Anglicanization gathered momentum. In the early years of the college, the institution was shaped by Yale, the University of Aberdeen, and Johnson's Berkeleyanism. With Cooper, the educational model which served the college was no longer Yale but Oxford.[56] This jovial and sociable poet wished to make New York's college not only into a university complex with its own secondary academy, medical school, and hospital, but he desired that King's College should become a royally chartered institution which would serve as the educational center of the Episcopal church throughout the colonies. Cooper sought to institute "Oxonian" higher faculties of law, medicine, and theology, to promote loyalty to church and crown, and to make his college a bulwark of the established order of Britain's empire.[57] Cooper was unable to obtain his royal charter, despite a trip to England for that purpose. Southern support for the college proved equally elusive in spite of Cooper's trips south. The most he could do was to make use of the New York-New Jersey high church axis, but by then it was too late. Revolution quashed the dream, and Cooper returned to England in May 1775.

Episcopalian Enlightenment theology, whether in its more conservative form at King's or in its more radical form at the College of Philadelphia, was by no means limited to these two institutions. The rationalist bent of a significant portion of the church is represented by important names in the history of revolutionary America: George Washington (1732–1799), George Mason (1725–1792), Edmund Pendleton (1721–1803), and John Marshall (1755–1835). These deistical statesmen—all Virginians—were hardly aware of exalted high church assertions. All that their God required of them was that they should "better their mental powers" and love him and his creatures.[58] In the case of Washington, for whom being a vestryman was a matter of course, Christology was the least of religious doctrines. It was simply not a matter of interest or importance to him "to believe in the divinity and resurrection of Christ and his atonement for the sins of man and to participate in the sacrament of the Lord's Supper . . . as requisites for Christian faith." He took the things of religion "as he found them existing,

215

and was content in his observance of worship according to the received forms of the Episcopal Church in which he was brought up." The doctrine of divine providence was about as far as the father of the country cared to go theologically. As one recent historian has wryly observed, it was fortunate for the public image of the Episcopal church during and after the revolution that he and others like him went at least that far.[59]

There were other deistical Episcopalians in the middle colonies. They are of greater interest, but confirmation was no more attainable for them than for the Virginians. Chief among the most vocal deists who frequented Episcopalian places of worship were Cadwallader Colden of New York and Benjamin Franklin of Philadelphia. Both wrote on the subject of religion as well as being political figures in their day.[60]

Colden, who served as a member of the governor's council for fifty-five years, was a fussy administrator, forever full of plans to set matters right. His chief concerns were the protection of the frontier in New York, just treatment of the Indians, and stopping the inequities of colonial land grabbing. Often he lambasted the provincial aristocracy of the Hudson River valley for their ostentation.[61] Time and again he sought firmer gubernatorial control and closer ties to Great Britain.[62] Historian, mathematician, botanist, and philosopher, he corresponded with the greatest scientists of his day.[63] He was a founder of the American Philosophical Society.

For Colden, the "Archeus of Nature" (God) was the originator of a grand system of the universe. In deistic terms, Colden allowed that this intelligent being "gives the action [of the universe] such direction as best suits its own purpose."[64] Colden, however, rejected Berkeleyan idealism in which the universe was in the mind of God. He wondered that anyone could believe such nonsense and was incredulous that it had "extended to America, where you will find men of sense advocates of it."[65] Somewhere between his deism and his materialism lurked Christian morality and the Bible. But neither Christianity nor its scripture should invite theological speculation on scientific matters. The sole purpose of religion was to instruct in morality.[66] It was a position well described by Nelson Burr as "Pious Utilitarianism."[67] Colden banned from the circle of the enlightened all priests, popish and pagan alike, especially the Jesuits. He thought Protestant clergy ought to be barred from controlling education. Jesus was for the western world what Confucius was for the eastern: the teacher of "certain Rules of Living well."[68] This meant that Jesus emerged as an antirevolutionary, conservative, Lockean Whig who supported the SPCK and the SPG and who might, as Colden was, be made an honorary member of the Mohawk tribe.

While Colden concerned himself with the politics of right living, his friend Benjamin Franklin interested himself in the liturgy which might accompany it. In the spring of 1773, Thomas Jefferson received a package from Benjamin Franklin. It contained a book titled *Abridgement of the Book of Common Prayer*. Within the flyleaf was inscribed: "To Thomas Jefferson from his friend Benjamin Franklin, February 3, 1773."[69] The two authors of this work were Franklin and Francis Dashwood (d. 1781), an English nobleman. *Abridgement* was something of a first: never before in the Church of England had laymen alone undertaken the task of revising the prayer book. They would not do so again. There is no doubt that Franklin and Dashwood were quite serious in their desire that the work be used by Episcopalians. That Anglicans in England and their fellow churchmen in America rejected the efforts of the two reformers is understandable for the book reflected the deism, however moderate, of the English and American Enlightenment. Not even a sizeable minority was ready then or later for such an unorthodox change. Subsequently Episcopalian church historians of the nineteenth and twentieth centuries have failed even to mention the existence of Franklin's and Dashwood's revision, despite the fact that Jefferson's personal copy has been available to scholars in the Library of Congress for over 150 years. This silence would be curious were it not explainable by the universal embarrassment which the prayer book caused.

Franklin and Dashwood achieved their surprising, deistic results without changing a single word. They merely excised what they did not like. Their excisions from the original text of the Book of Common Prayer turned out to be all of the longer, uniquely historical references to the words and acts of Jesus himself. In addition the authors removed whatever allusions they could to the sinfulness of the world and man as it stood in relation to the holiness of God. Divine pardon was made general and lenitive rather than personal and humbling. Gone from the service of Holy Communion were the rehearsal of Christ's words of institution at the last Supper and the "prayer of humble access" before the communion of the faithful. From the baptismal office, Franklin and Dashwood removed the reference to "the devil and all his works, the vain pomp and glory of the world, and the sinful desires of the flesh."[70] Franklin introduced the book with a preface whose benignty must have overjoyed the hearts of those restless with the archaisms of long services. There were, declared the Pennsylvanian, too many repetitions so that "the mind wanders and the fervency of devotion is slackened." The Lord had "given us a short prayer as an example, and censured the Heathen for thinking to be heard because of much speaking."[71]

If these changes were not enough to make the conservers of tradition wince, the circumstances surrounding the revision by Franklin and Dashwood would, if they had been fully known, have shocked many. As Alfred Aldridge had described him, Dashwood was a vigorous lecher "with

217

a taste for spectacular sex, blasphemy, and the macabre."[72] Dressed as Franciscan friars the members of Dashwood's infamous group, the Hell-Fire Club, as it was known, or sometimes as the Monks of Medmenham Abbey, conducted lascivious, mock-religious rites. At these affairs prostitutes and other female visitors dressed as nuns and joined in as "devotional" participants. Probably Franklin witnessed and participated in Dashwood's ceremonies and "sacraments." At West Wycombe mockery of medieval "superstition," that is, whatever contradicted deistic faith in nature and reason, was given full reign. Since celibacy was seen as notoriously unenlightened, it was overtly rejected in the name of right living. On the other hand, Dashwood and Franklin had a genuine interest in medieval style and liturgy and thought it worthy of emulation. It was a long way from the Old South Church in Puritan Boston to Medmenham Abbey at West Wycombe, yet for Franklin an occasional *mésalliance,* not itself lacking in benevolence, was one thing, industriousness and doing one's duty, quite another.

To what extent can Franklin be called an Episcopalian? The answer is: in a limited sense. For one thing, he knew nothing intellectually of the liberal Anglican tradition with which he might in the normal course of things have acquainted himself.[73] Only at its most extended line of influence was he touched by the latitudinarians.[74] He read Tillotson, but so did everyone else. Franklin cared little for the particulars of Anglican theology. He agreed with Shaftesbury that virtue was not dependent upon religion at all but upon the subordination of selfish to social affections. No doubt God first implanted the seed in the human minds from which the moral order grew. Franklin did not care to prove the point. Enough to look into his own heart for evidence of morality and to accept without cavil the Shaftesburian assumption that moral integrity pervaded the universe.[75]

Beyond that, he found to his liking a non-Calvinist church which appeared in its stately liturgy and ministerial orderliness to best exemplify these beliefs and which promised on their basis to assure the formation of pious and useful citizens. Franklin could even agree with the conclusion of his friend Granville Sharp (1735–1813) when the latter wrote that it would be advantageous to restore "the *primitive Apostolic form of Episcopal Government* and the ancient Freedom of Election to Ecclesiastical Offices."[76] Such views were not uncongenial to other Episcopalians and even to such freethinking members of the English hierarchy as Jonathan Shipley (1714–1788), bishop of St. Asaph, with whom Franklin maintained close, personal ties.[77] Finally, the very fact that he went to the effort of careful abridgement and publication of his prayer book indicates a more than ordinary concern for the larger affairs of the church in which he habitually worshiped.

When Franklin was laid to rest at Christ Church, the preacher for the occasion was his old archenemy William Smith. In the utter incongruity and unsuitableness of the choice of preacher, we may discern a symbolic appropriateness: the Enlightenment proved a more enduring bond than politics. As with the two deistical churchmen, Franklin and Smith, so with Johnson, Colden, Auchmuty, and, in England, Sharp and Shipley; they constituted a circle of friends and correspondents. Some were loyalists in the Revolution, others, patriots; some were more radical religiously than others; some, high churchmen, others not. But what unified them all was a degree of trust in human rationality, a concurrent demythologizing of Christian faith, and the belief that it was up to humankind, not God, to see that men and women lived happily in this life because they lived morally.

CHAPTER 10
Loyalists, the Episcopate, and the Revolution

In England in 1748, Thomas Sherlock (1678–1761), the court prelate, was elevated from the bishopric of Salisbury to that of more prestigious London. Sherlock was the leader of the Tory party in the Hanoverian church. At Fulham Palace, London, he succeeded the hard-working Whig bishop Edmund Gibson (1669–1748), who had exercised considerable organizational influence on the American church for over 25 years. Where Gibson had welcomed responsibility for the colonial churches, Sherlock showed himself to be the opposite. The new bishop of London sought to divest himself of the financial albatross of plantation affairs. Sherlock determined that a clean, swift break would suffice: he simply refused to seek confirmation of his authority over the colonial church—a necessary legal step for each succeeding bishop in the capital. Never one to stir himself unnecessarily, Sherlock sat tight and did nothing. It could not have been a more unpropitious moment for inaction. The Episcopal church in America was just beginning to enjoy the fruits of the antirevivalist backlash. She needed counsel, aid, and inspiration in order to consolidate her gains. Bishop Sherlock's answer to this opportunity was to suggest that the ecclesiastical care of the colonies be divided among his brethren on the episcopal bench of the House of Lords. With that in mind, he delivered to Archbishop of Canterbury Thomas Herring (1693–1757) a "Scheme for parcelling out ye Plantation Jurisdiction." It was an unwelcome document on the desk of Herring. The archbishop expressed dubiety: fellow bishops would be unlikely to receive with gratitude the additional paperwork, not to mention the extra expense.[1]

The issue was further complicated when the SPG met on 7 April 1749 to discuss the settlement of Nova Scotia, a province within the usual jurisdiction of the bishop of London. While Sherlock was absent from the meeting, an unusually large crowd of clergy and laity were in enthusiastic attendance. Nor was the conversation limited to Nova Scotia. The question of the state of the American church in general was raised, along with the prickly issue of an American episcopate. As a result of the SPG's meeting, Sherlock quickly abandoned his scheme to parcel out American jurisdictions to fellow bishops. Ever one to recognize an opportunity, he assumed with unaccustomed celerity the leadership in the reawakened episcopal cause. Here was the perfect way in which to rid himself of his vexatious American problem. Speedily Sherlock dispatched a Mr. A. Spencer to take the American pulse on the episcopal issue. At the same time he requested from the government a deputy to carry out the day-to-day work of colonial administration.

By June 1749, Spencer had reported back to his superior that, while objections had been raised to an American bishop in Philadelphia and New York, he had been able to allay fears. "I replied," wrote the agent, "that I believed that he [a suffragan bishop] would have no more Power over the Laity, than what the Commissaries in the colonies already had."[2] This information found its way to London in company with ominous rumbles of nonconformist thunder emanating from far-off Connecticut and Massachusetts. The government sensed difficulty, and, as the summer wore on, Sherlock discovered that he could not even get a reply to his request for aid from the duke of Newcastle. It was now the government's turn to sit tight. Might he not, Sherlock wrote the duke, have "Bps. [bishops] abroad & some help for myself at home?"[3] When Newcastle finally replied, it was to accuse the bishop of laziness, lack of public spirit, and lack of trust in those wise men who had long had the welfare of the American church under consideration.[4] Hurriedly, Sherlock tried to cover his mistake. The London prelate assured the duke that none was more loyal to the crown or more interested in "putting the Ch[urch] abroad on a true and primitive footing" than he. Were he to be an instrument of such a work, concluded Sherlock blandly, "I shou'd indeed think it the glory of my life."[5]

Bishop Sherlock had achieved his point. The issue of the welfare of the American church and the possibility of an episcopal presence in the colonies had been raised in earnest, and, whatever his motives, the bishop of London had become the central figure in the drama. He would continue to be so, though by a strange twist of fate the credit for raising the episcopal issue in relation to America would go to another.

In the meantime, the agents of New England nonconformity, Eliakim Palmer (1707–1749) and the Britisher, Dr. Benjamin Avery (d. 1764), were busy. These able lobbyists against an American bishop were momentarily victorious against what Palmer described as "Ecclesiastical Tyranny." Palmer and Avery assured provincials in Massachusetts "that for the present a Stop is put to it." When the House of Representatives in the Bay Colony foolishly responded with a public declaration of thanks that the

221

"mischievous . . . design" for an American bishop had been dropped, Archbishop Herring lost all patience. To Herring it seemed "harsh . . . to be told in some sort by an Assembly of Dissenters, That Episcopacy is contrary to the Liberties of a Protestant Country at a time when Independents enjoy uncontrolled Toleration under the Establishment."[6] Legally it was a good point, justly, if haughtily, made. The feeling now grew among the hierarchy of the church that something must be done to put the American church in regular order. Once again it was Thomas Sherlock who came forward with yet another plan entitled "Some Considerations humbly offered by Thomas[,] Bishop of London relating to Ecclesiastical Government in his Majesty's Dominions in America,"[7] and which included what has up to this time been misnamed the "Butler Plan."

This plan questioned the entire arrangement whereby supervision of colonial churches had fallen to the bishop of London. That responsibility rested, Sherlock boldly claimed, in the crown alone by virtue of the Act of Supremacy. Since as bishop he had not taken out the customary patent of jurisdiction with the solicitor-general, he was not now, nor had he been since 1748, the ecclesiastical authority for America. Moreover, judged Sherlock, the bishop of London's patent in the past had been so severely limited as to make a mockery of ecclesiastical control. While he might have power over commissaries and clergy, he had no authority over churchwardens, nonconformist ministers, or counterfeit parsons of the colonial church. Laymen could not testify before him. If he handed down poor judgment, appeal was not made to the church hierarchy but to secular officers of the state and, ultimately, to the king in council. If the bishop of London found a commissary's policy or a clergyman's action improper, the sentence which the bishop handed down became an accusation as both defendent and plaintiff stood equally before the bar of higher secular authority.[8] With these criticisms went Sherlock's suggestions for nonpolitical, nontax supported bishops for America.

"Some Considerations" was a stunning document. Sherlock had challenged custom, policy, and tradition. This intrepid ecclesiastic had attempted to influence directly the government's colonial policy on the extremely sensitive issue of religion. Moreover, the church in America was a pawn in the hands of cynical politicians. This announcement, made in the early months of 1750, was not addressed to the Pelham ministry or to the bishops in convocation but directly to the king in council. In addition, Sherlock boldly decided to go public. He arranged for two thousand copies of his composition to be printed. In shunning back room politics, he was guilty of an un-British breach of etiquette. On 8 May, Sherlock added his final touch by laying his proposal for nonpolitical bishops for America before a mass meeting of the SPG.[9] He had chosen his moment well: Herring was absent from the capital, and George II was off in his beloved Hanover. Once again the government moved to quash what Prime Minister Horace Walpole called this "improper and irregular Step." In addition Sherlock's action raised for Walpole the "distinction of High Church & Low Church wch has occasioned great Mischiefs in this divided Country in former Reigns, and has happily laid a Sleep for some years."[10]

To the end Sherlock maintained the charade of unselfish concern. As late as 1752 he wrote to Samuel Johnson that he "should be tempted to throw off all this care [of the bishopric of London] . . . were it not for the sake of preserving even an appearance of an Episcopal Church in the plantations." Others, he more truthfully confided, "who have more power and influence do not see the thing in the light we do."[11]

How did Sherlock's proposals for an American bishop come to be called the Butler Plan, and how did the name of the famous Joseph Butler, bishop of Durham and author of the *Analogy of Religion,* come to be associated with the episcopal cause in the American colonies? The answer serves to illuminate the politics of the bishop controversy. The name Butler Plan was attached in the 1760s to Bishop Sherlock's "Some Considerations" by the Reverend East Apthorp (d. 1816).[12] It was a brilliant exchange of names, one likely to further the high church campaign for a bishop by disarming Congregational resistance. Sherlock was a Tory; Butler, a Whig. What is more, the bishop of Durham did not believe in competition with dissenters in American missionary activity on the part of the Church of England. In 1739, Butler had preached a sermon before the SPG in which he suggested that the "design before us [of ecumenical missionary endeavor] being . . . unquestionably good, it were much to be wished that serious men *of all denominations would join it.* "[13] Among liberal Congregationalist ministers in New England, Butler, then bishop of Bristol, was considered, as Jonathan Mayhew (1720–1766) put it, "A great ornament of the episcopal order, and of the Church of England; the clearness of whose head, the precision of whose language, and the goodness of whose heart, are so conspicuous in all his writings."[14] Such an ornament, thought Apthorp, ought to prove useful. If New Englanders would listen to Butler, then Butler they would have.

In 1763, the bishop controversy in America was in full swing, and Apthorp, Arthur Browne of Portsmouth, and Thomas Secker, the new archbishop of Canterbury, were engaged in vigorous debate with Mayhew. In response to criticism that the SPG was proselyting among Congregationalists, Apthorp had written a pamphlet in which he declared that the purpose of the society was simply to provide maintenance for Episcopal ministers in the colonies.[15] He further cited authorities who did not believe in competing with American nonconformity. Unconvinced, Mayhew answered Apthorp's disclaimer with a sonorous blast in which he accused Episcopalians of setting altar against altar.[16] In so doing, Mayhew quoted Bishop Butler at length and made skillful use of the appeals of that apologist for charity, ecumenicity, and mutual encouragement.[17] At that point, Browne and Secker entered the scene. Browne failed even to mention Butler, though he dealt in detail with an episcopate for America.[18] In an anonymous reply to Mayhew, Archbishop Secker struck a conciliatory note and added, in response to the Congregationalist's mention of Butler, that the bishop of Durham had indeed been a friend to the SPG and had bequeathed £500 to the society.[19] Unlike Apthorp, who had flatly stated that Congregational worship was no better "to the Episcopalians than Popery or Mahometanism,"[20] Secker sought to smooth ruffled, nonconformist feathers. Members of the Church of England, he reassured Massachusetts liberals, intended to behave like gentlemen.[21] They meant to hatch no plot to root out New England's Protestant establishments and were not above altering the measures of the SPG to prove it. While the case of an Episcopal church without bishops "never had its parallel in the Christian World," let New England know, Secker reassured his readers, that American bishops would not be vested with "any authority now exercised by Provincial Governors or subordinate Magistrates or infringe or diminish any Privileges and Liberties enjoyed by any of the Laity, even of our own Communion."[22]

The lesson was not lost on Apthorp, who proved himself to be almost too apt a pupil. When his next move in the debate came, he took his cue from Archbishop Secker. Aware of Mayhew's use of Butler's charitable attitude, Apthorp noted that "there have been many proposals for bishops in America. One of them perhaps may have peculiar weight with the Doctor [Mayhew]. I mean that made in the year 1750 by the excellent Bishop Butler, in the doctor's own judgment 'a great ornament of the episcopal order and of the Church of England.' "[23] Butler quickly replaced Sherlock. Apthorp nearly protested too much: he had been favored by an unnamed gentleman of distinction in Boston with a copy of the plan for nonpolitical bishops which had been in Butler's own handwriting. This plan, he continued smoothly, was so exactly similar to the one in Secker's anonymous *Answer to Dr. Mayhew's Observations* "that it cannot be doubted, they are the same, and that it is the only one intended to be put into execution."[24] Thus the name Butler Plan came into common usage. The bishop of Durham's authorship was not doubted then, nor has it been ever since.[25]

In the 1760s, with the elevation of Thomas Secker to the see of Canterbury, issue of an American episcopate came to a head. Unlike Bishop Sherlock of London, there is little doubt of Secker's genuine interest in the

American church. Samuel Johnson himself recognized this fact. In 1760, three years before the Mayhew controversy, Johnson acted boldly. The old king, George II, had died. Through Secker, Johnson wished to capture the attention and aid of young George III, who had just assumed his royal responsibilities. Johnson thought he knew the mind of his clerical superior in England. The new archbishop had known the new king since childhood, had baptized, confirmed, and crowned him, and in the coming year would solemnize his marriage. In a letter to Secker written on 12 July 1760, Johnson had appended fourteen far-reaching "Questions Relating to the Union and Government of the Plantations."[26] Johnson's "Questions" were to be sent to William Pitt and the Earl of Halifax if Secker saw fit; Secker did not. Nor would that discerning prelate adopt Johnson's suggestion that the "Questions" appear in the London press. The American had had the temerity to suggest that not only should the colonial church receive a bishop but that the entire provincial system in the New World should be reordered. "Questions" was a powerful and thorough document. It went far beyond earlier episcopal schemes and, given the new political situation in England, was conceived with far greater hope of success. Long winter evenings during a temporary retirement at Stratford in 1759 and "conversations with several gentlemen of good understanding and public spirit" had hatched the strategy.[27] The next move must come from Canterbury.

Secker was appalled by the blitheness of Johnson in seeking to instruct England's men of affairs in public. The American's provincial enthusiasm was politically insane. Johnson had misjudged the archbishop's mind. To publish such blatant queries "to the world beforehand, instead of waiting till the time comes and then applying privately to the persons whose advice the King will take about them is likely to raise opposition and prevent success." No doubt Johnson's ideas were "in the main right, so far as they may be practicable," but "you will pardon the frankness with which I tell you my thoughts. Whatever good I can make of your notions, I will. But the use which you propose is not agreeable to my judgment."[28] Secker was the best friend American Episcopalians ever had.[29] The somber defender of Christianity against rationalists and enthusiasts alike had spent a quarter of a century in quiet diplomacy in behalf of the American church.[30] It was to no avail.

The intercolonial debate went on between Episcopalians and their liberal Congregational opponents. With the retirement of Apthorp in 1765, the deaths of Mayhew in 1766 and Secker in 1768, and with the advancing age of Johnson, the cudgels were taken up by fresh contestants, Thomas Bradbury Chandler for the Episcopalians and Charles Chauncy (1705–1787) for the Congregationalists.

Chandler was a man of high seriousness with respect to the "importance of the sacerdotal office."[31] He was also a lover of music, a convivial host, and a notable trencherman. Chandler was as diligent in his study of the church fathers as he was witty and apt with his pen. Despite the fact that he believed he should "be continually advancing towards a higher degree of perfection, and shining more and more unto the perfect day," he could laugh at himself and in doing so employ vivid simile. In the midst of convention business in 1766, he confided to Samuel Johnson that his desk was piled high "with convention papers as a Dutchman sometimes is with those oyster-shells after supper."[32] His favorite theologians were Jerome, Chrysostom, Basil of Caesarea, and above all Erasmus of Rotterdam.[33] Conspicuous by their absence were Luther and the English reformers. From much study, Chandler developed high conceptions of the disciplines of the priest, who occupied a "hazardous station" demanding "unremitting application." Not surprisingly, his own twenty-eight year ministry at St. John's Church, Elizabeth Town, New Jersey (1747–1775), paid off in remarkable growth. The church became one of the largest and most influential in the middle colonies.[34] Its vigorous rector tried publicly to show "Charity, Candor and moderation" toward dissenters. With kindliness Chandler comforted the sick of whatever denomination, and he exercised generosity outwardly in "his appraisal of a fellow minister's weakness."[35] Yet in his private correspondence he vented his spleen at the "craft of the Jesuits [revivalistic dissenters]," whose words sank "into the language of fisherwomen." To waste time confuting them was "like charging a cannon for the destruction of vermin." A "small squib or flash would do better execution."[36] His fellow clergy of the Church of England did not escape his acid pen; not even Thomas Secker escaped censure. When that unfortunate archbishop failed to deliver the episcopate to his American charges, Chandler judged him of "timid disposition." "What has the Church ever gained," cried the New Jersey minister, "and what have its enemies not gained by that thing which the courtesy of England calls prudence?" Let the church just once follow the maxim "honesty is the best policy."[37]

It was love and respect for tradition, both ecclesiastical and political, which Chandler brought to the second stage of the bishop controversy and his debate with Charles Chauncy. In June 1767 at the instigation of the aging Samuel Johnson, the New Jersey rector began to assume the role of chief American defender of episcopacy. That order had ruled the church in the lost catholic world of Richard Hooker, and Chandler approved the succession which was the key element in the continuation of that world.[38] Thereafter he cited the usual points: the need for regular church government, the lack of episcopal supervision in the American Episcopal church, the difficulties Episcopalians had encountered whenever they suggested nonpolitical bishops, and their right as an American denomination to "Perfect Equality."[39] There was little new in the argument itself or in the way in which it was conducted. After Chauncy's reply,[40] the point-counterpoint conduct of the controversy became apparent, and the participants, not to mention the reading public, were soon exhausted. In the year 1771, Chandler threw diplomacy and discretion to the winds and attacked the basis of the dissenters' ministry itself. New Englanders in the seventeenth century had begun ministerial "Succession *de novo*."[41] Until that time, Chandler argued, authority had been unitary.

For three years Chandler fell silent. Then in 1774 he published his *Friendly Address to All Reasonable Americans on the Subject of Our Political Confusions*. In that work the Elizabeth Town rector went far beyond the ecclesiastical issues which separated Episcopalians from dissenters. Now the point of contention was loyalty to the crown. He implored his fellow countrymen to awake to common sense and to "avoid the wrath of powerful England."[42] Even here he could not let go of the religious issue. As he saw the specter of disloyal democracy looming on the political horizon, he declared that Great Britain's national church had always "been a great obstacle in the way of those republican fanaticks." No republic, he cried, would ever tolerate the Church of England. All citizens would be encumbered "with that Presbyterian yoke of bondage."[43] However much he acknowledged the Butler Plan for nonpolitical bishops, church and crown continued to occupy opposite sides of the same coin.[44] On the ecclesiastical side, he held that "rather than say that without religion there is no Church, Chandler would say that without the Church there is no religion." On the political side "he would admit that without the king there can be no state."[45] As the unhappy churchman had once attacked the hierarchy of the English church, so now he found himself more and more dependent upon the waning power and popularity of the imperial government which supported that hierarchy.

If Chandler failed to bring bishops to his church or stem the tide of revolution, he did discover a new way of ordering ecclesiastical affairs, a way which would bear immensely important consequences for the future: conventions. If other Americans could meet in congresses and assemblies of protest, Episcopalians could do the same. The result was the prologue to self-government.[46] At Perth Amboy in October 1765 and again at Shrewsbury a year later, the first representative conventions of leading northern Episcopalian clergy took place. From New York, Connecticut, Pennsylvania, and New Jersey, delegates learned a measure of cooperation which amounted to a revolutionary step for American churchmen. Hence-

227

forth, Episcopalians took matters into their own hands more often. It was a lesson not to be forgotten in the 1780s when the new denomination had to be organized, now in the American republic. No matter that for all his adroit chairmanship Chandler's alliance fell apart.[47] Through his efforts, churchmen learned that they could meet and act together.

"One thing above all is clear," wrote Carl Bridenbaugh of the years 1766–1776: "the colonial clergy [of the Church of England] formed the core of the American Tories."[48] Samuel Auchmuty, Jonathan Boucher (1736–1804), Thomas Chandler, Samuel Johnson, Samuel Seabury, John Vardill (1752–1811), Isaac Wilkins (d. 1830), and Charles Inglis (1734–1816) gave clear expression and occasional eloquence to the loyalist cause. There were other less well-known Episcopalian clergy, mostly New Englanders, who, from the days of the Stamp Act, helped write the loyalist platform: William Agar (fl. 1760–1776), Marmaduke Brown (d. 1771), James Scovil (1733–1808), Ebenezer Thompson (d. 1775), Joshua Wingate Weeks (d. 1804), and John Wiswall (d. 1812).[49]

What the "Anglican Tories"—really conservative Whigs—wrote in the 1770s should have been written in the 1750s or even earlier. By 1776 it was too late; the process of polarization had gone on too long. In the final analysis, all that these American loyalists could do was rely upon the power of British military presence, though "adherence to Britain was, at the time, only an incident in their battle with other Americans over what kind of institutions America ought to have."[50]

Preeminent among those who spoke for the cause of king and Parliament was Charles Inglis, rector of Trinity Church in New York, acting president of King's College from 1771 to 1776, loyalist pamphleteer, and intelligence agent for the crown. Charles Inglis was born in Ireland in 1734. For four generations his clerical family had displayed marked high church leanings. His great-grandfather, Archibald Inglis, was a Nonjuring clergyman who had moved to Ireland after 1689. For the next two generations, the Inglis family had served the Irish church. Charles was ordained to the ministry of England's establishment in 1758. He had first come to America in 1755. Ten years later he was assistant minister at Trinity Parish in New York. As a member of the board of governors of King's College, his influence in the city increased rapidly. With the imminent threat of revolution in 1775 he took it upon himself to tour the province and make determination of the size and ardor of loyalist support. In the process he learned of patriot movements and passed that information to Governor Tryon. When in July 1776 the governor, under the protection of the British army, fortified himself on Staten Island, Inglis wisely joined him.[51] The rector of Trinity Parish had shortly before closed his church rather than omit the requisite prayers for the king. Such an omission for Inglis would have desecrated the liturgy.[52]

Five months earlier, in February 1776, he had added pen to deed and answered Tom Paine's *Common Sense*. Written in less than a month, Inglis's *True Interest of America* remains the greatest loyalist pamphlet of the war, both for its political as well as for its philosophical perception. Publication was by no means easy. "At Risque not only of my Liberty, but of my Life," wrote the New York rector, "I drew up an Answer & had it printed here, but the Answer was no sooner advertised, than the whole Impression was seized by the Sons of Liberty and burnt."[53]

True Interest of America, along with James Chalmer's (1727?–1806) *Plain Truth,* has been termed by one historian the most important of "several spirited and lengthy responses" to Paine's *Common Sense.*[54] On the subject of Anglo-American history, the author of *The True Interest of America* showed that he was far from grandfather Archibald's Nonjuring views. In contrast to his forbear, Inglis spoke with the accent of a conservative Whig. Americans should beware, he wrote, lest they subvert the liberties won so conspicuously in 1688. At that crucial turning point in history, Americans and Britons became one people, he declared. Mutiny now and the "common bond that tied us together and by which our property is secured [will be] snapt asunder." When Parliament rid itself of James II, the constitution, he insisted, was fixed. It was an "aera ever memorable in the fair annals of Liberty." Precise limits had been set to the powers of both king and people. The Glorious Revolution produced no "darkened and slavish time," as Paine held, but a time when science's lamp burned brightly, "when Patriots of fame adorned the cause of freedom."[55] At that time democracy was assured for England and America. Indeed it had graced the House of Commons for six hundred years. England had the best of all possible governments, a mixed one, whose constituent parts were democracy, aristocracy, and monarchy. In all this Inglis argued fairly and ably.

It is with respect to aristocracy and monarchy that the truly revolutionary character of the American Revolution becomes clear. While all used the language of constitutionalism in the eighteenth century, Americans went far beyond Inglis. The rector of Trinity Parish would have been content to erect barriers against encroaching power on the settlement of 1689. Otherwise the world should remain the same. Patriots like Adams and Jefferson wished to "formulate new and more explicit charters of the people's liberties."[56] These, so they hoped, would root out tyranny forever. There lay their difference from Inglis. They found the hereditary distinctions of rank and class, implied as they were in the existence of monarchy and aristocracy, to

229

be tyrannous. Inglis found such inequalities healthy. They made for stability and order.

In Inglis's view, the rights of monarch, aristocrat, and democrat would be assured, each in its proper relation to the others. These were the same rights that had been won in 1689 and which in 1776 were being threatened by the rebellion. The colonials failed to see that such a balanced society was ordained by God. Inglis, in his reliance upon Richard Hooker's integrated world, recoiled from the mad assemblies of the revolutionaries. He wanted respect for tradition and for God, who through his established national church decreed those traditions. Paine had argued that society was produced because people have wants and that government was produced because they were wicked. Inglis chose to assault this argument by way of theology. "We may reasonably presume," he wrote, "there are neither wants nor wickedness in Heaven. According to this doctrine [Paine's] then, there can be no society nor government there; and yet we are assured to the contrary."[57] Not only in heaven but on earth as well, the existence of both society and government precede the individual. We are born into them. Whoever, he asked, was born out of them? As society cannot be without government, so government cannot be without law. They are all one, and anyone who tries to separate them is a fool. The constitutions of communities were not separate, *ad hoc* documents written in contractual form, but "that assemblage of laws, customs and institutions which form the general system; according to which the several powers of the state are distributed, and their respective rights secured to the different members of the community."[58]

In Inglis's view of the good society, unity and even more important, continuity were of the essence. They bolstered each other. Without unity, that is, mutual respect on the part of unequals for the laws which governed all persons and circumscribed their several powers, there could be only republican rage. That baneful passion had been exhibited all too clearly in the revolutionary committees and assemblies. Without continuity there would be fanatical enthusiasm and rejection of the "religious wisdom of the ages." For Inglis the "illustrious patriots" who settled the Hanoverian succession were the political guarantors of that wisdom, while the bishops of the church were its sanctified and sanctifying purveyors. When people challenged that wisdom and attacked the right of king and Parliament to pass laws for the empire, they gave evidence of an unholy desire to "loose the bands of society and overturn governments that have been founded on the wisdom of the ages, to make way for their own crude systems and thereby entail ruin and misery upon millions."[59]

American revolutionaries were going against what God ordained. That is why Episcopalian clergy like Inglis took up the pen in defense of church and nation. They felt themselves engaged in the defense of a holy cause: the right of God's community to be what he ordained it to be. For Adams, Otis, Jefferson, and others, the principles of the good society must be separated from those capricious authorities which governed the citizens of that society. Those principles should be written down in a constitution to which even Providence might on occasion refer for the refreshment of memory. For Inglis and the high church Episcopalians, a written constitution was a scrap of paper which could be changed at will. It was no substitute for the embodiment of authority in the person of a bishop, king, or prime minister in a continuous succession, whether apostolic, royal, or civil. Given such an incarnation in a fixed authority, law and principle would take care of themselves. While those individuals in whom such an embodiment took place might on occasion prove themselves to be sinful, in the long run through the persuasion of the church they would learn to behave morally, traditionally, and customarily.

For conservative Episcopalian Whigs like Inglis, the guarantors of the morality of society were the bishops. For the revolutionaries, bishops were no better than other men and no doubt, if memory served them correctly, a lot worse. As Ezra Stiles gently but very firmly informed Samuel Seabury in 1785, as the new Episcopal bishop of Connecticut he would be welcome at Yale's graduation ceremonies, but he could expect no special treatment since he would be in company with numerous other "bishops," i.e., the Congregational ministers, all as good as he. For Stiles, the traditional palliatives of ordination, dress, and address were unimpressive. For Seabury they were the outward signs of an invisible grace with which God clothed sinful men.

Three questions are of concern here and should be answered. First, did the desire for the episcopate and espousal of the loyalist cause represent a majority of Episcopalians and therefore the mind of the church? Second, what constituency did Charles Inglis and the other pro-British pamphleteers represent? Third, how did that constituency fit into the larger picture of loyalism in the revolutionary period?

Was the church as a whole in favor of obtaining the episcopate and was it predominately loyalist? On both counts the answer is no. Until very recently the impression was given that members of the Church of England in colonial America generally pined away because they did not have bishops.[60] The work of Frederick V. Mills, Sr., indicates clearly that nothing could be further from the truth. Wherever the church was established and at least nominally strong, those responsible for establishment and control of affairs saw no need to change the status quo. This attitude included clergy as well as laity. Richard Bland of Virginia not only did not want a resident bishop, but was averse to the bishop of London intermeddling in church affairs at all in

231

the tidewater. In South Carolina, episcopal oversight was not only resisted passively by that colony's self-satisfied ministers, but the Reverend Charles Martyn warned that it would be positively unsafe for a bishop to set foot in Charles Town. Along the Gold Coast, says Mills, there was never an episcopal controversy because there was no one to champion the cause of episcopal control.[61] As late as 1787, the Episcopal church in South Carolina instructed its delegates to the General Convention of the newly formed, postrevolutionary denomination to "insist as a condition of union that she [the church in South Carolina] should not be compelled to receive a bishop."[62] In Georgia not even the bishop of London received jurisdiction.

Only in Maryland are a few exceptions to the general apathy to an episcopate to be found. There Thomas Cradock sought episcopal supervision for pragmatic, not theological, reasons: the clergy needed to be kept in order and parishes delivered from those "Monsters of Wickedness [the Vestries]" whom they "sometimes labor under."[63] The Maryland clergy on the whole, however, did not want a bishop because such a presence "might upset their security and subject them to an ecclesiastical official who would discipline or coerce them into following a policy contrary to the interest of their parish."[64]

It was in Virginia in the early 1770s that the most dramatic opposition occurred. In an attempt to restore their besmirched clerical image, some of the clergy openly opposed the episcopal scheme. The Virginia House of Burgesses passed a resolution expressing its appreciation to the outspoken ministers,[65] and "this event spread like a news flash to Annapolis, Philadelphia, New York, and Boston."[66] Clergy in the Old Dominion who actively sought an American bishop were seen to be disrespectful to the legislature which had for so long overseen the affairs of the establishment. Even in high church Connecticut the laity showed no enthusiasm, while the SPG dragged its feet and did not encourage an American episcopate lest they themselves lose prestige.

Coupled with low church apathy about bishops went adherence to the more radical Whig patriot cause. It was people holding such views who made up the majority of Episcopalians in America, not the high church conservatives. The patriot Episcopalians' center of population was the Chesapeake Bay, and it is there that loyalism was weakest and resistance to an American episcopate was greatest.[67] If the colonial Church of England supplied a higher number of loyalists than any other single denomination, it must also be pointed out that on the whole an astonishing thing had happened, at least in the South: England's church had become American to the extent that it could claim more signers of the Declaration of Independence than any other. However nominal theologically those signers turned out to be, that fact would remain to tempt facile apologists in the future. In addition, in Virginia, the church's most populous province, approximately three-fifths of the lay members of the church supported the cause of independence from Great Britain.[68]

What was the composition of the constituency which Inglis and the other Tory pamphleteers addressed just prior to independence? These clerical, loyalist apologists were a distinct if vocal minority of the church's clergy. A mere handful, they were the ones who agitated most for a bishop and for closer ties with Britain. They even raised the level of the debate with the patriots to a discussion of the kind of society America should become. They did this as individuals and not as part of a unified, transcolonial loyalist movement. No doubt their constituents were among the 63 out of 286 solidly loyalist clergy of the colonial church in 1775, as well as being among the 2,908 loyalist claimants who filed for permanent compensation after the war.[69] Political unity for purposeful action simply did not exist among the newer, urban immigrants who tended to make up the bulk of the loyalists. No single leader or group of leaders emerged within loyalism as a whole to galvanize its followers.

If the clerical, Episcopalian pamphleteers were unable to speak with authority for a majority of their own church or even for their own order within the church, they surely were not representative of the religious caste of loyalism as a whole. Recent studies of loyalist refugees in both New Brunswick and Nova Scotia indicate that, far from being universally Anglican, the émigrés represented many different religious persuasions.[70] In Nova Scotia, it has been remarked both by contemporaries and by modern historians that Anglicans made up less than half of the total population of loyalist settlements in that province.[71] Whether the Episcopalian loyalist leaders could have served as a unifying factor for their cause seems doubtful. The best that can be said about their politics is that they shared with others the sense of weakness, fear, and distrust which marked those conscious minorities of the loyalist cause.[72] They tried to give voice to that cause, but, precisely because there was little common heritage to begin with, they failed. They did not reach out to other loyalist groups among Quakers, Congregationalists, Presbyterians, blacks, and Indians. Rather, they sought to convince their fellow clergy of the justice of their cause. It would seem then that we cannot really speak of the colonial clergy as forming the core of the American Tories, only of those who were already Episcopalian and already loyal to crown and mitre.

Conclusion

Legislators often try to impose uniformity without any clear view of the susceptibility of their subjects to that uniformity. Diversities are often increased rather than diminished by such attempts, and, unless local customs are taken into account, authority ultimately comes to reside in other hands, usually in the hands of those who have kept a finger on the pulse of local usage. England's royal church in America was involved in this process, not only in terms of its relations with other churches but also in terms of its inner structure. The efforts of the imperially minded to legislate in spiritual matters were insignificant in the long run. For a variety of reasons, Americans slowly came to think that diversity and pluralism were not in themselves bad things. Recognition of this fact bred mutual respect and willingness to live in peace with those of differing opinions.

In religion as in politics, Americans also decided that, whatever sovereignty was in theory, in practice it was divisible. Whether they were inconsistent in this and strangers to subtlety is a matter for conjecture. They parceled out authority as it suited them and not always fairly. By 1787, the divisions they had caused became particularly apparent, but the idea, the tendency, had been there all along. Americans who were also Episcopalians were no exception to the division of sovereignty. For a long time they retained the source of ecclesiastical authority, the episcopate, even when throughout the entire colonial period they had no bishop. Moreover, at the same time that they acknowledged that their ministers must have episcopal ordination with the requisite laying on of "apostolic" hands, a majority within the church resisted having a bishop transported to their shores at all. Thus, local abusage severely limit the indispensable source of power without actually repudiating it. Rather they depended on churchmanship to make episcopal power as palatable as possible.[1]

In the 1780s when Episcopalians first got one bishop, then two more, they changed radically the inherited ideas about the episcopate by dismantling

234

the medieval, hierarchical pretensions of that office.[2] The church's laity and lower clergy were so successful in their efforts to divide episcopal sovereignty that, as a result, each bishop became the servant, not the lord, of the people within his diocese. From their ranks he had come, to them he owed his exalted position, and for their sakes he must labor. Henceforth, bishops were responsible first and foremost to their diocesan conventions. Clearly local usage had won out. This is not to say that authority ultimately resided in the state or diocesan conventions. Episcopalians were neither "states' righters" nor did they model their church on the Articles of Confederation. For that matter, they did not adopt the federalism of the Constitution of 1787. Rather, they chose to divide sovereignty differently. The laity and the lower clergy were episcopally minded enough to retain the traditional unitary power of central government in their General Convention. The word of that body became church law, binding on all those who voluntarily chose to place themselves under its spiritual guidance. Episcopalians were able to do this because they made sure that their convention remained general, i.e., representative of all orders in the church. What is more, the laity and the lower clergy were thoroughly and powerfully represented by voice and vote in a true convention, a meeting of free individuals in which legislation was initiated and then approved or disapproved. Bishops were given a special and "higher" place where they alone met to do the church's business, but that business was not theirs alone to perform. They had to share sovereignty with clerical and lay deputies. Moreover, by a strange American custom the unitary power of the General Convention was decentralized, placing authority for month-to-month local church business in the hands of the servant-bishop and those to whom he owed his election. Thus did Episcopalians revere, change, and limit the inherited source of authority in their body and so come to share sovereignty.

The seeds of this future revolutionary development are to be found in the care for the church from 1619 on by Virginia's General Assembly, in Blair's conventions of clergy, and, ironically, in the actions in the 1760s of such high churchmen as Thomas Bradbury Chandler. In the latter case, conventions of ministers across provincial boundaries provided a pattern for future organizing conventions in the 1780s which Chandler would not have approved. Both sets of conventions were in and of themselves strangely unepiscopal by traditional standards, since there were no bishops present. All of these played their part in making a royal, hierarchical church astoundingly democratic in a short span of time.

Was this a triumph of "Americanization"? Considering the role of the laity in this history, we might say that Americanization is simply another term for laicization. There is no doubt that in colonial America the laity,

235

particularly in the southern vestries, contributed markedly to the democratization of the church to the extent that their voices carried unusual authority. This is true of George Thorpe, Sir Thomas Dale, Governor Berkeley, even for all his prejudice Colonel John Dodman, and, by way of contrast, Nathaniel Bacon and Elias Neau. But Americanization cannot simply be equated with laicization, for, despite the Virginia and South Carolina vestries, not all of the laity sought to reshape their church along more democratic, American lines. A considerable group of laity sought to make the church more, not less, hierarchical. This was particularly true in New England, though not exclusively. One thinks here of John Checkley, longer a layman than a clergyman, and, before him in Massachusetts, Thomas Lechford. There were royal governors: Cranfield, Andros, Cornbury, Tryon; provincial officials such as Heathcote and Colden; and, above all, Francis Nicholson and the wealthy nobility in England who supported the SPG with their funds. All these sought a church run by the clergy. Yet these same laity were intensely loyal to America or, more accurately, to their provinces. Americanization and laicization did not always go hand in hand.

In the larger sense, Americanization, understood as deference to provincial habits and prejudices, was a shared attitude which involved clergy and laity alike, Tory and Whig, high and low church people, even the imperially minded, as well as the provincially minded. We are not surprised at the report of Hugh Jones that Virginia planters had developed a sense of superiority toward Great Britain, that they "for the most part have contemptible notions of England" due to their contact with "common dealers, sailors, and servants."[3] These planters were the ideological progenitors of Patrick Henry, Jefferson, Washington, and Madison. Similarly, it was not surprising when Virginia Episcopalian Richard Bland displayed American distaste for the hierarchical pretensions of the Church of England by calling its higher orders a "relic of the papal encroachments on the common law."[4] But when East Apthorp spoke glowingly of the superiority of American manners over English ones and loyalist Jonathan Boucher castigated British politicians who denied American rights, it was puzzling.[5] Even among those high churchmen who agitated the loudest for an American episcopate, there was often a desire to put some distance between themselves and the mother country. Even Samuel Johnson was not above taking England to task for her neglect of the colonies. Johnson, who often felt diminished by English rebuffs, stated his "intense affection for this my native country," as well as the "highest veneration for our ancient mother country." He wondered aloud why Great Britain did not take more interest in the "joint weal of these her daughters . . . as becomes the wisdom and goodness of the mother."[6] As British Americans, high churchmen like Johnson called for obedience to the crown, but that fealty was enjoined for the sake of provincial welfare as much as for anything else.[7] As William H. Nelson has observed, "It was the war that made the British enemies rather than mere antagonists," and it "was the war that cut the Tories out of American society and set up a new sovereignty."[8]

Until that time, the most avid proponents of the clericalization of the church might be considered guilty of advocating the Americanization of the church in terms of purity of manners in the New World, ingenuousness, and freedom from vice and affectation. In 1764, Apthorp judged that American "simplicity and frugality" were much to be preferred to English opulence. There was too much wealth in England said one of Boston's leading high churchmen, and, as a result, the English were perverted by the "grosser pleasures of vice and luxury." America by contrast enjoyed greater composure of spirit, "holy cheerfulness and serenity."[9] Bishops, others kept insisting, would be nonpolitical in America, and insistence on that point eventually led them to a sense of superiority about the whole matter of their own episcopate once they got it. In America, they were to claim in the 1780s, the primitive episcopate of the early church had been reborn.

Americanization involved not only laicization but adaptation to national customs, prejudices, and racisms. It meant accepting the idea that spiritually powerfully clergy could live side by side with powerful laity, each sovereign in his own sphere. The Americanization of the Church of England meant rewriting popular church history to suit the temper of the times, whether that rewriting corresponded to the facts or not. This process reached something of a crescendo in the midnineteenth century. In 1859 for instance, George Duyckinck (1823–1863) attempted to square the Laudian episcopate with the revolutionary ideas of the Founding Fathers. Duyckinck boldly asserted that Bishop Thomas Ken's (1637–1711) loyalty to the Roman Catholic James II and Ken's refusal to take the oath of allegiance to William and Mary in 1689 made that prelate a "great example of successful legal resistance" in what came to be the American tradition. In his anxiety to declare that Episcopalians made loyal citizens of the United States and in his even stronger desire to commend Anglo-Catholicism, Duyckinck was led to opine that Ken was "one of the precedents for our fathers in 1776 . . . one who did good service in preparing deep-laid foundations of our American liberties."[10] Thus was a Nonjuring bishop Americanized and placed in the pantheon of liberty without losing his spiritual episcopal prerogatives.

Duyckinck was not alone in espousing both American republicanism and English religion. Both Calvin Colton (1789–1857) and James Fenimore Cooper (1789–1851) evidenced staunch loyalty to America and at the same time sought to build bridges to England's church and civilization.[11] They were Americanized to the extent that they believed their own society, both religious and political, comprised nearly the best of all possible worlds. When viewed from one angle, the Americanization of this church was an extraordinary achievement; when viewed from another, it was simply a matter of permitting time and circumstance to work their inevitable change. The most monarchical and magisterial Protestant church in Europe did not grow small and disappear over the horizon in the new American republic. Still only partially reformed in its ministry and liturgy, it was able to adapt to the first democracy in the western world. In that democracy, a thoroughly reformed and even sectarian tradition which was foreign and inimical to Anglicanism proved far more influential. Nevertheless, Episcopalians learned to live side by side in peace with others of different religious persuasions. They did so in a prudent and marvelous manner: they retained and went on in the next century to elaborate and increase the inherited, medieval trappings of religion, while at the same time repudiating that absolute, hierarchical sovereignty of which the trappings were the expression in the first place. To those who required stately, historical forms for ceremony, language, buildings, and clothings, this church offered them to all, and for that offering there was much to be said.

Abbreviations

AHR	*American Historical Review*
AL	*American Literature*
ATR	*Anglican Theological Review*
CH	*Church History*
DAB	*Dictionary of American Biography*
DNB	*Dictionary of National Biography*
HLQ	*Huntington Library Quarterly*
HM	*Historical Magazine of the Protestant Episcopal Church*
JAH	*Journal of American History*
JHI	*Journal of the History of Ideas*
JNH	*Journal of Negro History*
JSH	*Journal of Southern History*
MHM	*Maryland Historical Magazine*
NCHR	*North Carolina Historical Review*
NEQ	*New England Quarterly*
NNHM	*Northern Neck Historical Magazine*
PMHB	*Pennsylvania Magazine of History and Biography*
SAQ	*South Atlantic Quarterly*
SPCK	Society for Promoting Christian Knowledge
SPG	Society for the Propagation of the Gospel in Foreign Parts
TQHGM	*Tyler's Quarterly Historical and Genealogical Magazine*
VMHB	*Virginia Magazine of History and Biography*
WMQ	*William and Mary Quarterly*

Notes

Notes to the Introduction

1. *Report upon Weights and Measures* (Washington, D.C., 1821), 91.
2. Ibid., 13.
3. For the complexities of this establishment see Sarah McCulloch Lemmon, "The Genesis of the Protestant Episcopal Diocese of North Carolina, 1701–1823," *NCHR* 28 (October 1951): 426–62 passim.
4. Disestablishment occurred in Maryland and North Carolina in 1776, in New York and Georgia in 1777 (and ultimately in the latter state in 1798), in South Carolina in 1778, and in Virginia in 1779 with the withholding of payment of clerical salaries from tax revenue and with final and full disestablishment in 1787.
5. See, for instance, Carl Bridenbaugh, *Mitre and Sceptre: Transatlantic Faith, Ideas, Personalities, and Politics* (New York, 1962), 54, 118, 119, 131, 339.
6. F. W. Buckler, "The Establishment of the Church of England: Its Constitutional and Legal Significance," *CH* 10, no. 4 (December 1941): 301.
7. Ibid., 336.
8. Frederick V. Mills, Sr., in his study *Bishops by Ballot: An Eighteenth-Century Ecclesiastical Revolution* (New York, 1978), shows the remarkable and energetic reconstituting of the church into a new denomination in the 1780s after the dismantling process which is in part the concern of this study.
9. Elizabeth H. Davidson, *The Establishment of the English Church in the Continental American Colonies* (Durham, N.C., 1936).
10. Ibid., 88.
11. Ibid., 37. The reason for this lack is that New York already had an establishment, the Dutch Reformed Church, and Episcopalians had to tread warily.
12. Charles A. Barker, *American Convictions: Cycles of Public Thought, 1680–1850* (Philadelphia and New York, 1970), 121.
13. See Joseph Tracy, *The Great Awakening* (New York, 1845), 377f.; Wesley M. Gewehr, *The Great Awakening in Virginia, 1740–1790* (Durham, N.C., 1930), 40f.; and George William Pilcher, *Samuel Davies: Apostle of Dissent in Colonial Virginia* (Knoxville, 1971), 54f.
14. *The Life of the Reverend Devereux Jarratt* (Baltimore, 1806; New York, 1969), 119.
15. See Kenneth Coleman, *Colonial Georgia, A History* (New York, 1976), 40, 48–49, 52, 158, 224, 226–27, 235.
16. Dawson to the bishop of London, 16 August 1751, in *Historical Collections of the American Colonial Church*, ed. William Stevens Perry, 5 vols. (Hartford, 1878; New York, 1969), 1:364.
17. Joan Gundersen, "The Anglican Ministry in Virginia, 1732–1776" (Ph.D. diss., University of Notre Dame, 1972), 249.
18. Vestry of Caratuck Parish to the secretary, 25 August 1710, SPG Letters, Series A, 5, no. 174. See James Adams to the secretary, 27 March 1710, ibid., no. 137, for his own account of his ministry.
19. Vestry of Chown Parish to the bishop of London, 24 August 1708, ibid., 4, no. 118.
20. Colonel [Caleb] Heathcote to the secretary, 9 November 1705, ibid., no. 117. See George Muirson to the secretary, 22 May 1706, 3, nos. 75, 168; 4, no. 149; 7, no. 150, for examples of commendations of both clergy and concerned laity in the middle colonies.
21. "Anglican Missions in America, 1701–1725: A Study of the Society for the Propagation of the Gospel in Foreign Parts" (Ph.D. diss., Northwestern University, 1962). Nelson includes for commendation such figures as Samuel Thomas (d. 1706) (p. 211), Francis

Le Jau (1665–1717) (p. 220), and Gideon Johnston (d. 1716) (p. 236) in South Carolina; John Bartow (d. 1725) (p. 309f.), Aeneas Mackenzie (1675–?) (p. 322f.), John Thomas (d. 1729) (p. 317f.), Peter Stoupe (d. 1760) (p. 347f.), and Thomas Barclay (d. 1726) (p. 375) in the province of New York; Edward Vaughan (d. 1747) (p. 397) in New Jersey; Evan Evans (1671–1721) (p. 409f.) in Pennsylvania; George Ross (1679?–1754) (p. 431f.) in Delaware; James Honeyman (d. 1750) (p. 477f.), James McSparran (1679–1757) (p. 495f.), and John Usher (1700?–1775) (p. 505f.) in Rhode Island; and Samuel Myles (1664–1728) (p. 56lf.) and Ebenezer Miller (1703–1763) (p. 567f.) in Massachusetts. No such selective list is complete without mention of South Carolina's gentleman missionary to the destitute poor in the Piedmont Charles Woodmason (c. 1722–1777), colonial America's Jonathan Swift.

In addition to those listed by Nelson, there were other, less well known parsons who contributed significantly to the larger well-being of their communities: John Ogilvie (1724–1774), the perspicacious missionary to the Mohawks who translated the Book of Common Prayer into the Mohawk tongue; Augur Treadwell (1734–1765), a Yale graduate who was both minister and teacher; Oxonian Philip Reading (1720–1778); the patient and skillful former French Recollet Michael Houdin (1706–1766); Boston Brahmin and Harvardian Samuel Auchmuty (1722–1777) of Trinity Church, New York; and the English aristocrat and Etonian Leonard Cutting (1724–1794), who became the secretary of the Episcopalian House of Bishops after the Revolution.

22. Edwin L. Goodwin, *The Colonial Church in Virginia* (Milwaukee, 1927), 252, 276, 310f., 294. For fuller treatment of the clergy in Virginia, see Chapters 1 and 4 below.

23. See n. 21 above.

24. The figures are based on John Clement, ''Clergymen Licensed Overseas by the Bishops of London, 1696–1710 and 1715–1716,'' *HM* 16 (1947): 318–49. Were solid information available, the numbers of English would no doubt be higher.

25. John Clement, ''Anglican Clergymen Licensed to the American Colonies, 1710–1744,'' *HM* 17 (1948): 207–50.

26. Nelson, ''Anglican Missions,'' 619.

27. Gundersen, ''Anglican Ministry,'' 38, 86. Gundersen notes that, of the approximately 294 Episcopalian ministers who served at one time or another between 1723 and 1776, at least one-half were residents of the colony or came to Virginia from other continental colonies; for a further breakdown of these figures, see ibid., 40–48. It should be noted here that Virginia was not staffed by the SPG.

28. Nelson, ''Anglican Missions,'' 206, 342–79, 469.

29. Ibid., 346, 353, 360, 372.

30. ''Clergy Convention at Burlington in the Plantations Address for a Suffragan Bishop,'' 2 November 1705, SPG Journals, A, 1, 84, 509.

31. Sources reveal a continuing desire to reach foreign language groups and in some cases to insist upon the use of native tongues; see Patrick Gordon, ''Proposals,'' 16 January 1701, SPG Journals, Appendix 1, 8, 60 and 66, for the initial desire to teach Indians English, but then see Sir William Ashurst to the secretary, 30 June 1703, SPG Letters, A, 1, no. 92, for the learning of Indian tongues; ''The Humble Memoriall of Robert Livingston, Secretary for Indian Affairs,'' 17 September 1703, SPG Journals, A, 1, no. 29 (Iroquois); Bishop of London to the secretary, 1702, SPG Letters, A, 1, no. 25 (Welsh); Henry Nichols to the secretary, 20 March 1704, ibid, no. 84 (Welsh); Caleb Heathcote to the secretary, 10 April 1704, ibid., no. 182 (French); Lewis Morris to the secretary, ? May 1704, ibid., no. 171 (Dutch); Elias Neau to the secretary, 22 June 1704, ibid., 2, 1 (French); Governor Robert Hunter to the secretary, 9 April 1715, ibid., no. 10 (Iroquois); William Andrews to the secretary, 12 July 1715, ibid., no. 185 (Iroquois); and at the end of the century, see William Smith to the Bishop of London, 18 December 1766, Fulham Papers, A, 8, 31–3 (German); Richard Peters to the Bishop of London, 30 August 1768, ibid., 38 (Swedish); William Smith to the Bishop of London, 3 May 1771, ibid., 46 (Swedish); T. F. Illing to the Bishop of London, 6 October 1773, ibid. (German).

32. On the question of primacy of the English language, it is interesting to note the numbers of Frenchmen who achieved eminence in the church's ministry in the eighteenth century: Virginia's Lewis Latané (1672–1732), South Carolina's Francis Le Jau, New York's Peter Stoupe, and French nobleman and scholar Daniel Bondet (d. 1722), as well as such prominent layment as Elias Neau (d. 1722) and Rhode Island's Gabriel Bernon. See also Robert M. Kingdon, "Why Did the Huguenot Refugees in the American Colonies Become Episcopalian?" *HM* 49 (December 1980): 317–35 passim.

33. From the Yorkshire-Cumberland area in the north of England came Myles Cooper (1737–1785), future president of King's College in New York; Jonathan Boucher (1737–1804); and Virginia's John Camm (1718–1779). From Scotland came a host of major figures: James Blair (1656–1744), the powerful leader of Virginia's church; missionary George Keith (1639–1716); James Honeyman; Alexander Garden (1685–1757), the commissary of South Carolina; William Smith (1727–1803), president of the College of Philadelphia; George Muirson (d. 1708), missionary to Connecticut; George Ross, Thomas Crawford (fl. 1700–1709), and a host of Virginia's ministers: Alexander Cruden (1721–1792), David Currie (d. 1791), John Wingate (1741–1789), William Douglas (d. 1777), John Buchanan (1748–1822), Thomas Johnson (d. 1790), and Christopher MacRae (d. 1808). From Ireland came South Carolina's first commissary, Gideon Johnston; McSparran; New Hampshire's Arthur Browne (1699–1773); and New York's prominent loyalist pamphleteer Charles Inglis (1734–1816). From Wales came Oxonian Gilbert Jones (1687–fl. 1722), Pennsylvania's Evan Evans, Thomas Jenkins (d. 1709), John Clubb (d. 1715), and Jacob Henderson (d. 1751).

34. Nelson, "Anglican Missions," 446.

35. In addition, there were 28 Presbyterian, 33 Baptist, and 22 Roman Catholic churches. When these figures are combined with Lutheran and Dutch Reformed churches and Quaker meeting houses, the number of all churches comes to 116. See Edwin S. Gaustad, *Historical Atlas of Religion in America* (New York, 1962), 1976), 3, 4.

36. Gaustad, *Historical Atlas* (1962), figs. 8, 10, 12, 14, and 16. Assuming that in 1700 there were approximately 65,000 Episcopalians in North America in 111 churches out of a total population of 269,000, that would mean one church to every 585.5 persons in the denomination. In 1750 the total population had increased to 1,170,000. At that time Episcopalians numbered perhaps 175,000. However, with 289 churches they were clearly keeping up with their own growth in terms of church buildings, for the ratio at that time was 1 church to every 605.5 persons. By 1780 Episcopalians had dropped to fourth place; they were outbuilt by both Baptists and Presbyterians.

   All of these figures are only approximations since there was never a colonial census. Moreover, the word *church* here is ambiguous, for it covers both preaching stations and large, settled congregations.

37. Gaustad, *Historical Atlas,* 7 (1976); see in particular fig. 8.

38. Maryland and Virginia had 700,000 population in 1775. Estimated New England population at the time was 589,500, while that of New York, New Jersey, and Pennsylvania was 600,000. See Robert V. Wells, *The Population of the British Colonies in America before 1776* (Princeton, 1975), 284.

39. James Potter, "Growth of Population," in *Population in History,* ed. D. V. Glass (London, 1965), 640. Virginia, along with New England, experienced slower growth; in the latter case, the percentage declined from 39 percent of the total population in 1700 to 26 percent in 1790. An exception was New Hampshire, which experienced a 5.4 percent increase (Wells, *Population of British Colonies,* 260). New Hampshire was second only to Georgia, where the annual rate of increase was 9.7 percent at midcentury. The overall rate of increase for the North American colonies from 1690 to 1790 was an explosive 34.5 percent per decade. By 1790 nearly 50 percent of the total population lived in the South.

40. By way of contrast, the periods of slowest colonial increase were the 1700s, 1710s, 1750s, and 1770s.

41. Frederick V. Mills, Sr., "Anglican Expansion in Colonial America," *HM* 39 (September 1970): 315–24.

42. These figures break down as follows for the middle colonies and the South: fifteen to New York, twelve to New Jersey, fifteen to Pennsylvania, twenty-nine to Maryland, eighty-eight to Virginia, twenty to North Carolina, and thirty-four to South Carolina. The rest were scattered or did not arrive.
43. In the period 1760 to 1775, sixteen to eighteen new churches were built in North Carolina under the energetic leadership of Governor William Tryon (1729–1788).
44. See Mills, "Anglican Expansion," 316. In Connecticut he counts 30 parishes in 1761 and 47 in 1774 and an additional 20 congregations not yet housed in church buildings. Despite growth in Connecticut and the Deep South, on the eve of the Revolution Maryland and Virginia still accounted for more than half (144) of all Episcopal churches in America.
45. Bridenbaugh, *Mitre and Sceptre*.
46. "Sermon Preached after the Victory over Scotch Rebels in the Battle of Culloden, 1746," Maryland Diocesan Archives, 2. See also David C. Skaggs and F. Garner Ranney, "Thomas Cradock Sermons," *MHM* 47 (1972): 179–80; and David C. Skaggs, "The Chain of Being in Eighteenth Century Maryland: The Paradox of Thomas Cradock," *HM* 45 (June 1976): 155–64, for a description of Cradock's significance.
47. Wallace E. Anderson, ed., *Jonathan Edwards: Scientific and Philosophical Writings* (New Haven, 1980), 17.
48. Among the classical Anglican writings which represented the church's theological position during the sixteenth-century reformation and immediately thereafter were the works of Richard Hooker (1553–1600); John Davenant (1576–1641), bishop of Salisbury and Lady Margaret Professor of Divinity at Cambridge; Joseph Hall (1574–1656), bishop of Norwich; Miles Smith (d. 1624), bishop of Gloucester; and the sometime Puritan and Erastian trimmer of sails Samuel Parker (1640–1688). High churchmen were represented by Robert Nelson (1656–1715), author of a life of Bishop Bull and compiler of the feasts and fasts of the Church of England; William Sherlock (1641?–1707), the anti-Puritan dean of St. Paul's; Richard Bentley (1662–1742), the Anglican church historian; William Cave (1637–1713), the early church historian; Robert South (1634–1716); Richard Allestree (1619–1681), supporter of Charles I and author of the popular *Whole Duty of Man*; Launcelot Andrewes (1555–1626), bishop of Lincoln; and Jeremy Taylor (1613–1667), bishop of Down and Connor and author of *Holy Living* and *Holy Dying*. Nonjurors were Henry Dodwell (1641–1711), who found his way to New Haven, and the future Jacobite plotter Francis Atterbury (1662–1732), bishop of Rochester and for a time chief of the high church party; the latitudinarian Whig contingent was represented in Richard Kidder (1633–1703), bishop of Bath and Wells and the bane of the high churchmen; by Gilbert Burnet (1643–1715), bishop of Salisbury, church historian and zealous advocate of toleration; by White Kennett (1660–1728), bishop of Peterborough and strong Whig partisan; Edward Stillingfleet (1635–1699), latitudinarian bishop of Worcester; and Henry More (1614–1687), the Cambridge Platonist. Less susceptible to easy classification but notably within the church were Simon Patrick (1626–1707), bishop of Ely, whose interest in the SPCK and the SPG was notable; John Harris (1666?–1719), the clerical satirist; Ezekiel Hopkins (1634–1690), bishop of Derry; Robert Sanderson (1587–1663), bishop of Lincoln and moderator of the Savoy Conference; James Ussher (1581–1656), the famous bishop of Armagh; John Strype (1643–1737), Tudor historian and the ardent Hanoverian bishop of St. Asaph; and William Fleetwood (1656–1723). Contemporary controversialists were William Whiston (1667–1752) and Daniel Whitby (1638–1726) and Cambridge University's homegrown Anglican Calvinist John Edwards (1637–1716). These all rested next to the works of Calvin, Beza, Owen, Sibbs, Prynne, Milton, Grotius, Descartes, and Eusebius. See Anne Stokely Pratt, "Books Sent from England by Jeremiah Dummer to Yale College," in *Papers in Honor of Andrew Keogh, Librarian of Yale University* (New Haven, 1938), 7–44.
49. Theodore Hornberger, "Samuel Johnson of Yale and King's College: A Note on the Relation of Science and Religion in Provincial America," *NEQ* 8 (1935): 379.
50. Barker, *American Convictions*, 119; for the charter of the college, see Richard Hofstadter and Wilson Smith, eds., *Documentary History of American Education* (New York, 1961),

1:33–49. William and Mary became an important center from which ideas of the moderate enlightenment were disseminated; see Merle Curti, *The Growth of American Thought* (New York, 1943), 110; cf. John M. Jennings, *The Library of the College of William and Mary, 1693–1793* (Charlottesville, Va., 1968), 57–80.

51. Coleman, *Colonial Georgia,* 239. This occurred in 1764. Whitefield refused to accept the recommendation of the Archbishop of Canterbury that only Anglicans be allowed to teach, and the idea died.

52. Graham P. Conroy, "Berkeley and Education in America," *JHI* 21 (1960): 213; cf. Benjamin Rand, *Berkeley's American Sojourn* (Cambridge, Mass., 1932); Alice Brayton, *George Berkeley in Newport* (Newport, 1954); and Norman J. Catir, Jr., "Berkeley's Successful Failure," *HM* 33 (1964): 65–82.

53. A. A. Luce, *The Life of George Berkeley, Bishop of Cloyne* (London, 1949), 136–52.

54. For a discussion of this work relative to the American influence, see Luce, *Berkeley,* 133–35. *Alciphron* was published in London in 1731.

55. *Catechetical Lectures on the Preliminary Questions and Answers of the Church Catechism in Four Volumes* (London, 1696).

56. Hildreth to Daniel Burton, New York, 17 October 1772, SPG Letters, B, 3, no. 168.

57. *Discourses on Various Subjects* (New York, 1793), 1:15, 22f.

58. "Lectures Upon the Church Catechism," n.d., General Theological Seminary, MF 32845: 39, 42. Written in Seabury's hand, we may be sure that the document is pre-Revolutionary, since it enjoins prayers for the king and royal family. For Seabury's life, see Bruce Steiner, *Samuel Seabury, 1729–1796: A Study in the High Church Tradition* (Athens, Ohio, 1972).

59. Seabury, "Lectures," 42.

60. Burr, *Church in New Jersey,* 175–78.

61. Donald Richard Friary, "The Architecture of the Anglican Church in the Northern American Colonies: A Study of Religious, Social, and Cultural Expression," (Ph.D. diss., University of Pennsylvania, 1971), 23. See also James McAllister, Jr., "Architecture and Change in the Diocese of Virginia," *HM* 45 (September 1976): 298–99, for a discussion of southern colonial architecture in churches. For the gothic survival in seventeenth-century Virginia, see Calder Loth and Julius Trousdale Sadler, Jr., *The Only Proper Style* (Boston, 1975), 5–8.

62. Friary, "Architecture," 18. An interesting example of such accommodation is to be seen in Virginia's cruciform churches, built in the eighteenth century and modeled on Christ Church, Lancaster County ("King" Carter's church). Here we find in Carter's beautiful building an example of Christopher Wren's influence on America, but more than that, an example of "the central-type domed or Greek-cross plan family memorial mausoleum" which in turn was influenced by Scottish models; see Alan Gowans, *King Carter's Church* (Victoria, B.C., 1969), 26.

63. Samuel Gaillard Stoney, *Colonial Church Architecture in South Carolina* (Charleston, 1953), 1–2.

64. Mills, *Bishops by Ballot,* 7; of the 65, 60 were converts from Congregationalism.

65. Ibid., 12. Mills notes 289 Episcopal churches in 1750, 400 in 1770; 132 Baptist in 1750, 350 in 1770; 465 Congregationalist in 1750, 675 in 1770; 79 Dutch Reformed in 1750, 125 in 1770; 90 German Reformed in 1750, 175 in 1770; 138 Lutheran in 1750, 225 in 1770; 233 Presbyterian in 1750, 390 in 1770; 30 Roman Catholic in 1750, 54 in 1770.

These figures do not tell all of the story by themselves, however. What is perhaps more instructive than Mills's bare figures is the percentage rate of growth for each denomination in the same twenty-year period. When one figures that, the picture changes quite markedly. On the basis of Mills's numbers of churches constructed between 1750 and 1770, the percentage rate of growth is as follows: Baptist, 62.3 percent; German Reformed, 48.5 percent; Presbyterian, 40.3 percent; Lutheran, 38.7 percent; Congregationalist, 31.1 percent; Episcopalian, 27.8 percent; Dutch Reformed, 26.3 percent; Roman Catholic, 25.9 percent. On the other hand, Mills's assertion that the 1760s represent a period of marked

Episcopalian expansion is born out, for in that decade the percentage rate of Episcopalian growth was second only to that of the Baptists and on a par with or ahead of all the others. The figures are as follows: Baptists, 31.4 percent; Presbyterians, 23 percent; German Reformed, 22.9 percent; Episcopalians, 22.5 percent; Dutch Reformed, 16 percent; Lutherans, 15.5 percent; Congregationalists, 14.8 percent; Roman Catholics, 12.9 percent.

66. The figures are drawn from Mills, *Bishops by Ballot*; Holmes, "Episcopal Church and the American Revolution"; and Gaustad, *Historical Atlas*. The breakdown is as follows for New England and the middle colonies: New Hampshire, two churches, two ministers; Maine (then still part of Massachusetts), five churches, one minister; Massachusetts, twenty churches, twelve ministers (Holmes, 262); Rhode Island, seven churches, seven ministers (Gaustad, 9); Connecticut, forty churches, twenty ministers, with communicant strength approximately 7 percent of the total population; New York, twenty-four churches, twenty ministers; New Jersey, twenty-four churches, twelve ministers (Holmes, 262); Pennsylvania, twenty-two churches, nineteen ministers (Mills, 62). The Chesapeake Bay area is as follows: Maryland, forty-four churches, forty-four ministers (Mills, 86); Virginia, ninety-five churches, ninety ministers (Mills, 86). In the southern colonies, North Carolina had eleven churches with an additional nineteen projected and eleven clergy (Mills, 112, and Holmes, 263); South Carolina had twenty-four churches and twenty-two ministers (Holmes, 263), while Georgia had twelve parishes, many of them on paper only, and two ministers (Holmes, 263).

While Episcopalians numbered approximately three hundred thousand out of a total population of 2.5 million on the eve of the Revolution, their percentage of the population in any given area varied markedly. In Virginia and Maryland, Episcopalians were in the majority and outnumbered all other denominations. In South Carolina, Episcopalians accounted for nearly half the population, but, elsewhere, particularly in New England, Pennsylvania, Delaware, and North Carolina, they remained a tiny minority.

67. Otto Lohrenz, "The Virginia Clergy and the American Revolution, 1774–1799" (Ph.D. diss., University of Kansas, 1970), 22.

Of the 129 clergy in Virginia during the Revolution, Lohrenz counts 10 who became loyalist refugees, 10 who supported the loyalist cause but remained in the colony and eventually yielded to the republican form of government, 11 who were politically irresolute, 22 who were "passive Whigs" and failed to support actively the patriot cause, and 31 who were active Whigs, participated in committees of safety, or served with the Congressional forces. Most of the refugee clergy were from the tidewater area or were more recent arrivals in the colony; conversely, most of the 31 patriot ministers had deeper ancestral roots in Virginia. By contrast, of the 100 Baptist and 30 Presbyterian ministers, all who can be accounted for were patriots.

68. *The Story of the Diocese of Connecticut* (Hartford, 1962), 126.

Notes to Chapter 1

1. For a discussion of the religious orientation of the various English colleges, see V. H. H. Green, *Religion at Oxford and Cambridge* (London, 1964), and H. C. Porter, *Reformation and Reaction in Tudor Cambridge* (Cambridge, 1958), particularly 233–35 and 239 for discussion of the ties between Cambridge and Virginia.

2. For a brilliant and painstaking discussion of seventeenth-century social and economic developments in Virginia, see Edmund S. Morgan, *American Slavery, American Freedom: The Ordeal of Colonial Virginia* (New York, 1975).

3. See Morgan, *American Slavery,* 395–432, for a detailed study of Virginia's population in general; for death rates, see pp. 115, 158–80; cf. Charles M. Andrews, *The Colonial Period of American History* (New Haven, 1934), 1:133–34. Comparison with death rates in New England is startling; average life expectancy for seventeenth-century Virginians in

Norfolk County was 49 years (Morgan, 161), while for native-born residents of Andover, Massachusetts, for the same period it was 71.8 years. See Philip J. Greven, Jr., *Four Generations: Population, Land, and Family in Colonial Andover, Massachusetts* (Ithaca, N.Y., 1970), 26; similar figures hold for Plymouth Colony in John Demos, *A Little Commonwealth: Family Life in Plymouth Colony* (New York, 1970), 192–93.

4. Additional breakdown is as follows: 13 served 2 years or less, 31 from 3 to 5 years, 7 from 6 to 10 years, and 16 for over 10 years.

5. Twelve served 30 years and over; 14 served 20 to 29 years; 38 served 10 to 19 years, and 80 served 1 to 9 years.

6. These ratios are as follows (from my own research): 1615, 15 ministers to 350 lay people (1:23.3); 1622, 16 to 1,250 (1:78.1) before the Good Friday massacre of that year; 1625, 6 to 1,300 (1:216.6); 1630, 5 to 2,600 plus (1:520); 1640, 8 to 8,100 (1:1012.5); 1650, 7 to 14,000 (1:2000); 1660, 11 to 25,000 (1:2272.7); 1675, 12 to 31,900 plus (1:2658.3); 1682, 24 to 40,600 (1:1691.6); 1699, 36 to 62,800 (1:1744.4); and 1710, 44 to 70,000 (1:1590.9).

7. George McLaren Brydon, *Virginia's Mother Church* (Richmond, 1947), 1:361–407.

8. Morgan, *American Slavery,* 73–75.

9. "A sermon Preached to the Honourable Company of the Virginia Plantation, 13 November 1622," in *The Sermons of John Donne,* ed. George R. Potter and Evelyn M. Simpson (Berkeley and Los Angeles, 1959), 4:265–82.

10. *A Good Speed to Virginia* (London, 1609; Edinburgh, 1970), C2.

11. R. T. Kendall, *Calvin and English Calvinism* (London, 1979), 5f., summarizes debates on the meaning of the term *Puritan.* To Kendall's limitation of the term to theological points, knowledge of saving faith in a "thoroughly predestinarian" context, one would want to add both personal and ecclesiastical reforming tendencies. Puritan theologian William Perkins was indeed, *contra* Kendall, an ecclesiastical reformer; he laid down quite specific standards, for instance, for episcopal comportment, as well as dealing with the more general doctrine of the ministry.

12. Peter Force, ed., *Tracts and Other Papers* (Gloucester, Mass., 1963), 3, 9–19.

13. "Religion and Society in the Early Literature of Virginia," *Errand into the Wilderness* (Cambridge, Mass., 1956), 99–140.

14. Edmund S. Morgan, "The Labor Problem at Jamestown, 1607–17," *AHR* 76 (June 1971): 602.

15. Force, *Tracts,* 3:63–68.

16. Irene D. Hecht, "The Virginia Colony, 1607–1640: A Study in Frontier Growth" (Ph.D. diss., University of Washington, 1969). Hecht counts 32 voyages between 1608 and 1613 bringing a total of 1,477 colonists or an average of 246 per year; between 1617 and 1624 there were 101 voyages bringing between 4,789 and 5,114 colonists or an average of 684 per year. The peak year for immigration was 1620, when 1,325 came to Virginia. The total number of immigrants from 1607 to 1624 is somewhere in the neighborhood of 6,400, of which approximately 5,400 died. While losses were staggering, it must be remembered that in other English military expeditions it was expected that many of the poorer people would perish in large numbers, but when in 1616 the population after nearly ten years was only 351, it became clear that even by current standards and expectations the Virginia Company had less to show for its efforts than was acceptable. See John E. Pomfret, *Founding the American Colonies, 1583–1660* (New York, 1970), 35.

17. Jurgen Herbst, "The New Life of Captain John Smith," *HM* 44 (March 1975): 59; cf. Alden T. Vaughan, *American Genesis: Captain John Smith and the Founding of Virginia* (Boston, 1975), 174.

18. For a discussion of these differences see Michael T. Malone, "The Doctrine of Predestination in the Thought of William Perkins and Richard Hooker," *ATR* 52 (April 1971): 103–17. See also Kendall, *English Calvinism,* 55f., for Perkins's views.

19. William S. Powell, "Books in the Virginia Colony before 1624," *WMQ,* 3rd Series, 5 (April 1948): 177–84, draws attention to the additional though less well known works sent

to the colony in 1619: Lewis Bayly's *Practice of Piety* and Gervase Babington's *Works*. Of the two, Bayly (d. 1631), bishop of Bangor, was a pronounced Puritan, thoroughly disliked in the royal court of James I and in his own diocese in Wales. Babington (1550–1610), successively bishop of Landall, Exter, and Worcester, was connected with both Oxford and Trinity College, Cambridge. This hard student of theology and biblical exegete was enormously popular in his day. He was not, however, a polemical man, avoiding the Puritan-Anglican debates on the nature of the church. See also David B. Quinn, ed., "A List of Books Purchased for the Virginia Company," *VMHB* 77 (July 1969): 358; cf. Richard B. Davis, "Volumes from George Sandys Library Now in America," *VMHB* 65 (October 1957): passim.

20. Kendall, *English Calvinism,* 61–66. For Calvin full assurance came to the believer at the point where he or she saw the freely given promise of Christ to all, Kendall argues. Perkins made full persuasion less available, it would seem, by putting it "out of reach" of the "first calling" and making it contingent upon the believer's diligence "to make our election sure, and to gather manifold toakens thereof." Kendall's analysis is more detailed, but this much indicates Perkins's misreading and changing of Calvin's thought.

21. William Perkins, *The Works of that Famous and Worthie Minister of Christ in the University of Cambridge* (London, 1608), 2:671, 684.

22. Babette M. Levy, *Puritanism in the Southern and Island Colonies* (Worcester, 1960), 95f. Zacharias Ursinus (1534–1583) was a Calvinist theologian and disputant with Lutherans. He and Olevianus composed the Heidelberg Catechism; before that Ursinus had written two other catechisms, the *Catechesis minor* and the *Summa Theologiae,* but which one of these the "Ursinaer Catechism" refers to is unknown. See also "Books in Colonial Virginia," *VMHB* 10, 403.

23. Quoted in Susan M. Kingsbury, *The Records of the Virginia Company of London* (Washington, D.C., 1906), 1:152.

24. H. C. Porter, "Alexander Whitaker: Cambridge Apostle to Virginia," *WMQ,* 3rd Series, 14:317–43.

25. See particularly Richard B. Davis, *George Sandys: Poet Adventurer* (New York, 1955), chapters 5–7.

26. While we must await a thorough examination of Virginia's seventeenth-century clergy, it seems certain that the following were securely in the Puritan camp. In order of their first appearance in the colony after 1624 they are: Nathaniel Eaton (d. 1648), John Rosier (d. 1647), William Thompson (d. 1642), Thomas Bennett (fl. 1630s), Thomas Harrison (fl. in Virginia 1640–1648), William Durand (fl. 1640s), Sampson Calvert (fl. 1647–1653), John Munro (fl. 1650s), Francis Doughty (fl. 1649–1660), Andrew Jackson (d. 1710), Daniel Richardson (fl. 1670–1676), and Jonathan Davis (fl. 1679–1682). Nor should the presence of French Calvinist Huguenots be overlooked: Michael Zyperne (fl. 1680s), Stephen Fouace (d. 1702), James Boisseau (fl. 1689–1705), John or Jean Bertram (d. 1710), and Nicholas Moreau (fl. 1697). For references to these see Goodwin, *Colonial Church,* 245–312, and Levy, *Puritanism,* 117–44. Possibly Puritan in their leanings, but definitely conforming to the Church of England, were Francis Bolton (d. 1652), John Lyford (d. 1630), Thomas Hampton (d. 1682), Robert Bracewell (d. 1688), David Lindsey (d. 1667), William Thompson (fl. 1662–1680), and Jonathan Davis (fl. 1680). All of these attended "Puritan" colleges at Oxford or Cambridge.

27. Ibid. We may place the following in the high church camp: George Alford (fl. 1658), Alexander Murray (fl. 1665–1672), Thomas Teakle, Philip Mallory (fl. 1634–1661), Morgan Godwyn (fl. 1662–1681), John Gwynn (fl. 1659–1688) and Edward Folliott (fl. 1650–1690).

28. [John Gauden ?], *Eikon Basilike: The Portraiture of His Sacred Majesty Charles I in His Solitudes and Sufferings* (London, 1649), was written in reply to John Milton's *Eikonoklastes* (London, 1649). Gauden's work was to be found in many Virginia libraries of the seventeenth and eighteenth centuries and was standard fare for royalists, though one might judge that Virginians read it more out of curiosity than ardent loyalty. The copy in the

Carter library may well have come into the possession of the family from Sarah Ludlow, Robert Carter's mother, or from the libraries of either of John Carter's first two wives, Judith Armistead and Betty Landon.

29. Lyon G. Tyler, ed., "Libraries of Colonial Virginia," *WMQ*, 1st Series, 8 (July, 1899):18–19.

30. Louis B. Wright, "Pious Reading in Colonial Virginia," *JSH* 6 (August 1940): 383–92; cf. George K. Smart, "Private Libraries in Colonial Virginia," *AL* 10 (March 1938): 24–62, and E. G. Swem, "The Observations on the 'Virginia Historical Index' by Dr. Howard Mumford Jones in His Address on 'Desiderata in Colonial Literary History,' " *VMHB* 56 (1948): 314–22, where Swem argues that Virginia was just as literary as New England.

31. Laugher, *Thomas Bray's Grand Design, Libraries of the Church of England in America, 1695–1785* (Chicago, 1973), 4.

32. John J. Jennings, *The Library of the College of William and Mary in Virginia, 1693–1793* (Charlottesville, Va., 1968), 22; Edwin Wolf, *The Dispersal of the Library of William Byrd of Westover* (Worcester, Mass., 1958), 47; Tyler, "Libraries," 2, 4, 248, 250; 3, 133; 6, 159; 8, 77, 146, and 10, 390, 401. Similarly, in the libraries of the SPG in the northern colonies, this volume appeared regularly; see Laugher, *Bray's Design,* 92, 96, and 100. Whitefield's distaste arose from the fact that Allestree regarded faith as a human duty rather than as a gift of divine grace.

33. For Hammond, see Tyler, Libraries," 2, 248; Laugher, *Bray's Design,* 87, 88, 89. For Taylor, Tyler, "Libraries," 2, 171; 9, 164; Laugher, *Bray's Design,* 88, 96. For Boyse, Tyler, "Libraries," 2, 171; 8, 77. For Hales, Tyler, "Libraries," 2, 174. For a description of this school of Anglican thought, see C. F. Allison, *The Rise of Moralism: The Proclamation of the Gospel from Hooker to Baxter* (New York, 1966).

34. Tyler, "Libraries," 174.

35. Laugher, *Bray's Design,* 89, 93, 94, and 100; Jennings, *Library of William and Mary,* 22; and Wolf, *Library of Byrd,* for the lack thereof in Byrd's library. For a definition of "Nonjuror," see chapter 4, n. 70.

36. Allison, *Rise of Moralism,* 15.

37. For Sanderson, Laugher, *Bray's Design,* 89, 93, and 96. For Barrow, Laugher, *Bray's Design,* 88, and Tyler, "Libraries," 2, 247; 6, 163; 8, 20; and 9, 166. For Sherlock, Laugher, *Bray's Design,* 88, 89, 94, and 97; Jennings, *Library of William and Mary,* 23; Tyler, "Libraries," 6, 161; 9, 164. For Downame, Laugher, *Bray's Design,* 88 and 92. For Ussher, Laugher, *Bray's Design,* 94 and 96; Tyler, "Libraries," 2, 170.

38. For Moore, Laugher, *Bray's Design,* 91, 97, and 98; Wolf, *Library of Byrd,* 86. For Stillingfleet, Laugher, *Bray's Design,* 88, 89, 93, and 94; Jennings, *Library of William and Mary,* 24; Tyler, "Libraries," 9, 166; "Books in Colonial Virginia," *VMHB* 10 (April 1903): 404. For Tillotson, Laugher, *Bray's Design,* 89 and 96; Jennings, *Library of William and Mary,* 22 and 24; Tyler, "Libraries," 6, 161; "Books in Virginia," 404.

39. For homilies, Laugher, *Bray's Design,* 96; Tyler, "Libraries," 2, 170. For Cranmer, Jennings, *Library of William and Mary,* 22. For Hooker, Laugher, *Bray's Design,* 90 and 97; Jennings, *Library of William and Mary,* 22; Tyler, "Libraries," 2, 249 and 251; Lucy Temple Latané, *Parson Latané, 1672–1732* (Charlottesville, Va., 1936), 46. See also John R. Williams, comp., "A Catalogue of Books in the Library of 'Councillor' Robert Carter at Nomini Hall, Westmoreland County," *WMQ*, 1st Series, 10:232–41.

40. Edward W. James, comp., "Libraries of Colonial Virginia," *WMQ*, 1st Series, 3:43–45, and Lyon G. Tyler, comp., "Libraries of Colonial Virginia," ibid., 250. For a discussion of Purchas, see Chapter 2.

41. Laugher, *Bray's Design,* 87, 88, 90, 92, 97, 98, and 99; Jennings, *Library of William and Mary,* 24; Wolf, *Library of Byrd,* 51 and 59; Tyler, "Libraries," 2, 174; 3, 133 and 250; 8, 19.

42. Joseph Blount Cheshire, ed., "List of Books Illustrating the History of the Church in North Carolina," in Cheshire, *Sketches of Church History in North Carolina . . .* (Wil-

mington, Del., 1892), 435; for Milton, see also Martha Custis Washington, comp.[?], "Catalogue of the Library of Daniel Parke Custis," *VMHB* 17:404, 407, and 409.

43. Wolf, *Library of Byrd,* 51, and [?] Dexter, "Books in Colonial Virginia," *VMHB* 10:390–405.

44. Laugher, *Bray's Design,* 2. The smallest libraries, those of backcountry farmers in Virginia and North Carolina, had, as Jackson Turner Main has observed, "only a Bible, a few other volumes of a religious nature, and a spelling book. . . . Probably most people of small income in the cities had the same sort of reading material." See Main, *The Social Structure of Revolutionary America* (Princeton, N.J., 1965), 258–59. Richard Beale Davis in his *Literature and Society in Early Virginia, 1608–1840* (Baton Rouge, La., 1973), 46, notes the prevalence of handbooks on epistolary style and declares that the presence of such volumes shows colonial interest in good writing. We may perhaps say the same for their selection of theological works.

45. Laugher, *Bray's Design,* 35.

46. Gundersen, "Anglican Ministry," 177.

47. Levy, *Puritanism,* 127–30.

48. Jon Butler, ed., "Two Letters from Virginia Puritans," *Massachusetts Historical Society, Proceedings* 94 (1972): 100.

49. Ibid., 105. See also Charles Francis Adams, *History of Braintree Massachusetts (1639–1708)* . . . (Cambridge, Mass., 1891), 15–18. I am indebted to Jane Wilson of Minneapolis, Minn., for drawing my attention to this volume.

50. Ibid., 107–9.

51. See, for instance, Morgan, *American Slavery,* chapters 1 and 2.

52. *The Church of England and Non-Episcopal Churches in the Sixteenth and Seventeenth Centuries* (London, 1949), 4.

53. *Queen Elizabeth* (London, 1950), in particular 181, 184, 230, 273, and 295; see also Winthrop Hudson, *The Cambridge Connection and the Elizabethan Settlement of 1559* (Durham, N.C., 1980), 29–60, 90–109, and 145–48.

54. Probably sixty thousand left England in the period 1630 to 1643, twenty thousand of whom came to Massachusetts Bay, perhaps nine thousand to Virginia, and the rest to Ireland, Bermuda, and the Caribbean. See Andrews, *The Colonial Period,* 1:396; for Virginia in the seventeenth century as a whole, see Morgan, *American Slavery,* 405–10. For a discussion of events leading up to the migration, see Williams B. Mitchell, *The Rise of the Revolutionary Party in the English House of Commons, 1603–1629* (New York, 1957); William Haller's classic *The Rise of Puritanism* (New York, 1938); and David Little, *Religion, Order, and Law: A Study in Prerevolutionary England* (New York, 1969).

55. Brian Manning, "The Nobles, the People, and the Constitution," in *Crisis in Europe, 1560–1660,* ed. Trevor Aston (Garden City, N.Y., 1967), 277.

56. Harold Hulme, "Charles I and the Constitution," in *Conflict in Stuart England, Essays in Honour of Wallace Notestein,* ed. W. A. Aiken and B. D. Henning (London, 1960), 103. I have not discovered the writings of Archbishop Laud in any seventeenth-century libraries in Virginia.

57. In seventeenth-century England, a tyrant was viewed as a traitor; he was considered a rebel against the people and could be killed on sight. See John N. Figgis, *The Divine Right of Kings* (Cambridge, 1914), 364–65.

58. *Antichrist in Seventeenth-Century England* (London, 1971), 69.

59. Ibid., 77.

60. David B. McIlhinny, "The Protestantism of the Caroline Divines," *HM* 44 (June 1975): 154.

61. J. Mills Thornton III, "The Thrusting Out of Governor Harvey: A Seventeenth-Century Rebellion," *VMHB* 76 (January 1968):16.

62. *Purchas his Pilgrimage or Relations of the World and the Religions Observed in All Ages discovered from the Creation unto this Present* (London, 1613), 42.

63. Quoted in Loren E. Pennington, "Hakluytus Posthumous: Samuel Purchas and the Promo-

tion of English Overseas Expansion," *Emporia State Research Studies* 14 (March 1966): 26, 631; cf. "The Second Charter to the Treasurer and Company for Virginia . . . May 23, 1609," *Statutes at Large, Being a Collection of all the Laws of Virginia from the First Session of the Legislature in the Year 1619*, ed. William H. Hening (New York, 1823), 1:97f.; Kingsbury, *Records*, 3:14, 446, for further evidence of anti-Roman Catholic thinking.

64. *The Present State of Virginia* . . . , ed. Richard L. Morton (Chapel Hill, N.C., 1956), 104, 83.

65. Lawrence J. Friedman and Arthur H. Shaffer, "The Conway Robinson Notes and Seventeenth-Century Virginia," *VMHB* 78 (July 1973): 262f.; see also Morgan, *American Slavery*, 129, 163, 176–77, 179, 225, 235–70, and Bernard Bailyn, "Politics and Social Structure in Virginia," in *Seventeenth-Century America*, ed. James M. Smith (Chapel Hill, N.C., 1959), 95.

66. Hening, *Statutes*, 1:359–61.

67. Morgan, *American Slavery*, 145–49.

68. *Virginia under Charles I and Cromwell, 1625–1660* (Williamsburg, Va., 1957), 61.

69. Nicholas Varga, "The English Parliament's Authority over Virginia," *VMHB* 62 (1954): 288; cf. Hening, *Statutes*, 1:368.

70. Joseph Frank, ed., "News From Virginny, 1645," *VMHB* 65 (1957): 85f.

71. Hening, *Statutes*, 1:240; cf. Levy, *Puritanism*, 130.

72. Hening, *Statutes*, 1:341–42.

73. There is some evidence (Levy, *Puritanism*, 132–34) that perhaps three hundred did so, moving not to Massachusetts Bay with those leaders with whom they had been in contact but to the Severn in Maryland. That colony, ever eager to attract new settlers, had a new governor, William Stone, a Protestant acceptable to any Puritan group.

74. Ibid., 131.

75. Hening, *Statutes*, 1:368.

76. Brydon, *Virginia's Mother Church*, 1:123, 131.

77. Gaustad, *Historical Atlas* (1976), 6.

78. Gundersen argues convincingly against the traditional view of the self-perpetuating power of the vestries in the eighteenth-century colonial church in Virginia. That after 1720 vestries could not eject clergy from their livings at will is, in her words, "the greatest irony of Virginia church history." Joan Gundersen, "The Myth of the Independent Virginia Vestry," *HM* 44 (June 1975): 133–41.

79. John F. Woolverton, "Address Commemorating the 300th Anniversary of St. Mary's White Chapel," *NNHM* 19 (December 1969): 1961–69. See also Isaac W. K. Handy, "Josias Mackie," in *Annals of the American Pulpit*, ed. William B. Sprague (New York, 1857–69), 3:6f., and Brydon, *Virginia's Mother Church*, 1:254–56.

80. Bailyn, "Politics and Social Structure," 96f.

81. Hening, *Statutes*, 1:412.

82. Brydon, *Virginia's Mother Church*, 1:123. More recently, Warren M. Billings in his "Virginia's Deplored Condition, 1660–1676: The Coming of Bacon's Rebellion" (Ph.D. diss., Northern Illinois University, 1968) has noted the population explosion during the two decades 1640–1660 and its positive effect upon the decentralization of authority. Virginia in 1640 had a population of eight thousand; by 1660 the total was thirty-three thousand, an increase of 87.5 percent in the first decade and 120 percent in the second. The bulk of these immigrants were, he judges, "rather ordinary, middling sorts of Englishmen, many of whom came as indentured servants." Cf. Morgan, *American Slavery*, 159, 234, 405–10.

83. James Kimbrough Owen, "The Virginia Vestry: A Study in the Decline of a Ruling Class" (Ph.D. diss., Princeton University, 1947), 23.

84. *Political Thought in England: From Locke to Bentham* (New York, 1920), 84.

85. Little, *Religion, Law, and Order*, 33–131.

86. Lacey Baldwin Smith, *This Realm of England, 1399–1688* (Boston, 1966), 292–93.
87. *The Church of England and Non-Episcopal Churches*, 3. The Latin reads: "the holy English church, the most excellent and highest in repute of all the Protestant churches."
88. "Sermon on Education," Maryland Diocesan Archives, 3.
89. "Sermon during the French and Indian Wars," Maryland Diocesan Archives, 4.
90. "Sermon Preached after Victory over Scotch Rebels," Maryland Diocesan Archives, 4.
91. See my "John Williamson Nevin and the Episcopalians: The Debate on the 'Church Question,' 1851–1874," *HM* 49 (December 1980): 361–87, for criticisms by Nevin of Episcopalian and Anglican anti-Catholicism.

Notes to Chapter 2

1. For a succinct and popular summary, see Wesley F. Craven, *The Virginia Company of London, 1606–1624* (Williamsburg, Va., 1957).
2. David Bertelson, *The Lazy South* (New York, 1967), 24–27.
3. Ibid., 46.
4. Purchas, *Pilgrimage*, verso facing Contents.
5. Maxwell Ford Taylor, "The Influence of Religion on White Attitudes toward Indians in the Early Settlement of Virginia" (Ph.D. diss., Emory University, 1970), 145. Perry Miller in his *Errand* was the first to recognize the importance of Purchas's theology of divine providence; see particularly pp. 115–22.
6. Purchas's reference here is to Julius Africanus (c. 160–240), a Christian and author of a world history, *Chronographia*, fragments of which were used by Eusebius of Caesarea in his *Ecclesiastical History* (c. 323). Purchas, *Pilgrimage*, 41.
7. Joseph Scaliger (1540–1609) was a Frenchman who established the modern science of chronology in his *De Emendatione* (1583) and in the larger and more famous *Thesaurus Temporum* (1606).
8. Purchas, in *Pilgrimage*, 43.
9. Purchas of course refers to the story found in the Greek poet Masaeus (*Grammaticus*), as well as in Virgil (*Georgics*, 3) and Ovid (*Heroides*, 18 and 19).
10. Purchas, *Pilgrimage*, 631.
11. See "Letters Patent to Sir Thomas Gates . . . April 10, 1606," Hening, *Statutes*, 1:58. For similar sentiments, compare Hening, *Statutes*, 1:68–69, 97; Kingsbury, *Records*, 3:14–15, 446.
12. George Percy, "Observations gathered out of a Discourse of the Plantation of the Southerne Colonie in Virginia by the English, 1606," in *Genesis of the United States*, ed. Alexander Brown (Boston, 1890), 1.
13. George Percy, "A Trewe Relacyon of the Procedings . . . which have hapned in Virginia . . . 1609 until . . . 1612," *TQHGM* 3 (1922): 260–82.
14. Percy, "Observations," in Brown, *Genesis*, 1:164.
15. Purchas, *Hakluytus Posthumus or Purchas His Pilgrims*, (London, 1625), 4:1770–71. The Puritans at the Hampton Court conference had suggested that the use of the surplice, ever a bone of contention, be made optional, since to them it was "Popish attire"; see Porter, *Reformation*, 239.
16. Alexander Whitaker, *Good Newes from Virginia* (London, 1613), 32–33.
17. Ralph Hamor, *A true discourse of the present state of Virginia . . . till the 18 of June, 1614* (London, 1615), 48.
18. See John Rolfe, *A true relation of the state of Virginia . . . in May last, 1616* (New Haven, 1951); Robert Johnson, *Nova Britannia . . .* (London, 1609), in Force, *Tracts*, 1:6.
19. Philip A. Bruce, *Institutional History of Virginia* (New York, 1910), 1:6; see instructions to Governor Yeardley, 1618, in Kingsbury, *Records*, 3:102.
20. Kingsbury, *Records*, 3:446.

21. Robert Evelin, *A Description of the Province of New Albion* (London, 1648), in Force, *Tracts,* 2:4, 5.
22. *A Perfect Description of Virginia* (London, 1649), 8, in Force, *Tracts,* 2:7; see William Bullock, *Virginia impartially examined* . . . (London, 1649).
23. Edward Williams, *Virgo Triumphant: or, Virginia richly and truly valued* . . . (London, 1650), in Force, *Tracts,* 3:11, 4–8.
24. John Hammond, *Leah and Rachel, or, two fruitfull sisters, Virginia and Maryland: their present condition, impartially stated and related* (London, 1656), in Force, *Tracts,* 3:14, 6.
25. Hammond, *Leah and Rachel,* 9; see also [Lionel Gatford], *Publick good without private interest. Or, A compendious remonstrance of the present sad state and condition of the English colonie in Virginea* (London, 1657).
26. Hammond, *Leah and Rachel,* 16, 9, 12, and 13.
27. Nathaniel Shrigley, *A true relation of Virginia and Maryland* (London, 1669), in Force, *Tracts,* 3:7.
28. Roger Greene, *Virginia's Cure: or An Advisive narrative concerning Virginia. Discovering the true ground of that churches unhappiness, and the only true remedy* (London, 1662), in Force, *Tracts,* 15:4.
29. Howard Mumford Jones, *The Literature of Virginia in the Seventeenth Century* (Charlottesville, Va., 1968), 104. Jones fails to mention Morgan Godwyn, John Hammond, Robert Evelin, William Bullock, Lionel Gatford, and Nathaniel Shrigley in his survey.
30. Greene, *Virginia's Cure,* 5–6.
31. Ibid., 15; see also 6, 17, 9, and 16.
32. Ibid., 18.
33. Ibid., 19.
34. See, for instance, Sir William Berkeley, *A Discourse and View of Virginia* (London, 1663; Norwalk, 1914); [Thomas Ludwell], *A Description of the Government of Virginia* (London, 1666); *VMHB* 5 (1897): 54–59; *Strange News from Virginia, being a true relation of a great tempest* . . . (London, 1667); John Ogilby, *America: Being the latest, and most accurate description of the New World* (London, 1671); *An Account of the Advantage of Virginia for Building Ships* (London, 1673); Thomas Glover, *An Account of Virginia* (London, 1676; Oxford, 1904); John Purvis, *A Collection of all Laws of Virginia* . . . (London, 1684?).
35. John Clayton, *A Letter* . . . *to the Royal Society* (London, 1688, 1723); also his *A Letter to Dr. Grew,* in answer to several queries (London, 1687); John Bannister, *Some Observations Concerning Insects Made in Virginia* (London, 1701).
36. Morgan Godwyn, *The Negro's and Indian's Advocate suing for their Admission into the Church* (London, 1680); see p. 62.
37. William Byrd to Charles, Earl of Orrery, June 1731, *VMHB* 32 (1924): 34–35.
38. William Byrd to Charles, Earl of Orrery, July 5, 1726, ibid., 27.
39. Byrd to Orrery, February 3, 1728. Morgan judges that "repeating widoes often married repeating widowers"; for a discussion of such marriages, see *American Slavery,* 164–68.
40. Sister Loan de Lourdes Leonard, "Operation Checkmate: The British and the Death of a Virginia Blueprint for Progress," *WMQ,* 3rd Series, 19:44–74.
41. Richard Morton, *Colonial Virginia,* (Chapel Hill, N.C., 1960), 1:32.
42. H. S. Smith, R. T. Handy, and L. Loetscher, *American Christianity* (New York, 1960–63), 1:42–44, for full text, as well as Brydon, *Virginia's Mother Church,* 1:4, and Miller, *Errand,* 105.
43. Second Charter . . . May 23, 1609, Hening, *Statutes,* 1:97f.; cf. Francis Bacon, *Advancement of Learning* (London, 1605), 1:v, 4; Charles Gibson, *Spain in America* (New York, 1966), 80f.; and *New Catholic Encyclopedia* 12:165, for discussion of the "Reductions of Paraguay" (*reducciones* were Indian villages run by the Jesuit order from which Europeans were excluded; the term was common seventeenth-century coinage).
44. Purchas, *Pilgrimage,* 639.

45. Kingsbury, *Records*, 3:102; see also 14 and 15.
46. W. Stitt Robinson, "Tributary Indians in Colonial Virginia," *VMHB* 67 (1959): 49.
47. Michael Kammen, *People of Paradox: An Inquiry Concerning the Origins of American Civilization* (New York, 1972), 201.
48. Clifford Geertz, "The Integrative Revolution: Primordial Sentiments and Civil Politics in the New States," in *Old Societies and New States: the Quest for Modernity in Asia and Africa*, ed. Clifford Geertz (New York, 1963), 105–7, quoted in John Higham, "Hanging Together: Divergent Unities in American History," *JAH* 61 (1974): 7.
49. Lurie, "Indian Adjustment," 35; Lurie's discussion of the work of Clifford J. Lewis, S.J., and Albert J. Loomie, S.J., *The Spanish Jesuit Mission in Virginia, 1570–1572* (Chapel Hill, N.C., 1953), concludes that proof of such a Spanish mission on the York River has not been established despite Lewis and Loomie's "exhaustive study." For further treatment of Virginia Indians, see Wesley Frank Craven, *White, Red, and Black and Seventeenth-Century Virginia* (Charlottesville, Va., 1971), especially 39–67, and Craven's "Indian Policy in Early Virginia," *WMQ*, 3rd Series, 1 (1944): 65–82, as well as William S. Powell, "Aftermath of the Massacre: The First Indian War, 1622–1632," *VMHB* 61 (1953): 44–75; Ben C. McCrary treats Indian culture in Virginia in his *Indians in Seventeenth-Century Virginia* (Williamsburg, Va., 1957), while a summary of the reaction of all Indians east of the Rocky Mountains to white English/American advance is to be found in Harold E. Driver, *The Indians of North America* (Chicago, 1961), especially 353–54.
50. For discussion of Smith's tough but unenlightened Indian policy see Morgan, *American Slavery*, 77–79.
51. Samuel Eliot Morison, *The European Discovery of America* (New York, 1971), 647; see also Silvio Zavala, "A General View of the Colonial History of the New World," *AHR* 66 (October 1960–July 1961): 920.
52. Lurie, "Indian Adjustment," 45.
53. For example, see Percy, "Observations," in Brown, *Genesis*, 1:156; cf. William Kellaway, *The New England Company, 1649–1776: Missionary to the American Indians* (London, 1961), 82, for reference to the supposed satanism of the Indians.
54. Ibid., 132.
55. [Robert Johnson], *Nova Britannia*, in Force, *Tracts*, 1, 6.
56. "Such continence on the part of English sailors," remarked Admiral Morison, "is hard to believe." *Discovery*, 647.
57. William Byrd, *History of the Dividing Line betwixt Virginia and North Carolina in the Year of Our Lord, 1728* (Cambridge, Mass., 1966), ed. Louis B. Wright, 160–61, and Introduction, where Wright quotes a letter by Byrd, 26.
58. Purchas, *Pilgrimage*, 546.
59. Winthrop D. Jordan in his *White over Black* (Chapel Hill, N.C., 1968), 92, argues otherwise. Writes Jordan, "The importance and persistence of the tradition which attached slavery to heathenism did not become evident in any positive assertions that heathens might be enslaved." Jordan surmises that it was not until after 1660, when slavery had been legally established in Maryland and Virginia, that the tradition that heathens made natural slaves emerged. Even then, he claims, there was no attempt to place heathenism and slavery in a one-for-one relationship. It is here argued otherwise.
60. *The Tempest* has, in its relation to American colonization, received a good deal of treatment but so far not in relation to English attitudes about color, race, and religion. In his "Shakespeare's American Fable" Leo Marx deals with the conflict between order and disorder in society and in nature. Marx proposes that the encounter here is between humane and humorless self-mastery (Prospero, from *prosperare*, "to cause to succeed") and profane susceptibility to music and landscape (Caliban). See chapter 2 of his *The Machine in the Garden: Technology and the Pastoral Ideal in America* (New York, 1964).

Perry Miller in his *Errand* deals with *The Tempest* as a gauge of the impact of America on English imagination generally. A. L. Rowse in his *The Elizabethans and America*

(London, 1959) notes that in *The Tempest* the American Indian sits for his portrait in the person of Caliban (196f.), but fails to analyze sufficiently the linking of race, color, heathenism, and slavery to form a common attitude toward the savage. Analysis of the joining of these factors is attempted in what follows.

61. William Shakespeare, *The Tempest* (New Haven, Conn., 1918), act 1, scene 2, lines 319, 17.
62. Ibid., act 2, scene 2, lines 119, 42.
63. Ibid., act 1, scene 2, lines 354–58.
64. Ibid., lines 363–65; the plague referred to is the bubonic plague.
65. Ibid., lines 308, 314, 321, 345, 353, and 375.
66. Ibid., lines 344–48.
67. Citations are from, respectively: act 5, scene 1, lines 272 and 275, 88f.; act 1, scene 2, lines 353, 18. With respect to the darkness of skin pigmentation and the impact of the contrast upon fair-skinned Englishmen of the sixteenth century, see Jordan, *White over Black,* 7.
68. Shakespeare, *Tempest,* act 1, scene 2, lines 283–84, 15.
69. Ibid., lines 244–45.
70. Ibid., act 5, scene 1, lines 316–18, 82.
71. Taylor, "Influences," 257.
72. Calvin wrote in the sermons on Galatians (6:9–11), "We cannot but behold our face in those who are poor and despised . . . even though they are utter strangers to us. Even in dealing with a Moor or a Barbarian, from the very fact of his being a man he carries about with him a looking-glass in which we can see that he is our brother and our neighbor." For his part, William Perkins specifically denied concepts of natural servitude derived from Aristotle and "proceedeth not from nature but hath his original from the laws of nations. . . . For all men are by nature equally and indifferently free, none more or less than others." William Perkins, "Practical Writings," *Work of William Perkins* (Appleford, England, 1970), 16, 436.
73. Carl Degler, "Slavery and the Genesis of American Race Prejudice," *Essays in American Colonial History,* ed. Paul Goodman (New York, 1967), 228.
74. Jordan, *White over Black,* 210.
75. In addition to the works of Morgan and Jordan already cited, attention should be drawn to a helpful summary of the patterns of the development of slavery in north and south America in Denzil T. Clifton, "Anglicanism and Slavery." Two classic studies amid a vast literature on the subject deserve particular mention as well. They are John Hope Franklin, *From Slavery to Freedom: A History of the Negro Americans* (New York, 1967), and David Brion Davis, *The Problem of Slavery in Western Culture* (Ithaca, N.Y., 1966).
76. Clifton, "Anglicanism," 69.
77. Henry R. McIlwaine, ed., *Journals of the House of Burgesses of Virginia, 1659/60–1693* (Richmond, Va., 1914), 34.
78. Hening, *Statutes,* 2:260.
79. Ibid., 197.
80. Ibid., 3:460–61; 2:270.
81. Godwyn, *Negro's and Indian's Advocate,* 34–35.
82. Richard Blome (?–1705) was the author of *A Geographical Description of the four parts of the World* (London, 1670) and *A Description of the Island of Jamaica, with other Isles and Territories in America, to which the English are related . . . ,* 8 vols. (London, 1672). Blome was anti-Quaker, like Godwyn; see his *The Fanatick History, or an exact relation and account of the Old Anabaptists and New Quakers* (London, 1660).
83. Godwyn, *Advocate,* 96; cf. Bede, *Ecclesiastical History* (various editions), 3:7 and 4:12.
84. Ibid., 96, italics Godwyn's.
85. Ibid., 37f.
86. Ibid., 38.
87. Ibid., 73.

88. Ibid., 80.
89. Ibid., 36.
90. For discussion of this subject, see Marion D. de B. Kilson, "Towards Freedom: An Analysis of Slave Revolts in the United States," in *The Making of Black America,* ed. August Meier and Elliott Rudwick (New York, 1969), 1:165–78. Kilson lists the following uprisings in the colonial period, some planned, others spontaneous: Virginia, 1663, 1687, 1691, 1712, 1722; Maryland, 1739; New York, 1708, 1712; North Carolina, 1776; South Carolina, 1711, 1720, 1730, 1740; Georgia, 1774 (see tables, 166 and 167). Kilson omits Bacon's rebellion since that was a white revolt primarily; it would also seem that some of the "slave" uprisings listed for Virginia were not necessarily black insurrections but those of white indentured servants or even a combination of the two. Morgan asserts that "no white person was killed in a slave rebellion in colonial Virginia." *American Slavery,* 309.
91. McIlwaine, *Minutes of the General Court,* 205, 226–27.
92. Brydon, *Virginia's Mother Church,* 1:507–8.
93. Godwyn, *Advocate,* 167–74, for the full text; also in Brydon, *Mother Church,* 1:503–16.
94. It is probable that Godwyn derived some of his royalist views from his father; see *Alumni Oxoniensis,* 1:585.
95. Thad W. Tate, *The Negro in Eighteenth-Century Williamsburg* (Charlottesville, Va., 1965), 116; cf. Marcus W. Jernegan, "Slavery and Conversion in the American Colonies," *AHR* 21 (1916): 504–27.
96. Arthur Lyon Cross, *The Anglican Episcopate and the American Colonies* (Cambridge, Mass., 1902), 4–5.
97. Margaret S. Harrison, "Commissary James Blair of Virginia: A Study in Personality and Power" (M.A. thesis, College of William and Mary, 1958), 8.
98. Gundersen, *Anglican Ministry,* 7.
99. For reference to the development of lay power in the Church of England in the eighteenth century, see Norman Sykes, *Church and State in England in the 18th Century* (Cambridge, 1934), 379; E. R. Norman, *Church and Society in England, 1770–1970* (Oxford, 1976), 15.
100. James Truslow Adams, *Provincial Society, 1690–1763* (New York, 1927), 151; cf. Spencer Irvin, "The Establishment, Government, and Function of the Church in Colonial Virginia," *HM* 26 (1957): 76. Generally speaking, instructions to governors show that guidance was indeed given and policy settled; see, for example, the instructions given to Governors Berkeley and Culpeper, in Perry, *Historical Collections,* 5:1–3; cf. "Secret Instructions Sent by James II to Governor Dongan, of New York," in *Ecclesiastical Records of the State of New York* (Albany, 1901), 5:11, 915–16, to Governor Sloughter, 991, to Governor Fletcher, 1033–34, to the Earl of Bellomont, 1213.

   Finally, comparison of the size alone of the church in Virginia with that of the mother country is revealing: Virginia had but 50 parishes as late as 1700 (Gundersen, *Anglican Ministry,* 10), whereas in the greater metropolitan area of London at the same time there were 145 churches, 97 of which were within the environs of the old city itself; see D. V. Glass, "Two Papers on Gregory King," *Population in History,* 174.
101. Morgan, *American Slavery,* 129.
102. Henry R. McIlwaine, *Minutes of the Council and General Court of Colonial Virginia* (Richmond, Va., 1924), 22.
103. The term *vestry* initially refers to that room adjacent to either chancel or choir in which vestments, communion vessels, and parish records were kept, a room, that is, belonging to those who vest, i.e., the clergy. The vestry also became the place where church business was transacted by laymen and clergy alike. In time those laymen who conducted church business became known collectively as the vestry whether they met in the vestry room or not.
104. Act of Supremacy, 1559, in G. R. Elton, *The Tudor Constitution, Documents and Commentary* (Cambridge, 1965), 366.

105. Kingsbury, *Records,* 3:14.
106. Force, *Tracts,* 3, no. 2, 11. Much attention has been given to the development of the vestry system in Virginia. Some of these studies are: James K. Owen, *The Virginia Vestry;* George McC. Brydon, "The Origin of the Rights of the Laity in the American Episcopal Church," *HM* 12 (1943): 313–38; William H. Seiler, "The Anglican Parish Vestry in Colonial Virginia," *JSH* 20 (1956): 310–37; Bradford Spangenberg, "Vestrymen in the House of Burgesses: Protection of Local Vestry Autonomy during James Blair's Term as Commissary," *HM* 32 (1963): 77–99. More recently Joan R. Gundersen has challenged the idea that seventeenth-century lay control went either unchallenged or unchanged in the eighteenth century in "The Myth of the Independent Virginia Vestry," *HM* 44 (1975): 133–41. A study of the vestry system in Maryland is supplied by Gerald Hartdagen in "The Anglican Vestry in Colonial Maryland: A Study in Corporate Responsibility, *HM* 40 (1971): 461–79.
107. Hening, *Statutes,* 1:180.
108. Ibid., 182.
109. Ibid., 183. Cf. E. Brooks Holifield, *The Covenant Sealed: The Development of Puritan Sacramental Theology in Old and New England, 1570–1720* (New Haven, Conn., 1974), 160.
110. Hening, *Statutes,* 1:183.
111. Ibid., 1:341, 433; 2:46, 47, 51, 54, and 144; 3:150, 362, 441, and 446.
112. Ibid., 184–85.
113. Bailyn, "Politics and Social Structure in Virginia," 95.
114. Brydon, *Virginia's Mother Church,* 1:82–83, 91–93.
115. Hening, *Statutes,* 1:240–42.
116. Ibid., 290–91.
117. Billings, "Virginia's Deplored Condition," 41.
118. Hening, *Statutes,* 1:433.
119. Billings, "Virginia's Deplored Condition," 79.
120. Hening, *Statutes,* 2:44–45.
121. Alan Kenneth Austin, "The Role of the Anglican Clergy in the Political Life of Colonial Virginia" (Ph.D. diss., University of Georgia, 1969), 36.
122. Wesley Frank Craven, *The Southern Colonies in the Seventeenth Century, 1607–1689* (Baton Rouge, La., 1949), 360–61; Wilcomb E. Washburn, *The Governor and the Rebel* (Chapel Hill, N.C., 1957), particularly chapters 1 and 10; and Billings, *Virginia's Deplored Condition,* 53. For a contemporary account see Robert Beverley, *The History and Present State of Virginia,* ed. Louis B. Wright, (Chapel Hill, N.C., 1957), 74.
123. Hening, *Statutes,* 2:356.
124. "A Petition of the Inhabitants and Housekeepers of St. Stephen's Parish in the County of New Kent," Council Papers 1682, 1683, 1684, printed in *VMHB* 41 (1933): 200–201.

Notes to Chapter 3

1. Edward Carpenter, *The Protestant Bishop: Being the Life of Henry Compton, 1632–1713, Bishop of London* (London, 1956), 82; for the full story of Compton's role in the Glorious Revolution, see chapter 8.
2. In the early part of the century the bishop of London sat on the board of the Virginia Company, and, since he had "manifested some interest in the church beyond the seas, the charge was entrusted to him, and from the precedent thus established may be traced the beginnings of the diocesan control of the bishops of London over the English plantations." So writes Cross in *Anglican Episcopate,* 8f.; see A. W. F. Ingram, *The Early English Colonies* (Milwaukee, Wis., 1908), 57–83.
3. Yeo to Sheldon, 25 May 1676, in *American Christianity,* ed. H. S. Smith, R. T. Handy, and L. A. Loetscher (New York, 1960–63), 1:54; see also M. G. Hall, L. H. Leder, and

M. G. Kammen, eds., *The Glorious Revolution in America* (Chapel Hill, N.C., 1964), 152.

4. Levy, *Puritanism*, 241.

5. Andrews, *Narratives*, 4. For comment on how Maryland's colonial prejudices continued to color historical judgments throughout the nineteenth century, see Theodore C. Gambrall, *Studies in the Civil, Social, and Ecclesiastical History of Early Maryland* (New York, 1893), vi.

6. William N. Sainsbury and J. W. Fortescue, *Calendar of State Papers, America and the West Indies, 1677–1680*, no. 337, 117.

7. See Carpenter, *Compton*, chapter 14.

8. William F. Troutman, "Respecting the Establishment of Religion in America" (Ph.D. diss., Duke University, 1959), 67.

9. Compton, "Memorandum to the Lords of Trade and Plantations, August 28, 1680," Sainsbury, *Calendar*, no. 1448, 590.

10. Troutman, "Establishment of Religion," 68.

11. Sixty-one were in England and Wales, fifty overseas, and the majority in North America. Bray's American libraries comprised 33,000 volumes for a population of 308,600 in 1710.

12. Quoted in H. P. Thompson, *Thomas Bray* (London, 1954), 103.

13. Richard Rawlinson, "A Short Historical Account of the Life and Designs of Thomas Bray, D.D.," in *Rev. Thomas Bray*, ed. Bernard C. Steiner (Baltimore, 1901), 12.

14. Social mobility did, however, exist in the established church. Among those who came from families of modest means were, besides Bray, Edmund Gibson (1699–1748), future bishop of London, and John Potter (1674–1747), who was destined to be one of the most scholarly archbishops of Canterbury since the Reformation.

15. Rawlinson, "Bray," 14.

16. Ibid., 22.

17. Thompson, *Bray*, 37.

18. Ibid., 42, 76.

19. Norman Sykes, "The Theology of Divine Benevolence," *HM* 16, (1947): 290.

20. Nelson, "Anglican Missions," 8f.

21. Bray, *A Memorial Representing the Present State of Religion on the Continent of North America* (London, 1700); for an account of Bray's visitation, see "Journal of Dr. Bray's Visitation," Fulham Papers, 1, A, 141–59.

22. Nelson, "Anglican Missions," 14.

23. Ibid., 17.

24. William Dawes, *A Sermon Preach'd before the Society for the Propagation of the Gospel in Foreign Parts, at the Parish-Church of St. Mary-le-Bow, on Friday February 18, 1708/9* (London, 1709), 21, quoted in Nelson, "Anglican Missions," 17, n. 37.

25. Melvin B. Endy, Jr., *William Penn and Early Quakerism* (Princeton, N.J., 1973), 193. The debate in England between Quakers and Puritans is complex and cannot be dealt with here. One example will suffice: to Quakers the "worship" of Scripture was superseded by the law written on the heart by the new light. Scripture alone was not sufficient for salvation for Quakers. Roman Catholics of the seventeenth century were, as Professor Endy remarks, "intent on proving that Scripture was not an adequate replacement for the church" (191).

26. Nelson, "Anglican Missions," 408; see also 92 and 406.

27. Bray, *Memorial*, 9.

28. John Calam, *Parsons and Pedagogues: The S.P.G. Adventure in American Education* (New York, 1971), 9.

29. Nelson, "Anglican Missions," 24.

30. Ibid., 27–28.

31. Ibid., 31.

32. Calam, *Parsons and Pedagogues*, 8f.

33. Ibid., 54.

34. White Kennett, *An Account of the Society for Propagating the Gospel in Foreign Parts . . .* (London, 1706), 8.

35. See "Instructions for the Clergy Employed by the SPG," in C. F. Pasco, *Two Hundred Years of the SPG: An Historical Account of the SPG, 1701–1900* (London, 1901), 2:837–39. For a discussion of the selection of missionaries, see Alfred W. Newcombe, "The Appointment and Instruction of SPG Missionaries," *CH* 5 (1936): 340–58.

36. Pascoe, *Two Hundred Years,* 838.

37. Ibid., 839.

38. Nelson, "Anglican Missions," 84.

39. Kirby, *Keith,* 39.

40. For a discussion of Keith's theological position, see Chapter 5.

41. George Keith to Thomas Bray, 26 February 1703, SPG Letters, A, 1, 88.

42. George Keith, *A Journal of Travels from New Hampshire to Caratuck On the Continent of North-America* (London, 1706), ed. E. L. Pennington, *HM* 33 (December 1951): 377.

43. [George Keith], "An Account of the State of the Church in North America by Mr. George Keith & others," 19 March 1702, SPG Journals, Appendix 1, 26, 177–90. Keith time and again described the New England colonies with the comment "All Dissenters." Nevertheless, he pointed to the fact that there were Episcopalians in Swansee, Naragensett, Siconet, Braintree, Salem, Ipswich, and Piscataway. People in Swansee and Piscataway had petitioned the bishop of London for ministers. In Naragensett he noted that there was "no form of Public Religion" yet, i.e., worship according to the Book of Common Prayer. In the English counties of New York (those nearest the city), only Suffolk was without a legal establishment. In addition Keith recorded that there were two churches in Queens, one in Westchester, and a large church (Trinity) in the city itself. There was a chapel at Fort Henry and, he noted, some pro-Church of England settlers in Ulster County and at Albany. Philadelphia and its environs had four congregations and but two ministers. The Jerseys had seven parishes, while Maryland had twenty-six "well supplied with ministers." Virginia had forty parishes "not fully supplied with ministers and schools." There were no recordings for either North or South Carolina.

44. Mr. [John] Talbot to the secretary, 1 September 1703, SPG Letters, A, 1, 125; cf. Churchwardens of Burlington, New Jersey, to the secretary, 4 September 1703, ibid., 128; Talbot to the secretary, 2 April 1704, ibid., 181; "An Extract of Letters Lately Received," 27 February 1701, SPG Journals, Appendix 1, 9; "Extracts from Several Foreign Letters Relating to Governor Nicholson's Benefactions," 20 October 1704, ibid., 59; "Mr. Keith's Account of the Benefactions of Colonel Nicholson," 17 November 1704, ibid., 9; Clergy of South Carolina to the secretary, 12 July 1722, SPG Letters, A, 16, 76.

45. Dorothy Louise Noble, "Life of Francis Nicholson" (Ph.D. diss., Columbia University, 1958), 33–54.

46. Ibid., 678f.

47. Ibid., 49; see also 44f., 667–68, 732–46.

48. Ibid., 789.

49. Steven Saunders Webb, "The Strange Career of Francis Nicholson," *WMQ,* 3rd Series, 23 (1966): 513–48.

50. Ruth M. Winton, "Governor Francis Nicholson's Relations with the Society for the Propagation of the Gospel in Foreign Parts," *HM* 17 (1948): 274–86.

51. For the association of these men with each other, see Colonel Lewis Morris to the secretary, 30 May 1709, SPG Letters, A, 4, 149.

52. "Character of the Revd. Mr. Vesey Taken out of the Newspapers, vizt, New York, July 14, 1746," quoted in Morgan Dix, *A History of the Parish of Trinity Church in the City of New York* (New York, 1898), 1:231.

53. Ibid., 141f., 193, 221.

54. Ibid., 194.

55. Secretary to Elias Neau, 23 August 1715, SPG Letters, A, 10, 270.

56. William Vesey to the secretary, March 1713, SPG Letters, A, 8, 120.
57. Ernest Hawkins, *Historical Notices of the Mission of the Church of England* (London, 1845), 143. While the rest of the figures mentioned here appear prominently in this history, Lilliston is less well known. He received his B.A. from Jesus College, Oxford, in 1676 and then served as vicar of Ilmer, Buckinghamshire. He came to Maryland in 1681; ten years later he was appointed rector of St. Paul's Church, Queen Anne County, where he served until his death (Percy G. Skirven, *The First Parishes of the Province of Maryland* [Baltimore, 1923], 145). He was recommended for suffragan bishop around 1704. See also Nelson W. Rightmyer, *Maryland's Established Church* (Baltimore, 1965), 197–98.
58. The origin of the term *whig* is not sure. It may come from the Scottish *whiggam*, the driving of horses, or *whiggamore*, a drover or farmer. The association here is with the Scottish Presbyterians. In 1648 a band of whiggamores, who usually went to Leith for farm supplies, marched instead to oppose Charles I. The issue was royal prerogative vs. the rights of local government. The term *whig* was also used as an acrostic of the Scottish Covenanters' motto "We hope in God." By the enemies of the whigs, the term was also associated with whey or sour milk, an uncomplimentary reference to the dour faces of Presbyterian lowlanders of the commonwealth period who ate such fare.

　　The term *Tory* derives from the Gaelic "Ta a Ri," "Come O King." The reference is to the Stuart kings.
59. Rightmyer, *Maryland's Church*, 172.
60. Parke Rouse, Jr., *James Blair of Virginia* (Chapel Hill, N.C., 1971), 81.
61. Elias Neau to the secretary, 15 October 1712, SPG Letters, A, 7, no. 39.
62. Elias Neau to the secretary, 9 June 1709, SPG Letters, A, 4, 160.
63. Joseph Hildreth to Daniel Burton, New York, 17 October 1772, SPG Letters, B, 3, no. 168.
64. Richmond Pugh Bond, *Queen Anne's American Kings* (Oxford, 1952), 17, quoted in Nelson, "Anglican Missions," 679. For a fascinating description of Episcopalian "humanitarianism" in the mission of William Andrews to the Mohawks in New York from 1712 to 1719, see Nelson, 712–33. Nelson shows that the failure of this important mission was due to a number of factors: the strangeness of Indian customs to the English (such as wife swapping), the language barrier (Andrews had to use a Dutch interpreter), unimaginative catechetical instruction, the resulting Indian boredom (despite bribery in gifts for attendance at the mission school), and Andrews's own disillusionment with the Mohawks' "filthy brutish lives."
65. Frank J. Klingberg, *Anglican Humanitarianism in Colonial New York* (Philadelphia, 1940), 49.
66. John Talbot to Richard Gillingham, 24 November 1702, SPG Letters, A, 1, 56.
67. George Muirson to the secretary, 4 August 1708, SPG Letters, A, 4, 168.
68. Lawrence H. Leder, *Robert Livingston, 1654–1728 and the Politics of Colonial New York* (Chapel Hill, N.C., 1961), 212.
69. Ibid.
70. "A Letter from the Lords Commissioners of Trade and Plantations to the Archbishop of Canterbury Concerning the Conversion of the Indians," 25 October 1700, SPG Journals, Appendix 1, 5, 34.
71. Godfrey Dellius to the secretary, 29 May 1702, SPG Letters, A, 1, 7; cf. ibid., 72.
72. Ibid.
73. Governor Spotswood to Bishop Robinson, 27 January 1715, Fulham Papers, 1, A, 11, 223f.
74. SPG Journals, A, Appendix 1, 88.
75. Talbot to Gillingham, SPG Letters, A, 61; cf. "Memorial of the Council of War appointed to Her Majesty for Managing Ye Expedition to Port Royal, Nova Scotia to the Society," 9 October 1710, ibid., 10, 288, and Ashurst to the secretary, ibid., 1, 92.
76. Livingston, Memoriall, Journals, A, Appendix 1, 29.

77. Robert Stevens to the secretary, 3 February 1708, SPG Letters, A, 4, 19; cf. "A True and Just Account of Mr. Blair's Mission to North Carolina," 17 November 1704, SPG Journals, Appendix 1, 49, where the "French Interest" is also spoken of.
78. Indian Princes Address to the Queen . . . ," SPG Journals, Appendix 1, 138.
79. Ibid.; cf. The Board of Trade to the archbishop of Canterbury, 25 October 1700, SPG Journals, Appendix 1, no. 5, for an earlier expression of readiness on the part of the Iroquois for missionaries.
80. Indian sachems to the Society, 22 May 1710, SPG Letters, A, 5, nos. 88 and 93.
81. John Talbot to the secretary, 1 September 1703, ibid., A, 1, 125. Nevertheless, Talbot may have been right. The Iroquois attached great significance to the presence among them of officers representing the state as well as the church, and bishops were, after all, lords spiritual.
82. Gordon, Proposals, Appendix 1, 60.
83. Elias Neau to the secretary, 15 April 1704, SPG Letters, A, 1, 178; cf. Samuel Thomas to the secretary, n.d. (1704?), ibid., 79.
84. See, for instance, SPG Journals, 2, 261, pertaining to Indian education in Virginia and South Carolina; cf. Charles Smith, Memoriall, n.d. (1703?), ibid., Appendix 1, 32 and 36, and C. Congreve, State of the Church in the Province of New York, A 1704, ibid., 48, 250, and Charles Smith to the secretary, 5 October 1703, SPG Letters, 1, 102.
85. Governor John Wentworth to Bishop Terrick, 28 April 1770, Fulham Papers, I, A, 6, 114.
86. Henry Barclay to the secretary, 2 December 1746, SPG Letters, B, 14, 97; cf. Henry Barclay to the secretary, 18 February 1747, ibid., 124, and John Fordyce to the secretary, 6 October 1746, ibid., 14.
87. Gerald J. Goodwin, "Christianity, Civilization, and the Savage: The Anglican Mission to the American Indian," *HM* 42 (June 1973): 110.
88. Thomas Cradock, "Sermon Preached after the Victory over Scotch Rebels in the Battle of Culloden, 1746," Maryland Diocesan Archives, 2. See also David C. Skaggs and F. Garner Ranney, "Thomas Cradock Sermons," *MHM* 67 (1972): 179–80, and David C. Skaggs, "The Chain of Being in Eighteenth Century Maryland: The Paradox of Thomas Cradock," *HM* 45 (June 1976): 155–64, for a description of Cradock's significance.

Notes to Chapter 4

1. Cotton Mather, *Diary of Cotton Mather*, ed. W. C. Ford (New York, n.d. [1957?]), 1:133f. The tract referred to was Increase Mather's *A Brief Discourse concerning the Unlawfulness of Common Prayer Worship*. Use of the Book of Common Prayer had been known in Boston since 16 May 1681, when Governor Joseph Dudley brought the Anglican minister Robert Ratcliffe with him.
2. Samuel Sewall, *The Diary of Samuel Sewall*, ed. M. H. Thomas (New York, 1973), 1:127.
3. Ibid.
4. Ibid., 122, 132, 133.
5. Ibid., 133, 140–45.
6. Edgar L. Pennington, *Anglican Beginnings in Massachusetts* (Boston, 1941), 41.
7. Robert C. Winthrop, ed., *Life and Letters of John Winthrop* (Boston, 1869), 1:11.
8. Sprague, *Annals*, 5:1. Blackstone or Blaxton was a graduate of Emmanuel College, Cambridge, M.A. 1621; he came to Massachusetts in 1625 but did not exercise his ministry; see *Alumni Cantabrigiensis*, 1:1, 162. It is not likely that he was killed in King Philip's War, which did not begin until June 1675; Blackstone died on May 26. See Benjamin Church, *Diary of King Philip's War* (Chester, Conn.: 1975), 30.
9. Goodwin, *Colonial Church*, 288. Lyford received his M.A. from Oxford in 1602; see *Alumni Oxoniensis*, 3–4:953. For the Puritan caste of Magdelen College, see Green, *Religion*, 107. Lyford is also dealt with in Pennington, *Anglican Beginnings in Mas-*

sachusetts, 8f.; Dudley Tyng, *Massachusetts Episcopalians, 1607–1957* (Pascoag, R.I., 1960), 3f.

10. *DNB*, 13:984; *Alumni Cantabrigiensis*, 1:3, 214. Morrell received his B.A. in 1614.

11. Pennington, *Anglican Beginnings in Massachusetts*, 4–7; Slotkin, *Regeneration through Violence*, 58–65; and, most recently, Robert M. Bartlett, *The Faith of the Pilgrims* (New York, 1978), 175–78, to name a few. Thomas Morton of Merry Mount may have been the same Thomas Morton who matriculated at Balliol College, Oxford, in 1610 (*Alumni Oxoniensis*, 3–4:1039). This man was from Dorset. We are told that the American Thomas Morton "practised [law] chiefly in the west of England" (*DNB*, 13:1055). Both are listed as "gent."

12. Thomas Morton, *New English Canaan; or New Canaan* (London, 1632), 79.

13. Kenneth B. Murdock, *Increase Mather, the Foremost American Puritan* (Cambridge, Mass., 1925), 8.

14. William Bradford, *History of Plymouth Plantation, 1620–1647* (Boston, 1912), 1:70.

15. Quoted in J. Hammon Trumbull, "A Sketch of the Life of Thomas Lechford," in *Note-Book Kept by Thomas Lechford Esq., Lawyer*, ed. Edward Everett Hale (Cambridge, Mass., 1885), xi.

16. Thomas Lechford to Hugh Peters, 11 March 1638, in Hale, *Lechford*, 49.

17. Thomas Lechford to [recipient not given], 28 May 1640, in ibid., 274f.

18. Ibid., 275.

19. Ibid., 276.

20. Ibid., 277.

21. See Thomas Lechford, *Plain Dealing: or Newes from New-England* (London, 1642).

22. It has been claimed that Eaton took holy orders in the 1630s before coming to America (*DNB* 6:337f.). I find no record of ordination. Furthermore, Eaton studied under William Ames in the early 1630s at Franeker in Holland. There he proved himself to be a strict sabbatarian. Elected first "president" of Harvard, he proved to be a tyrannous and disastrous disciplinarian and administrator. While in Cambridge, he was "not yet sealed and sanctified by the Cambridge brethren" (Samuel Eliot Morison, *The Founding of Harvard College* [Cambridge, Mass., 1935], 203). In other words, he was not a church member in the Congregational way. Upon moving to Virginia, Eaton became clerk at Hungar's Parish, Northampton County, from 1639 to 1645. While this action indicates a reversion to the Anglican faith of his father's vicarage in England, it does not tell us whether he was in orders, for a clerk in the Church of England might or might not be ordained. During the interregnum, Eaton gained a Ph.D. and an M.D. from the University of Padua (1647). After that, he lived privately in Cromwell's England. However, in 1661 he conformed to the Church of England and may have been ordained at that time. As it was, Eaton then became a "bitter persecutor of dissenters" (Cotton Mather, *Magnalia Christi Americana*, 4:127). For such loyalty to church and crown he received the rich rectorship of Bideford in Devonshire. Erratic and often dishonest behavior caught up with him, and he died in debtors' prison in 1674 (Goodwin, *Colonial Church*, 266; Levy, *Puritanism*, 142f.).

23. Maverick had a fortified house in present-day Cheslsea and also owned Noddles Island in Boston Harbor. He left Massachusetts in 1650. He then published a *Briefe Description of New England* (London, 1660). He returned in 1664 to Massachusetts as one of four royal commissioners and eventually settled in New York. See *DNB* 12:432–33.

24. Child received his M.A. from Cambridge in 1635; he then studied medicine at Leyden and took an M.D. from the University of Padua in 1638. He came to Massachusetts in 1644, where he was imprisoned for his religious views. Released in 1647, he returned to England where he settled in Kent. See *Alumni Catabrigiensis*, 1:1, 333.

25. Quoted in Peter Oliver, *The Puritan Commonwealth* (Boston, 1856), 423.

26. For a description of this case, see G. L. Kittredge, "Dr. Robert Child the Remonstrant," Publication of the Colonial Society of Massachusetts, 146, 21, and John Child, *New-England's Jonah Cast Up at London* (London, 1647).

27. William Pynchon to John Winthrop, 9 March 1647, *Winthrop Papers*, 2:13; cf. Joseph H.

Smith, ed., *Colonial Justice in Western Massachusetts (1639–1702): The Pynchon Court Record* (Cambridge, Mass., 1961), 19–20.

28. Quoted in Pennington, *Massachusetts,* 29.

29. Ibid., 34.

30. David Humphreys, *An Account of the Incorporated Society for the Propagation of the Gospel in Foreign Parts* (London, 1730 [New York, 1969]), 312.

31. John M. Murrin, ''Anglicizing an American Colony: The Transformation of Provincial Massachusetts'' (Ph.D. diss., Yale University, 1966), 197.

32. William Manross, *A History of the American Episcopal Church* (New York, 1935), 31.

33. Jeremy Belknap, *The History of New Hampshire,* (New York, 1833 [1970]), 1:104–8; see also Edwin D. Sanforn, *History of New Hampshire from Its First Discovery to the Year 1830* (Manchester, 1875), 85.

34. Patricia U. Bonomi, *A Factious People: Politics and Society in Colonial New York* (New York, 1971), 54f.

35. William G. McLoughlin, *New England Dissent, 1630–1833* (Cambridge, Mass., 1971), 1:201.

36. Henry W. Foote, *Annals of King's Chapel* (Boston, 1882), 1:95f.; see also Susan M. Reed, *Church and State in Massachusetts* (Urbana, Ill., 1914), chapter 6.

37. For example, Braintree (1702), Scituate (1727), Taunton (1742), Marshfield (1742), Bridgewater (1747), Canton (1755), and Dedham (1756) on the South Shore; Newbury (1712), Marblehead (1714), Salem (1733), and Amesbury (1762) on the North Shore. Christ Church, Cambridge, was formed in 1759, while further afield parishes were started in Hopkinton (1738), Great Barrington (1761), and Lanesborough (1763). Timothy Cutler speaks of baptizing persons in Sudbury, Gloucester, Woburn, and Billerica. See Dudley Tyng, *Massachusetts Episcopalians, 1607–1957* (Pascoag, R.I., 1960), 10–17. Tyng reports that by 1735 there were four parishes in Rhode Island, headed by St. Paul's, Wickford (1706), and St. Michael's, Bristol (1722); St. John's in Portsmouth, New Hampshire (1735), marked the furthest northerly reach of the Church of England to that date.

38. Murrin, ''Transformation,'' 65, 78–82.

39. Ibid., 157, 160, 173.

40. Ibid., 263–66.

41. Clifford K. Shipton, *Biographical Sketches of Those Who Attended Harvard College* (Cambridge, Mass., 1933), 7:92–100. Miller was in the class of 1722.

42. Ibid., 12:110–12.

43. Franklin Bowditch Dexter, *Biographical Sketches of the Graduates of Yale College* (New York, 1885), 2:731–33.

44. Sewall, *Diary,* 1:119, 171.

45. Ibid., 172.

46. Checkley to Read, 24 December 1720, in Edmund F. Slafter, ed., *John Checkley or the Evolution of Religious Tolerance in Massachusetts* (Boston, 1897), 2:147.

47. Francis L. Hawks and William S. Perry, eds., *Documentary History of the Protestant Episcopal Church in the United States of America* (New York, 1863–64), 1:20–21, 27, and 38.

48. McLoughlin, *Dissent,* 1:208. McLoughlin is not, apparently, aware of Read's identity and thinks he sounds like a Baptist in the case involving Recompense Wadsworth (1711). For descriptions of Read, see Shipton, *Harvard Graduates,* 4:369–78, and cf. David H. Flaherty, ed., *Essays in the History of Early American Law* (Chapel Hill, N.C., 1969), 422, 423.

49. See Shipton, *Harvard Graduates,* 4:377.

50. Suffolk Court Files, No. 18112, Paper No. 1, quoted in Slafter, *Checkley,* 2:44.

51. Mather, *Diary,* 2:716, 605, 703.

52. Mather to Dr. James Durin, 21 May 1723, in Kenneth Silverman, ed., *Selected Letters of Cotton Mather* (Baton Rouge, La., 1971), 359.

53. Mather, *Diary,* 364, also 353, 359; see Murrin, ''Transformation,'' 38.

54. See Thomas Walter, *Choice Dialogue between John Faustus, a Conjurer, and Jack Tory, his Friend* (Boston, 1720).

55. Noble, "Nicholson," 402f.

56. Mather, *Diary,* 2:290.

57. Ibid., 291.

58. Sewall, *Diary,* 2:735.

59. Ibid., 743–45.

60. For comment on Thomas Dudley, Winthrop's deputy governor in the early days of the Bay Colony and Joseph's father, see Darrett Rutman, *Winthrop's Boston* (Chapel Hill, N.C., 1965), 31; see Selma R. Williams, *Kings, Commoners, and Colonists* (New York, 1974), 107f. For further comment on Joseph Dudley, see Perry, *History,* 1:175–81; John Gorham Palfrey, *A Compendious History of New England* (Boston, 1873), 2:291–313; 3, chapter 8.

61. Slafter, *Checkley,* 1:143.

62. Gerald J. Goodwin, "The Anglican Middle Way in Early Eighteenth Century America: Anglican Religious Thought in the American Colonies, 1702–1750" (Ph.D. diss., University of Wisconsin, 1965), 41.

63. Slafter, *Checkley,* 1:144.

64. Ignatius of Antioch (fl. 90) was a Syrian churchman, bishop of Antioch, who wrote seven letters to churches in Asia Minor while on his way to execution in Rome.

65. For helpful definitions of deism see the following: *New Catholic Encyclopedia,* 4:721–24; Ernst Cassirer, *The Philosophy of the Enlightenment,* tr. F. Koelln and J. Pettegrove (Princeton, N.J., 1951); Herbert Morais, *Deism in 18th Century America* (New York, 1960); and G. Adolph Koch, *Religion of the American Enlightenment* (New York, 1968), originally published under the title *Republican Religion* (New York, 1922).

66. Goodwin, "Middle Way," 38f.

67. Checkley, "Appendix," *Defence,* 2.

68. Checkley, *Modest Proof,* in Slafter, *Checkley,* 232.

69. Checkley, "Discourse concerning Episcopacy," in Charles Leslie, *A Short and Easie Method* (8th ed., Boston and London, 1723), 41–42, 45, quoted in Goodwin, "Middle Way," 59.

70. Checkley, *Defence,* in Slafter, *Checkley,* 84, and Goodwin, "Middle Way," 54.

71. Slafter, *Checkley,* 1:7. Nonjurors were those English and Scottish bishops and lower clergy who refused to break their oaths of allegiance to James II, even though they detested his Roman Catholicism.

72. Murrin, "Transformation," 31.

73. Checkley does so, for instance, in *A Modest Proof* (Slafter, *Checkley,* 1:223f.) and in his "A Discourse Showing Who is a True Pastor of the Church of Christ" (Slafter, *Checkley,* 1:246).

74. Wesley F. Craven, *The Colonies in Transition* (New York, 1958), 247.

75. Goodwin, "Middle Way," 62f.

76. Cotton Mather, *Bonifacius,* ed. David Levin (Cambridge, Mass., 1966), in particular 17–34.

77. Checkley to John Read, 30 January 1720, in Slafter, *Checkley,* 2, 149.

78. Ibid., 150.

79. Thomas C. Reeves, "John Checkley and the Emergence of the Episcopal Church in New England," *HM* 34 (December 1965): 352.

80. Nelson, "Anglican Missions," 561.

81. Foote, *King's Chapel,* 1:224.

82. Arthur Bernon Tourtellot, *Benjamin Franklin: The Shaping of Genius, the Boston Years* (Garden City, N.Y., 1977), 281.

83. References to the above named are as follows: John Gibbin, in Shipton, *Harvard Graduates,* 5:315–17; William Douglass, in Massachusetts Historical Society, *Collections,* 4th Series, 2:182, for Douglass's correspondence with New York's Episcopalian

deist Cadwallader Colden (see below, Chapter 9); for George Steward, see Edward J. Forster, *From the Professional and Industrial History of Suffolk County, Massachusetts: A Sketch of the Medical Profession* (Boston, 1894), 279; John Eyre, in Shipton, *Harvard Graduates*, 6:240–42; Thomas Fleet, in *DNB*, 6:457–58; John Valentine, in ibid., 383. For further discussion of Franklin's religion, see Chapter 9.

84. Benjamin Franklin, *Autobiography* (New Haven, Conn., 1964), 67.
85. Tourtellot, *Franklin*, 287.
86. *Alumni Oxoniensis*, 1–2:655. Harris was a fellow of Jesus College, Oxford, even while he was in Boston, which points to a degree of theological acumen or at least fashionableness.
87. Greene and Harrington, *American Population*, 6–7, 89, 106.
88. Nelson, "Anglican Missions," 255.
89. See Leder, *Robert Livingston*, chapter 6.
90. Colonel Lewis Morris to the secretary, 1707, SPG Journals, Appendix B, no. 121.
91. Nelson, "Anglican Missions," 275. Nelson notes the imprisonment not only of the well-known Francis Makemie, the pioneer Presbyterian organizer, but also that of the Episcopalian minister in New Jersey Thoroughgood Moore.
92. Thomas Prichard to the secretary, 6 June 1704, SPG Letters, A, 1, no. 169.
93. Morris, Journals, Appendix B., no. 121.
94. Morris to the secretary, 30 May 1709 SPG Letters, A, 4, no. 149, quoting Colonel Richard Ingoldsby of New Jersey.
95. Morris to the secretary, 13 June 1714, SPG Letters, A, 7, 164; cf. "Memorial of the Clergy relating to Mr. Poyer and the Church in Jamaica to the Bishop of London," n.d. [1712], ibid., 295f., and "Address of the Clergy of New York to R[obert] Hunter," 20 February 1712, ibid., B, 1:445. The issue involved the incumbency of the Reverend Thomas Poyer at the Episcopal church in Jamaica (a place and cure of continuous contention between Presbyterians and successive Anglican governors) and Hunter's renovation of the chapel at New York's fort in opposition to Vesey's Trinity Church. See Nelson, "Anglican Missions," 287–301.
96. Nelson, "Anglican Missions," 255.
97. Ibid., 258.
98. Heathcote's missionary concern is seen in his petition to King William for a minister in Westchester County; see *Calendar of State Papers, Colonial Series* (London, 1912), 17. For Heathcote's importance as lawyer and landowner, see ibid., no. 166, 187, 328, and 341. Heathcote's biographer is Dixon Ryan Fox, *Caleb Heathcote, Gentleman Colonist: The Story of a Career in the Province of New York, 1692–1721* (New York, 1926).
99. Hawks and Perry, eds., *Documentary History, Connecticut*, 20.
100. Samuel Johnson to the secretary, 20 September 1727, SPG Letters, B, 1:224, for a description of the parish.
101. See Clifford K. Shipton, *New England Life in the 18th Century* (Cambridge, Mass., 1963), 79–101, for a sketch of Cutler's personality.
102. Quoted in Shipton, *New England Life*, 84. Cutler in his turn described Edwards—thirty years later—as "a man of much sobriety and gravity and of more decent language than the Mayhew faction, but odd in his principles, haughty, stiff and morose." Shipton is incorrect in supposing this to be a description of Cutler (99); cf. Herbert and Carol Schneider, eds., *Samuel Johnson . . . His Career and Writings* (New York, 1929), 4:318.
103. Hawks and Perry, *Documentary History, Connecticut*, 56.
104. For a discussion of the "broad and catholick" atmosphere which permitted full membership for dues-paying members, ritual use of the Lord's Prayer, and acceptance of the Presbyterian ministry by John Leverett and William and Thomas Brattle, see Sydney E. Ahlstrom, *A Religious History of the American People* (New Haven, Conn., 1972), 161f. For treatment of the impact of Solomon Stoddard on the churches of the Connecticut valley, see Paul R. Lucas, *Valley of Discord: Church and Society along the*

Connecticut, 1636–1725 (Hanover, N.H., 1976); Lucas draws attention to the Presbyterian influence on Stoddard, i.e., "open communion," a national church, and a "complicated apparatus of clerical organizations" (149).

105. See Perry Miller, *The New England Mind: From Colony to Province* (Cambridge, Mass., 1953), 417; cf. Goodwin, "Middle Way," chapter 3, Raymond W. Albright, *A History of the Protestant Episcopal Church* (New York, 1964), 63f., and Richard Warch, *School of the Prophets, Yale College, 1701–1740* (New Haven, Conn., 1973), 96–121, to name a few.

   Besides Cutler and Samuel Johnson who are treated at length in this study, the remaining five were as follows: Daniel Browne (1698–1723), who accompanied Cutler and Johnson to London, was ordained in the Church of England and died a month later, Dexter, *Yale Graduates,* 1:118–20; John Hart (1686–1730), who did not become a priest in the Church of England, Dexter, *Yale Graduates,* 1:13–17; Samuel Whittelsey (1686–1752), like Hart, remained in the Congregational church, Dexter, *Yale Graduates,* 1:40–44; Jared Eliot (1685–1763) likewise remained a Congregationalist, an Old Light in the Great Awakening, Dexter, *Yale Graduates,* 1:52–56; James Wetmore (1695–1760) was ordained in the Church of England, though some months later than Cutler and Johnson. Thereafter he became minister in Westchester County, New York, Dexter, *Yale Graduates,* 1:133–38.

106. Henry F. May, *The Enlightenment in America* (New York, 1976), 77.

107. Hawks and Perry, eds., *Documentary History, Connecticut,* 58.

108. Pigot to the secretary of the SPG, 3 October 1722, ibid., 59.

109. See above n. 105.

110. Goodwin, "Middle Way," 85.

111. Burr, *Diocese of Connecticut,* 26.

112. Shipton, *Harvard Graduates,* 5:58. Cutler, together with Samuel Myles, also memorialized the Board of Trade against the synod. They received, however, a reprimand on 23 June 1725 for their efforts. Rectors Myles (of King's Chapel) and Cutler were told that they had overstepped the bounds of decorum and that their memorial contained an "indecent reflection on the proceedings of this Board." See *Calendar of State Papers, Colonial Series 1724–5* (London, 1936), no. 739. For biographical material on Myles, see *Appleton's Encyclopedia of American Biography,* 4:474.

113. John Nichols, *Illustrations of the Literary History of the Eighteenth Century* (London, 1817–58), 4:279, quoted in Shipton, *New England Life,* 91.

114. Curwin Mss, 12 April 1711, quoted in Shipton, *New England Life,* 82.

115. He lost one son from sickness in early 1739 after he had sent the boy on a Mediterranean voyage for his health. See Shipton, *Harvard Graduates,* 9:393.

116. Jonathan Edwards to Timothy Edwards, 21 July 1719, in Dexter, *Documentary History of Yale University* (New Haven, Conn., 1916), 195. See also Samuel Myles to Bishop Robinson, n.d. [1722], *Fulham Papers,* A, 4:84–85. Myles called attention to Cutler's "Unblemisht character," his mature deliberation, and his sincerity in becoming an Episcopalian.

117. Such an attitude was common on the part of eighteenth-century high churchmen and other Episcopalians of an aristocratic nature. See, for instance, Timothy Cutler, "Mr. Cutler's Re-presentation," in Hawks and Perry, *Documentary History, Connecticut,* 80; the letters of George Pigot, ibid., 56f.; and Cadwallader Colden, "Account of the Government of the New England Colonies," Cadwallader Colden Papers (New-York Historical Society, 1918), 9:245.

118. John Checkley to Francis Nicholson, 11 December 1725, in Slafter, *Checkley,* 2:182–84.

119. John Checkley to the secretary, 6 November 1740, ibid., 194.

120. Ibid., 196.

121. John Checkley to the Rev. Mr. Black, 27 December 1727, ibid., 186.

122. Stenerson, "Anglican Critique," 478.

123. Gabriel Thomas, *An Historical and Geographical Account of the Province and Country of Pensilvania; and of West-New Jersey* (London, 1698), quoted in George M. Hills, *History of the Church in Burlington, New Jersey* (Trenton, N.J., 1876), 17; see also Albert C. Myers, ed., *Narratives of Early Pennsylvania, West New Jersey, and Delaware, 1630–1707* (New York, 1912), 313–37, for the full text of Thomas's work.

124. Jeremiah Bass, "History of the Church at Burlington," n.d. [1715], SPG Journals, A, 10:226.

125. Robert M. Duncan, "A Study of the Ministry of John Talbot in New Jersey, 1702–1727: On 'Great Ripeness'[,] Much Dedication, and Regrettable Failure," *HM* 42:238.

126. See in particular Edgar L. Pennington, *Apostle of New Jersey: John Talbot, 1645–1727* (Philadelphia, 1938). Talbot was from Norfolk in the north of England and the son of a gentleman. He attended Christ College in Cambridge and took his M.A. from Peterhouse in 1671. Talbot was rector in Suffolk, England, from 1673 to 1689. It is said that he came to Virginia after 1689—as an émigré Jacobite. In 1695 he returned to England, where he had a cure in Gloucestershire. When Talbot joined Keith and settled in Burlington he was already fifty-nine years old. See Burr, *Anglican Church*, 38–43, 642–44.

127. Duncan, "Talbot," 241; Nelson, "Anglican Missions," 390.

128. George Keith to Thomas Bray, February 1703, in Pennington, *Apostle*, 28f.

129. Nelson, "Anglican Missions," 389.

130. Talbot to Whitefield, SPG Letters, A, 2:24. Francis Bugg (1640–1724?) was an ex-Quaker whose philippics against the Society of Friends were notorious (see *DNB*, 3:226–28).

131. Ibid.

132. There were approximately twelve thousand people in East Jersey and eight thousand in West Jersey, of whom six hundred were Episcopalians. In terms of churches, there were seven Dutch Reformed, seven Quaker, three Congregational, three Presbyterian, two Baptist, two Episcopalian, and one Lutheran in 1701. By 1725 there were only three Episcopal congregations served with any regularity (Burlington, Elizabeth Town, and Perth Amboy), though there were some churchmen at Hopewell, Salem, and Shrewsbury, where missionaries had been known briefly. See Burr, *Anglican Church*, iii, 60; Nelson, "Anglican Missions," 380, 406.

133. Nelson, "Anglican Missions," 384.

134. John Talbot to the secretary, 1 September 1703, SPG Letters, A, 1:125.

135. See SPG Journals, 1, 2:245; Letters, A, 11:335; Hills, *Church in Burlington*, 154–56, 160; Pennington, *Apostle*, 38–39, 96. Talbot was not the only one calling for episcopal authority; his Whig adversary in the church Lewis Morris made the same request (Morris, Memoriall, Journals, Appendix 1, 2).

136. Pennington, *Apostle*, 50, 52.

137. For the accusation see Pennington, *Apostle*, 58. Those who find good evidence, to use Nelson's term, for Talbot's consecration are, besides that historian (Nelson, "Anglican Missions," 397), Henry Broxap, *The Later Non-Jurors* (Cambridge, Mass., 1924), 88–90; Pennington, *Apostle*, 72–79; John Fulton, "The Non-Juring Bishops in America," in William S. Perry, *The History of the American Episcopal Church, 1587–1883* (Boston, 1885), 1:541–60; Hills, "John Talbot, The First Bishop in North America," *PMHB*, 3, 1 (1879): 32–55.

138. William W. Manross, "Apostle to New Jersey, John Talbot, 1645–1727," *HM* 8 (1939): 96–98, and Duncan, "Talbot," 255–56.

139. Duncan, "Talbot," 249.

140. Governor [Robert] Hunter to the Society, 9 April 1715, SPG Letters, A, 10:178.

141. John Talbot to the Society, 23 August 1715, in Pennington, *Apostle*, 59. The reference to Philadelphia is to Governor Gookin of Pennsylvania, who also charged Talbot with being a Jacobite; see Duncan, "Talbot," n 69, 250.

142. SPG Minutes, 16 October 1724, quoted in Nelson, "Anglican Missions," 397.

143. John Talbot to the secretary, 20 August 1708, quoted in Pennington, *Apostle*, 118.

144. John Talbot to the secretary, 5 December 1716, SPG Letters, A, 12:180.
145. Pennington, *Apostle*, 118.
146. John Talbot to the SPG, 24 August 1708, quoted in Pennington, *Apostle*, 119f.

Notes to Chapter 5

1. These were as follows: John Lilliston (1656–1709) from Jesus College (*Alumni Oxoniensis*, 2:914); Benjamin Noble (fl. 1700), Clare College (*Alumni Cantabrigiensis*, 2, 3, 259); Christopher Platts (fl. 1705), Peterhouse (*Alumni Cantabrigiensis*, 1, 3, 370); George Tubman (1668–1701), Queen's College (*Alumni Oxoniensis*, 2:1514); Hugh Jones, Gloucester Hall (*Alumni Oxoniensis*, 1:822); Henry Hall (1676–1722), Peterhouse, Cambridge (Rightmeyer, *Maryland's Church*, 186); Edward Top (fl. 1706), Brasenose (*Alumni Oxoniensis*, 3:1496); George Trotter (1667–1721), Peterhouse (*Alumni Cantabrigiensis* 1, 4, 268); Joseph Colebatch (fl. 1700), Oriel College, Oxford (Rightmeyer, *Maryland's Church*, 172); Stephen Bordley (1673–1709), Christ's College (*Alumni Cantabrigiensis*, 1, 4, 45); Jonathan White (fl. 1717), Jesus College, Cambridge (Rightmeyer, *Maryland's Church*, 219).
2. Charles M. Andrews, *Narratives of Insurrection, 1675–1690* (New York, [1915] 1959), 4.
3. Charles A. Barker, *The Background of the Revolution in Maryland* (New Haven, Conn., [1940] 1967), 1.
4. Quoted in A. Moss Ives, *The Ark and the Dove: The Beginning of Civil and Religious Liberties in America* (New York, [1936] 1969), 237.
5. No doubt a high degree of infant mortality, unbalanced sex ratios, maladministration in government, proprietary nepotism, heavy taxation upon the poor, and the deprivation of the franchise to the landless contributed to the disquiet. See Lois G. Carr and David W. Jordan, *Maryland's Revolutionary Government, 1689–1692* (Ithaca, N.Y., 1974), 180–88.
6. Francis Nicholson to Henry Compton, May 1694, Fulham Mss., Maryland, no. 145.
7. Gerald E. Hartdagen, "The Anglican Vestry in Colonial Maryland" (Ph.D. diss., Northwestern University, 1965), 17.
8. Carr and Jordan, *Maryland's Government*, 200f.
9. Hartdagen, "Anglican Vestry," 18.
10. *Alumni Oxoniensis*, 1–2:319.
11. Hartdagen, "Anglican Vestry," 17.
12. Carr and Jordan, *Maryland's Government*, 245f.
13. Michael G. Hall, Lawrence H. Leder, and Michael G. Kammen, eds., *The Glorious Revolution in America* (Chapel Hill, N.C., 1964), 172f.
14. Maryland Archives, 8:192–93.
15. Hall, Leder, and Kammen, *Glorious Revolution*, 161.
16. For example, in the same year the Reverend William Hunter, S.J., built, consecrated, and openly celebrated mass in the old capitol, St. Mary's. For this act he was arraigned before the governor and there defended by fellow Roman Catholic and lawyer Charles Carroll. See John Tracy Ellis, *Catholics in Colonial America* (Baltimore, 1965), 345, and Thomas O'Gorman, *A History of the Roman Catholic Church* (New York, 1895), 235.
17. It is hard to imagine that English lawyers vetoed the act of 1696 solely because of legal technicalities of language, as Hartdagen argues ("Anglican Vestry," 25). This historian does not reap the reward of his own research. The denial by the king of the act of 1696 reads as follows: "therein is a clause declaring all the Laws of *England* to be in force in *Maryland*; which Clause is of another nature than that which is set forth by the Title of the said Law." The point is that the imperial lawyers in London understood only too well that their Maryland counterparts were professing to follow England's laws while, in fact, curtailing them severely. Whitehall, far from fussing unnecessarily about the technicalities

of legal language, saw only too clearly that basic English rights, however newly granted, were being threatened in America.

18. Rightmeyer appears to regret England's evenhandedness in the matter (*Maryland's Church,* 20).

19. W. W. Abbot, *The Colonial Origins of the United States: 1607–1763* (New York, 1975), 65.

20. Endy, *Penn,* 193.

21. Thomas Bray, *A Memorial Representing the Present State of Religion* (London, 1700), in Steiner, *Bray,* 160. For reference to Bray's conversation with Keith, see Ethyn W. Kirby, *George Keith* (New York, 1942), 114.

22. Perry, *Historical Collections, Maryland,* 12.

23. Ibid., 1.

24. Ibid., 10.

25. Fulham Papers, Maryland, 1:A, ii, 102.

26. Ibid., 51–52.

27. See Steiner, *Bray,* passim. For the *Journal of Dr. Bray's Visitation* (to Maryland), see Fulham Papers, 1:A, ii, 141–59.

28. James Blair, *A Paraphrase on Our Saviour's Sermon on the Mount* (London, 1729), 44.

29. "Some Remarks Upon the Minutes of the Clergy of Virginia," 29 August 1705, Perry, *Historical Collections,* 1:157.

30. James Blair, *Our Saviour's Divine Sermon on the Mount,* 2nd ed. (London, 1740), 147–48.

31. "Some Remarks," Perry, *Historical Collections,* 1:168.

32. Ibid., 169.

33. Clergy to Queen Anne, 22 April 1703, Great Britain, Colonial Office 5, Board of Trade, Original Correspondence, Letters, 1313:303.

34. Clergy to the Bishop of London, 23 August 1703, Fulham Papers, A, 3:48.

35. "Some Remarks," Perry, *Historical Collections,* 1:154. Crambo is a word game in which one player gives a word or line of verse to which each of the others have to find a rhyme.

36. Clergy of Virginia to Henry Compton, 25 August 1703, Fulham Papers, 1:A, xi, 170–72.

37. For examples of the variety of assessment, see Samuel R. Mohler, "Commissary James Blair, Educator and Politician of Colonial Virginia (Ph.D. diss., University of Chicago, 1940), ii; Brydon, *Virginia's Mother Church,* 2:57; Meade, *Old Churches,* 1:154; Rouse, *Blair,* 257–61.

38. Leonard Labaree, *Conservatism in Early American History* (Ithaca, N.Y., 1959), 6; cf. Jack P. Greene, "Foundations of Political Power in the Virginia House of Burgesses, 1720–1776," *WMQ,* Series 3, 16 (October 1959): 484–506, and Greene's *The Quest for Power: The Lower House of the Assembly in the Southern Colonies, 1689–1776* (Chapel Hill, N.C., 1963), 28–31, 344–50, for particular reference to Virginia.

39. Hamilton J. Eckenrode, "Separation of Church and State in Virginia," *Sixth Annual Report of the Library Board of the Virginia State Library, 1908–1909* (Richmond, Va., 1909), 17–18; see also Perry, *American Episcopal Church,* 1:128; Troutman, *Establishment,* 71; Gundersen, "Anglican Ministry," 20f.

40. Troutman, *Establishment,* 93.

41. Rouse, *Blair,* 69. Rouse hints at Blair's Whig allegiance but never develops the theme; see in this regard 63, 64, 110, 134, 153.

42. "A Memoriall Concerning £2000 raised out of the Quitt Rents now begg'd for ye Colledge of Virginia," quoted in Rouse, *Blair,* 69f.

43. Ibid., 133.

44. While numerous histories of the period attest to gubernatorial Toryism, the following may prove helpful: for Andros, David S. Lovejoy, *The Glorious Revolution* (New York, 1972), 283, 331, 373; Rouse, *Blair,* 153; Andrews, *Colonial Period,* 3, 124; for Nicholson, Lovejoy, *Revolution,* 283; Rouse, *Blair,* 134, 153. For Spotswood, see Greene, *Quest,* 26, 29; Rouse, *Blair,* 193–94; and John C. Rainbolt, *From Prescription to Persuasion:*

Manipulation of Eighteenth-Century Virginia Economy (Port Washington, N.Y., 1974), 164–65.

45. For Drysdale, see Greene, *Quest*, 28, 245; Rouse, *Blair*, 207. For Gooch, see *DAB*; Greene, *Quest*, 28; and Rouse, *Blair*, 224. Gooch was closely associated with Edmund Gibson, bishop of London, an avowed Whig who built a "fence of prohibition" against Tories in the church. See Sykes, *Church and State*, 36.

46. James Blair, "Mr. James Blair's affidavit relating to the mal-administration of Col. Nicholson, Governor of Virginia, 25 April 1704," Perry, *Historical Collections*, 1:109.

47. Ibid., 106.

48. "Memorial Concerning Maladministration," 20 May 1703, Colonial Office, 5:1314, 63.

49. "Some Remarks," Perry, *Historical Collections*, 1:173.

50. Rouse, *Blair*, 185–86.

51. Perry, *Historical Collections*, 1:187–88.

52. Ibid., 1:192; Rouse, *Blair*, 194. See also R. A. Brock, ed., *Spotswood Letters* (Richmond, Va., 1884), 1, 126, for Spotswood's concern for the religious education of blacks and Indians; cf. McIlwaine, *Executive Journals of the Council*, 3:364, and the Spotswood letters to the bishop of London in Perry, *Historical Collections*, 1:191, and Brock, *Letters*, 2:19. Jerome W. Jones claims that Spotswood was, racially speaking, "Virginia's most perspicuous governor" (*JNH*, 46 [January 1961]: 17). The Spotswood letters, however, show the governor's primary political interest.

53. The South Farnham vestry declared that Latané's French accent offended their ears. It is more likely that his theology offended them even more, for, as one historian has put it, Latané "preached the doctrines of grace . . . from the pulpit; they [the parishioners] preferred a kind of preaching that dwelt more on moral principles and duties than on Christian faith." See W. H. Foote, *The Huguenots; or, Reformed French Church* (New York, 1870), quoted in Lucy Temple Latané, *Parson Latané, 1672–1732* (Charlottesville, Va., 1936), 28.

54. Greene, *Quest*, 346; also *Spotswood Letters*, 1:27, 66–67, 2:137, 158, 198, 203–8, 236–37, 292–94, as well as Perry, *Historical Collections*, 1:128, 245. Spotswood appealed to and was upheld by the solicitor general, Sir William Thompson (1678–1739), while Blair and the Ludwell faction appealed to Sir Robert Raymond (1673–1733), the attorney general and reputedly the better lawyer. Raymond upheld the vestry, in this case that of St. Anne's Parish, Essex County. Raymond, like Thompson, was a Tory, but tended to be more apolitical. For discussion of Thompson and Raymond, see *DNB*, 19:706 and 16:788–89, respectively. Raymond became lord chief justice in 1725.

55. For the letters see Perry, *Historical Collections*, 1:200–203; cf. Rouse, *Blair*, 204; also Perry, 209, 246, for Hugh Jones's questioning of Blair's ordination, in Jones to the bishop of London, 30 May 1719. John Robinson was appointed bishop of London at the end of Queen Anne's reign. He was the last English prelate to hold secular office as well as an ecclesiastical one: Robinson was lord privy seal and a Tory diplomat who helped negotiate the Treaty of Utrecht at the conclusion of the War of Spanish Succession. See Sykes, *Church and State*, 43–44; *DNB*, 17:22–26.

56. See Brock, *Spotswood Letters*, as follows: Spotswood to the bishop of London, 31 March 1713, 2:63; ibid., 23 May 1716, 158; and ibid., 13 June 1717, 253–55. See also 2:44, 88–93, 137–38.

57. P. G. Scott, "James Blair and the Scottish Church: A New Source," *WMQ*, 3rd Series, 33 (April 1976): 301. From 1690 on, Whiggism, Scotland, Presbyterianism, and illegal trade were to the Tories practically synonymous terms (see Noble, "Nicholson," 206). The charge of Presbyterianism was probably much overblown at the time (Gundersen, "Anglican Ministry," 48f.).

58. "A true Account of a Conference at Lambeth," 27 December 1697, Perry, *Historical Collections*, 1:37; see also 38–40.

59. Ibid., 18.

60. Rouse, *Blair*, 5.

61. Scott, "Blair," 300, 303.
62. Ibid., 308.
63. See, for example, "Queries to be Answered by Every Minister" (1724), in Perry, *Historical Collections,* 1:261–318. Parishes were large, twenty, thirty, fourty, sometimes one-hundred twenty miles in length, sometimes "fifty miles in circumference," with at times one to four hundred families. Often, besides the church proper, ther were "Chappels" in outlying areas. See Seiler, "Anglican Parish," and A. P. Flory, C. E. Hamilton, Jr., F. Nevitt, and A. M. Jones, eds., *Minutes of the Vestry: Truro Parish, Virginia, 1732–1785* (Lorton, Va., 1974), 1, 90, 104. All of this meant that attendance at Sunday services was irregular, and ministers often preached, read the marriage office, and buried the dead in places other than the church building proper. See Hugh Jones, *Present State of Virginia,* ed. Richard L. Morton (Chapel Hill, N.C., 1956), 125.
64. Scott, "Blair," 306, with reference to Samuel McCulloch, ed., "James Blair's Plan to Reform the Clergy of Virginia," *WMQ,* erd Series, 4 (1947): 72f., 74. Blair was not trying to establish English Tudor ecclesiastical courts in the tidewater.
65. James Blair, "Some of the Chief Grievances of the present constitution of Virginia, with an Essay towards the Remedies thereof," in McCulloch, "Blair's Plan," 84; cf. Michael Kammen, ed., "Virginia at the Close of the Seventeenth Century: An Appraisal by James Blair and John Locke," *VMHB* 74 (1966):167.
66. McCulloch, "Blair's Plan," 78, 82, 84.
67. Ibid., 84.
68. Thomas Bell, ed., *Records of the Meeting of the Exercise of Alford* (Aberdeen, 1897), 59, quoted in Walter Roland Foster, *Bishop and Presbytery: The Church of Scotland, 1661–1688* (London, 1958), 75.
69. See James K. Cameron, ed., *The First Book of Discipline* (Edinburgh, 1972), 97f.
70. Foster, *Bishop and Presbytery,* 62.
71. Cameron, *First Book of Discipline,* 36; see also 24, 31, 175.
72. Gundersen, "Virginia Vestry," 136; see Cameron, *First Book of Discipline,* 36. Gundersen counts 113 vestry elections between 1720 and 1776; 28 of these elections were unrelated to divisions of parishes.
73. Cameron, *First Book of Discipline,* 101; for Virginia see Chapter 2 above.
74. See, for instance, Hening, *Statutes,* 4:204–8; Brydon, *Virginia's Mother Church,* 1:238; and Gundersen, "Virginia Vestry," 138. Blair was never one to skimp on his own income: he received £330 per annum, while many of his clergy got between £80 and £100. Blair's salary may have exceeded the intake of many planters themselves, who were generally cash-hungry.

  Rouse makes the point that Blair himself had learned to compromise with local circumstances, and that whereas he had at first demanded induction, better glebe houses, more cows, books, and even slaves for his clergy, over the decades he became less strident in his requests. See *Blair,* 144–48, and also 150 and 205 for special reference to his reversal of policy on permanent tenure.
75. See Jones, *Present State,* 118. This enemy of Blair complained to the bishop of London that "vice, prophaneness, and immorality are not suppressed so much as might be: The people hate the very name of the bishop's court. There are no visitations."
76. James Blair, "Queries to be Answered by Persons who were Commissaries to my Predecessor," in Perry, *Historical Collections,* 1:260.
77. See Gundersen, "Anglican Ministry," 86, 89, 248. The breakdown of Gundersen's figures for 1723–1776 are as follows: forty-five received training at William and Mary; Oxford trained thirty-nine, with ten of that number having graduated from Queen's College, which took poor northern England students on scholarship (see J. Wells, *Oxford and Its Colleges* [London, 1899], 110–11; cf. Sykes, *Church and State,* 190–95); among the Queen's students was Edmund Gibson, future bishop of London and diocesan for Virginia. Cambridge educated twenty; four went to unspecified Scottish universities; thirteen to Edinburgh; seventeen to Aberdeen; ten to Glasgow; two to St. Andrews; eleven to Trinity

College, Dublin; one to Halle University; two to Catholic seminaries and ten "some-where" (Gundersen, 88). At least one of these "somewhere"'s was Yale; cf. John Clement, "Clergymen Licensed Overseas by the Bishops of London, 1696–1710," *HM* 16 (1947): 318–46, and his "Anglican Clergymen Licensed to the American Colonies, 1710–1744," *HM* 17 (1948): 207–50.

78. See Jones, *Present State.* Jones was influenced by his mentor John Wynne (1667–1743), the principal of Jesus College, Oxford, where Jones matriculated in 1709. Wynne was Lady Margaret Professor of Divinity and bishop of St. Asaph (1715). He was for "un-blushing Whig Propagandism" (*DNB*, 21:1177–78).

79. Jones, *Present State,* 117, 118.

80. Ibid., 98.

81. Perry, *Historical Collections,* 202–3, and particularly Mr. Jones to the bishop of London, 30 May 1719, 246.

82. In 1719, Blair did not have the English connections he had maintained in the 1690s. In 1691 he had knelt in the presence of William and Mary, a humble suppliant after a college charter. Then he had known John Locke (1632–1704), a member of the Board of Trade and Plantations; successive archbishops of Canterbury John Tillotson (1639–1694) and Thomas Tenison (1636–1715); and for a time William Wake (1657–1737); as well as the bishop of Salisbury, Gilbert Burnet (1643–1715); Winchester's Edward Stillingfleet (1635–1699); and London's Compton. By 1719, the commissary of Virginia had been transformed from an international churchman to a provincial leader. Blair remained such for the rest of his life.

83. Jones, *Present State,* 118f.

84. Gundersen, "Anglican Ministry," 249.

85. Brydon points out that the average length of tenure reported by twenty-eight ministers in 1724 was twenty-one years, *Virginia's Mother Church,* 1:374–83; cf. Brydon, "New Light upon the History of the Church in Colonial Virginia," *HM* 10 (1941): 78–83. For other sympathetic assessments, see Boorstin, *Americans: The Colonial Experience,* 123–31, and Arthur P. Middleton, "The Colonial Virginia Parson," *WMQ,* 3rd Series, 26:425–40. Nineteenth- and twentieth-century critical judgments can be found in Meade, *Old Churches,* 1:14–17, and Carl Bridenbaugh, *Myths and Realities: Societies of the Colonial South* (New York, 1963), 30–34. The latter volume echoes Meade's evangelical dislike for his "evil living" forebears.

86. Louis B. Wright, ed., *The Prose Works of William Byrd of Westover* (Cambridge, Mass., 1966), 49. A pistole was a gold coin, either Spanish (worth about 18 shillings in 1592), or the French louis d'or (1640), or, more probably, the Scottish twelve-pound piece of William III (1701), worth one English pound. For dullness in preaching, see "Journal of Col. James Gordon of Lancaster County, Va," *WMQ,* 1st Series, (1903), 109.

87. William Gooch to Thomas Gooch, 9 June 1728, quoted in Gundersen, "Anglican Minis-try," 143.

88. James Blair to Bishop Gibson, 27 July 1738, quoted in Gundersen, "Anglican Ministry," 144.

89. Gerald Fothergill, *A List of Emigrant Ministers to America* (London, 1904), 24.

90. "Marriage Bonds in Lancaster County," *WMQ,* 1st Series, 12 (October 1903): 99, 106.

91. Potter, "Growth of Population", 642, 638. Between 1700 and 1740, thirty-two thousand Africans were imported through the slave trade. The next decade saw an increase of fourteen thousand, while the peak decade for Virginia's slave trade was 1760–1770, when thirty thousand were imported and sold.

92. Adam Dickie to Henry Newman, 27 June 1732, Fulham Papers, 12:182–83. Newman was secretary of the SPG and forwarded the letter to Bishop Gibson, as Dickie requested.

93. James Blair to Bishop Gibson, 14 May 1731, Fulham Papers, 12:163–64.

94. Dickie to Newman, 27 July 1732, Fulham Papers, 12:183.

95. Ibid.

96. Henry Newman to Bishop Gibson, 15 November 1732, *Fulham Papers,* 12:183. Eight

years earlier, in 1724, Bishop Gibson had queried the colony's ministers as to the state of their cures. Responses concerning the instruction of the black population were discouraging. See Perry, *Historical Collections,* 1:257–318. Nevertheless, by means of the answers to such questionnaires as those supplied by the bishop of London, the English churchmen learned of conditions in America among the Afro-Americans. It is often claimed that the English had a monumental misconception of American conditions (Jordan, *White over Black,* 208), but in the light of reports from Godwyn to Dickie, one wonders if they were so naive after all: firsthand reports had been coming across episcopal desks for some time. Those reports came from Americans who were often shocked by their own conditions.

97. See, respectively, Thomas Dell to the bishop of London, 1 June 1724, Perry, *Historical Collections,* 1:255, and 278, 264, 301, and for Garzia, North Farnham Parish Register, 1672–1800, Virginia State Archives, quoted in Gundersen, "Anglican Ministry," 121.

98. See Robert A. Bennett, "Black Episcopalians: A History from the Colonial Period to the Present," *HM* 43 (1974): 231–45.

99. See Jordan, *White over Black,* 210.

100. Rhys Isaac, "Religion and Authority: Problems of the Anglican Establishment in Virginia in the Era of the Great Awakening and the Parsons' Cause," *WMQ* 30 (January 1973): 3f.

Notes to Chapter 6

1. Gideon Johnston to the secretary, 5 July 1710, printed in Frank J. Klingberg, ed., *Carolina Chronicle: The Papers of Commissary Gideon Johnston, 1707–1716* (Berkeley and Los Angeles, 1946), 60.

2. Gideon Johnston to the bishop of Sarum, 20 September 1708, in ibid., 22.

3. "Mr. Samuel Thomas's Remonstrance in Justification of Himself to the Honourable Society," n.d. (1704?), SPG Journals, A, 79:466.

4. Samuel Thomas to the SPG, 18 January 1706, SPG Journals, A, 211–12.

5. Nelson, "Anglican Missions," 197.

6. Levy, *Puritanism,* 264.

7. Ibid., 261f.

8. *Colonial and State Records of North Carolina* (Raleigh, N.C., 1886), 1:204.

9. It is not quite correct to say then that Carolina trustees and proprietors were "in a secular tradition," as does Darrett B. Rutman, *Morning of America, 1603–1789* (Boston, Mass., 1971).

10. S. Charles Bolton, "The Anglican Church of Colonial South Carolina, 1704–1754: A Study in Americanization" (Ph.D. diss., University of Wisconsin, 1973), 14–29, for a discussion of this change of policy.

11. The 1670 revision of the Fundamental Constitutions, quoted in ibid., 27.

12. Quoted in Levy, *Puritanism,* 258f.

13. Johnston to the bishop of Sarum, in Klingberg, *Carolina Chronicle,* 23.

14. Sykes, *Church and State,* 35. The vote on this bill was nearly evenly divided between Whig and Tory bishops, i.e., those appointed by William III and those appointed by Charles and James.

15. Levy, *Early Puritanism,* 259; cf. Greene, *Quest,* 457, for listing of governors. Dissenting chief executives served twenty-three of the thirty-nine years which separated the founding of the colony from Johnston's arrival.

16. See Bolton, "Anglican Church," 106.

17. Commissary Johnston to the secretary of the SPG, 13 February 1713, in Klingberg, *Carolina Chronicle,* 121.

18. Andrews, *Colonial Period,* 3:202; see also Greene, *Quest,* 32.

19. E. T. James, J. W. James, and P. S. Boyer, eds., *Notable American Women 1607–1950: A Biographical Dictionary* (Cambridge, Mass., 1971), 2:281–82; cf. James Thomas

Flexner, *First Flowers of Our Wilderness: American Painting, the Colonial Period* (New York, [1947] 1969), 91, 293.

20. Gideon Johnston to the SPG, 27 January 1716, in Klingberg, *Carolina Chronicle,* 156; cf. 127, 142, 151, 161–62.

21. SPG *Papers,* A, 3, no. 114, 266–67.

22. M. Eugene Sirmans, "Politics in Colonial South Carolina: The Failure of Proprietary Reform, 1682–1694," *WMQ,* 3rd Series, 23 (October 1966): 39.

23. Peter H. Wood, *Black Majority: Negroes in Colonial South Carolina from 1670 to the Stono Rebellion* (New York, 1974), 9; cf. Bolton, "Anglican Church," 10, and Eugene Sirmans, *Colonial South Carolina, a Political History, 1663–1763* (Chapel Hill, N.C., 1966), 3–6.

24. Richard S. Dunn, "The Barbados Census of 1680: Profile of the Richest Colony in English America," *WMQ,* 3rd Series, 26 (1969): 11. Dunn has shown that in the Barbados, the largest English colony in the New World next to those of Virginia and Massachusetts, 6.9 percent of the population owned 93.1 percent of the wealth. In 1684 there were 19,568 whites in Barbados, 46,602 black slaves, and 2,381 indentured white servants. More of the immigrants from Barbados came to South Carolina, New York, and Virginia. They brought with them the aristocratic concept of the good life, based upon their former experience in the Caribbean.

25. Albert Sidney Thomas, *A Historical Account of the Protestant Episcopal Church in South Carolina, 1820–1957* (Columbia, S.C., 1957), 3f.

26. Jackson Turner Main states that the Episcopal clergy of South Carolina were the best paid of all colonial ministers of the church in the southern colonies (*Social Structure,* 97). While this may have been true by midcentury, original sources do not bear out the contention for the period before 1725. Durward T. Stokes argues, not wholly convincingly, that these same clergy were also the best educated of any Episcopalian parsons in prerevolutionary America. He notes that of the fifty-four ministers who served South Carolina parishes between 1680 and 1766, when the SPG was eased out of the ecclesiastical picture, there were twenty-one M.A.s: fourteen from Oxford, five from Trinity College, Dublin, and one each from Cambridge and Edinburgh. This is commendable but does not seem much different from other colonies. See his "The Clergy of the Carolinas and the American Revolution" (Ph.D. diss., University of North Carolina, 1968), 192.

27. Wood, *Black Majority,* 144. Wood estimated the total population of South Carolina to be 9,580 in 1708, of which 4,080 were white, 4,100 were black slaves, and 1,400 were Indian slaves. The colony as a whole was only one-seventh the size of Virginia at that time. For comparative population figures, white and black, in both colonies, see Robert V. Wells, *The Population of the British Colonies in America before 1776* (Princeton, N.J., 1975), 160–68.

28. Klingberg, *Carolina Chronicle,* 123.

29. See Frank J. Klingberg, *An Appraisal of the Negro in Colonial South Carolina, a Study in Americanization* (Washington, D.C., 1941). Pp. 121, 69, and 50 show complaints corresponding to those of Johnston; cf. Francis Le Jau to the SPG, 20 February 1712, SPG Letter Books, A, 7:396, where he treats slave owner recalcitrance as well as the difficulties of pastoral visitation of slaves.

30. Le Jau, ibid. The biblical reference is to Exod. 21:26: "When a man strikes the eye of his slave, male or female, and destroys it, he shall let the slave go free for the eye's sake. If he knocks out a tooth of his slave, male or female, he shall let the slave go free for the tooth's sake."

31. Klingberg, *An Appraisal,* 50.

32. Robert M. Weir, " 'Ye Harmony We Were Famous For': An Interpretation of Pre-Revolutionary South Carolina Politics," *WMQ,* 3rd Series, 26 (1969): 474.

33. Klingberg, *An Appraisal,* 79.

34. Wood, *Black Majority,* 139.

35. Ibid., 138.

36. See, for instance, the reference to the *South Carolina Gazette* for 17 and 24 April 1742, quoted in Jordan, *White over Black*, 185f.

37. As an example, see Bishop Gibson's "Pastoral Letter to the Masters and Mistresses of Families in the English Plantations abroad: Exhorting them to encourage and promote the Instruction of their Negroes in the Christian Faith," 19 May 1727, in Dalcho, *Historical Account*, 104–12.

38. See Verner W. Crane, *The Southern Frontier, 1670–1732* (Ann Arbor, Mi., [1929] 1956), 151–61.

39. Le Jau to the bishop of London, 17 May 1721, *Fulham Papers*, A, 9:31–32.

40. Gary B. Nash, "The Image of the Indian in the Southern Colonial Mind," *WMQ*, 3rd Series, 29 (1972): 222.

41. Le Jau to the secretary, 22 April 1708, in Frank J. Klingberg, *Carolina Chronicle of Dr. Francis Le Jau* (Berkeley, Calif., 1956), 38f.; see Bolton, "Anglican Church," 166.

42. Le Jau to Philip Stubbs, 15 April 1707, quoted in Bolton, "Anglican Church," 166.

43. Clergy of South Carolina to the bishop of London, 13 October 1715, in Klingberg, *Carolina Chronicle*, 147.

44. Bolton, "Anglican Church," 150, 151, 215, 145.

45. Levy, *Puritanism*, 260.

46. Samuel Thomas, the first missionary to come to South Carolina from the SPG, appears to have been free in omitting the sign of the cross at baptism as well as not insisting upon kneeling at the Holy Communion, all of which would be in keeping with reformed tradition (Bolton, "Anglican Church," 88; C. F. Pascoe, *Classified Digest of the Records of the SPG* [London, 1895], 850). John Maitland (d. 1711) also had Calvinistic leanings (Bolton, "Anglican Church," 80–81). Robert Maule (d. 1717), a graduate of Trinity College, Dublin, in 1703, is harder to place theologically, though it is significant that Calvinist Le Jau admired him greatly and spoke of him as "a very pious, good, and honest man" (Fulham Papers, 9:27–28; SPG Letters, B, 4, 1:102–8). Ebenezer Taylor, who resided in the colony from 1711 to 1717, was a former Presbyterian. Taylor got into trouble with Gideon Johnston for continuing to preach "after the Method of the meanest and most ignorant of the Presbyterians" (Bolton, "Anglican Church," 86, 129; Pascoe, *Digest*, 850). Philip De Richebourg, minister at St. James, Santee, after 1720, was a Huguenot who continued his Genevan ways (Bolton, "Anglican Church," 110, 115). James Gignillat was also a French Calvinist (c. 1710) (Pascoe, *Digest*, 850). Le Jau himself, who took Anglican orders after leaving France, was a canon of St. Paul's Cathedral in London, spent six years in Antigua, and in 1706 became rector of the church at Goose Creek (Bolton, "Anglican Church," 58). John La Pierre (d. 1755) was still another Calvinist of Huguenot background; he became minister at Orange Quarter and St. Dennis's Parish (Bolton, "Anglican Church," 83, and Clement, "Clergy Licensed, 1695–1716," 334). Welshman Lewis Jones was one of the most significant and dedicated missionaries on the frontier, friend of George Whitefield, and rector of St. Helena's Parish from 1725 to 1744 after graduation from Oxford in 1724 (Bolton, "Anglican Church," 284–87; Pascoe, *Digest*, 850). Francis Varnod, a Frenchman, was ordained in the Church of England in 1722 and became rector of St. George's Parish in 1723, serving until 1736; he proved himself to be a remarkable observer of Indian ways and a leading frontier missionary (Bolton, "Anglican Church," 287–90; Clement, "Clergymen Licensed, 1710–1744," 248).

47. Johnston's own efforts to make his clergy conform by regularly saying Morning and Evening Prayer and to avoid "all Conceiv'd or Extemporary Prayers," together with his dislike of any leniency in this regard, would also lead one to suspect that many episcopally ordained ministers did not adhere strictly to Anglican rubrics. See Klingberg, *Carolina Chronicle*, 56.

48. See Bolton, "Anglican Church," 91–92, 134–37.

49. George C. Rogers, Jr., *Church and State in Eighteenth-Century South Carolina*, Dalcho Papers, No. 12 (Charleston, S.C., 1957), 11.

50. Bolton, "Anglican Church," 42–43.
51. Rogers, *Church and State*, 14.
52. Davidson, "Establishment," 64.
53. Report of the Commons House to Edward Marston, 18 October 1704, quoted in Frederick Dalcho, *An Historical Account of the Protestant Episcopal Church in South Carolina* (Charleston, S.C., 1820; New York, 1972), 55–56. The biblical reference is to Numbers 16:1–35. For questioning Moses' authority, Korah, Dathan, and Abiram were swallowed up, whereupon "they, and all that appertained to them, went down alive into the pit, and the earth closed over them." The pit refers to Sheol.
54. Memorial of Dessenters to the House of Lords, January-February 1706, quoted in Dalcho, *Historical Account*, 65.
55. Address to the Queen, Dei Martii 12, 1706, quoted in Dalcho, *Historical Account*, 67f.
56. John Lederer, *The Discoveries of John Lederer in Several Marches from Virginia to the West of Carolina* (London, 1672), translated by Sir William Talbot.
57. Ibid., 12–13.
58. Ibid., 12, 3.
59. John Lawson, *A New Voyage to Carolina* (London, 1709), 236.
60. Ibid., 237.
61. Ibid., 236.
62. Ibid., 238.
63. This was the name given the most northern colony of the Carolinas from which North Carolina emerged. At Cape Fear, New Englanders first established a settlement in 1662. As early as 1665, the proprietary colony which had developed there under the same fundamental constitutions as operated to the south was allowed to have its own governor, elected legislature, and courts. See William S. Powell, *North Carolina: A History* (New York, 1977), 24.
64. Greene and Harrington, *American Population*, 156, 172.
65. Nelson, "Anglican Missions," 127.
66. Colonial Records of North Carolina, 1:21, quoted in Nelson, "Anglican Missions," 134.
67. Powell, *North Carolina*, 29–42. For the French, see Henry Savage, *River of the Carolinas: The Santee* (New York, 1956). For Germans (Moravians), see Gilliam L. Gollin, *Moravians in Two Worlds: A Study of Changing Communities* (New York, 1967).
68. Powell, *North Carolina*, 26.
69. Nelson, "Anglican Missions," 135f.
70. North Carolina did not become a royal colony until 1729.
71. Powell, *North Carolina*, 30.
72. William Byrd, "History of the Dividing Line," in *The Prose Works of William Byrd of Westover*, ed. Louis B. Wright (Cambridge, Mass., 1966), 194.
73. William Byrd, "Secret History of the Dividing Line," ibid., 44, 49. A pistole was a gold coin, either Spanish, worth approximately 18 shillings (1692), or the French louis d'or of Louis XIII, or, more probably in this case, the Scottish twelve-pound piece of William III (1701), worth one English pound.
74. Ibid., 195.
75. Nelson, "Anglican Missions," 141. No copy of the vestry act of 1701 survives.
76. John Blair, "The Reverend John Blair's Mission to North Carolina, 1704," *Narratives of Early Carolina, 1650–1708* (New York, [1911] 1953), 216.
77. Ibid., 217.
78. For a discussion of this see Nelson, "Anglican Missions," 172–94, especially 172–78.
79. John Urmstone to the secretary, 21 July 1721, SPG Letters, A, 15:52; Urmstone to the secretary, 5 February 1721, ibid., 42; Urmstone to the secretary, 15 February 1720, ibid., 14:68, quoted in Nelson, "Anglican Missions," 177.
80. Powell, *North Carolina*, 31.
81. See Greene, *Quest*, 352–53, for a discussion of these measures.

Notes to Chapter 7

1. While Johnson himself attests the influence of Bacon, it has been pointed out that Johnson's autobiographical remarks should be used with care, since they were made in 1770 when he was seventy-four; see Norman S. Fiering, "President Samuel Johnson and the Circle of Knowledge," *WMQ*, 3rd Series (1971), 209. The Samuel Johnson/Daniel Brown correspondence in Schneiders, *Career*, 2:189–99, indicates otherwise: clearly, at the time of his early intellectual development (1716), Johnson himself bore witness to Bacon's influence. In addition, Thomas Bradbury Chandler, Johnson's midlife student and spiritual son, also spoke of the importance of Bacon on the mind of the older man; see Thomas Bradbury Chandler, *The Life of Samuel Johnson* (New York, 1824), 6f.

   While Johnson was without doubt the first American to recognize the importance of Bacon's *Advancement of Learning,* the book was by no means absent from American libraries. See for instance Dorothy Flower Livingston and Mollie Marjorie Patton, "Contributions to a Bibliography of Francis Bacon, Editions before 1700 in Yale Libraries," *Papers in Honor of Andrew Keogh*, 95–143. See also Samuel Eliot Morison, *The Intellectual Life of Colonial New England* (New York, 1956), 49, and his *Harvard College in the Seventeenth Century* (Cambridge, Mass., 1936), 1:130; Perry Miller, *The New England Mind: From Colony to Province* (Cambridge, Mass., 1953), 13; Davis, *Sandys,* 235; Charles Evans, *American Bibliography* (New York, 1941), 1:75; Fiering, "Johnson," 210, for other references. Livingston and Patton count six copies of *Advancement of Learning* in America, either separately or together with editions of Bacon's works, by roughly 1680; Fiering judges that there were some twenty-five copies of the *Advancement* in the colonies by 1715, which may be a bit high. In any event Johnson was wrong in thinking that the copy he read in 1714 was the only one in the colonies (Schneiders, *Career,* 1:7).

2. See, for instance, Moody E. Prior, "Bacon's Man of Science," JHI 15 (1954): 352. It should be noted that the scientific revolution of the seventeenth century was not based on Bacon's suggestion that one should approach nature without a hypothesis but precisely on the hypothetic-deductive method. See Arthur C. Danto, *Analytical Philosophy of History* (Cambridge, 1965), 101; Danto suggests that had science heeded Bacon it would have ground to a halt. This is in fact an overstatement, for Bacon himself sought the unification of all learning; see Robert McRae, "The Unity of the Sciences: Bacon, Descartes, and Leibnitz," JHI 18 (1957): 27.

3. For Bacon's popularization of this ideal see *Advancement of Learning,* 17–24.

4. Schneiders, *Career,* 1:6–7.

5. Ibid., 2:61.

6. Ibid., 1:6; see also 1:499 with reference to Johnson's rereading the *Advancement of Learning* in 1722.

7. Daniel Brown to Samuel Johnson, 3 August 1716, Schneiders, *Career,* 2:195.

8. Ibid., 197. For further details on Johnson's classification of history among the sciences, see ibid., 2:214–15; cf. Bacon, *Advancement of Learning,* 2:46–61. In 1716 in his "Revised Encyclopedea," Johnson placed history under the *cognoscenda* of theology. Later in the same year, in his last letter to Daniel Brown, he reclassified history under "Creature, works of"; the point is that this follows Bacon's classification even more closely.

9. Schneiders, *Career,* 2:199.

10. Samuel Johnson, "My Present Thoughts of Episcopacy," ibid., 3:3.

11. Samuel Johnson, "A Second Letter from a Minister of the Church of England To his Dissenting Parishioners, 1734," Schneiders, *Career,* 3:54 (surplice), 50 ("middle way of Erasmus"), 81–83 ("bodily worship").

12. Amos 5:24.

13. Johnson, "Present Thoughts," 3: 7.

14. See Bacon, *Advancement,* 9:301. He notes that the Saviour's coat was seamless "but the garment of the church is of many colors." Bacon would not arbitrarily "cut off men from

the body of the Church and exclude them from the communion of the faithful." The Cambridge Platonists seldom quoted Bacon, and, as C. A. Patrides has noted, they were opposed to the earlier philosopher because he refused to ground his thought in "religion" and because he espoused "materialism." C. A. Patrides, *The Cambridge Platonists* (Cambridge, 1970), 187. Henry More in his "Brief Discourse of the True Grounds for Certainty of Faith in Points of Religion," spoke of the "comprehension of . . . the points of faith always and everywhere held by all Christian Churches from the apostles time till now." See G. R. Cragg, ed., *The Cambridge Platonists* (New York, 1968), 147. No doubt Johnson's own ecclesiology was derived more from those like More than Bacon.

15. See David Douglas, *English Scholars, 1660–1730* (London, 1951).
16. William King, *A Discourse Concerning the Inventions of Men in the Worship of God* (Philadelphia, 1828), 18.
17. Ibid., 59.
18. Johnson, "Second Letter," 3:77–78; see Schneiders, *Career,* 1:11; 3:81–84.
19. King, *Discourse,* 104.
20. Johnson, "Second Letter," 3:84.
21. Joseph J. Ellis, "The Puritan Mind in Transition: The American Samuel Johnson (1696–1772)," (Ph.D. diss., Yale University, 1969), 73–94. Published as *The New England Mind in Transition: Samuel Johnson of Connecticut, 1696–1772* (New Haven, Conn., 1973). References are from the original dissertation.
22. Peter King, *An Enquiry into the Constitution, Discipline, Unity and Worship of the Primitive Church* (London, 1691).
23. William Sclater, *Original Draught of the Primitive Church* (Oxford, 1740), 2:352f., 263.
24. It was superseded by Edwin Hatch's Bampton Lectures of that year published as *The Organization of the Early Christian Church* (London, 1881).
25. Sykes, *Church and State,* 292.
26. John 18:36.
27. Bailyn, *Ideological Origins,* 37–38.
28. Schneiders, *Career,* 1:21.
29. Johnson, "Second Letter," 3:87–92.
30. Schneiders, *Career,* 3:38; cf. Ellis, *Transition,* 122.
31. Johnson, "Present Thoughts," 3:3, 7. Scott was rector of St. Giles-in-the-Fields. He graduated from New Inn Hall, Oxford, in 1658, received his D.D. in 1685, and politically was a Whig. He defended the idea of particular, national churches as diverse branches off a parent trunk, the roots of which were to be found in the primitive church of apostolic times. Johnson quoted with approval Scott's *The Christian Life from its beginning to its Consummation in Glory . . .* (London, 1681). See *Works of the Learned and Reverend John Scott* (Oxford, 1826), 2:498–99. For his life, see *DNB,* 17:979.
32. Potter was the son of a tradesman in Yorkshire. He received his B.A. from University College, Oxford, 1692; M.A., 1694; and D.D., 1706. In 1707, he became Regius Professor and, in 1715, bishop of Oxford. A classical scholar, his *Antiquities of Greece* went through fifteen editions by 1837.
33. Schneiders, *Career,* 1:13; see Johnson, "Present Thoughts," 3:5.
34. John Potter, *A Discourse on Church-Government* (London, 1839), 46.
35. Samuel Johnson to Thomas Secker, 12 July 1760, Schneiders, *Career,* 1:300.
36. Potter, *Discourse,* 110.
37. Sclater, *Original Draught,* 209.
38. Johnson, "Present Thoughts," 3:5. Later he would reject this; here Johnson refers to the lay ministry in Calvinist churches of the reformation period and thereafter. Elders were of two types, teaching elders, whose function was pastoral, and ruling elders, who were laymen set apart by ordination to assist the minister in the government of the church. Also, deacons were laymen who either administered the alms or cared for the poor and the sick. Supposedly, elders and deacons were chosen by the congregation. "In reality," writes Michael Walzer, "they were coopted by the existing church leadership" (*Revolution of the*

Saints, [1965], 52). Such "inferior ministry" helped overcome the moral gap between laymen and their clerical governors. For the history of the Anglican-Puritan debate on the ministry, see Norman Sykes, *Old Priest and New Presbyter: Episcopacy and Presbyterianism since the Reformation with Especial Relation to the Churches of England and Scotland* (Cambridge, 1956); for the Puritan ministry in America in the colonial period, see David D. Hall, *The Faithful Shepherd, a History of the New England Ministry in the Seventeenth Century* (Chapel Hill, N.C., 1972).

39. Schneiders, *Career,* 1:22.
40. Johnson, "Elementa Philosophica," Schneiders, *Career,* 2:429.
41. Ibid., 434.
42. Ibid., 435.
43. Goodwin, *Anglican Middle Way,* 136.
44. Johnson, "Second Letter," 3:27.
45. George Keith, *A Reply to Mr. Increase Mather's Printed Remarks on a Sermon . . .* (New York, 1703), 4.
46. Ibid., 14.
47. George Keith, *The Anti-Christs and Sadducees Detected* (London, 1696), 40; cf. Keith's *The Notes of the True Church . . .* (New York, 1704), "Epistle," n.p. and 5; also his *The Spirit of Railing Shimei and of Baal's Four Hundred Lying Prophets Entered into Caleb Pusey and His Quaker Brethren in Pennsilvania* (New York, 1703), 2, and *The Power of the Gospel in the Conversion of Sinners* (Annapolis, 1703), 12f. and 18.
48. Thomas Cradock, Sermon on education, Maryland Diocesan Archives, 3.
49. Edward Bass, Sermon to the congregation at Newburyport, Massachusetts, 14 October 1759, Maryland Diocesan Archives, 18f.
50. Schneiders, *Career,* 3:38.
51. Johnson, "Second Letter," 50.
52. Ibid; see Book of Common Prayer (1979), 871.
53. The term *Arminian,* after Jacobus Arminius (1560–1609), a Dutch theologian, was by the eighteenth century in America a common term of derision rather than a precisely defined theological position. When used by Puritans, it designated a doctrinal deviant who appeared to put too much emphasis on man's ability to choose or reject salvation rather than on God's free will in choosing some for salvation and rejecting others, regardless of merit. Originally an Arminian was one who believed that the efficacy of God's grace depended upon man's ability to accept or reject it; Arminianism thus denied implicitly that God's grace was irresistible. Calvinists at the Synod of Dort (1618–19) condemned Arminianism and reasserted that God's election of men depended upon no human capacity and was solely a function of his arbitrary will. The Arminian position is contained in the "Arminian Remonstrance of 1610." When Anglican Henry Bettenson edited *Documents of the Christian Church,* he included the Arminian Remonstrance but not the celebrated "five points" of Calvinism, which were reaffirmed at Dort, perhaps lending some credence to the charge that Episcopalians tend to be Arminian. See Bettenson, *Documents* (1967), 268, for the Arminian Remonstrance, and Philip Schaff, *The Creeds of Christendom* (New York, 1877), 3:581–97, for the "five points" of Calvinism.
54. Ibid., 90.
55. Johnson, "A Discourse Concerning the Nature of God . . . ," in Schneiders, *Career,* 3:490.
56. Ellis, "Transition," 175.
57. A solifidian was one who believed that he was made righteous by grace through faith alone. An antinomian is generally one who defies the law. In the passage from Blair's sermon, the term refers to those who, believing themselves set free by God's grace, think themselves liberated from all restraints, moral and religious.
58. Blair, *Our Saviour's Divine Sermon,* 83. Similar concern for morality in Virginia may be found in Jones, *Present State,* 98, 11, and 122.

59. Goodwin, "Anglican Middle Way," 153.
60. C. C. Goen, making use of the work of F. Ernest Stoeffler (*The Rise of Evangelical Pietism*, 1965), writes, "A competent recent study has defined pietism as the extension to individual Christian experience of principles which the Reformers had applied 'chiefly, though by no means exclusively, to areas of doctrine and polity,' resulting in a surging reassertion of Christianity's experiential tradition in post-Reformation Protestantism. . . . Always strongly biblical and intensely missionary, pietism encouraged lively preaching to persuade unbelievers and complacent church members to commit themselves cordially to the obedience of faith. In short the character of pietism required it to be aggressively conversionist" (*The Great Awakening* [New Haven, Conn., 1972], 1). Pietism thus emphasized the quality of life rather than orthodoxy of belief. It emphasized not only individual but social reform, though, unlike Puritanism, without political interest or force.
61. Keith, *Christian Catechisme*, 54.
62. Keith, *The Power of the Gospel*, 2, 4, 6.
63. Ibid., 12; see Keith, *Sermon . . . Turner's Hall*, 10.
64. Keith, *Refutation*, 1–3. The term "Ranter" probably does not refer to a self-conscious sect in the period of the English Civil War but to those "Seekers" who, like spiritualists and others, represented an extreme of antinomianism. See Norman Cohn, *Pursuit of the Millennium* (New York, [1957] 1961), and G. F. S. Ellens, "The Ranters Ranting: Reflections on a Ranting Counter Culture," *CH* 40 (1971).
65. Checkley, *Choice Dialogues*, 1:155.
66. Thomas Bray, *A Short Discourse Upon the Doctrine of our Baptismal Covenant . . .* (London, 1697), 126.
67. Checkley, "Mr. Checkley's Letter to Jonathan Dickinson," Slafter, *Checkley*, 2:130.
68. William Haller, *The Rise of Puritanism* (New York, 1938), chapter 6, esp. 238–48.
69. In this regard, see Stephen Foster, *Their Solitary Way: The Puritan Social Ethic in the First Century of Settlement in New England* (New Haven, Conn., 1971), passim.
70. Robert S. McGinnis, Jr., "A Model for Theological Education in Eighteenth-Century America: Samuel Johnson D.D. of King's College" (Ph.D. diss., Vanderbilt University, 1971), 72.
71. Johnson, "Elementa Philosophica," 2:503; see Johnson, "A Sermon Concerning the Intellectual World . . . 1747," 3:504.
72. Johnson, "Elementa Philosophica," 447, 486, where Johnson asserts that God is primarily truth; see also 379 and cf. McGinnis, "Model," 70, where Johnson's concept of human "light" in relation to God's light is spelled out in greater philosophical detail.
73. Ellis, "Transition," 218.
74. Johnson, "Preface" to "A Second Vindication of God's Sovereign and Free Grace . . . By John Beach, M.A.," Schneiders, *Career*, 3:209. The original text reads "self-exerting Power."
75. See Ellis, "Transition," 194, 198, 206–14, 221–23, for discussion of Johnson's position; also McGinnis, "Model," 63. Johnson followed Berkeley in the latter's rejection of Lockean sensationalism and affirmed that perception is the sole criterion for existence (we do not perceive matter, but only ideas of matter). Johnson was also influenced by Berkeley in matters of causality as well as in epistemology: all real causality belongs to God, and Newton's first law is only descriptive of events by correlation and inference from one to the other. Through Edwards America followed John Locke. Lockean sensationalism proved nothing short of sensational; i.e., one sought in the ordinary motions and emotions of religious revival the sensate actions of God upon his creatures.
76. Heimert, *American Mind*, 46.
77. Johnson, *Elementa Philosophica*, 2:514.
78. Ellis, "Transition," 203; for a full discussion of Johnson's relation to his Puritan heritage, see 200–205.
79. Schneiders, *Career*, 2:19; cf. McGinnis, "Model," 72.

Notes to Chapter 8

1. George Whitefield, *A Short Account of God's Dealings With the Reverend Mr. George Whitefield . . . (1714–1736),* in Whitefield, *Journals* (London, 1960), 62.
2. See Gerald J. Goodwin, "The Anglican Reaction to the Great Awakening," *HM* 35 (1966).
3. George Whitefield, *Journals* (London, 1960), 457–59; see also Timothy Cutler to Edmund Gibson, 5 December 1740, Fulham Papers, 5:269–70. Price was commissary of Massachusetts from 1730 to 1748; he was a graduate of Balliol College, Oxford, and became rector of King's Chapel in 1729. Whitefield described Price as having "little learning and less experience, with principles inconsistent and contradictory, in opposition to Scripture and reason." See Mary Plummer Salsman, "The Reverend Proger Price," *HM* 15 (1945): 193–229.
4. Cutler to Gibson, 5 December 1740, Fulham Papers, 5:269.
5. Whitefield, *Journals,* 458.
6. The rubric Cutler referred to reads, "It is certain by God's word, that children which are baptized, dying before they commit actual sin, are undoubtedly saved." See Archibald John Stephens, ed., *The Book of Common Prayer 1666 . . . With Notes, Legal and Historical* (London, 1849–1854), 2:1274.
7. Whitefield, *Journals,* 459.
8. Ibid. The subject under discussion was sin after baptism; Cutler and Whitefield were quoting from Article Seventeen of the Thirty-nine with minor misquotes.
9. Cutler to Gibson, 5 December 1740, Fulham Papers, 5:270.
10. Ibid. For Whitefield's castigations on the clergy of the church, see J. W. Weeks to the secretary (of the SPG) 4 September 1770 in Perry, *Historical Collections,* 3:551.
    Samuel Willard (1640–1707), author of *Compleat Body of Divinity* (1726), graduated from Harvard in 1659 and was ordained in 1664. In 1678 he became assistant minister and then minister of the Old South Church. Learned theologically, Willard scorned both the enthusiasm of the Baptists and the Arminianism of the Episcopalians. He did not wish toleration in Massachusetts. In 1700 he became vice-president of Harvard College. Married twice, Willard had eighteen children. See Seymour Van Dyken, *Samuel Willard, 1640–1707: Preacher of Orthodoxy in an Era of Change* (Grand Rapids, Mi., 1972); also Ernest Benson Lowrie, *The Shape of the Puritan Mind: The Thought of Samuel Willard* (New Haven, Conn., 1974), passim.
    Thomas Shepard (1604–1649) author of *The Sound Believer, Or a Treatise of Evangelical Conversion,* 8 vols. (London, 1645). Shepard graduated from Emmanuel College, Cambridge, in 1623, taking his M.A. in 1627. Ordained in the Church of England, he was subsequently forbidden by Laud to exercise his ministry in the diocese of London due to his strong Puritan leanings. In 1635 he arrived in Boston with his wife and there played a leading role in the founding of Harvard College. Shepard also interested himself in Indian missions. The leading Puritan in Massachusetts, he placed the efficacy of the law at the center of his thought about the process of conversion, not as a means to salvation itself but as an efficacious restraint. Though he did not offer extensive instructions for self-examination, Shepard did much to make clear the stages of conversion Puritans might expect. For a comparison of Shepard with other American Puritans, see Norman Pettit, *The Heart Prepared: Grace and Conversion in Puritan Spiritual Life* (New Haven, Conn., 1966), 101–14. Also for Shepard's spiritual autobiography, see Michael McGiffert, ed., *God's Plot: The Paradoxes of Puritan Piety* (Amherst, Mass., 1972), passim.
    Solomon Stoddard (1643–1729), author of *The Safety of Appearing at the Day of Judgement, in the Righteousness of Christ: Opened and Applied . . .* (Boston, 1687), was a graduate of Harvard (1662), the first librarian of the church in Northampton, and the grandfather of Jonathan Edwards. There he presided over numerous revivals of religious zeal which anticipated the Great Awakening of his grandson.

What is curious about Whitefield's mentioning these three works in the same breath is that seemingly "Stoddardianism" flies in the face of Shepard's emphasis on the process of conversion. Stoddard lowered the bar completely to the Lord's Supper and admitted those who could make no profession of experiential faith. In fact, Stoddard remained deeply concerned about conversion, feeling that the Lord's Supper was a converting ordinance. Stoddard encouraged a return to the sanctity of the inner life. Norman Pettit comments that "he was able to encourage the unregenerate while assuming the highest standards of unspoken piety" (*The Heart Prepared*, 205).

11. Timothy Cutler to Edmund Gibson, 28 May 1739, in "An Anglican Critique of the Early Phase of the Great Awakening in New England: A Letter by Timothy Cutler," ed. Douglas C. Stenerson, *WMQ*, 3rd Series (1973), 487; see Kenneth W. Cameron, ed., *The Church of England in Pre-Revolutionary Connecticut* (Hartford, Conn., 1976), 55.

12. Mr. Brockwell to the secretary (of the SPG), 8 February 1742, in Perry, *Historical Collections*, 3:353; see also Cutler to the secretary, 11 June 1741, 355; Brockwell to the bishop of London, 15 June 1741, 356; Brockwell to the secretary, 15 June 1741, 356–57; Cutler to the secretary, 25 September 1741, 357; Cutler to the secretary, 30 June 1742, 362f.; Cutler to the secretary, 26 December 1744, 388; Cutler to the secretary, 26 June 1746, 396; Mr. Weeks [Joshua Wingate Weeks] to the secretary, 10 November 1770, 553–54.

13. Henry Caner to the secretary of the SPG, 10 May 1744, in *Letter Book of Henry Caner from 1728 through 1778*, ed. Kenneth W. Cameron (Hartford, Conn., 1972), 12; see ibid., 96, 97, 205, 206; Ebenezer Punderson to the secretary, 30 March 1742, in Cameron, *Pre-Revolutionary Connecticut*, 59. See, for a general reaction to the awakening in Connecticut, Godfrey Malbone to Simon?, 13 February 1772, 177–79. Kenney, "Whitefield," 85–88, notes the urban orientation of Whitefield's New England campaign: of the forty-five days of his first visit, nineteen were spent in Boston, New Haven, and Northampton, while only thirteen were allotted for an additional forty New England towns; the rest of the time was spent on horseback. Whitefield, concludes Kenney, judged his success by the size of his crowds, which would obviously be greater in urban areas.

14. Adverse reactions in New York included those of James Wetmore to the secretary, 28 September 1741, SPG Letters, B, 9:73; Isaac Brown to the secretary, 16 June 1741, ibid., 79; 19 October 1741, ibid., 80; 24 March 1742, ibid., 93; Thomas Colgan to the secretary, 15 December 1741, 9:66; and Jonathan Arnold to the secretary, 10 November 1742, ibid., 10:82.

15. Whitefield, *Journals*, 346.

16. Ibid., 349.

17. Cadwallader Colden to Samuel Johnson, 12 April 1746, in Colden Papers, *NYHS*, 3, 202–3.

18. For comments from the Pennsylvania clergy on the Whitefieldian cabal, see William Currie to the secretary (of the SPG), 7 July 1740, 208–9; Richard Blackhouse to the secretary, 23 August 1740, 205; Richard Blackhouse to the secretary, 25 July 1741, 216; Richard Blackhouse to the secretary, 31 October 1741, 218; Archibald Cummings to the secretary, 14 November 1739, 210; and Alexander Howie to the secretary, 27 September 1741, 221–23, in Perry, *Historical Collections*, 2. For Episcopalian reactions to Whitefield in Delaware, see Nelson W. Rightmyer, *The Anglican Church in Delaware* (Philadelphia, 1947), 111–16; for New Jersey, see Burr, *Church in New Jersey*, 67–85.

19. See Francis L. Hawks, *A Narrative of Events Connected with the Rise and Progress of the Protestant Episcopal Church in Maryland* (New York, 1839), 224; also Whitefield, *Journals*, 365, 366, 388, and James S. M. Anderson, *A History of the Church of England in the Colonies* (London, 1856), 3:188–213.

20. For the particulars of Blair's reception of Whitefield, see Whitefield, *Journals*, 371, 379, 388. Blair's later attitude is found in Blair to the bishop of London, 29 May 1740, Perry, *Historical Collections*, 1:362.

21. Henry, *Whitefield*, 138–41; Goodwin, "Middle Way," 260–70; Bolton, *Anglican Church*, 297–309, 311–15; Anderson, *Episcopal Church*, 522–53; Perry, *American Church*, 1:386–89; Albright, *Episcopal Church*, 33–34.
22. David Taft Morgan, "The Great Awakening in the Carolinas and Georgia, 1740–1775" (Ph.D. diss., University of North Carolina, 1967), 140.
23. Alexander Garden, *Regeneration, and the Testimony of the Spirit . . .* (Charleston, S.C., 1740), in Heimert and Miller, *The Great Awakening*, 56.
24. Whitefield, *Journals*, 439f.
25. Whitefield's trial in the ecclesiastical court convened in St. Philip's Church on 15 July 1740 was something of a first in American law: the summons issued to the revivalist required that he appear and answer questions for "the mere good of his soul"; see L. W. Labaree, *Conservatism in Early American History* (New York, 1948), 86f., and Morgan, *Awakening in Carolinas*, 137.
26. William H. Kenney III, "George Whitefield and Colonial Revivalism: The Social Sources of Charismatic Authority, 1737–1770" (Ph.D. diss., University of Pennsylvania, 1966), 4.
27. Stuart C. Henry, *George Whitefield: Wayfaring Witness* (New York, 1957), 179.
28. Whitefield, *Journals*, 472; the date was Sunday, 12 October.
29. Ibid.
30. Of these, Willard and Cooper were particularly strong friends of Whitefield and Jonathan Edwards. Willard described Whitefield as "a man fearing God" and added, "Oh, that the Lord would make me worthy of so great a Favour. . . . There has been so evidently the Finger of God directing you into this Province . . . and in the wonderful Success that has attended . . . your Ministry . . . that many that like the work are sadly put to it to keep their Eyes shut against the evidences of it" (Shipton, *Harvard Graduates*, 4:429). Cooper was a firm friend of Edwards, a Calvinist of the New Light variety, and a popular preacher himself; see Shipton, *Harvard Graduates*, 5:624–33. Benjamin Coleman, though a more urbane preacher with a "Catholick Air," told Whitefield after their first meeting that "it was the most pleasant Time he ever enjoyed in that Meeting House through the whole course of his Life" (Shipton, *Harvard Graduates*, 4:120–37).
31. Jonathan Edwards to George Whitefield, 12 February 1739/40, quoted in Henry Abelove, "Jonathan Edwards Letter of Invitation to George Whitefield," *WMQ*, 3rd Series, 29 (1972): 487–89; cf. Edwards's references to Whitefield as another Alexander the Great and Oliver Cromwell in Edwards, "Some Thoughts Concerning the Revival," in *Jonathan Edwards, the Great Awakening*, ed. C. C. Goen, (New Haven, Conn., 1972), 508–9.
32. Gerald J. Goodwin, "The Anglican Reaction to the Great Awakening," *HM* 35 (1966).
33. Patrick Henry to Commissary William Dawson, 14 October 1745, *WMQ*, 2nd Series, 1 (1921):266–67.
34. George Ross to the secretary of the SPG, 4 August 1741, Perry, *Historical Collections*, 5:84.
35. George Ross to the secretary of the SPG, 3 June 1742, ibid., 85.
36. George Ross to the secretary of the SPG, 6 March 1745, ibid., 86; see ibid., 2:204.
37. John Pugh to the SPG, 17 November 1740, in SPG Records, Series B, 9, no. 102.
38. William Beckett to the SPG, 25 April 1741, ibid., 95.
39. Alexander Howie to the SPG, 17 July 1740, Perry, *Historical Collections*, 2:207–8.
40. William Currie to the secretary of the SPG, 7 July 1740, ibid., 209.
41. Samuel C. McCulloch, "Thomas Bradbury Chandler: Anglican Humanitarian in Colonial New Jersey," in *British Humanitarianism*, 107; Samuel A. Clark, *A History of St. John's Church, Elizabeth Town, New Jersey* (Philadelphia, 1857), 147.
42. Alexander Malcolm to the secretary, 10 May 1742, SPG Letters, B, 10:31.
43. Donald J. D'Elia, *Benjamin Rush: Philosopher of the American Revolution* (Philadelphia, 1974), 83.

44. Benjamin Rush to John Adams, 24 February 1790, in *Letters of Benjamin Rush*, ed. Lyman H. Butterfield (Princeton, 1951), 1:533.
45. For Rush's comments on the Thirty-nine Articles, see Benjamin Rush to Richard Peters, 20 May 1786, ibid., 1:389.
46. Benjamin Rush to John Adams, 5 April 1808, ibid., 2: 963, and Rush to James Montgomery, 5 July 1808, ibid., 969.
47. Jarratt, born in Kent County, Virginia, was largely self-educated, but received ordination in 1763 despite his lack of training. Thereafter, he was rector of Bath Parish, Dinwiddie County, for the next thirty-eight years. His *A Brief Narrative of the Revival in Virginia in a Letter to a Friend* went through three editions in his lifetime, two of which were published in London. His *Life of the Reverend Devereux Jarratt* is one of the best-known autobiographies of eighteenth-century America. See *DAB*, 9:616–17.
48. Jarratt, *Life*, 28.
49. *DNB*, 7:253.
50. *DNB*, 9:733–35.
51. Jarratt, *Life*, 57.
52. Ibid. For statements of his theological position, see pp. 58, 315, and 320. For his itinerating activities, see pp. 97 and 109.
53. David Lynn Holmes, Jr., "William Meade and the Church in Virginia" (Ph.D. diss., Princeton University, 1971), 54. Among the early leaders in England was Augustus M. Toplady, an Anglican Calvinist and indefatigable admirer of Whitefield. To Toplady, Whitefield was par excellence the spiritual unifier of the transatlantic Church of England, indeed "the apostle of English and Calvinist Empire." See Augustus M. Toplady, *The Complete Works of Augustus M. Toplady B.A.* (London, 1857), 494.
54. Hunter Dickinson Farrish, ed., *Journal & Letters of Philip Vickers Fithian* (Williamsburg, Va., 1965), 61.
55. Bolton, *Anglican Church*, 334.
56. Ibid., 445, 438.
57. Samuel Peters, *General History of Connecticut* . . . ([London, 1781] New York, 1877), 161–62; the work may also be found in Kenneth W. Cameron, ed., *The Works of Samuel Peters of Hebron, Connecticut* . . . (Hartford, Conn., 1967). Peters graduated from Yale in 1757 and received an M.A. from King's College in New York in 1761 after ordination in England in 1758. From 1760 to 1774 he held the Episcopal church at Hebron in his charge. Peters was a loyalist and a slave holder. During hostilities he returned to England and remained there until 1806. In 1794 he was elected bishop of Vermont but was never consecrated. He was a satirist, folklorist, and historian of his native Connecticut. For his biography see *DAB*, 14:511. For Peters's churchmanship see Steiner, *Seabury*, 259. Peters also admired those who were "very rubrical"; see Samuel Peters to the secretary, 12 May 1766, in Perry, *Documentary History*, 2:89, and cf. ibid., 106, an "impressive preacher" much like Whitefield himself. For this see E. C. Chorley, ed., "Letters of the Reverend Doctor Ebenezer Diblee of Stamford to the Reverend Doctor Samuel Peters, Loyalist Refugee in London, 1784–1793," *HM* 1 (1932): 79. Peters was also not above preaching in non-Episcopalian churches; see Peters to the secretary, 27 December 1764, in Perry, *Documentary History*, 2:74.
58. Benjamin Franklin to George Whitefield, 2 July 1756, in *The Papers of Benjamin Franklin*, ed. William B. Willcox (New Haven, Conn., 1959–74), 15:468–69.
59. Franklin, *Papers*, 20:438. Franklin was not always so laudatory and often employed sarcasm and insult in his letters to Whitefield as the condescending minister tried, unsuccessfully, to convert his deistic American friend; see ibid., 3:88, 383, 11:231–32. For an analysis of reactions to Whitefield in Franklin's *Pennsylvania Gazette*, as well as in other newspapers, see Melvin H. Buxbaum, *Benjamin Franklin and the Zealous Presbyterians* (University Park, Pa., 1975), 141–45, 238–39.
60. Franklin to Wimberly Jones, 5 March 1771, in Franklin, *Papers*, 18:53.

61. William White, *Comparative Views of the Controversy between the Calvinists and the Arminians* (Philadelphia, 1817), 2:189. For discussion of White's theological position, see John F. Woolverton, "Philadelphia's William White: Episcopalian Distinctiveness and Accommodation in the Post-Revolutionary Period," *HM* (1974): 279–96.
62. Bird Wilson, *Memoir of the Life of the Right Reverend William White* (Philadelphia, 1839), 15.
63. Henry, *Whitefield*, 61.
64. Martin Gardner, *The Flight of Peter Fromm* (Los Altos, Calif., 1973), 16.
65. Henry, *Whitefield*, 24, 82. For Whitefield's reading, see 53–54, 56; also Martin Schmidt, *John Wesley: A Theological Biography*, 1 (1962): 48.
66. Henry, *Whitefield*, 27.
67. Ibid., 96.
68. Josiah Smith, "A Sermon on the Character, Preaching, &c. of the Rev. Mr. Whitefield (1740)," in *The Great Awakening, Documents Illustrating the Crisis and Its Consequences*, ed. Alan Heimert and Perry Miller (Indianapolis, Ind., 1967), 63, 68.
69. Kenney, "Whitefield," 49, quoting Sidney E. Mead, *The Lively Experiment: The Shaping of Christianity in America* (New York, 1963), 29. Kenney seems also to approve Stuart Henry's assertion in his *Whitefield* that the evangelist had a "non-critical and highly subjective" approach to the Bible (98). It should be clear by now that the thesis here argued is that together with Whitefield's properly tropological view of scripture went a clearly defined theological position.
70. See Aeneas Ross to the secretary, 1 August 1740, in Perry, *Historical Collections*, 204; cf. ibid., Alexander Howie to the secretary, 17 July 1740, 207, and Archibald Cummings to the secretary, 31 July 1740, 211. Howie reported that Whitefield "desired a great auditory to burn it [*Whole Duty of Man*], telling them he would burn as many as came to his hand." Judging from the popularity of the book, it would have made quite a bonfire! For further references to Tillotson, see Whitefield, *Journals*, 404, 407, 438, 462.
71. Heimert, *American Mind*, 367.
72. *Virginia Gazette*, no. 181, 18 January 1740, 2; cf. *Pennsylvania Gazette*, no. 571, 22 November 1739, 2.
73. *Virginia Gazette*, no. 953, 24 August 1769; see *Pennsylvania Gazette*, no. 151, 30 March 1769.
74. Richard Hofstadter, *America at 1750* (New York, 1971), 207.
75. Quoted in Robert H. Dunn, *Old St. John's at Portsmouth and Her Distinguished Colonial Flock* (New York, 1947), 18f.
76. Bruce E. Steiner, "New England Anglicanism: A Genteel Faith?" *WMQ*, 3rd Series, 27 (1970): 135.
77. Lawrence N. Crumb, "The Anglican Church in Maine," *HM* 23 (1964): 258f.
78. John Wentworth to Joseph Harrison, 24 September 1769, Fulham Papers, 6:106–7.
79. Belknap, *New Hampshire*, 1:340.
80. Wentworth to Harrison, n.d., Fulham Papers, 6:107.
81. William Tryon to the secretary, 31 July 1765, Fulham Papers, 6:304–5.
82. Richard J. Hooker, ed., *The Carolina Backcountry on the Eve of the Revolution* (Chapel Hill, N.C., 1953), xxxv.
83. "Remonstrance of 1767," in Hooker, *Carolina Backcountry,* 215.
84. Hooker, *Carolina Backcountry,* 121f.
85. Quoted in ibid., xxx. Woodmason had been a provincial official, a member of the social St. George's Society, and was, in his own words, "greatly caressed, and ev'ry one's favorite." When he came to South Carolina, c. 1752, he left a wife and son in England whom he intended to send for once he had become established. Sometime later, he underwent a severe and painful accident: he was thrown from his horse, kicked in the genitals, and rendered incapable of sexual intercourse. As a result, his wife refused to join him in America, and his vestry—he had by then become a parson—ridiculed his plight. In 1766, he removed to the Piedmont.

86. Samuel Davies, *The State of Religion among the Protestant Dissenters in Virginia* . . . (Boston, 1751), 10–11, quoted in Rhys Isaac, "Religion and Authority: Problems of the Anglican Establishment in Virginia in the Era of the Great Awakening and the Parsons' Cause," *WMQ*, 3rd Series, 30 (January 1973): 22. For the attitude of the awakened to the Church of England in Virginia, see Joseph Tracy, *The Great Awakening* (New York, 1845), 375.
87. Isaac, "Religion and Authority," 10; see also 20 and 5.
88. Bishop of London to the Board of Trade, 14 June 1759, Perry, *Historical Collections,* 1: 461.
89. Not all the cases in the Parsons' Causes involved financial matters. The Lunenberg Parish affair involving William Kay had to do with security of tenure, the Brunskill Case (1757), with episcopal vs. gubernatorial authority, and the William and Mary Visitation affair (1757), something close to the issue of academic freedom. For a discussion of these and others, see Isaac, "Religion and Authority."
90. Perry, *Historical Collections,* 1: 364.
91. A. Shrady Hill, "The Parson's Cause," *HM,* 46 (1977), 27.
92. James Maury to William Douglas, 20 November 1759, Maury Letterbook, quoted in Isaac, "Religion and Authority," 34.
93. Isaac, "Religion and Authority," 34.
94. Ibid., 35f.
95. Samuel Davies to the bishop of London, 10 January 1752, in Foote, 1: 180, quoted in George William Pilcher, *Samuel Davies: Apostle of Dissent in Colonial Virginia* (Knoxville, 1971), 130.
96. J. H. Plumb, *Sir Robert Walpole, The Making of a Statesman,* 2 vols. (London, 1956), 1: 42.

Notes to Chapter 9

1. Less well known now, though not in his own time, Clarke, a disciple of Newton, was as widely read as Tillotson. "For a great many Englishmen in the colonies and at home," remarks Henry F. May, "Dr. Samuel Clarke, probably the most famous liberal Anglican divine, was an authority almost equal to Locke or Newton" (May, *Enlightenment,* 11). In a larger context this graduate of Caius College, Cambridge (1695), and rector of St. James, Westminster, was one of the first in a long line of mediating theologians who have sought to "prove" the truth of Christianity. Occupants of this line, declares Hans Frei, whatever their differences, are—down to our own time—"John Locke, Samuel Clarke, Joseph Butler, Johann Salomo Semler, Johann Joachim Spalding, Friedrich Schleiermacher, Albrecht Ritschl, Wilhelm Herrmann, Emil Brunner, Rudolph Bultmann, Karl Rahner, Gerhard Ebeling, Wolfhart Pannenberg, and Jurgen Moltmann" (Frei, *Eclipse,* 128). These have agreed that the meaningfulness of Christianity must be "perspicuous through its relation to other accounts of general human experience." For Samuel Clarke, writes May, the task of theology in addition was to bring to that study, "the exactitude and certainty possessed by mathematics." For Clarke "any kind of truth so demonstrated was irresistible to human reason." Revelation was for the ignorant. Jesus's doctrines, though not always discoverable by the light of nature, were clearly the work of an utterly rational deity and at the same time conformable to human reason. Clarke then rejected scepticism. Christianity was a rational system of belief, proven by miracle and prophecy. Clarke's rhetoric was orthodox; his Christology tended in an Arian direction. He was, as a result, held in suspicion by the deistic disciples of Locke as well as by the orthodox. His most famous work was *The Scripture Doctrine of the Trinity* (1712). See *DNB,* 4, 443–46.
2. Samuel Johnson to George Berkeley, [Jr.], 10 December 1756, in Schneiders, *Career,* 2, 339.
3. Ibid., 1, 23.

4. Samuel Johnson to William Samuel Johnson, 30 January 1757, ibid., 270.

5. George Whitefield, "A Letter to the Reverend the President, and Professors, Tutors, and Hebrew Instructor of Harvard College (Boston 1745)," in *American Higher Education, A Documentary History,* ed. Richard Hofstadter and Wilson Smith, 2 vols. (Chicago, 1961), 1: 64.

6. May, *Enlightenment,* 11.

7. For reference to the relation between Hogarth and Fielding and Richardson, see Michael Levey, *Rococo to Revolution: Major Trends in Eighteenth-Century Painting* (New York, 1966), 124–28; also E. H. Gombrich, *Art and Illusion* (New York, 1960), 338. For a discussion of the painting of Smibert, see Flexner, *First Flowers,* 112–29.

8. See John Redwood, *Reason, Ridicule and Religion: The Age of Enlightenment in England* (Cambridge, 1976), 118. At the College of William and Mary in 1752, President William Stith took pains to assure the bishop of London that he—Stith—was neither a "Clarkist" nor tainted with "Clarkism." Stith denied that he had even read Clarke's *The Scripture Doctrine of the Trinity.* See William Stith to the bishop of London, 15 August 1752, in Herbert L. Gantner, "Documents Relating to the Early History of the College of William and Mary and to the History of the Church in Virginia," *WMQ,* 2nd Series, 20 (1940), 232.

9. Ibid., 112. For a summary of Clarke's mathematical methodology see, Robert H. Hurlbutt III, *Hume, Newton, and The Design Argument* (Lincoln, 1965), 32.

10. May, *Enlightenment,* 80.

11. William Smith, *A General Idea of the College of Mirania* (New York, 1753), 10.

12. Ibid., 11.

13. Ibid., 59.

14. Lawrence A. Cremin, *American Education: The Colonial Experience, 1607–1783* (New York, 1970), 380.

15. Frederick Rudolph, *The American College and University* (New York, 1962), 32.

16. See Richard Hofstadter and Walter P. Metzger, *The Development of Academic Freedom in the United States* (New York, 1955), 187; Edward Potts Cheyney, *History of the University of Pennsylvania, 1740–1940* (Philadelphia, 1940), 41.

17. Cremin, *American Education,* 379.

18. Thomas Firth Jones, *A Pair of Lawn Sleeves: A Biography of William Smith (1727–1803)* (Philadelphia, New York, and London, 1972), 9f.

19. Population figures for Pennsylvania and its capital are less readily available than those for other colonies. It has been estimated that the population of the colony as a whole in 1731 was around 45,000 (Wells, *Population of the British Colonies,* 143); in 1775 the figure had jumped to 300,000. This made Pennsylvania the second largest colony in North America after Virginia and before Massachusetts (Wells, 284). By 1750 Philadelphia had begun to challenge the commercial primacy of Boston. At that time Philadelphia was larger than either Boston or New York (Wells, 78f. and 111). Cremin computes the population of New York in 1755 at 13,719 and in 1770 at 21,885. Philadelphia city in 1755 was 12,140 and 13,115 in 1770 (Cremin, *American Education,* 539). However the county of New York was coterminous with the city (ibid., 571), while Philadelphia's outlying communities were not considered part of the city. When one takes into account what today would be called "greater Philadelphia" the population jumps, in 1769, to 34,412 which would make that city larger than New York at approximately the same time by some 12,527 people. It is likely that in the 1750s Philadelphia's entire population, surrounding communities included, was around 20,000. New York in 1749 had a population of 13,275.9 or 18.1 percent of the total for the colony, which in that year was 73,348 (Wells, 112).

20. Jones, *Lawn Sleeves,* 23.

21. For a description of Hopkinson's contribution to church music see Oscar G. T. Sonneck, *Francis Hopkinson, The First American Poet-Composer (1737–1791) and James Lyon, Patriot Preacher, and Psalmodist (1735–1794)* (New York, 1967).

22. See Arthur Hobson Quinn, *Representative American Plays* (New York and London,

1938). *Prince* is a tragedy which shows the influence of *Hamlet, Julius Caesar, Macbeth,* and *Romeo and Juliet;* its blank verse tends to be full of "darksome shades," "chilling fear," and "panting bosom[s]."

23. Jones, *Lawn Sleeves,* 28.
24. Richard Slotkin, *Regeneration through Violence, the Mythology of the American Frontier, 1600–1820* (Middletown, 1973), 231.
25. William Smith, *Historical Account of the Expedition against the Ohio Indians* (Cincinnati, 1868), 19.
26. Slotkin, *Regeneration,* 231.
27. H. Trevor Colbourn, *The Lamp of Experience* (Williamsburg, 1965), 14.
28. William Smith to the archbishop of Canterbury, 1 July 1760 in Perry, *Historical Collections,* 2, 320.
29. Melvin H. Buxbaum, "Benjamin Franklin and William Smith: Their School and Their Dispute," *HM* (1970), 373.
30. Benjamin Franklin, "Preface," *Abridgement of the Book of Common Prayer . . .* (London, 1773), iii, vii.
31. Besides the work of Buxbaum, see Ralph Ketchum, "Benjamin Franklin and William Smith: New Light on an Old Philadelphia Quarrel," *PMHB* 78 (1964): 142–63, and James H. Hutson, "Benjamin Franklin and William Smith: More Light on an Old Philadelphia Quarrel," *PMHB* 93 (1969): 109–13, wherein are treated Smith's role as pamphleteer for the proprietary Penn family and the personal animosity between the two men.
32. Franklin in the preface to his abridgement of the Book of Common Prayer states, "He [Franklin] professes himself to be a Protestant of the Church of England, and hold in the highest veneration the doctrines of Jesus Christ." *Abridgement,* iii.
33. Carl and Jessica Bridenbaugh, *Rebels and Gentlemen: Philadelphia in the Age of Franklin* (London, 1968), 119.
34. Franklin, Papers, 8, 35.
35. Quoted in L. H. Butterfield, *John Witherspoon Comes to America, A Documentary Account* (Princeton, 1953), 20.
36. L. H. Butterfield, ed., *Diary and Autobiography of John Adams,* 4 vols. (Cambridge, 1962), 2, 118; cf. Butterfield, ed., *Adams Family Correspondence,* 2 vols. (Cambridge, 1963), 1, 400–401.
37. Ibid., 2, 115.
38. Benjamin Rush, *Commonplace Book,* quoted in Don Roy Byrnes, "The Pre-Revolutionary Career of Provost William Smith, 1751–1780" (Ph.D. diss., Tulane University, 1969), 197.
   Others as well as Rush recognized Smith's learning. He received honorary D.D.s from Aberdeen, Oxford (where he trumped Franklin's bid for one), and Dublin. However, it is a fact that the contentiousness which Smith possessed and bred in others persists today in the jog trots of academics; one recent biographer of Smith characterizes a current competitor as "a graduate student in the pay of his [Smith's] descendents." See Jones, *Lawn Sleeves,* 198.
   Not all of Smith's love of conflict can be blamed on his personality, however. Soon after his arrival in Pennsylvania he was accused of libel, thrown in jail, and then underwent a trial, the injustices of which were notable. See Leonard W. Levy, *Freedom of Speech and Press in Early American History: Legacy of Suppression* (New York, 1963), 56–61.
39. See in this regard, Cremin, *American Education,* 382–83; David Churchill Humphrey, "King's College in the City of New York, 1754–1776" (Ph.D. diss., Northwestern University, 1968), 436–46, 476–78; Herbert Baxter Adams, "The College of William and Mary . . .," *Contributions to American Education,* ed. H. B. Adams (Washington, D.C., 1887), 20; Morison, *Harvard,* 174–76; Warch, *School of the Prophets,* 198–200; and, Thomas J. Wertenbaker, *Princeton, 1746–1896* (Princeton, 1946), 12, 29, and 92.
40. See Humphrey, "King's," 384–87.

41. William Wollaston was a follower of Clarke. He was a graduate of Sidney-Sussex College, Cambridge, and received his M.A. in 1681. Wollaston was a fine Hebrew scholar who contributed to Johnson's idea of divine benevolence, though King's president felt that in his *Religion of Nature* Wollaston failed to realize that, had it not been for scripture, he never could have written about God in the natural order (Schneiders, *Career*, 1, 23; *DNB*, 21, 781–82).

Francis Hutcheson, philosopher and Presbyterian minister, occupied the chair of moral philosophy at the University of Glasgow for nearly twenty years until his death. Hutcheson was a close follower of Shaftesbury. He is best known for his Scottish or "common sense" realism. (Sydney E. Ahlstrom, *A Religious History,* 355–56). Scottish realism extended to the nineteenth century in America, where, in the persons of Francis Wayland, Thomas C. Upham, Noah Porter, Mark Hopkins, and Francis Bowen, it dominated university and seminary education in moral philosophy until the Civil War. Wayland's *Elements of Moral Science* (1835) was standard fare in all centers of theological education in the Episcopal church as well as in other denominations.

Paul de Rapin, enormously popular in England as well as in the colonies, was a French Protestant intellectual who fled his native France at the revocation of the Edict of Nantes in 1685. Rapin was the author of *L'Histoire D'Angleterre,* published in eight volumes in The Hague in 1724. This and his *Dissertation sur les Whigs et les Torys* (1717) were basic reading in modern history at both Smith's academy and at King's in New York. Rapin's contribution to the Whig interpretation of history earned him a place on nearly every colonial bookshelf of consequence. See Colbourn, *Lamp of Experience.* Rapin's republicanism also commended him to English liberals and radicals of the eighteenth century. See Carolina Robbins, *The Eighteenth-Century Commonwealthmen* (Cambridge, 1959), 274.

42. Robert Dodsley (1703–1764) was a poet, dramatist, satirist, and bookseller who wrote the *Chronicle of the Kings of England* (London, 1740) a sham history written in mock-biblical style. *The Preceptor,* lauded by Boswell, was a kind of self-improvement course which included some subjects not taught at the universities, such as natural history, geometry, and geography (*DNB,* 5, 1075–79).

David Fordyce (1711–1751) was professor of moral philosophy at Marischal College, University of Aberdeen, from which he had received his M.A. in 1728. Smith may well have known and even studied under Fordyce (Humphrey, "King's," 400). He was the author of *Elements of Moral Philosophy* (London, 1754) and *Dialogues Concerning Education* (London, 1754–1758) (*DNB,* 7, 432).

Charles Rollin (1661–1741) was professor of Latin eloquence at the Collège Royale and then principal of the Collège Beauvais. He was author of *Histoire Ancienne* (1730–1738), *Histoire Romaine* (1738), and also of the widely read *Le Traite des études . . .* (1726–1731), which appeared in English as *Method of Studying and Teaching the Belles Lettres* (6th ed., London, 1768). Rollin was a pro-Jansenist which could not have failed to endear him to Protestants in England (*Nouvelle Biographie Générale,* 41–42, 570–71).

43. Humphrey, "King's," 401.
44. Ibid., 399f.
45. Schneiders, *Career,* 4, 228.
46. Humphrey, "King's," 405.
47. King's College averaged only twenty-five students per year in its first fifteen years and grew to forty-five in the decade before the Revolution. Harvard and Yale each had over one hundred students in the 1760s (Cremin, *American Education,* 510, Warch, *School of the Prophets,* 257). In 1765 the College of Philadelphia graduated twelve students from its senior class (Cheyney, *Pennsylvania,* 90). The entire college served only forty to sixty students. By way of contrast, in 1760 Harvard graduated twenty-seven, Yale, thirty-three; in 1770 Harvard granted thirty-four B.A. degrees to Yale's nineteen. In 1760 Princeton graduated eleven and in 1770, twenty-two (Cremin, 554). William and Mary averaged some sixty students for the seventy years prior to the Revolution (Adams, "College," 29).

48. William Smith never lost his interest in the sciences nor did he find them threatening to his religious views, no doubt due to the liberality of the latter. Johnson, on the other hand, in later life embraced the "fundamentalist" claim of John Hutchinson (1674–1737) that Genesis had scientific value in opposition to the very Newtonian physics which Johnson had once labored to introduce in American education. Hutchinson attempted to establish the scientific value of the Bible and argued against Newtonian philosophy that gravity was either the work of a universal fluid or of the cherubim! See Theodore Hornberger, "Samuel Johnson of Yale and King's College, A Note on the Relation of Science and Religion in Provincial America," *NEQ* 8 (1935), 393; cf. Humphrey, "King's," 459–65.

49. Cremin, *American Education,* 512.

50. Humphrey, "King's," 507; see also Cheyney, *Pennsylvania,* 89.

51. Byrnes, *Smith,* 60; Cheyney, *Pennsylvania,* 85. William Smith's own views tended toward unitarianism and, by Episcopalian standards, heresy. For example, after the Revolution he came to preside over the committee to revise the Book of Common Prayer for the new Episcopal church. Under Smith's influence, the Athanasian Creed and the Nicene Creed were dropped from what became the ill-fated prayer book of 1785. He also deleted the phrase "He descended into Hell" from the Apostles' Creed. Presumably, suggests one of Smith's biographers, the deletion "was a logical extension of liberal Episcopalian thought: if none of *us* must go to hell, why must Jesus?" See Jones, *Lawn Sleeves,* 153; the Apostles' Creed is of course the basic statement of faith of the Episcopal church (Book of Common Prayer, 304–5); cf. Benjamin Franklin to Granville Sharp, 20 May 1786, MS 1373 f. 1., Lambeth Palace Library.

52. William Smith, "The Editor's Preface," *Elementa Philosophica,* in Schneiders, *Career,* 2, 349.

53. *New York Gazette, or Weekly Post-Boy,* 3 June 1754, ibid., 4, 223.

54. Byrnes, *Smith,* 60.

55. Humphrey, "King's," 252–53. The aristocratic make-up of the college was only gradually changed to include the sons of tradesmen; see 335–44; cf. 246.

56. Myles Cooper was a graduate of Queen's College (B.A. 1756, M.A. 1760). In 1761 he had been appointed chaplain to Queen's, *DAB,* 4, 408–9.

57. Humphrey, "King's," 257–58, 261, 280, 284, and 302–4.

58. Herbert M. Morais, *Deism in Eighteenth-Century America* (New York, 1960), 73. Nothing like full-blown skepticism emerged in America until the 1790s, and even then, writes Henry F. May, "the skeptical Parisian Enlightenment had a far less important influence than its moderate, rationalist, English predecessor" (*Enlightenment,* 132).

59. Martin E. Marty, *Righteous Empire, The Protestant Experience in America* (New York, 1970), 20.

60. Colden has not received the attention he deserves; there has been one biography of him so far, the barely readable Alice M. Keys, *Cadwallader Colden: A Representative Eighteenth-Century Official* (New York, 1906). Franklin of course has received a stunning press beginning with Carl Van Doren's classic study and moving to Verner W. Crane's short and lively *Benjamin Franklin and a Rising People* (Boston, 1954), Paul W. Conner's political study, *Poor Richard's Politics: Benjamin Franklin and His New American Order* (New York, 1965), and Alfred O. Aldridge's study of Franklin's religion, *Benjamin Franklin and Nature's God* (New York, 1967).

61. Colden Papers, 9, 242f.; cf. *Zenger's New York Weekly Journal,* 8 August 1737.

62. See his "Observations on the Balance of Power in Government," Colden Papers, 9, 251–55 (c. 1744), "Account of the Government of New England," ibid., 245f., Colden to Sir William Johnson, 3 March 1765, New Netherlands volume, Folio 69, "Paper on Public Affairs, 1744–5," Colden Papers, Box 12, no. 65, "Comments on Government in General," ibid., 371–82, Colden to Benjamin Franklin, May–June [?], 1754, ibid., 4, 449–51.

63. Colden's friends and correspondents included John Rutherford (1694–1768), professor of medicine at the University of Edinburgh; Robert Whytt (1714–1766) that university's

professor of the theory of medicine; William Porterfield (fl. 1759) of Edinburgh's Royal College of Physicians and Surgeons; John Bevis (1693–1771), astronomer and physician; and Lord Macclesfield (1697–1764), president of the Royal Society (1752–1764) and one of the most renowned astronomers of the century. In the field of botany in which Colden had an avid interest, he corresponded with Peter Collinson (1694–1768); Carolus Linnaeus (1707–1778), the great Swedish scientist; the Dutchman Johann Friedrich Gronovius (1690–1760); and finally John Bartram (1699–1777), the Philadelphia Quaker and abolitionist, whose botanical pursuits placed him in the forefront of that science in America. Other close friends of Colden were James Alexander (1691–1756), the foremost lawyer in New Jersey in his day and William Douglass (1691–1752), the physician who had opposed Cotton Mather in the debate over the smallpox inoculation in Boston in the 1720s.

64. Colden, "Of Intelligent Being," Colden Papers, 6, 120.

65. Colden, "An Introduction to the Study of Phylosophy wrote in America for the use of a younge gentleman," (1760?), 7, 708. Johnson's Christian theism and Berkeleyanism clashed during the 1760s with Colden's deistic and humanistic materialism; see Cornelius Ryan Fay, *An Essay Describing Colden's "The First Principles of Morality"* (M.A. thesis, Columbia University, 1950), 22f.; for a general description of Colden's philosophical position see I. Woodbridge Riley, *American Philosophy the Early Schools* (New York, 1907). Fay corrects Riley's assertion that Thomas Hobbes influenced Colden; according to Fay it was John Locke. For further anti-Berkeleyanism, see Colden, "Inquiry into the Principles of Vital Motion," Unprinted Scientific and Political Papers, Colden Papers, 7, 96.

66. Cadwallader Colden to Samuel Pike, November 1753, Colden Papers, 7, 359. Pike was an overly eager apologist who, upon reading Colden's *The Principles of Action in Matter*, published in London in 1751, decided that Colden's scientific observations were in fact corroborated by scripture itself! What in fact the American scientist had unearthed through the observation of natural phenomena had lain in the Bible all along uncrecognized. In 1753 Pike revealed his startling discovery in a book, the title of which made Colden wince, *Philosophia Sacra*. For his part Colden hoped for reactions from the British scientific community to his *Principles of Action*. All he got for his efforts was the eager apology of Samuel Pike, hardly a suitable reward for his efforts. Had not Pike sent Colden a copy of *Philosophia Sacra* with his letter of explanation, "I would have suspected him," wrote Colden to Franklin, "of being a Wag." See Colden to Franklin, 29 November 1753, Franklin Papers, 5, 123.

67. Nelson Burr, *A Critical Bibliography of Religion in America*, vols. 3 and 4 of "Religion in American Life Series," 4 vols. (Princeton, 1961), 4, 1013.

68. Colden, "Essay on the Art of Right Living," Unprinted Scientific and Political Papers, Colden Papers, 7, 375.

69. *Abridgement of the Book of Common Prayer* (London, 1773), Thomas Jefferson Collection, Rare Book Room, Library of Congress, Washington, D.C.

70. See *Book of Common Prayer* (1928), 276.

71. *Abridgement*, iii.

72. Aldridge, *Franklin and Nature's God*, 106.

73. For a discussion of this liberal line of descent from the loins of Hooker, see John E. Booty, "Hooker and Anglicanism," in *Studies in Richard Hooker, Essays Preliminary to an Edition of His Works*, ed. W. Speed Hill (Cleveland and London, 1972), 207–39, especially 229.

Franklin's association with and attendance at King's Chapel in Boston and then Christ Church, Philadelphia, are matters of fact. Franklin, no doubt through his wife's influence, became a pewholder at Christ Church, made regular financial contributions to it, saw that his children were baptized there, and he and Deborah Read Franklin interred their son there in 1736 (see Franklin Papers, 2, 188, n.4). Franklin also supported the Presbyterian minister in Philadelphia (Alfred O. Aldridge, *Benjamin Franklin: Philosopher and Man*

[New York, 1965], 50f.). Nevertheless, the weight of evidence provided by Arthur Bernon Tourtellot in *Benjamin Franklin: The Shaping of Genius, The Boston Years* (Garden City, 1977) indicates that if Franklin can be said to have exhibited loyalty to any denomination, it was to the Church of England. Tourtellot writes: "The only church with which he himself ever became even informally affiliated (he supported it regularly and was buried in its churchyard, though he never became a communicant) was the Church of England." (287). Franklin sought to present the church in a good light and appears to have approved "the moderation of the present church of England towards Dissenters" (Franklin Papers, 8, 341). Buxbaum, however, only states that Franklin "thought well of the Church of England" (*Benjamin Franklin*, 41).

While I am aware of the dangers of designating Franklin as an Episcopalian, these comments in addition to his abbreviation of the Book of Common Prayer have led me to include him within the deistical wing of the church. Other than serving as a vestryman, there is little difference between Franklin's and Washington's participation. Franklin's own declaration that others saw him "of no sect at all" should be taken with a grain of salt, since the *Autobiography* is a notoriously political and self-serving document (see 134 for the above comment). In it Franklin would not be about to tip his hand as to church preference. Nor did he.

Further comment on Franklin's religion which shows his involvement with Christ Church, Philadelphia, is to be found in Carl Van Doren, *Benjamin Franklin* (New York, 1938), 131–32.

74. Van Doren, *Franklin*, 191; see also Aldridge, *Franklin and Nature's God*, 108.
75. Ibid., 81. Shaftesbury's writings in moral philosophy were collected under the title *Characteristics of Men, Manners, Opinions, Times* (London, 1711 and 1713) with which Franklin was acquainted.
76. Quoted in ibid., 186.
77. Ibid., 162. Aldridge mistakenly calls Shipley "Joseph." Aldridge, *Franklin and Nature's God*, 58.

Notes to Chapter 10

1. See Edward Carpenter, *Thomas Sherlock, 1678–1761* (London, 1936), 196–98.
2. A. Spencer to Thomas Sherlock, 12 June 1749, printed in Cross, *Anglican Episcopate*, 310.
3. Sherlock to Newcastle, 3 September 1749, ibid., 320.
4. Ibid., 320–21; interestingly, Cross omits the more self-incriminating statements of Sherlock's in which personal considerations play a large role. Cf. Carpenter, *Sherlock*, 201.
5. Ibid., 322. For Sherlock's subsequent account of his activities, see *Fulham Papers*, A, 6 (North Carolina), 270–75.
6. Quoted in Carpenter, *Sherlock*, 203f.
7. The full text is to be found in Belby Porteus, *A Review of the Life and Character of Archbishop Secker* (London, 1773), 109f.
8. Ibid., 110–11.
9. Papers of the SPG in the Lambeth Palace Library, *Minutes 1745–50*, 5, 279.
10. Horace Walpole to Thomas Sherlock, 29 May 1750, in Cross, *Anglican Episcopate*, 326.
11. Thomas Sherlock to Samuel Johnson, 21 April 1752, quoted in Chandler, *Life of Johnson*, 171.
12. Arthur Cross not only accepted without question the notion that Butler was the perpetrator of the proposal of 1750 but fails to get that bishop's name straight when he refers to "William Butler, Bishop of Durham, author of the celebrated *Analogy*" (*Anglican Episcopate*, 122).
13. Quoted in Jonathan Mayhew, *Observations on the Charter and Conduct of the Society for the Propagation of the Gospel in Foreign Parts* (Boston, 1763), 34.

14. Ibid., 32. Eighteenth-century American appreciation of Butler is noted in Conrad Wright, *The Beginnings of Unitarianism* (Boston, 1955), 75–76, 112, 148, and 246. Jonathan Edwards knew the *Analogy,* albeit second hand; see Clyde Holbrook, *Original Sin* (New Haven, 1970), 17, 72–73. In William J. Norton, *Bishop Butler, Moralist and Divine* (New Brunswick, 1940), it is suggested that Butler's relation "to his age was largely of an academic nature" (6). This is not born out in L. H. Butterfield, ed., *Adams Family Correspondence,* 2 vols. (Cambridge, 1963), 2, 241, where Abigail Adams approved Butler's comments regarding personal ethics. Both Norton's and Leslie Stephens's assertion (*DNB,* 3, 523f.) that the profundities of Butler's thought deterred contemporaries from venturing into his arguments are contradicted elsewhere, especially in L. H. Butterfield, ed., *The Diary and Autobiography of John Adams,* 4 vols. (Cambridge, 1962), 1, 25, 26 and 106; Lester Capon, ed., *The Adams-Jefferson Letters,* 2 vols. (Chapel Hill, 1959), 2, 534; Timothy Dwight, *Travels in New England and New York,* 4 vols. (Cambridge, 1969), Barbara M. Solomon, ed., 1, 378. See also Bernard Bailyn, ed., *Pamphlets of the American Revolution, 1750–1776,* vol. 1 (Cambridge, 1965), 200; and May, *Enlightenment,* 23–24, 353.
15. East Apthorp, *Considerations on the Institution and Conduct of the Society for the Propagation of the Gospel in Foreign Parts* (Boston, 1763), 11.
16. Mayhew, *Observations,* 156.
17. Ibid., 32–38.
18. Arthur Browne, *Remarks on Dr. Mayhew's Incidental Reflections Relative to the Church of England As contained in his Observations on the Charter and Conduct of the Society* (Portsmouth, 1763), 22–27.
19. [Thomas Secker], *An Answer to Dr. Mayhew's Observations on the Charter and Conduct of the Society for the Propagation of the Gospel in Foreign Parts* (London, 1764), 53.
20. Apthorp, *Considerations,* 13; see also Richard J. Hooker, "The Mayhew Controversy," *Church History,* 5 (1936), 249.
21. For discussion of the issue of who evidenced the greatest civility and antirevivalistic good breeding, Episcopalians or liberal Congregationalists, see Heimert, *Religion and the American Mind,* 361–64.
22. Secker, *Answer,* 50, 51.
23. East Apthorp, *A Review of Dr. Mayhew's Remarks on the Answer to his Observations on the Charter and Conduct of the SPG* . . . (London, 1765), 55.
24. Ibid., 56.
25. Suspicion that Butler was not the author of the Butler Plan was aroused in my mind by the fact that in a long letter written by Secker to Horace Walpole in the winter of 1750 which discussed at length the fracas raised by Thomas Sherlock's activities, Secker nowhere mentions the name of Butler. He contented himself with the declaration: "Yet I believe there scarce is, or ever was a Bishop of the Church of England, that hath not desired the establishment of Bishops in our colonies. Archbishop Tenison, who was surely no High-Churchman, left by his Will 1000 £ towards it." Thomas Secker, *A Letter* . . . *to Horace Walpole, Written, January 9, 1750/1* (London, 1769), 9. Surely if Butler had been the author of the plan of 1750, Secker would have mentioned so important a fact.
26. See Schneiders, *Career,* 1, 297–301, and Johnson's letter to Secker, 293–97. Johnson's letter of 1760 was by no means the first or only petition for an American bishop to emanate from the colonies. Among the better known petitions are: Evan Evans, "The State of the Church in Pennsylvania, 18 September 1707," in William White Papers, 1, 1 (Archives of the Episcopal Church), reprinted in the *Episcopal Magazine,* 1 (January, 1820), 16–21; "Queries humbly offered to the Consideration of the Friends of Protestant Episcopacy in North America, April 1764," Smith Papers, 1, 43, in which it is argued that a bishop might be located in Canada where ordination might be received without upsetting dissenters. See also "Thoughts upon the present State of the Church of England in America, June 1764," Smith Papers, 1, 45, and White Papers, 1, 12, wherein it is urged that the bishop of London be given four suffragan bishops in America, one each at Burlington, New Jersey,

William and Mary College in Virginia, Charleston, South Carolina, and at Codrington College, Barbados; Massachusetts Clergy to the archbishop of Canterbury, 17 June 1767. With respect to Burlington, New Jersey, the SPG, in the first decade of the eighteenth century, bought an "episcopal palace," the "stately home of John Tatham Esq." (Hill, *Church in Burlington*, 172–74, 265–66; Burr, *Church in New Jersey*, 342–48). Finally among the most important petitions, since it represented the mind of a convention, was that of Thomas Bradbury Chandler to the SPG, 3 October 1765 and 17 February 1766 in SPG Letters, Series B (1701–1786), [B] 24, Part 2, 314.

Among the most interesting letters having to do with an American episcopate are those of Thomas Herring to William Smith, 19 January 1755, Maryland Diocesan Archives, and Thomas Secker to William Smith, 27 September 1758, Smith Papers, 1, 25. Both of these epistles manifest concern for dissenting consciences. The reluctance of the London government to send a bishop to America is noted in Richard Terrick to William Smith, 10 November 1764, Maryland Diocesan Archives. See also letters from the archbishop of York to Richard Peters, 11 August 1764 and 28 May 1765, White Papers, 1, 13.

Petitions and letters from Episcopal clergy in Massachusetts constitute a special case. There, while lip service was paid to the efforts to obtain the episcopate, as early as 1760, before the clergy as a whole had petitioned the English hierarchy, Henry Caner (1700–1792), rector of King's Chapel, judged an American bishop to be "an expedient too remote to be thought of" (Perry, *Historical Collections*, 3, 459). In August 1763, Caner wrote Thomas Secker to the effect already established *de jure* if not *de facto*—a bit of special pleading (ibid., 504). Thereafter, Caner vaguely argued for "some person vested with to convene the brethren" (Fulham Papers, 54–55). Not until 17 June 1767 did the Massachusetts clergy petition formally (Perry, *Historical Collections*, 3, 531). The following year, however, they did not renew their request and instead blandly stated that the church "was in as good condition as can reasonably be expected under the present troublesome state of these Colonies" (ibid., 541). In Boston and environs the issue was simply too controversial.

27. See Bridenbaugh, *Mitre and Sceptre*, 135f.
28. Thomas Secker to Samuel Johnson, 4 November 1760, Schneiders, *Career*, 4, 72.
29. Samuel Johnson to Bishop Robert Lowth, 25 October 1768, ibid., 449.
30. For characterizations of Secker and his role in colonial religious history, see Gerald R. Cragg, *The Church in the Age of Reason* (New York, 1961), 127 and 129; E. Edwards Beardsley, *Life and Correspondence of the Right Reverend Samuel Seabury* (Boston, 1881), 13; and Samuel C. McCulloch, "Thomas Bradbury Chandler: Anglican Humanitarian in Colonial New Jersey," *British Humanitarianism* (Philadelphia, 1950), 116.
31. Chandler, *Life of Johnson*, 137. Descriptions of Chandler appear in McCulloch, "Chandler," 108; Dexter, *Yale Graduates*, 23–28; Perry, *History of the American Episcopal Church*, 1, 413–18; Sprague, *Annals*, 5, 137–42.
32. Thomas Bradbury Chandler to Samuel Johnson, October 1766, Schneiders, *Career*, 1, 369.
33. Chandler, *Life of Johnson*, 136f.
34. Dexter, *Yale Graduates*, 24.
35. McCulloch, "Chandler," 107.
36. Thomas Bradbury Chandler to Samuel Johnson, n.d., Schneiders, *Career*, 1, 166.
37. Thomas Bradbury Chandler to Samuel Johnson, ibid., 1, 357.
38. Thomas Bradbury Chandler, *An Appeal to the Public, in Behalf of the Church of England in America* . . . (New York, 1767), 19f. Chandler quotes Hooker's *Laws of Ecclesiastical Polity* indicating that the episcopal line must not be broken.
39. Ibid., 26–33, 42, 55, 95, and 117.
40. Charles Chauncy, *An Appeal to the Public Answered* (Boston, 1766).
41. Thomas Bradbury Chandler, *An Appeal Farther Defended in Answer to the Farther Misrepresentation of Dr. Chauncy* (New York, 1771), 81–82.

42. Chandler, *Address to Americans,* 18.
43. Ibid., 24.
44. Chandler, *Appeal Farther Defended,* 210, and *A Free Examination of the Critical Commentary on Archbishop Secker's Letter to Mr. Walpole* (New York, 1744), 5.
45. Harry A. C. Read, "Thomas Bradbury Chandler: His Life and Times" (Term paper, Virginia Theological Seminary, 1975), 25.
46. Burr, *Church in New Jersey,* 288–90; see Edgar L. Pennington, "Colonial Church Conventions," *HM* 1 (1939): 179–89.
47. Chandler wished to do away with the system of commissaries in favor of episcopacy. Such a radical step was too much for the New Yorker Samuel Auchmuty and Philadelphia rector Richard Peters (1704–1776). The former wanted other aid as well, while the latter wanted to expand the commissariat to include greater territorial responsibility.
48. Bridenbaugh, *Mitre and Sceptre,* 256.
49. Hooker, *Anglican Church and the American Revolution,* 36–45, discusses these clergy. For sympathetic but not uncritical discussion of all of these and others in context, see North Callahan, *Flight from the Republic: The Tories of the American Revolution* (Indianapolis, 1967); William H. Nelson, *The American Tory* (Oxford, 1961), especially 72–81; Wallace Brown, *The King's Friends* (Providence, 1965), and Leonard W. Labaree, "The Nature of American Loyalism," *Proceedings of the American Antiquarian Society,* New Series, 54, Part 1 (1944), 15–58, which deserves special attention. These and a host of periodical literature now join older studies such as Alexander Flick, *Loyalism in New York during the American Revolution* (London, 1901) and C. H. Van Tyne, *The Loyalists in the American Revolution* (New York, 1902, and Gloucester, 1959).
50. Nelson, *American Tory,* 1f.
51. Flick, *Loyalism in New York,* 105. At the time Tryon with Inglis's help was recruiting loyal Americans for a provincial regiment.
52. Ibid., 154; see Brown, *King's Friends,* 99.
53. Ibid., 166–67; see Van Tyne, *The Loyalists,* 108f.
54. Gordon Wood, *The Creation of the American Republic, 1776–1787* (Chapel Hill, 1969), 94.
55. [Charles Inglis], *The True Interest of America Impartially Stated in Certain Strictures on a Pamphlet Entitled Common Sense* (Philadelphia, 1776), 15.
56. Wood, *American Republic,* 135f.
57. [Inglis], *True Interest,* 10.
58. Ibid., 18.
59. Ibid., 10.
60. It was a nineteenth-century English visitor to America, the Reverend Henry Caswall, who intiated the idea that a majority of colonial Episcopalians desired episcopal supervision. Caswall observed in 1839, "Sensible of their necessities, the members of the Church of England in America had exerted themselves as early as the reign of Charles II, to obtain an Episcopate from their mother country. Their letters and memorials supplied for a whole century a connected chain of expostulations and petitions to this effect." *America and the American Church* (London, 1851), 132. This misrepresentation was subsequently reduced by Samuel D. McConnell in his *History of the American Episcopal Church* (New York, 1890): "From this side of the water the cry for a bishop was never silent" (177); see Charles C. Tiffany, *A History of the Protestant Episcopal Church in the United States of America* (New York, 1895), 268; Perry, *American Episcopal Church,* 1, 397, 401, 405, 406, 410, and 420f.; and Raymond W. Albright, *A History of the Protestant Episcopal Church* (New York, 1964), 96. Only Perry and William Manross in his *A History of the American Episcopal Church* (New York, 1935) note that Virginians had a lack of interest in the subject (Manross, 154f.).
61. Frederick V. Mills, Sr., "Anglican Resistance to an American Episcopate" (Ph.D. diss., University of Pennsylvania, 1967), 137. In addition, historiography on the controversy follows. Bridenbaugh's *Mitre and Sceptre* deals with the dissenters who opposed an

American episcopate. Within that area of research, Heimert's *Religion and the American Mind* makes the point that it was not so much the Calvinist ministers of the Great Awakening who opposed bishops as the liberal Congregationalist leaders who, prior to the Revolution, vied with resurgent northern Episcopalianism in an effort to capture the more urbane followers of the moderate enlightenment. May (*Enlightenment in America*) notes that the bishop controversy split the forces of religious liberalism (87). Arthus L. Cross's older *Anglican Episcopate* deals chronologically with high church attempts to settle bishops in America, and Mills's "Anglican Resistance" discloses the hitherto ignored attitudes of those Episcopalians who actively and passively stood against the importation of the episcopate.

62. Edwin A. White and Jackson A. Dyckman, *Annotated Constitution and Canons,* 2 vols. (Greenwich, 1954), 1, 10–11.
63. Thomas Cradock, Sermon Preached at Annapolis, 1753, Maryland Diocesan Archives.
64. Mills, "Anglican Resistance," 104.
65. John P. Kennedy, ed., *Journals of the House of Burgesses, 1770–1772* (Richmond, 1906), 122.
66. Mills, "Anglican Resistance," 115.
67. William Warren Sweet, "The Role of Anglicans in the American Revolution," *HLQ,* 9 (November, 1947), 52; Brown, *King's Friends,* 281.
68. Otto Lohrenz, "The Virginia Clergy and the American Revolution, 1774–1799" (Ph.D. diss., University of Kansas, 1970), 22. Of the 129 clergy in Virginia during the Revolution, Lohrenz counts 10 who became loyalist refugees, 10 who supported the loyalist cause but remained in the colony and eventually yielded to the republican form of government, 11 who were politically irresolute, 22 who were passive Whigs and failed to support actively the patriot cause, and 31 who were active Whigs, participated in committees of safety, or served with the congressional forces. Most of the refugee clergy were from the tidewater area or were more recent arrivals in the colony; conversely, most of the 31 patriot ministers had deeper ancestral roots in Virginia. By contrast, of the 100 Baptist and 30 Presbyterian ministers who can be accounted for, all were patriots.
69. Brown, *King's Friends,* 290–344, gives tables with figures for Episcopalian, loyalist clergy from each state. As Brown clearly warns, beyond this an accurate count of the number of loyalists, clerical and otherwise, can never be made (252). Regarding general loyalist strength, Brown notes that from New York the seaboard towns of Greenwich, Stamford, Norwalk, Fairfield, and Stratford contained 56 percent of Connecticut's loyalists, Newport, R.I., 89 percent; Boston, 52.5 percent. Similar figures are given for loyalist claimants for the other areas. Beyond that there were loyalist pockets, notes Brown, in Virginia's seaport towns such as Norfolk and Portsmouth, Charleston, and Savannah—all of them urban, coastal areas.
70. Esther Clark Wright, *The Loyalists of New Brunswick* (Fredericton, N.B., 1972), 237.
71. Judith Fingard, *The Anglican Design in Loyalist Nova Scotia* (London, 1972), 41.
72. Nelson, *American Tory,* 91.

Notes to the Conclusion

1. For example, in 1722 Daniel Browne, one of the Yale "apostates," wrote home from England that Anglican bishops "we find are not such frightful People as you in that Country are made to believe" (Daniel Browne to Joseph Browne, 5 February 1722, Smith Papers, 1, 2). From that time on, Episcopalians sought, as we have seen, to commend the episcopate on a "nonpolitical" basis.
2. Mills, *Bishops by Ballot,* 282f. and especially 288–307.
3. Jones, *Present State,* 43; cf. Bailyn, *Ideological Origins,* 83–93 and 128–43.
4. Quoted in Mills, *Bishops by Ballot,* 106.
5. Letters of Jonathan Boucher, *MHM,* 8 (March 1913), 44, quoted in Anne Young Zimmer

and Alfred H. Kelly, "Jonathan Boucher: Constitutional Conservative," *JAH*, 58 (March 1972), 904.

6. Samuel Johnson to Thomas Secker, 12 July 1760, Schneiders, *Career*, 1, 298.

7. See for instance, Samuel Johnson, "Raphael or the Genius of English America," Schneiders, *Career*, 2, 556.

8. William H. Nelson, "The Revolutionary Character of the American Revolution," *AHR*, 70 (July 1965), 1004.

9. East Apthorp, *Of Sacred Poetry and Music, A Discourse at Christ's Church, Cambridge, at the opening of the ORGAN on Tuesday, 21 August, 1764* (Boston, 1764), 16–17.

10. George Duyckinck, *The Life of Thomas Ken, Bishop of Bath and Wells* (New York, 1859), viii. Duyckinck also wrote *The Life of George Herbert* (New York, 1858) and *The Life of Jeremy Taylor* (New York, 1860). Duyckinck made his mistake by attempting to read the history of his own time into that of Bishop Ken. He saw Ken as a proto-Tractarian who anticipated the Anglo-Catholicism of the nineteenth century in England with its "Isidorean" demand for the supremacy of the spiritual over the temporal. Nonjurors such as Ken, on the other hand, embraced royal supremacy zealously and declared James II the only true monarch of England. Constitutionally, the two were far apart. The American revolutionary Whigs rejected the supremacy of the king, particularly the king in Parliament, and opted for the sectarian "Brownist" position which declared that the state had no authority over the church. Duyckinck would have been on much firmer ground had he contented himself with the observation that the Tractarian demand for the freedom of the Church of England from the control by Parliament was the ecclesiastical counterpart of the American Declaration of Independence of the Hanoverian state. Instead, he attempted to link an earlier revolt against Parliament with radical American Whigism by simply ignoring the royal absolutism of the earlier "rebels."

11. See for instance, Calvin Colton, *The Americans* (1822), and James Fenimore Cooper, *The American Democrat* (1838). In addition, see John F. Woolverton, "Whither Episcopalianism? A Century of Apologetic Interpretations of the Episcopal Church, 1835–1964," *ATR* (Supplementary Series, 1, 1973), 142–49.

Bibliography

Primary Sources

Manuscript Collections

Bass, Edward. Papers. Maryland Diocesan Archives at the Maryland Historical Society, Baltimore, Maryland.
Board of Trade. Manuscript Letters. Great Britain. British Museum.
Colden, Cadwallader. Papers. New York Colonial Documents. New-York Historical Society, New York.
Collections, 4th Series. Massachusetts Historical Society, Boston, Massachusetts.
Cradock, Thomas. Papers. Maryland Diocesan Archives at the Maryland Historical Society, Baltimore, Maryland.
Fulham Papers. Lambeth Palace Library, London, England.
Letters and Journals. Society for the Propagation of the Gospel in Foreign Parts, London, England.
Seabury, Samuel. "Lectures Upon the Catechism." Papers. St. Mark's Library, The General Theological Seminary, New York.
Shaftesbury Papers. South Carolina Historical Society, Charleston, South Carolina.
Smith, William. Papers. Archives of the Episcopal Church with the Historical Society of the Episcopal Church, Austin, Texas.
White, William. Papers. Archives of the Episcopal Church with the Historical Society of the Episcopal Church, Austin, Texas.

Books

Adams, John Quincy. *Report upon Weights and Measures*. Washington, D.C., 1821.
Anderson, Wallace E., ed. *Jonathan Edwards: Scientific and Philosophical Writings*. New Haven, 1980.
Andrews, Charles M., ed. *Narratives of Insurrection, 1675–1690*. New York, [1915], 1959.
Apthorp, East. *Considerations on the Institution and Conduct of the Society for the Propagation of the Gospel in Foreign Parts*. Boston, 1763.
———. *A Review of Dr. Mayhew's Remarks on the Answer to his Observations on the Charter and Conduct of the SPG . . .* London, 1765.
———. *Of Sacred Poetry and Music, A Discourse at Christ's Church, Cambridge, at the opening of the ORGAN on Tuesday, 21 August, 1764*. Boston, 1764.
Bacon, Francis. *Advancement of Learning*. New York, 1919.
Bailyn, Bernard, ed. *Pamphlets of the American Revolution, 1750–1776*. Cambridge, 1965.
Banister, John. *Some Observations Concerning Insects Made in Virginia*. London, 1701.
Berkeley, Sir William. *A Discourse and View of Virginia*. London, 1663, and Norwalk, 1914.
Bettenson, Henry, ed. *Documents of the Christian Church*. 2d ed. London, 1967.
Beverley, Robert. *The History and Present State of Virginia*. Edited by Louis B. Wright. Chapel Hill, 1957.
Blair, James. *Our Saviour's Divine Sermon on the Mount*. 2d ed. London, 1740.
———. *A Paraphrase on Our Saviour's Sermon on the Mount*. London, 1729.
Blair, John. "The Reverend John Blair's Mission to North Carolina, 1704." In *Narratives of Early Carolina, 1650–1708*. Edited by A. S. Salley. New York, 1953.
Blome, Richard. *A Description of the Island of Jamaica, with other Isles and Territories in America, to which the English are related . . .* 8 vols. London, 1672.

————. *The Fanatick History, or an exact relation and account of the Old Anabaptists and New Quakers.* London, 1660.

————. *A Geographical Description of the four parts of the World.* London, 1670.

Bray, Thomas. *Catechetical Lectures on the Preliminary Questions and Answers of the Church Catechism in Four Volumes.* London, 1696.

————. *A Memorial Representing the Present State of Religion on the Continent of North America.* London, 1700.

————. *A Short Discourse Upon the Doctrine of our Baptismal Covenant. . .* London, 1697.

Brayton, Alice. *George Berkeley at Newport.* Newport, 1954.

Brock, R. A., ed. *The Official Letters of Alexander Spotswood, Lieutenant Governor of the Colony of Virginia, 1710–1722.* 2 vols. Richmond, 1882–1885.

Browne, Arthur. *Remarks on Dr. Mayhew's Incidental Reflections Relative to the Church of England As contained in his Observations on the Charter and Conduct of the Society.* Portsmouth, 1763.

Bullock, William. *Virginia impartially examined.* London, 1649.

Burnet, Gilbert. *History of My Own Time.* 2 vols. Oxford, 1897.

Butterfield, L. H., ed. *Adams Family Correspondence.* 2 vols. Cambridge, 1963.

————, ed. *Diary and Autobiography of John Adams.* 4 vols. Cambridge, 1962.

————, ed. *John Witherspoon Comes to America, A Documentary Account.* Princeton, 1953.

————, ed. *Letters of Benjamin Rush.* 2 vols. Princeton, 1951.

Byrd, William. *History of the Dividing Line betwixt Virginia and North Carolina in the Year of Our Lord, 1728.* Edited by Louis B. Wright. Cambridge, 1966.

Cameron, James K., ed. *The First Book of Discipline.* Edinburgh, 1972.

Cameron, Kenneth W., ed. *The Church of England in Pre-Revolutionary Connecticut.* Hartford, 1976.

————, ed. *Letter Book of Henry Caner . . . from 1728 through 1778.* Hartford, 1972.

————, ed. *The Works of Samuel Peters of Hebron, Connecticut.* Hartford, 1967.

Capon, Lester, ed. *The Adams-Jefferson Letters.* 2 vols. Chapel Hill, 1959.

Chandler, Thomas Bradbury. *An Appeal Farther Defended in Answer to the Farther Misrepresentation of Dr. Chauncy.* New York, 1771.

————. *An Appeal to the Public, in Behalf of the Church of England in America. . .* New York, 1767.

————. *A Free Examination of the Critical Commentary on Archbishop Secker's Letter to Mr. Walpole.* New York, 1744.

————. *A Friendly Address to All Reasonable Americans on the Subject of Our Political Confusions.* New York, 1774.

————. *The Life of Samuel Johnson.* New York, 1824.

Chauncy, Charles. *An Appeal to the Public Answered.* Boston, 1766.

Clayton, John. *A Letter to Dr. Grew, in answer to several queries.* London, 1687.

————. *A Letter . . . to the Royal Society.* London, 1688.

Colton, Calvin. *The Americans.* 1822.

Cooper, James Fenimore. *The American Democrat.* 1838.

Dawes, William. *A Sermon Preach'd before the Society for the Propagation of the Gospel in Foreign Parts, at the Parish-Church of St. Mary-le-Bow, on Friday February 18, 1708/9.* London, 1709.

Donne, John. ''A Sermon Preached to the Honourable Company of the Virginia Plantation, 13 November 1622." In *The Sermons of John Donne.* Edited by G. R. Potter and E. M. Simpson. Berkeley and Los Angeles, 1959.

Dwight, Timothy. *Travels in New England and New York.* 4 vols. Cambridge, 1969.

Edwards, Jonathan. *A Treatise Concerning Religious Affections.* New Haven, 1959.

Elton, G. R., ed. *The Tudor Constitution, Documents and Commentary.* Cambridge, England, 1965.

Evelin, Robert. *A Description of the Province of New Albion.* London, 1648.

Farrish, Hunter Dickinson, ed. *Journal & Letters of Philip Vickers Fithian*. Williamsburg, 1965.

Flory, A. P., Hamilton, C. E., Jr., Nevitt, F., and Jones, A. M., eds. *Minutes of the Vestry: Truro Parish, Virginia, 1732–1785*. Lorton, Virginia, 1974.

Force, Peter, ed. *Tracts and Other Papers*. 4 vols. Gloucester, 1963.

Franklin, Benjamin. "Preface." *Abridgement of the Book of Common Prayer*. London, 1773.

————. *Autobiography*. New Haven and London, 1964.

Garden, Alexander. *Regeneration, and the Testimony of the Spirit*. Charleston, 1740.

[Gatford, Lionel]. *Publick good without private interest. Or, A compendious remonstrance of the present sad state and condition of the English colonie in Virginea*. London, 1657.

[Gauden, John]. *The Portraiture of His Sacred Majesty [Charles I] in His Solitudes and Sufferings*. London, 1649.

Gibson, Edmund. *Pastoral Letter*. London, 1739.

Glover, Thomas. *An Account of Virginia*. Royal Society, 1676, and Oxford, 1904.

Godwyn, Morgan. *The Negro's and Indians Advocate suing for their admission into the church*. London, 1680.

Graye, Robert. *A Good Speed to Virginia*. Edinburgh, 1970.

Greene, Roger. *Virginia's Cure: or An Advisive narrative concerning Virginia. Discovering the true ground of that churches unhappiness, and the only true remedy*. London, 1662.

Hall, Michael G.; Leder, Lawrence H.; and Kammen, Michael G.; eds. *The Glorious Revolution in America*. Chapel Hill, 1964.

Hammond, John. *Leah and Rachel, or two fruitfull sisters Virginia and Maryland: their present condition, impartially stated and related*. London, 1656.

Hamor, Ralph. *A true discourse of the present state of Virginia till the 18 of June 1614*. London, 1615.

Hawkins, Ernest. *Historical Notices of the Mission of the Church of England*. London, 1845.

Hawks, Francis L., and Perry, William S., eds. *Documentary History of the Protestant Episcopal Church in the United States of America*. 2 vols. New York, 1863–1864.

Heimert, Alan, and Miller, Perry. *The Great Awakening, Documents Illustrating the Crisis and Its Consequences*. Indianapolis and New York, 1967.

Hofstadter, Richard, and Smith, Wilson, eds. *American Higher Education, A Documentary History*. 2 vols. Chicago, 1961.

Hooker, Richard J., ed. *The Carolina Backcountry on the Eve of the Revolution*. Chapel Hill, 1953.

[Inglis, Charles]. *Letters of Papinian*. New York, 1779.

————. *The True Interest of America Impartially Stated in Certain Strictures on a Pamphlet Entitled Common Sense*. Philadelphia, 1776.

Jarratt, Devereux. *The Life of the Reverend Devereux Jarratt*. New York, 1969.

[Johnson, Robert]. *Nova Britannia*. London, 1609.

Jones, Hugh. *The Present State of Virginia. . .* Edited by Richard L. Morton. Chapel Hill, 1956.

Keith, George. *The Anti-Christs and Sadducees Detected*. London, 1696.

————. *The Notes of the True Church*. New York, 1704.

————. *The Power of the Gospel in the Conversion of Sinners*. Annapolis, 1703.

————. *A Reply to Mr. Increase Mather's Printed Remarks on a Sermon . . .* New York, 1703.

————. *The Spirit of Railing Shimei and of Baal's Four Hundred Lying Prophets Entered into Caleb Pusey and His Quaker Brethren in Pennsilvania*. New York, 1703.

Kennedy, John P., ed. *Journals of the House of Burgesses, 1770–1772*. Richmond, 1906.

Kennett, White. *An Account of the Society for Propagating the Gospel in Foreign Parts*. London, 1706.

King, Peter. *An Enquiry into the Constitution, Discipline, Unity and Worship of the Primitive Church*. London, 1691.

King, William. *A Discourse Concerning the Inventions of Men in the Worship of God.* Philadelphia, 1828.

Kingsbury, Susan M. *The Records of the Virginia Company of London.* 4 vols. Washington, D.C., 1906–1935.

Klingberg, Frank J., ed. *Carolina Chronicle of Dr. Francis LeJau.* Berkeley, 1956.

————, ed. *Carolina Chronicle: The Papers of Commissary Gideon Johnston, 1707–1716.* Berkeley and Los Angeles, 1946.

Lawson, John. *A New Voyage to Carolina.* London, 1709.

Lechford, Thomas. *Plain Dealing: or, Newes from New-England.* London, 1642.

Lederer, John. *The Discoveries of John Lederer in several Marches from Virginia to the West of Carolina.* London, 1672.

————. *Minutes of the Council and General Court of Colonial Virginia.* Richmond, 1924.

Mather, Cotton. *Bonifacius.* Edited by David Levin. Cambridge, 1966.

————. *Diary of Cotton Mather.* Edited by W. C. Ford. 2 vols. New York, 1957.

————. *The Saviour with his Rainbow.* London, 1714.

Mather, Increase. *The Order of the Gospel Possessed and Practiced by the Churches of Christ in New England.* New York, 1972.

Maverick, Samuel. *Briefe Description of New England.* London, 1660.

Mayhew, Jonathan. *Observations on the Charter and Conduct of the Society for the Propagation of the Gospel in Foreign Parts.* Boston, 1763.

McIlwaine, Henry R. *Journals of the House of Burgesses of Virginia, 1659/60–1693.* Richmond, 1914.

Morton, Thomas. *New English Canaan: or New Canaan.* London 1632.

Myers, Albert C. *Narratives of Early Pennsylvania, West Jersey, and Delaware, 1630–1707.* New York, 1912.

Ogilby, John. *America: being the latest, and most accurate description of the New World.* London, 1671.

Percy, George. "Observations gathered out of a Discourse of the Plantation of the Southern Colonie in Virginia by the English, 1606." In *Genesis of the United States.* Edited by Alexander Brown. 2 vols. Boston, 1890.

Perkins, William. *The Whole Treatise of the Cases of Conscience.* Vol. 1 of *The Works of That Famous and Worthie Minister of Christ in the University of Cambridge.* London, 1609.

Perry, William Stevens. *Historical Collections of the American Colonial Church.* 5 vols. New York, 1969.

Peters, Samuel. *General History of Connecticut.* London, 1781 and New York, 1877.

————. *A History of the Rev. Hugh Peters A.M.* New York, 1807.

————. *A Letter to the Rev. John Tyler A.M. Concerning the Possibility of Eternal Punishments, and the Improbability of Universal Salvation.* London, 1785.

Porteus, Belby. *A Review of the Life and Character of Archbishop Secker.* London, 1773.

Potter, John. *A Discourse on Church Government.* London, 1839.

Purchas, Samuel. *Haklyutus Posthumus or Purchas His Pilgrims.* London, 1625.

————. *Purchas his Pilgrimage or Relations of the World and the Religions Observed in All Ages discovered from the Creation unto this Present.* London, 1613.

Rolfe, John. *A true relation of the state of Virginia . . . in May last, 1616.* New Haven, 1951.

Sainsbury, William N., and Fortescue, J. W., eds. *Calender of State Papers, America and the West Indies.* 10 vols. London, 1860–19.

Saint-Beuve, Charles-Augustin. *Causeries du lundi.* 15 vols. Paris, 1849–1861.

Saunders, William L., ed. *Colonial Records of North Carolina.* 10 vols. Raleigh, 1886–1890.

Schaff, Philip. *The Creeds of Christendom.* 3 vols. New York, 1877.

Schneider, Herbert and Schneider, Carol, eds. *Samuel Johnson, President of King's College: His Career and Writings.* 4 vols. New York, 1929.

Sclater, William. *Original Draught of the Primitive Church.* Oxford, 1740.

Scott, John. *The Christian Life from its beginning to its Consummation in Glory.* London, 1681.

Seabury, Samuel. *Discourses on Various Subjects.* 2 vols. New York, 1793.

[Secker, Thomas]. *An Answer to Dr. Mayhew's Observations on the Charter and Conduct of the Society for the Propagation of the Gospel in Foreign Parts.* London, 1764.

———. *A Letter . . . to Horace Walpole, Written, January 9, 1750/1.* London, 1769.

"The Second Charter to the Treasurer and Company, for Virginia . . . May 23, 1609." In *Statutes at Large, Being a Collection of all the Laws of Virginia from the First Session of the Legislature in 1619.* Edited by William H. Hening. New York, 1823.

Sewall, Samuel. *The Diary of Samuel Sewall.* Edited by M. H. Thomas. 2 vols. New York, 1973.

Shakespeare, William. *The Tempest.* New Haven, 1955.

Shepard, Thomas. *The Sound Beleever. Or a Treatise of Evangelical Conversion.* 8 vols. London, 1645.

Shrigley, Nathaniel. *A True relation of Virginia and Maryland.* London, 1669.

Silverman, Kenneth, ed. *Selected Letters of Cotton Mather.* Baton Rouge, 1971.

Slafter, Edmund F., ed. *John Checkley or the Evolution of Religious Tolerance in Massachusetts.* 2 vols. Boston, 1897.

Smith, H. S.; Handy, R. T.; and Loetscher, L. *American Christianity.* 2 vols. New York, 1960–1963.

Smith, Joseph H., ed. *Colonial Justice in Western Massachusetts (1632–1702): The Pynchon Court Record.* Cambridge, 1961.

Smith, Josiah. *A Sermon on the Character, Preaching, &c. of the Rev. Mr. Whitefield.* 1740.

Smith, William. *A Brief State of the Province of Pennsylvania.* Philadelphia, 1755.

———. *A Brief View of the Conduct of Pennsylvania.* Philadelphia, 1756.

———. *A General Idea of the College of Mirania.* New York, 1753.

[Smith, William]. *Historical Account of the Expedition Against the Ohio Indians.* Cincinnati, 1868.

Stephens, Archibald John, ed. *The Book of Common Prayer 1666 . . . With Notes, Legal and Historical.* 3 vols. London, 1849–1854.

Stoddard, Solomon. *The Safety of Appearing at the Day of Judgement, in the Righteousness of Christ: Opened and Applied.* Boston, 1687.

Thomas, Gabriel. *An Historical and Geographical Account of the Province and Country of Pensilvania; and of West-New Jersey.* London, 1698.

Toplady, Augustus. *The Complete Works of Augustus M. Toplady B.A.* London, 1857.

Walters, Thomas. *Choice Dialogue between John Faustus, a Conjurer, and Jack Tory, his Friend.* Boston, 1720.

Whitaker, Alexander. *Good Newes from Virginia.* London, 1613.

White, William. *The Case of the Episcopal Churches in the United States Considered.* Edited by Richard G. Salomon. Church Historical Society Publication 39. 1954.

———. *Comparative Views of the Controversy Between the Calvinists and the Arminians.* 2 vols. Philadelphia, 1817.

Whitefield, George. *Journals.* London, 1960.

Willcox, William B., ed. *The Papers of Benjamin Franklin.* 22 vols. New Haven and London, 1959– .

Williams, Edward. *Virgo Triumphant: or, Virginia richly and truly valued.* London, 1650.

Wilson, Bird. *Memoir of the Life of the Right Reverend William White.* Philadelphia, 1839.

Works of the Learned and Reverend John Scott. 6 vols. Oxford, 1826.

Wright, Louis B., ed. *The Prose Works of William Byrd of Westover.* Cambridge, 1966.

Periodicals

Boucher, Jonathan. "Letters of Jonathan Boucher." *MHM* 8 (March 1913).

Butler, Jon, ed. "Two Letters from Virginia Puritans." Massachusetts Historical Society. *Proceedings* 34 (1972).

Bibliography

Byrd, William. William Byrd to Charles, Earl of Orrery, June 1731. "Virginia Council Journals 1727–1753." *VMHB* 32 (1924).

Chorley, E. C., ed. "Letters of the Reverend Doctor Ebenezer Diblee of Stamford to the Reverend Doctor Samuel Peters, Loyalist Refugee in London, 1784–1793." *HM* (1932).

Gantner, Herbert L. "Documents Relating to the Early History of the College of William and Mary and to the History of the Church in Virginia." *WMQ*, 2nd Series (1940).

Gordon, James. "Journal of Col. James Gordon of Lancaster County." *WMQ*, 1st Series (1903).

Kammen, Michael, ed. "Virginia at the Close of the Seventeenth Century: An Appraisal by James Blair and John Locke." *VMHB* 74 (1966).

Keith, George. "A Journal of Travels from New Hampshire to Caratuck On the Continent of North-America. London, 1706." *HM* 20 (1951).

Ludwell, Thomas. "A Description of the Government of Virginia. London, 1666." *VMHB* 5 (1897).

"Marriage Bonds in Lancaster County." *WMQ*, 1st Series, 12 (1903).

Percy, George. "A Trewe Relacyon of the Procedings . . . which have hapned in Virginia . . . 1609 until . . . 1612." *TQHGM* 3 (1922).

St. Stephen's Parish. "A Petition of the Inhabitants and Housekeepers of St. Stephen's Parish in the County of New Kent. Council Papers, 1682, 1683, 1684." *VMHB* 41 (1933).

Secondary Sources

Dissertations and Theses

Austin, Alan Kenneth. "The Role of the Anglican Clergy in the Political Life of Colonial Virginia." Ph.D. diss., University of Georgia, 1969.

Bates, Geroge Edward. "The Emergence of the Modern Mind in Colonial America." Ph.D. diss., University of Illinois, Urbana-Champaign, 1970.

Billings, Warren M. "Virginia's Deplored Condition, 1660–1676: The Coming of Bacon's Rebellion." Ph.D. diss., Northern Illinois University, 1968.

Bolton, Sidney Charles. "The Anglican Church of Colonial South Carolina, 1704–1754: A Study in Americanization." Ph.D. diss., University of Wisconsin, 1973.

Byrnes, Don Roy. "The Pre-Revolutionary Career of Provost William Smith, 1751–1780." Ph.D. diss., Tulane University, 1969.

Ellis, Joseph J. "The Puritan Mind in Transition: The American Samuel Johnson (1696–1772)." Ph.D. diss., Yale University, 1969. Published as *The New England Mind in Transition: Samuel Johnson of Connecticut, 1696–1722*. New Haven, 1973.

Fay, Cornelius Ryan. "An Essay Describing Colden's 'The First Principles of Morality.' " Master's thesis, Columbia University, 1950.

Friary, Donald Richard. "The Architecture of the Anglican Church in the Northern American Colonies: A Study of Religious, Social, and Cultural Expression." Ph.D. diss., University of Pennsylvania, 1971.

Goodwin, Gerald J. "The Anglican Middle Way in Early Eighteenth Century America: Anglican Religious Thought in the American Colonies, 1702–1750." Ph.D. diss., University of Wisconsin, 1965.

Gundersen, Joan. "The Anglican Ministry in Virginia, 1723–1776." Ph.D. diss., University of Notre Dame, 1972.

Harrison, Margaret S. "Commissary James Blair of Virginia: A Study in Personality and Power." Master's thesis, College of William and Mary, 1958.

Hartdagen, Gerald E. "The Anglican Vestry in Colonial Maryland." Ph.D. diss., Northwestern University, 1965.

302

Hecht, Irene D. "The Virginia Colony, 1607–1640: A Study in Frontier Growth." Ph.D. diss., University of Washington, 1969.

Holmes, David Lynn, Jr. "William Meade and the Church in Virginia." Ph.D. diss., Princeton University, 1971.

Humphrey, David Churchill. "King's College in the City of New York, 1754–1776." Ph.D. diss., Northwestern University, 1968.

Kenney, William H., III. "George Whitefield and Colonial Revivalism: The Social Sources of Charismatic Authority, 1737–1770." Ph.D. diss., University of Pennsylvania, 1966.

Lohrenz, Otto. "The Virginia Clergy and the American Revolution, 1774–1799." Ph.D. diss., University of Kansas, 1970.

McGinnis, Robert S., Jr. "A Model for Theological Education in Eighteenth-Century America: Samuel Johnson D.D. of King's College." Ph.D. diss., Vanderbilt University, 1971.

Mills, Frederick V., Sr. "Anglican Resistance to an American Episcopate." Ph.D. diss., University of Pennsylvania, 1967.

Mohler, Samuel R. "Commissary James Blair, Educator and Politician of Colonial Virginia." Ph.D. diss., University of Chicago, 1940.

Morgan, David Taft. "The Great Awakening in the Carolinas and Georgia, 1740–1775." Ph.D. diss., University of North Carolina, 1967.

Murrin, John M. "Anglicizing an American Colony: The Transformation of Provincial Massachusetts." Ph.D. diss., Yale University, 1966.

Nelson, John K. "Anglican Missions in America, 1701–1725: A Study of the Society for the Propagation of the Gospel in Foreign Parts." Ph.D. diss., Northwestern University, 1962.

Noble, Dorothy Louise. "Life of Francis Nicholson." Ph.D. diss., Columbia University, 1958.

Overfield, Richard A. "The Loyalists of Maryland during the American Revolution." Ph.D. diss., University of Maryland, 1968.

Owen, James Kimbrough. "The Virginia Vestry: A Study in the Decline of a Ruling Class." Ph.D. diss., Princeton University, 1947.

Read, Harry A. C. "Thomas Bradbury Chandler: His Life and Times." Term paper, Virginia Theological Seminary, 1975.

Stokes, Durward T. "The Clergy of the Carolinas and the American Revolution." Ph.D. diss., University of North Carolina, 1968.

Taylor, Maxwell Ford. "The Influence of Religion on White Attitudes toward Indians in the Early Settlement of Virginia." Ph.D. diss., Emory University, 1970.

Troutman, William F. "Respecting the Establishment of Religion in America." Ph.D. diss., Duke University, 1959.

Zimmer, Anne Young. "Jonathan Boucher: Moderate Loyalist and Public Man." Ph.D. diss., Wayne State University, 1966.

Books

Abbot, W. W. *The Colonial Origins of the United States: 1607–1763.* New York, 1975.

Adams, Charles Francis. *History of Braintree Massachusetts (1639–1708), the North Precinct of Braintree (1708–1792) and the Town of Quincy (1792–1889).* Cambridge, Massachusetts, 1891.

Adams, Herbert Baxter. "The College of William and Mary." In *Contributions to American Education.* Edited by H. B. Adams. Washington, D.C., 1887.

Adams, James Truslow. *Provincial Society, 1690–1763.* New York, 1927.

Ahlstrom, Sydney E. *A Religious History of the American People.* New Haven and London, 1972.

Albright, Raymond W. *A History of the Protestant Episcopal Church.* New York and London, 1964.

Aldridge, Alfred O. *Benjamin Franklin: Philosopher and Man.* New York, 1965.

————. *Benjamin Franklin and Nature's God.* New York, 1967.

Allison, C. F. *The Rise of Moralism: The Proclamation of the Gospel from Hooker to Baxter.* New York, 1966.

Anderson, Fulton H. *Francis Bacon, His Career and Thought.* Los Angeles, 1962.

Anderson, James S. M. *A History of the Church of England in the Colonies.* 3 vols. London, 1856.

Andrews, Charles M. *The Colonial Period of American History.* 4 vols. London and New Haven, 1934–1938.

Bailyn, Bernard. "Politics and Social Structure in Virginia." In *Seventeenth-Century America.* Edited by James E. Smith. Chapel Hill, 1959.

————. "Politics and Social Structure in Virginia." In *Colonial America, Essays in Politics and Social Development.* Edited by Stanley N. Katz. Boston, 1971.

Barker, Charles A. *American Convictions: Cycles of Public Thought, 1680–1850.* Philadelphia and New York, 1970.

————. *The Background of the Revolution in Maryland.* New Haven, 1940, 1967.

Beardsley, E. Edwards. *Life and Correspondence of the Right Reverend Samuel Seabury.* Boston, 1881.

Belknap, Jeremy. *The History of New Hampshire.* 2 vols. New York and London, 1833, 1970.

Bennett, G. V. *The Tory Crisis in Church and State, 1688–1730: The Career of Francis Atterbury, Bishop of Rochester.* Oxford, 1975.

Berkovitch, Sacvan. *The Puritan Origins of the American Self.* New Haven and London, 1975.

————. *The American Jeremiad.* Madison and London, 1978.

Bertelson, David. *The Lazy South.* New York, 1967.

Boller, Paul Franklin. *George Washington and Religion.* Dallas, 1963.

Bond, Richmond Pugh. *Queen Anne's American Kings.* Oxford, 1952.

Bonomi, Patricia U. *A Factious People: Politics and Society in Colonial New York.* New York, 1971.

Boorstin, Daniel. *Americans: The Colonial Experience.* New York, 1958.

Booty, John E. "Hooker and Anglicanism." In *Studies in Richard Hooker, Essays Preliminary to an Edition of His Works.* Edited by W. Speed Hill. Cleveland and London, 1972.

Brayton, Alice. *George Berkeley in Newport.* Newport, 1954.

Bridenbaugh, Carl. *Cities in Revolt: Urban Life in America, 1743–1776.* New York, 1955.

————. *Mitre and Sceptre: Transatlantic Faiths, Ideas, Personalities, and Politics, 1689–1775.* New York, 1962.

————. *Myths and Realities: Societies of the Colonial South.* New York, 1963.

Bridenbaugh, Carl, and Bridenbaugh, Jessica. *Rebels and Gentlemen: Philadelphia in the Age of Franklin.* London, Oxford, and New York, 1968.

Brown, Wallace. *The King's Friends.* Providence, 1965.

Broxap, Henry. *The Later Non-Jurors.* Cambridge, 1924.

Bruce, Philip A. *Institutional History of Virginia.* 2 vols. New York, 1910.

Brydon, George McLaren. *Virginia's Mother Church.* 2 vols. Richmond, 1947–1952.

Burr, Nelson R. *The Anglican Church in New Jersey.* Philadelphia, 1947.

————. *The Story of the Diocese of Connecticut.* Hartford, 1962.

Buxbaum, Melvin H. *Benjamin Franklin and the Zealous Presbyterians.* University Park and London, 1975.

Calam, John. *Parsons and Pedagogues: The SPG Adventure in American Education.* New York and London, 1971.

Callahan, North. *Flight From the Republic: The Tories of the American Revolution.* Indianapolis, 1967.

Carpenter, Edward. *The Protestant Bishop: Being the Life of Henry Compton, 1632–1713, Bishop of London.* London, 1956.

————. *Thomas Sherlock, 1678–1761.* London, 1936.

Carr, Lois G., and Jordan, David W. *Maryland's Revolutionary Government, 1689–1692.* Ithaca and London, 1974.

Carse, James. *Jonathan Edwards and the Visibility of God.* New York, 1967.

Cassirer, Ernst. *The Philosophy of the Enlightenment.* Translated by F. Koelln and J. Pettegrove. Princeton, 1951.

Cheney, Edward Potts. *History of the University of Pennsylvania, 1740–1940.* Philadelphia, 1940.

Clark, Samuel A. *A History of St. John's Church, Elizabeth Town, New Jersey.* Philadelphia, 1857.

Cohn, Norman. *Pursuit of the Millennium.* New York, 1961.

Colbourn, H. Trevor. *The Lamp of Experience: Whig History and the Intellectual Origins of the American Revolution.* Williamsburg, 1965.

Coleman, Kenneth. *Colonial Georgia, A History.* New York, 1976.

Connor, Paul W. *Poor Richard's Politics: Benjamin Franklin and His New American Order.* New York, 1965.

Cragg, Gerald R., ed. *The Cambridge Platonists.* New York, 1968.

———. *The Church in the Age of Reason.* New York, 1961.

Crane, Verner W. *Benjamin Franklin and a Rising People.* Boston, 1954.

———. *The Southern Frontier, 1670–1732.* Ann Arbor, 1929, 1956.

Craven, Wesley Frank. *The Colonies in Transition, 1660–1713.* New York, 1958.

———. *The Southern Colonies in the Seventeenth Century, 1607–1689.* Baton Rouge, 1949.

———. *The Virginia Company of London, 1606–1624.* Williamsburg, 1957.

———. *White, Red, and Black and the Seventeenth-Century Virginian.* Charlottesville, 1971.

Cremin, Lawrence A. *American Education: The Colonial Experience, 1607–1783.* New York, 1970.

Cross, Arthur Lyon. *The Anglican Episcopate in the American Colonies.* New York, 1902.

Curti, Merle. *The Growth of American Thought.* New York and London, 1943.

Dalcho, Frederick. *An Historical Account of the Protestant Episcopal Church in South Carolina.* Charleston, 1820; New York, 1972.

Danto, Arthur C. *Analytical Philosophy of History.* Cambridge, England, 1965.

Dargan, Edwin Charles. *A History of Preaching.* 2 vols. New York, 1912.

Davidson, Elizabeth H., *The Establishment of the English Church in Continental American Colonies.* Historical Papers of the Trinity College Historical Society, Series 20. Durham, 1936.

Davis, David Brion. *The Problem of Slavery in Western Culture.* Ithaca, 1966.

Davis, Richard B. *George Sandys: Poet Adventurer.* New York, 1955.

———. *Literature and Society in Early Virginia, 1608–1840.* Baton Rouge, 1973.

Dawson, Raymond, ed. *The Legacy of China.* Oxford, 1964.

Degler, Carl. "Slavery and the Genesis of American Race Prejudice." In *Essays in American Colonial History.* Edited by Paul Goodman. New York, 1967.

Delattre, Roland A. *Beauty and Sensibility in the Thought of Jonathan Edwards.* New Haven and London, 1968.

D'Elia, Donald J. *Benjamin Rush: Philosopher of the American Revolution.* Philadelphia, 1974.

Demos, John. *A Little Commonwealth: Family Life in Plymouth Colony.* New York, 1970.

Dexter, Franklin Bowditch. *Biographical Sketches of the Graduates of Yale College.* New York, 1885.

———. *Documentary History of Yale University.* New Haven, 1916.

Dix, Morgan. *A History of the Parish of Trinity Church in the City of New York.* 4 vols. New York, 1898.

Douglas, David. *English Scholars, 1660–1730.* London, 1951.

Driver, Harold E. *The Indians of North America.* Chicago, 1961.

Dunn, Robert H. *Old St. John's at Portsmouth and Her Distinguished Colonial Flock.* New York, 1947.

Duyckinck, George. *The Life of George Herbert*. New York, 1858.

————. *The Life of Jeremy Taylor*. New York, 1860.

————. *The Life of Thomas Ken, Bishop of Bath and Wells*. New York, 1859.

Ellis, John Tracy. *Catholics in Colonial America*. Baltimore, 1965.

Endy, Melvin B., Jr. *William Penn and Early Quakerism*. Princeton, 1973.

Fergusson, Francis. *Dante's Drama of the Mind*. Princeton, 1953.

Figgis, John N. *The Divine Right of Kings*. Cambridge, England, 1914.

Fingard, Judith, *The Anglican Design in Loyalist Nova Scotia*. London, 1972.

Flaherty, David H., ed. *Essays in the History of Early American Law*. Chapel Hill, 1969.

Flexner, James Thomas. *First Flowers of Our Wilderness: American Painting, the Colonial Period*. New York, 1947, 1969.

Flick, Alexander. *Loyalism in New York during the American Revolution*. London, 1901.

Foote, Henry W. *Annals of King's Chapel*. 2 vols. Boston, 1882.

————. *The Huguenots; or, Reformed French Church*. New York, 1870.

Forster, Edward J. *From the Professional and Industrial History of Suffolk County, Massachusetts: A Sketch of the Medical Profession*. Boston, 1894.

Foster, Stephen. *Their Solitary Way: The Puritan Social Ethic in the First Century of Settlement in New England*. New Haven, 1971.

Foster, Walter Roland. *Bishop and Presbytery: The Church of Scotland, 1661–1688*. London, 1958.

Fothergill, Gerald. *A List of Emigrant Ministers to America*. London, 1904.

Fox, Dixon Ryan. *Caleb Heathcote, Gentleman Colonist: The Story of a Career in the Province of New York, 1692–1721*. New York, 1926.

Franklin, John Hope. *From Slavery to Freedom: A History of the Negro Americans*. New York, 1967.

Frei, Hans W. *The Eclipse of the Biblical Narrative: A Study in Eighteenth and Nineteenth Century Hermeneutics*. New Haven and London, 1974.

Fulton, John. "The Non-Juring Bishops in America." In *The History of the American Episcopal Church, 1587–1883*. Edited by W. S. Perry. Boston, 1885.

Gambrall, Theodore C. *Studies in the Civil, Social, and Ecclesiastical History of Early Maryland*. New York, 1893.

Gardner, Martin. *The Flight of Peter Fromm*. Los Altos, 1973.

Gaustad, Edwin S. *Historical Atlas of Religion in America*. New York, 1962, 1976.

Gay, Peter. *The Enlightenment: An Interpretation*. 2 vols. New York, 1966.

Geertz, Clifford. "The Integrative Revolution: Primordial Sentiments and Civil Politics in the New States." In *Old Societies and New States: The Quest for Modernity in Asia and Africa*. New York, 1963.

Gewehr, Wesley M. *The Great Awakening in Virginia, 1740–1790*. Durham, N.C., 1930.

Gibson, Charles, *Spain in America*. New York, 1966.

Glass, D. V. "Two Papers on Gregory King." In *Population in History*. London, 1965.

Goen, C. C. *The Great Awakening*. New Haven and London, 1972.

————. *Revivalism and Separatism in New England, 1740–1800*. New Haven and London, 1962.

Gollin, Gilliam L. *Moravians in Two Worlds: A Study of Changing Communities*. New York and London, 1967.

Gombrich, E. H. *Art and Illusion*. New York, 1960.

Goodwin, Edwin L. *The Colonial Church in Virginia*. Milwaukee, 1927.

Gowans, Alan. *King Carter's Church*. Victoria, B.C., 1969.

Green, V. H. H. *Religion at Oxford and Cambridge*. London, 1964.

Greene, E. V. and Harrington, V. D. *American Population Before the Federal Census of 1790*. New York, 1932.

Greene, Jack P. *The Quest for Power: The Lower House of the Assembly in the Southern Colonies, 1689–1776*. Chapel Hill, 1963.

Greven, Philip J., Jr. *Four Generations: Population, Land, and Family in Colonial Andover, Massachusetts*. Ithaca, 1970.

Grosseteste, Robert. *On Light*. Milwaukee, 1942.

Hall, David D. *The Faithful Shepherd, A History of the New England Ministry in the Seventeenth Century*. Chapel Hill, 1972.

Haller, William. *The Rise of Puritanism*. New York, 1938.

Handy, Isaac W. K. "Josias Mackie." In *Annals of the American Pulpit*. Edited by William Sprague. New York, 1857–69.

Hawks, Francis L. *A Narrative of Events Connected with the Rise and Progress of the Protestant Episcopal Church in Maryland*. New York, 1839.

Heimert, Alan. *Religion and the American Mind from the Great Awakening to the Revolution*. Cambridge, 1966.

Henry, Stuart C. *George Whitefield, Wayfaring Witness*. New York, 1957.

Herklots, H. G. G. *The Church of England and the American Episcopal Church*. London and New York, 1966.

Hill, Christopher. *Antichrist in Seventeenth-Century England*. London, 1971.

Hofstadter, Richard. *America at 1750*. New York, 1971.

———, and Metzger, Walter P. *The Development of Academic Freedom in the United States*. New York, 1955.

Holbrook, Clyde. *Original Sin*. New Haven, 1970.

Holifield, E. Brooks. *The Covenant Sealed: The Development of Puritan Sacramental Theology in Old and New England, 1570–1720*. New Haven and London, 1974.

Hudson, Winthrop. *The Cambridge Connection and the Elizabethan Settlement of 1559*. Durham, 1980.

Hulme, Harold. "Charles I and the Constitution." In *Conflict in Stuart England, Essays in Honour of Wallace Notestein*. Edited by W. A. Aiken and B. D. Henning. London, 1960.

Humphreys, David. *An Account of the Incorporated Society for the Propagation of the Gospel in Foreign Parts*. New York, 1969.

Hurlbutt, Robert H., III. *Hume, Newton, and the Design Argument*. Lincoln, 1965.

Ingram, A. W. F. *The Early English Colonies*. Milwaukee, 1908.

Ives, A. Moss. *The Ark and the Dove: The Beginning of Civil and Religious Liberties in America*. New York, 1936, 1969.

Jennings, John M. *The Library of the College of William and Mary, 1693–1793*. Charlottesville, 1968.

Johnson, Robert D. "Transportation of Vagrant Children from London to Virginia, 1618–1622." In *Early Stuart Studies*. Edited by Howard S. Reinmuth, Jr. Minneapolis, 1970.

Jones, Howard Mumford. *The Literature of Virginia in the Seventeenth Century*. 2d ed. Charlottesville, 1968.

Jones, Thomas Firth. *A Pair of Lawn Sleeves: A Biography of William Smith (1727–1803)*. Philadelphia, New York, and London, 1972.

Jordan, Winthrop D. *White over Black: American Attitudes toward the Negro, 1550–1812*. Chapel Hill, 1968.

Kammen, Michael. *People of Paradox: An Inquiry Concerning the Origins of American Civilization*. New York, 1972.

Kellaway, William. *The New England Company, 1649–1776: Missionary to the American Indians*. London, 1961.

Kendall, R. T. *Calvin and English Calvinism*. London, 1979.

Keys, Alice M. *Cadwallader Colden: A Representative Eighteenth-Century Official*. New York, 1906.

Kilson, Marion D. de B. "Towards Freedom: An analysis of Slave Revolts in the United States." In *The Making of Black America*. Edited by August Meier and Elliott Rudwick. New York, 1969.

Kirby, Ethyn W. *George Keith (1638–1716)*. New York, 1942.

Kitagawa, Joseph M., ed. *History of Religions in America: Essays in Methodology.* Chicago, 1959.

Klingberg, Frank J. *Anglican Humanitarianism in Colonial New York.* Philadelphia, 1940.

———. *An Appraisal of the Negro in Colonial South Carolina, A Study in Americanization.* Washington, D.C., 1941.

Koch, G. Adolph. *Religion of the American Enlightenment.* New York, 1968.

Labaree, Leonard. *Conservatism in Early American History.* Ithaca, 1959.

Laski, Harold J. *Political Thought in England: from Locke to Bentham.* New York, 1920.

Latané, Lucy Temple. *Parson Latané, 1672–1732.* Charlottesville, 1936.

Laugher, Charles T. *Thomas Bray's Grand Design, Libraries of the Church of England in America, 1695–1785.* Chicago, 1973.

Leder, Lawrence H. *Robert Livingston, 1654–1728 and the Politics of Colonial New York.* Chapel Hill, 1961.

Levey, Michael. *Rococo to Revolution: Major Trends in Eighteenth-Century Painting.* New York, 1966.

Levy, Babette M. *Puritanism in the Southern and Island Colonies.* Worcester, 1960.

Levy, Leonard W. *Freedom of Speech and Press in Early American History: Legacy of Suppression.* New York, 1963.

"List of Books Illustrating the History of the Church in North Carolina." In *Sketches of Church History in North Carolina.* Edited by Joseph Blount Cheshire. Wilmington, 1892.

Little, David. *Religion, Order, and Law: A Study in Pre-revolutionary England.* New York, 1969.

Livingston, Dorothy Flower, and Patton, Mollie Marjorie, "Contributions to a Bibliography of Francis Bacon, Editions Before 1700 in Yale Libraries." In *Papers in Honor of Andrew Keogh.* Edited by D. F. Livingston and M. M. Patton. New Haven, 1938.

Loomie, Albert J., S.J. *The Spanish Jesuit Mission in Virginia, 1570–1572.* Chapel Hill, 1953.

Loth, Calder and Sadler, Julius Trousdale, Jr. *The Only Proper Style.* Boston, 1975.

Lovejoy, David S. *The Glorious Revolution.* New York, 1972.

Lowrie, Ernest Benson. *The Shape of the Puritan Mind: The Thought of Samuel Willard.* New Haven and London, 1974.

Lucas, Paul R. *Valley of Discord: Church and Society Along the Connecticut, 1636–1725.* Hanover, New Hampshire, 1976.

Luce, A. A. *The Life of George Berkeley, Bishop of Cloyne.* London, 1949.

Lurie, Nancy Ostriech. "Indian Cultural Adjustments to European Civilization." In *Seventeenth-Century America.* Edited by James M. Smith. Chapel Hill, 1959.

Lydekker, John Wolfe. *The Life and Letters of Charles Inglis.* London, 1936.

Main, Jackson Turner. *The Social Structure of Revolutionary America.* Princeton, 1965.

Manning, Brian. "The Nobles, the People, and the Constitution." In *Crisis in Europe, 1560–1660.* Edited by Trevor Aston. Garden City, 1967.

Manross, William. *A History of the American Episcopal Church.* New York and Milwaukee, 1935.

Marty, Martin E. *Righteous Empire, The Protestant Experience in America.* New York, 1970.

Marx, Leo. *The Machine in the Garden: Technology and the Pastoral Ideal in America.* New York, 1964.

May, Henry F. *The Enlightenment in America.* New York, 1976.

Mazzeo, Anthony. *Structure and Thought in the Paradiso.* Ithaca, 1958.

McConnell, Samuel D. *History of the American Episcopal Church.* New York, 1890.

McCrary, Ben C. *Indians in Seventeenth-Century Virginia.* Williamsburg, 1957.

McCulloch, Samuel. "Thomas Bradbury Chandler: Anglican Humanitarian in Colonial New Jersey." In *British Humanitarianism.* Philadelphia, 1950.

McGiffert, Michael, ed. *God's Plot: The Paradoxes of Puritan Piety.* Amherst, 1972.

McLoughlin, William G. *New England Dissent, 1630–1833.* 2 vols. Cambridge, 1971.

Mead, Sidney E. *The Lively Experiment: The Shaping of Christianity in America.* New York, 1963.

Meade, William. *Old Churches, Ministers, and Families of Virginia.* Philadelphia, 1861.

Middlekauff, Robert. *Ancients and Axioms: Secondary Education in Eighteenth-Century New England.* New Haven and London, 1963.

Miller, Perry. "Religion and Society in the Early Literature of Virginia." In *Errand into the Wilderness.* Cambridge, 1956.

———. *The New England Mind: From Colony to Province.* Cambridge, 1953.

———. *The New England Mind: The Seventeenth Century.* Cambridge, 1954.

Mitchell, Williams B. *The Rise of the Revolutionary Party in the English House of Commons, 1603–1629.* New York, 1957.

Morais, Herbert. *Deism in 18th Century America.* New York, 1960.

Morgan, Edmund S. *American Slavery, American Freedom: The Ordeal of Colonial Virginia.* New York, 1975.

Morison, Samuel Eliot. *The European Discovery of America.* New York, 1971.

———. *Harvard College in the Seventeenth Century.* Cambridge, 1936.

———. *The Intellectual Life of Colonial New England.* New York, 1956.

Morton, Richard. *Colonial Virginia.* 2 vols. Chapel Hill, 1960.

Murdoch, Kenneth B. *Increase Mather, the Foremost American Puritan.* Cambridge, Mass., 1925.

Nammack, Georgiana C. *Fraud, Politics, and Dispossession of the Indians.* Norman, 1969.

Neale, John Ernest. *Queen Elizabeth.* London, 1950.

Nelson, William H. *The American Tory.* Oxford, 1961.

Nissenbaum, Stephen, ed. *The Great Awakening at Yale College.* Belmont, California, 1972.

Norman, E. R. *Church and Society in England, 1770–1970.* Oxford, England, 1976.

———. *The Conscience of the State in North America.* Cambridge, England, 1968.

Norton, William J. *Bishop Butler, Moralist and Divine.* New Brunswick, 1940.

O'Gorman, Thomas. *A History of the Roman Catholic Church.* New York, 1895.

Ong, Walter J., S.J. *Ramus Method and the Decay of Dialogue.* Cambridge, 1958.

Pacoe, C. F. *Classified Digest of the Records of the SPG* London, 1895.

———. *Two Hundred Years of the SPG: An Historical Account of the Society for the Propagation of the Gospel in Foreign Parts, 1701–1900.* London, 1901.

Palfrey, John Gorham. *A Compendious History of New England.* 4 vols. Boston and New York, 1873.

Patrides, C. A. *The Cambridge Platonists.* Cambridge, 1970.

Pelikan, Jaroslav. *Light of the World.* New York, 1952.

Pennington, Edgar L. *Apostle of New Jersey: John Talbot, 1645–1727.* Philadelphia, 1938.

Pettit, Norman. *The Heart Prepared: Grace and Conversion in Puritan Spiritual Life.* New Haven, 1966.

Pilcher, George William. *Samuel Davies: Apostle of Dissent in Colonial Virginia.* Knoxville, 1971.

Plumb, J. H. *Sir Robert Walpole, The Making of a Statesman.* 2 vols. London, 1956.

Pomphret, John E. *Founding the American Colonies, 1583–1660.* New York, 1970.

Porter, H. C. *Reformation and Reaction in Tudor Cambridge.* Cambridge, England, 1958.

Potter, J. "Growth of Population." In *Population in History.* Edited by D.V. Glass. London, 1965.

Powell, William S. *North Carolina: A History.* New York, 1977.

Pratt, Anne Stokely. "Books sent from England By Jeremiah Dummer to Yale College." In *Papers in Honor of Andrew Keogh, Librarian of Yale University.* New Haven, 1938.

Quinn, Arthur Hobson. *Representative American Plays.* New York and London, 1938.

Rainbolt, John C. *From Prescription to Persuasion: Manipulation of Eighteenth-Century Virginia Economy.* Port Washington, 1974.

Rand, Benjamin. *Berkeley's American Sojurn.* Cambridge, 1932.

Rapin, Paul de. *Dissertation sur les Whigs et les Torys.* The Hague, 1717.

———. *L'Histoire D'Angleterre.* 8 vols. The Hague, 1724.

Rawlinson, Richard. "A Short Historical Account of the Life and Designs of Thomas Bray D.D." In *Rev. Thomas Bray*. Edited by Bernard C. Steiner. Baltimore, 1901.

Redwood, John. *Reason, Ridicule and Religion: The Age of Enlightenment in England*. Cambridge, 1976.

Reed, Susan M. *Church and State in Massachusetts*. Urbana, 1914.

Rightmyer, Nelson W. *The Anglican Church in Delaware*. Philadelphia, 1947.

———. *Maryland's Established Church*. Baltimore, 1965.

Rightor, Anne. "Francis Bacon." In *The English Mind*. Edited by H. S. Davies and G. Watson. Cambridge, 1964.

Riley, I. Woodbridge. *American Philosophy, the Early Schools*. New York, 1907.

Robbins, Caroline. *The Eighteenth-Century Commonwealthmen*. Cambridge, 1959.

Rogers, George C., Jr. *Church and State in Eighteenth-Century South Carolina*. Dalcho Papers, No. 12. Charleston, 1957.

Rossiter, Clinton. *Conservatism in America, The Thankless Persuasion*. New York, 2d ed., 1962.

Rouse, Parke, Jr. *James Blair of Virginia*. Chapel Hill, 1971.

Rowse, A. L. *The Elizabethans and America*. London, 1959.

Rudolph, Frederick. *The American College and University*. New York, 1962.

Rutman, Darrett B. *Morning of America, 1603–1789*. Boston, 1971.

———. *Winthrop's Boston*. Chapel Hill, 1965.

Sanforn, Edwin D. *History of New Hampshire from Its First Discovery to the Year 1830*. Manchester, 1875.

Savage, Henry. *River of the Carolinas: The Santee*. New York, 1956.

Schmidt, Martin. *John Wesley: A Theological Biography*. London, 1962.

Shea, Daniel B. *Spiritual Autobiography in Early America*. Princeton, 1868.

Shipton, Clifford K. *Harvard Graduates*. Vols. 4–8. Cambridge and Boston, 1933–1951.

———. *New England Life in the 18th Century*. Cambridge, 1963.

Sibley, J. L. *Harvard Graduates*. Vols. 1–4. Cambridge and Boston, 1873–1885.

Simpson, Otto von. *The Gothic Cathedral*. Translated by C. C. Riedl. New York, 1956.

Sirmans, Eugene. *Colonial South Carolina, A Political History, 1663–1763*. Chapel Hill, 1966.

Skirven, Percy G. *The First Parishes of the Province of Maryland*. Baltimore, 1923.

Slotkin, Richard. *Regeneration through Violence, the Mythology of the American Frontier, 1600–1820*. Middletown, 1973.

Smith, Lacey Baldwin. *This Realm of England, 1399–1688*. Boston, 1966.

Smith, Page. *John Adams*. 2 vols. New York, 1962.

Sonneck, Oscar G. T. *Francis Hopkinson, the First American Poet-Composer (1737–1791) and James Lyon, Patriot, Preacher, and Psalmodist (1735–1794)*. Washington, D.C., 1905, and New York, 1967.

Steiner, Bruce. *Samuel Seabury, 1729–1796: A Study in the High Church Tradition*. Athens, Ohio, 1972.

Stoeffler, F. Ernest. *The Rise of Evangelical Pietism*. Leiden, 1965.

Stoney, Damuel Gaillard. *Colonial Church Architecture in South Carolina*. Publication of the Dalcho Society of the Diocese of South Carolina. Charleston, 1953.

Stromberg, Roland N. *Religious Liberalism in Eighteenth-Century England*. Oxford, 1954.

Sutherland, S. H. *Population Distribution in Colonial America*. New York, 1936.

Sykes, Norman. *Church and State in England in the Eighteenth Century*. Cambridge, 1934.

———. *The Church of England and Non-Episcopal Churches in the Sixteenth and Seventeenth Centuries*. Theology, Occasional Papers. New Series, 11. 2d ed. 1949.

———. *Old Priest and New Presbyter; Episcopacy and Presbyterianism since the Reformation with Especial Relation to the Churches of England and Scotland*. Cambridge, 1956.

Tate, Thad W. *The Negro in Eighteenth-Century Williamsburg*. Charlottesville, 1965.

Thomas, Albert Sidney. *A Historical Account of the Protestant Episcopal Church in South Carolina, 1820–1957*. Columbia, 1957.

Thompson, H.P. *Thomas Bray*. London, 1954.

Tiffany, Charles C. *A History of the Protestant Episcopal Church in the United States of America*. New York, 1895.

Tourtellot, Arthur Bernon. *Benjamin Franklin: The Shaping of Genius, the Boston Years*. Garden City, 1977.

Tracy, Joseph. *The Great Awakening*. New York, 1845.

Trumbull, J. Hammon. "A Sketch of the Life of Thomas Lechford." In *Note-Book Kept by Thomas Lechford Lawyer*. Edited by Edward Everett Hale. Cambridge, Massachusetts, 1885.

Tuveson, Ernest Lee. *Redeemer Nation: The Idea of America's Millennial Role*. Chicago, 1968.

Tyng, Dudley. *Massachusetts Episcopalians, 1607–1957*. Pascoag, R.I., 1960.

Van Doren, Carl. *Benjamin Franklin*. New York, 1938.

Van Dyken, Seymour. *Samuel Willard, 1640–1707: Preacher of Orthodoxy in an Era of Change*. Grand Rapids, 1972.

Van Tyne, C. H. *The Loyalists in the American Revolution*. New York, 1902, and Gloucester, 1959.

Vaughan, Alden T. *American Genesis: Captain John Smith and the Founding of Virginia*. Boston, 1975.

Walzer, Michael. *Revolution of the Saints*. Cambridge, Massachusetts, 1965.

Warch, Richard. *School of the Prophets, Yale College, 1701–1740*. New Haven, 1973.

Washburn, Wilcomb E. *The Governor and the Rebel*. Chapel Hill, 1957.

———. *Virginia under Charles I and Cromwell, 1625–1660*. Williamsburg, 1957.

Wells, J. *Oxford and Its Colleges*. London, 1899.

Wells, Robert V. *The Population of the British Colonies in America before 1776*. Princeton, 1975.

Wetenbaker, Thomas J. *Princeton, 1746–1896*. Princeton, 1946.

White, Edwin A., and Dyckman, Jackson A. *Annotated Constitution and Canons*. 2 vols. Greenwich, 1954.

Willey, Basil. *The Seventeenth-Century Background*. London, 1942.

Williams, Selma R. *Kings, Commoners, and Colonists*. New York, 1974.

Wolf, Edwin, II. *The Dispersal of the Library of William Byrd of Westover*. Worcester, 1958.

Wood, Gordon. *The Creation of the American Republic, 1776–1787*. Chapel Hill, 1969.

Wood, Peter H. *Black Majority: Negroes in Colonial South Carolina from 1670 to the Stono Rebellion*. New York, 1974.

Wright, Conrad. *The Beginnings of Unitarianism*. Boston, 1955.

Wright, Esther Clark, *The Loyalists of New Brunswick*. Fredericton, 1972.

Periodicals

Abelove, Henry. "Jonathan Edwards Letter of Invitation to George Whitefield." *WMQ*, 3rd Series 29 (1972).

Ahlstrom, Sydney E. "Religion, Revolution, and the Rise of Modern Nationalism." *CH* 44 (1975).

Bennett, Robert A. "Black Episcopalians: A History From the Colonial Period to the Present." *HM* 63 (1974).

Brewer, James H. "Negro Property Owners in Seventeenth-Century Virginia," *WMQ*, 3rd Series 12 (1955).

Brydon, George M. "New Light Upon the History of the Church in Colonial Virginia." *HM* 10 (1941).

———. "The Origin of the Rights of the Laity in the American Episcopal Church." *HM* 12 (1943).

Buckler, F. W. "The Establishment of the Church of England: Its Constitutional and Legal Significance." *CH* 5 (1941).

Buxbaum, Melvin H. "Benjamin Franklin and William Smith: Their School and Their Dispute." *HM* 39 (1970).

Catir, Norman J., Jr. "Berkeley's Successful Failure." *HM* 33 (1964).

Clement, John. "Anglican Clergymen Licensed to the American Colonies, 1710-1744." *HM* 17 (1948).

———. "Clergymen Licensed Overseas by the Bishops of London, 1696-1710." *HM* 16 (1947).

Conroy, Graham P. "Berkeley and Education in America." *JHI* 21 (1960).

Craven, Wesley Frank. "Indian Policy in Early Virginia." *WMQ,* 3rd Series 1 (1944).

Crumb, Lawrence N. "The Anglican Church in Maine." *HM* 33 (1964).

Davis, Richard B. "Volumes from George Sandys Library Now in America." *VMHB* 65 (1957).

Detweiler, Robert. "Robert Rose, 1704-1751: Effective and Popular Minister of Colonial Virginia." *HM* 41 (1972).

Duncan, Robert M. "A Study of the Ministry of John Talbot in New Jersey, 1702-1727: On 'Great Ripeness[,]' Much Dedication, and Regrettable Failure." *HM* 42 (1973).

Dunn, Richard S. "The Barbados Census of 1680: Profile of the Richest Colony in English America." *WMQ,* 3rd Series 26 (1969).

Eckenrode, Hamilton J. "Separation of Church and State in Virginia." *Sixth Annual Report of the Library Board of the Virginia State Library, 1908-1909.* Richmond, 1909.

Ellens, G. F. S. "The Ranters Ranting: Reflections on a Ranting Counter Culture." *CH* 40 (1971).

Ervin, Spencer. "The Establishment, Government, and Function of the Church in Colonial Virginia." *HM* 26 (1957).

Fiering, Norman S. "President Samuel Johnson and the Circle of Knowledge." *WMQ,* 3rd Series 28 (1971).

Frank, Joseph, ed. "News from Virginny, 1644." *VMHB* 65 (1957).

Friedman, Lawrence J., and Shaffer, Arthur H. "The Conway Robinson Notes and Seventeenth-Century Virginia." *VMHB* 78 (July 1973).

Goen, C. C. "Jonathan Edwards: A New Departure in Eschatology." *CH* 28 (1959).

Goodwin, Gerald J. "The Anglican Reaction to the Great Awakening." *HM* 35 (1966).

———. "Christianity, Civilization, and the Savage: The Anglican Mission to the American Indian." *HM* 42 (1973).

Greene, Jack P. "Foundations of Political Power in the Virginia House of Burgesses, 1720-1776." *WMQ,* 3rd Series 16 (October 1959).

Griswold, A. Whitney. "Three Puritans on Prosperity." *NEQ* 7 (1934).

Gundersen, Joan R. "The Myth of the Independent Virginia Vestry." *HM* 44 (1975).

Hartdagen, Gerald. "The Anglican Vestry in Colonial Maryland: A Study in Corporate Responsibility." *HM* 40 (1971).

Herbst, Jurgen. "The New Life of Captain John Smith." *HM* 44 (March 1975).

Higham, John. "Hanging Together: Divergent Unities in American History." *JAH* 41 (1974).

Hill, A. Shrady. "The Parson's Cause." *HM* 46 (1977).

Hills, George M. "John Talbot, The First Bishop in North America." *PMHB* 3 (1879).

Holmes, David L. "The Episcopal Church and the American Revolution." *HM* 47 (1978).

Hooker, Richard J. "The Mayhew Controversy." *CH* 5 (1936).

Hornberger, Theodore. "Samuel Johnson of Yale and King's College: A Note on the Relation of Science and Religion in Provincial America." *NEQ* 8 (1935).

Hutson, James H. "Benjamin Franklin and William Smith: More Light on an Old Philadelphia Quarrel." *PMHB* 93 (1969).

Isaac, Rhys. "Religion and Authority: Problems of the Anglican Establishment in Virginia in the Era of the Great Awakening and the Parsons' Cause." *WMQ* 30 (1973).

Jernegan, Marcus W. "Slavery and Conversion in the American Colonies." *AHR* 21 (1916).

Jones, Jerome W. "The Established Virginia Church and the Conversion of Negroes and Indians, 1620–1760." *JNH* 46 (1961).

Ketchum, Ralph. "Benjamin Franklin and William Smith: New Light on an Old Philadelphia Quarrel." *PMHB* 98 (1964).

Labaree, Leonard W. "The Nature of American Loyalism." *Proceedings of the American Antiquarian Society*, New Series 54 (1944).

Lemmon, Sarah McCulloch. "The Genesis of the Protestant Episcopal Diocese of North Carolina, 1701–1823." *NCHR* 28 (1951).

Leonard, Sister Loan de Lourdes. "Operation Checkmate: The British and the Death of a Virginia Blueprint for Progress." *WMQ*, 3rd Series 24 (1967).

Malone, Michael T. "The Doctrine of Predestination in the Thought of William Perkins and Richard Hooker." *ATR* 52 (1971).

Manross, William W. "Apostle to New Jersey, John Talbot, 1645–1727." *HM* 8 (1939).

McAllister, James, Jr. "Architecture and Change in the Diocese of Virginia." *HM* 45 (1976).

McCulloch, Samuel, ed. "James Blair's Plan to Reform the Clergy of Virginia." *WMQ*, 3rd Series, 4 (1947).

McIlhinny, David B. "The Protestantism of the Carolina Divines." *HM* 44 (1975).

McRae, Robert. "The Unity of the Sciences: Bacon, Descartes, and Leibnitz." *JHI* 18 (1957).

Middleton, Arthur P. "The Colonial Virginia Parson." *WMQ*, 3rd Series 26 (1969).

Mills, Frederick V., Sr. "Anglican Expansion in Colonial America." *HM* 39 (1970).

Morgan, Edmund S. "The Labor Problem at Jamestown, 1607–17." *AHR* 76 (1971).

Nash, Gary B. "The Image of the Indian in the Southern Colonial Mind." *WMQ*, 3rd Series 29 (1972).

Nelson, Andrew T. "Enthusiasm in Carolina, 1740." *SAQ* 44 (1945).

Nelson, William H. "The Revolutionary Character of the American Revolution." *AHR* 70 (1965).

Newcombe, Alfred W. "The Appointment and Instruction of SPG Missionaries." *CH* 5 (1936).

Pennington, Edgar L. "Colonial Church Conventions." *HM* 8 (1939).

Pennington, Loren E. "Hakluytus Posthumous: Samuel Purchas and the Promotion of English Overseas Expansion." *Emporia State Research Studies* 14 (1966).

Perrin, Porter G. "Possible Sources of Technologia at Early Harvard." *NEQ* 7 (1934).

Porter, H. C. "Alexander Whitaker: Cambridge Apostle to Virginia." *WMQ*, 3rd Series 14.

Powell, William S. "Aftermath of the Massacre: The First Indian War, 1622–1632." *VMHB* 61 (1953).

———. "Books in the Virginia Colony Before 1624." *WMQ*, 3rd Series 5 (1948).

Prior, Moody E. "Bacon's Man of Science." *JHI* 15 (1954).

Quinn, David B., ed. "A List of Books Purchased for the Virginia Company." *VMHB* 77 (1969).

Raab, Theodore K. "Sir Edwyn Sandys and the Parliament of 1604." *AHR* 49 (1964).

Rabe, Harry G. "Devereux Jarratt and the Virginia Social Order." *HM* 33 (1964).

Rand, Edward K. "Liberal Education in Seventeenth-Century Harvard." *NEQ* 6 (1933).

Reeves, Thomas C. "John Checkley and the Emergence of the Episcopal Church in New England." *HM* 34 (1965).

Robinson, W. Stitt. "Tributary Indians in Colonial Virginia." *VMHB* 67 (1959).

Salsman, Mary Plummer. "The Reverend Roger Price." *HM* 15 (1945).

Scott, P. G. "James Blair and the Scottish Church: A New Source." *WMQ*, 3rd Series 33 (1976).

Seiler, William H. "The Anglican Parish Vestry in Colonial Virginia." *JSH* 20 (1956).

Sirmans, M. Eugene. "Politics in Colonial South Carolina: The Failure of Proprietary Reform, 1682–1694." *WMQ*, 3rd Series 23 (1966).

Skaggs, David C. "The Chain of Being in Eighteenth-Century Maryland: The Paradox of Thomas Cradock." *HM* 45 (1976).

————, and Ranney, F. Garner. "Thomas Cradock Sermons." *MHM* 47 (1972).

Smart, George K. "Private Libraries in Colonial Virginia." *AL* 10 (1938).

Spangenberg, Bradford. "Vestrymen in the House of Burgesses: Protection of Local Vestry Autonomy During James Blair's Term as Commissary." *HM* 32 (1963).

Steiner, Bruce E. "New England Anglicanism: A Gentile Faith?" *WMQ*, 3rd Series 27 (1970).

Stenerson, Douglas C. "An Anglican Critique of the Early Phase of the Great Awakening in New England: A Letter by Timothy Cutler." *WMQ*, 3rd Series (1973).

Swem, E. G. "The Observations on the 'Virginia Historical Index' By Dr. Howard Mumford Jones in His Address on 'Desiderata in Colonial Literary History.' " *VMHB* 56 (1948).

Sykes, Norman. "The Theology of Divine Benevolence." *HM* 16 (1947).

Thornton, J. Mills, III. "The Thrusting Out of Governor Harvey: A Seventeenth-Century Rebellion." *VMHB* 76 (1968).

Tyler, Lyon G., ed. "Libraries of Colonial Virginia." *WMQ*, 1st Series 8 (1899).

Varga, Nicholas. "The English Parliament's Authority over Virginia." *VMHB* 62 (1954).

————. "The Rev. Michael Houdin (1706–1766)—A Shepherd in the Mist." *HM* 33 (1964).

Walsh, James J. "Scholasticism in the Colonial Colleges." *NEQ* 5 (1932).

Webb, Steven Saunders. "The Strange Career of Francis Nicholson." *WMQ*, 3rd Series 23 (1966).

Weir, Robert M. " 'Ye Harmony We Were Famour For': An Interpretation of Pre-Revolutionary South Carolina Politics." *WMQ*, 3rd Series 26 (1969).

Winton, Ruth M. "Governor Francis Nicholson's Relations with the Society for the Propagation of the Gospel in Foreign Parts." *HM* 17 (1948).

Woolverton, John F. "Address Commemorating the 300th Anniversary of St. Mary's White Chapel." *NNHM* 19 (1969).

————. "Conflict and Democratic Impulses in Colonial Maryland and the Establishment of the Anglican Church, 1690–1702." Address to the Convocation of Annapolis, May 10, 1967. Maryland Diocesan Archives, Baltimore.

————. "John Williamson Nevin and the Episcopalians: The Debate on the 'Church Question,' 1851–1874." *HM* 49 (1980).

————. "Philadelphia's William White: Episcopalian Distinctiveness and Accommodation in the Post-Revolutionary Period." *HM* (1974).

————. "Whither Episcopalianism? A Century of Apologetic Interpretations of the Episcopal Church, 1835–1964." *ATR*, Supplementary Series Number One (1973).

Wright, Louis B. "Pious Reading in Colonial Virginia." *JSH* 6 (August 1940).

Zavala, Silvio. "A General View of the Colonial History of the New World." *AHR* 66 (1960–1961).

Zimmer, Anne Young, and Kelly, Alfred H. "Jonathan Boucher: Constitutional Conservative." *JAH* 58 (1972).

Name Index

Subject Index

John Frederick Woolverton, a graduate of Harvard University (B.A., 1950) and Columbia University (Ph.D., 1963), received his Master of Divinity degree from the Episcopal Theological Seminary in Virginia in 1953. Currently rector of Trinity Church, Portland, Maine, and editor of the *Historical Magazine of the Protestant Episcopal Church*, he was for many years chairman of the Department of Church History at the Virginia Theological Seminary.

The manuscript was edited by Doreen Broder. The typeface for the text is Mergenthaler's VIP Times Roman, based on a design by Stanley Morison in 1932. The typeface for the display is Mergenthaler's VIP Cheltenham, based on a design by Bertram G. Goodhue in 1896.

The text is printed on 55-lb. Booktext Natural text paper, and the book is bound in Holliston Mills' Crown Linen cloth over binder's boards.

Manufactured in the United States of America.